Advances in
ARCHAEOLOGICAL
METHOD AND THEORY
Volume 1

Advisory Board

Advances in
ARCHAEOLOGICAL
METHOD AND THEORY
Volume 1

Edited by
MICHAEL B. SCHIFFER

Department of Anthropology
University of Arizona
Tucson, Arizona

ACADEMIC PRESS **New York** **San Francisco** **London** **1978**

A Subsidiary of Harcourt Brace Jovanovich, Publishers

The design of the logo stamped on the front
cover of this volume is taken from a thirteenth–
century St. John's Black–on–Red ceramic bowl
excavated in the El Morro Valley of New Mexico
by the Cibola Archaeological Research Project.
An analysis of the design can be found in
Charles L. Redman's article "The 'Analytical
Individual' and Prehistoric Style Variability"
in *The Individual in Prehistory*, edited by James
N. Hill and Joel Gunn, Academic Press, New York,
1977. Design courtesy of Charles L. Redman.

ACADEMIC PRESS, INC.
111 Fifth Avenue, New York, New York 10003

United Kingdom Edition published by
ACADEMIC PRESS, INC. (LONDON) LTD.
24/28 Oval Road, London NW1 7DX

ISSN 0162–8003

ISBN 0–12–003101–9

PRINTED IN THE UNITED STATES OF AMERICA

To my parents Louie and Frances-Fera

Contents

7 Independent Dating in Archaeological Analysis
JEFFREY S. DEAN

8 Advances in Archaeological Seriation
WILLIAM H. MARQUARDT

9 A Survey of Disturbance Processes in Archaeological Site Formation
W. RAYMOND WOOD and DONALD LEE JOHNSON

10 **Decision Making in Modern Surveys**

STEPHEN PLOG, FRED PLOG, and WALTER WAIT

List of Contributors

Numbers in parentheses indicate the pages on which the authors' contributions begin.

Jeffrey S. Dean (223), Laboratory of Tree-Ring Research, The University of Arizona, Tucson, Arizona 85721

Michael A. Glassow (31), Department of Anthropology, University of California, Santa Barbara, California 93106

Fekri A. Hassan (49), Department of Anthropology, Washington State University, Pullman, Washington 99164

Donald Lee Johnson (315), Department of Geography, University of Illinois, Urbana, Illinois 61801

Roger E. Kelly (1), National Park Service, Department of Interior, San Francisco, California 94102

William H. Marquardt (257), Department of Anthropology, University of Missouri, Columbia, Missouri 65201

Michael J. Moratto (1), Idaho Panhandle National Forests, Coeur d'Alene, Idaho 83814

Fred Plog (383), Department of Anthropology, Arizona State University, Tucson, Arizona 85721

Stephen Plog (143, 383), Department of Anthropology, Southern Illinois University, Carbondale, Illinois 62901

Alan P. Sullivan (183), Department of Anthropology, University of Arizona, Tucson, Arizona 85721

Joseph A. Tainter (105), Paleo-Indian Institute, Eastern New Mexico University, Portales, New Mexico 88130

Walter Wait (383), National Park Service, Southwest Region, Department of the Interior, Santa Fe, New Mexico 87501

W. Raymond Wood (315), Department of Anthropology, University of Missouri, Columbia, Missouri 65201

Preface

Definitions of archaeology ranging from the traditional "studies of man's past from material remains" to the avante garde "interdisciplinary science" have proliferated to the extent that a Kroeber–Kluckhohn compendium would be needed to contain them all. Despite much effort, and the belief held by every archaeologist that he or she has the answer, the problem of what archaeology is at the general level remains unsolved. Perhaps needed are fewer superficial attempts at definition and integration and more efforts to identify those areas, particularly in method and theory, where progress in research seems to be moving ahead briskly, for it is from productive lines of investigation that truly scientific disciplines emerge. *Advances in archaeological method and theory* will be a medium for distilling and disseminating progressive explorations in method and theory. Through its coverage, it will, perhaps, help to identify what archaeology is and is not.

The motive for establishing this new serial publication goes well beyond existential concerns and is rooted in the practical difficulties of simultaneously doing archaeology oneself and keeping up with advances in knowledge made by others. Many archaeologists, particularly those who accept the label "prehistorian," labor under a rather imposing set of research conditions. First, they strive to follow the ever-increasing stream of articles concerning their geographic area which are published in potentially hundreds of journals, monographs, and books, not to mention the ubiquitous "n.d.s." and "unpublished ms." And second, prehistorians must attempt to keep abreast of the latest developments in method and theory so that substantive studies can be evaluated critically and research can be designed and executed effectively. Fortunately it is relatively easy to predict where current studies on the prehistory of a specific geographic area may be found. On the other hand, an advance in archaeological method or theory may be reported virtually anywhere. A glance at the bibliography of any one of the chapters in this volume should demonstrate the near impossibility of controlling the entire current of primary literature on archaeological method and theory. Even those of us who are not basically prehistorians can barely keep pace with developments concerning our own pet topical interests. It is not surprising that today's contributors to archaeological method and theory are becoming rather specialized in their areas of expertise.

Advances in archaeological method and theory is established to help lighten the prehistorian's burden by integrating recent methodological and theoretical advances into authoritative and readable topical syntheses. I have chosen to call the chapters to be included "topical syntheses" in preference to the more conventional "review article." Review article connotes a sterile rendering of references and a bland panorama of people and ideas. Most contributions to this volume illustrate the fact that an article can serve the primary bibliographic function of a review article and at the same time provide insightful criticism of previous work, synthesize recent progress, and, of course, furnish new frameworks and ideas. Of course, not every contribution included achieves each of these goals, but each is in its own way much more than a bibliographic essay.

How a topic is approached depends in part on the history of the subject. For example, demographic archaeology, long a popular topic of research, has generated an expansive and sometimes abstruse literature. Hassan has taken a pragmatic, craftsman's approach and integrated a field so large that the next synthesis surely will be book length or will of necessity be handled by subtopic. Sullivan's treatment of archaeological inference, on the other hand, is more freely handled. Considering the embarrassingly little progress that has been made until very recently on what is perhaps archaeology's most fundamental problem, much of his contribution breaks new ground. I hope that in future volumes it will always be possible to present such a pleasing mixture of topics, old and new.

In order to insure that a wide range of expertise goes into the selection and preparation of manuscripts in every volume, a formal Advisory Board has been named. These Advisors are providing the Editor with ideas for articles and authors (with the exception of those in this Volume I which has been assembled under a streamlined schedule). In addition, they are playing an important role in the review process. Advice is also sought from other members of the profession, and the Editor welcomes unsolicited proposals and contributions. The final selection of topics and authors resides with the Editor, however, who, by reputation well deserved, is rather high-handed.

The articles that follow and those to appear in subsequent volumes need no introduction. Each stands alone as a contribution to knowledge. The customary justification for the selection of topics and their mode of treatment would be out of place in the present context. Although some of these articles naturally fall into clusters of related topics, they do not require that an overall organization be contrived and imposed on them. The order of presentation, in fact, is most of all in harmony with the Editor's aesthetic inclinations.

Advances in archaeological method and theory holds great promise both for the young science seeking its identity and the mature discipline charting its progress. Archaeology is both of these, and more. It is a peculiar and difficult subject, motivated partly by humanistic concerns, yet dependent upon and contributing to some of the most sophisticated method and theory produced by science. Perhaps in the pages of this serial publication we shall see unfold a new view of the human condition.

I thank Academic Press for it assistance and unflagging enthusiasm for archaeology in general and, in particular, this project. I do sympathize with the authors for enduring the rigors of my beastly production schedule. And finally, the many people who unselfishly contributed insightful but anonymous reviews deserve a special note of appreciation.

MICHAEL B. SCHIFFER

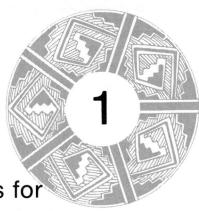

1

Optimizing Strategies for Evaluating Archaeological Significance

MICHAEL J. MORATTO
and ROGER E. KELLY

INTRODUCTION

The assessment of significance is central to archaeological research and management planning. Perceived significance influences such research decisions as which sites to investigate and what kinds of data to collect. Likewise, management decisions (that is, whether to preserve, alter, or destroy cultural resources) turn on the value of the resources vis-à-vis other planning considerations. At issue is the fact that the nation's archaeological remains are being methodically conserved or obliterated, depending on their adjudged significance (Moratto and Kelly 1977). Yet many of those who control the fate of cultural resources fail to appreciate the full complexity of the significance issue. Assessing significance may immerse the evaluator in "the most fundamental, intriguing problems of the discipline: the nature of archaeological data and the relationships between archaeology and society" (Schiffer and Gumerman 1977a: 239).

In this amplification of an earlier paper (Moratto and Kelly 1977), we emphasize that a broadly based strategy for appraising significance is needed to maximize the preservation and wise use of cultural resources. Here we use the terms "archaeological resources" and "cultural re-

1

Copyright © 1978 by Academic Press, Inc.
All rights of reproduction in any form reserved.
ISBN 0-12-003101-9

sources" interchangeably to refer to both historic and prehistoric cultural properties. Our objectives are, first, to set forth criteria by which the significance of cultural resources may be evaluated and, second, to suggest procedures for the optimal use of these properties in light of emerging policies for the long-range management of the nation's resources.

General Aspects of Significance

Scovill, Gordon, and Anderson (1972) were the first to examine significance in the arena of cultural resource management (CRM). In CRM, significance implies criteria or standards for evaluating properties as well as a resultant status. The significance of a resource may be derived from professional interests (such as research values) or social concerns (for example, symbolic values), and it may entail both potential and realized qualities.

Because the importance of a given resource depends on the context of assessment as well as its inherent qualities, there can be no universal or absolute measures of cultural worth (Grady 1977; Lipe and Grady 1975). Neither is it possible for archaeologists or planners to use a checklist of "standard" criteria as a recipe for brewing up a batch of significance. The criteria of significance change as the research goals of archaeology evolve and as public interests and priorities shift (Lipe and Grady 1975), and various measures of significance may augment, crosscut, or even contradict one another. Thus, archaeological significance is both dynamic and relative.

Significance may be arrayed within a hierarchy of cultural phenomena. *Intrasite* significance refers to the varying worth of subsite material in different judgmental contexts. In one research framework, fossil pollen may be deemed the most valuable site constituent; in another, ceramics in the same site might come out on top. At a higher level, the *site* may be the unit for which significance is appraised. Most CRM decisions affect sites rather than subsite entities. On yet a broader horizon, the quality of *intersite* significance emerges when a number of sites are evaluated as related parts of a larger system. Odum (1977: 1289), with reference to ecology, put it this way: "An important consequence of hierarchical organization is that as components, or subsets, are combined to produce larger functional wholes, new properties emerge that were not present or not evident at the next level below." Grady (1977) was dealing with significance on this plane when he noted that the importance of a given region may be greater than the sum of its archaeological parts.

Our levels are rather arbitrary, but we mention them to show that cultural resources can be assessed at various points on a continuum (that is, at the levels of artifact, site, region, area, etc.). It is critical, however, that evaluations consider the relationships between levels: Just as the value of artifacts is determined by their context in a site, the significance of a site is best seen with respect to regional data potentials and research designs.

Significance in Conservation Archaeology

For many years significance was judged, often intuitively, from the perspective of individual archaeologists. The site was the most common unit of interest, and a site's value was often thought of in terms of extent, depth, richness, age, uniqueness, or presumed scientific worth (Meighan 1974). Sites that failed to measure up with respect to great age, high yield of artifacts, etc., were often dismissed as unimportant. However, the recent enactment of certain laws and rules has forced the profession to rethink the concept of significance and its applications. During the 1970s, the focus of North American archaeology shifted from a mix of "pure research" and salvage work to an emphasis on CRM (Schiffer and House 1977b). This transformation led to the development of conservation archaeology, an approach with distinctive models, goals, methods, and its own extensive literature (Lipe 1974; Lipe and Lindsay 1974; McGimsey and Davis 1977; Schiffer and Gumerman 1977c).

The essence of conservation archaeology is planning for the best long-term use of cultural resources. If we assume that all cultural properties are actually or potentially jeopardized, such planning entails tactical options ranging from the preservation of resources intact to the recovery of some of their data—for instance, by excavation (McMillan *et al.* 1977). Selecting and justifying the best tactic depends on the accurate determination of the resource's significance (Schiffer and Gumerman 1977b). Indeed, if significance is not established in a timely and competent way, the resource will probably be destroyed. In present CRM frameworks the fate of archaeological properties depends largely on their explicit value; without *demonstrated* significance, such properties have little or no status in the planning process.

Yet significance—this pivotal management concept—seems ill-defined and misunderstood by many archaeologists and planners. Ideas on the matter range from the academic conviction that all sites were created significant (and are therefore worthy of eternal salvation) to the planners' view that sites were made to be "ranked" so that "expendable" ones can be consigned to the bulldozers while some of the "important" ones are preserved as monuments to their enlightened civic and ecological awareness. Obviously, neither extreme is a viable stance for those seeking a reasonable balance between domesticating the landscape and conserving the nation's partrimony (Moratto and Kelly 1977).

A basic question is how to translate professional concepts of significance into terms understandable to contemporary society. Many recent symposia and papers have grappled with this difficult issue (Glassow 1977; Glassow *et al.* 1976; Lipe and Grady 1975; May 1976; McMillan *et al.* 1977; Moratto 1975; Raab and Klinger 1977; Schiffer and Gumerman 1977a; Schiffer and House 1975, 1977a; Scovill *et al.* 1972).

Here we suggest that appraising significance requires not only a structure for evaluation, but also considerable flexibility in practice. Since significance can be measured only against some "frame of reference" (Schiffer and Gumerman 1977a), different frames of reference allow the archaeologist to identify various categories of significance. The basic elements of significance are information value and symbolic value; various permutations of these within different frames of reference may yield historic, scientific, ethnic, public, monetary, and legal aspects of significance—categories that are more often interdependent than mutually exclusive (Moratto and Kelly 1977). These heuristic units form neither a checklist nor a roster of the "types" of significance that might be imagined, and we offer them only to show the multifaceted nature of cultural resource assessments.

SOME CATEGORIES OF SIGNIFICANCE

Historical Significance

A cultural resource is historically significant if it can be associated with a specific individual event or aspect of history (Scovill *et al.*, 1972) or, more broadly, if it can provide information about cultural patterns during the historic era. For example, a property that may yield information on historic social interaction, use of space, or economic activities would be significant (Deetz 1977; NRHP 1977). Since "complete" histories do not exist for any locality, archaeology can provide a grasp of historical events and processes where written documentation is lacking.

A case in point is Vindolanda, a first- to fifth-century Roman garrison post in northern Britain. Contrary to traditional accounts, excavations at Vindolanda revealed that for nearly four centuries after the building of Hadrian's Wall the northern frontier garrisons interacted closely with nearby civilian communities. Moreover, the civilians linked to the outposts apparently enjoyed a standard of living higher than that of any other people in the area until the nineteenth century. Life along the northern frontier was previously known only from a few fragmentary documents. Recent archaeological work has produced so many new data (among them over 200 inscribed wooden slats) bearing on architecture, handicrafts, clothing, diet, and daily affairs in general that "when the excavations at Vindolanda are completed, it will be necessary to rewrite the history of the early Roman frontier in Britain" (Birely 1977: 46).

Historically significant sites often lend themselves to preservation combined with public interpretation. Ready American examples include the Southwest missions, California's gold-rush towns, colonial Jamestown, Fort Raleigh, etc. But, as Hickman (1977) pointed out, traditional historic preservation has emphasized standing structures over sites and less obvious entities, and has selected for structures reflective of the more flattering aspects of local history (such as fine homes, mills, schoolhouses, and public buildings). The record of less successful groups—tenant farmers, migrant workers, post-mission Indians, and the like—tend not to be preserved or highlighted (King and Hickman 1973). This is typically a major oversight in CRM today, although recent studies such as Deetz' (1977) *In Small Things Forgotten* promise to raise levels of awareness about the historical archaeology of common people. Thus, the value of historic properties depends chiefly on their representativeness of cultural patterns and the way that they can be used to study these patterns (Hickman 1977). When assessing significance, archaeologists should ensure "that properties important to all sorts of people, and to the understanding of all sorts of cultural phenomena, are intelligently and efficiently treated" (King *et al*. 1977:104).

Scientific (Research) Significance

Scientific significance involves the potential for using cultural resources to establish reliable facts and generalizations about the past. It is increasingly recognized that archaeological data are of great value not only to anthropology but also to many other sciences. Because archaeological remains permit the study of former environments as well as cultures, archaeology has much to offer toward the advancement of both natural and social sciences.

Values to Social Sciences

Archaeological resources are significant because they constitute a unique, nonrenewable data base for reconstructing the cultural past and for testing propositions about human behavior. During the last few decades, archaeology has made notable progress toward understanding major theoretical and specific issues: What factors govern the location and nature of settlements? How and why did agriculture and attendant social configurations evolve in Mesoamerica, Africa, and Western Asia? When and by whom was America first populated? Archaeology ultimately seeks to trace and explain the development of culture from its paleolithic origins to its postindustrial elaborations. Cultural resources that may provide data relevant to this goal are significant to the social sciences.

In this vein, Schiffer and House (1977a) defined four types of archaeological significance based on different types of research questions. A resource holds "substantive significance" when its data bear upon questions about specific events and times (for instance, why was northeastern Arkansas apparently abandoned during the Middle Archaic?). The key to measuring substantive research potential is the process of matching questions and "analytic units." Analytic units are "deposits or sets of deposits of archaeological materials produced by specified cultural and noncultural formation processes" (Schiffer and House 1977a:251). Archaeologists must have both research queries and analytic units before significance can be assessed.

"Anthropological significance" is defined by Schiffer and House as the extent to which the study of given resources might allow the testing of anthropological principles, especially those relating to long-term culture change and ecological adaptation. To illustrate, T. F. King (1974, 1976) used archaeological data from several parts of California to investigate the evolution of nonegalitarian political organization. King showed that high level political differentiation existed among certain hunter–gatherers earlier than 2000 B.P. He proposed that this was explicable "as a result of population pressures within and among sedentary nonagricultural societies," and that "such population pressures would be likely to result in both trade and warfare, both selecting for the development of managerial subgroups" (T. F. King 1976:x). These archaeological findings are significant to anthropology not only because they shed new light on the origins of complex social patterns among hunter–gatherers, but also because they call into question traditional interpretations that linked the rise of political differentiation with the origins of agriculture.

A third category of values is "social scientific significance"—the potential of cultural resources to answer questions germane to the social sciences generally (Schiffer and House 1977a). One might ask: How and why do civilizations develop? Why is there war? What factors limit social and cultural growth? The potential of specific archaeological remains to address such questions is seldom readily apparent. This form of significance becomes patent only when resources can be evaluated in terms of expansive research frameworks. Such a format allowed MacNeish and others to relate all manner of sites—from sherd scatters to ceremonial centers—to the problem of the origins of civilization in Mesoamerica (MacNeish and Byers 1967–1976).

Lastly, Schiffer and House (1977a) identify "technical, methodological, and theoretical significance." Technical or methodological innovations often emerge from substantive investigations. If there is potential for technical or theoretical advancement, even when the substantive value is low, the resource is significant.

Thus, each property that may expand our knowledge of the cultural past or lead to improved archaeological methods is significant. But, because significance is perceived in terms of research goals and designs, the importance of specific archaeological resources will vary according to the research interests of the evaluator:

> The archaeological investigator interested in cultural chronology would probably consider a stratified site more significant to those problems than a site occupied extensively but briefly, while the student interested in functional relationships within a single community would probably reverse the priority [McMillan et al. 1977:32].

Although the research focus may vary from one individual to another, it is imperative that CRM archaeologists make every effort to recognize aspects of significance beyond their immediate professional interests. This can best be accomplished by evaluating cultural properties in light of a regional or areal research design embracing the current interests of scholars working in the subject region or area (Raab and Klinger 1977).

It is also important to recognize that small, surface, and disturbed sites are sources of significant archaeological data more often than not. Given a thoughtful research design, such sites may yield valuable information concerning settlement patterns, activity loci, chronology, etc. (Talmage et al. 1977). Consequently, "it is not acceptable to decide, independent of other facts, that small, surface, or disturbed sites should be given little or no consideration in mitigation decisions" (Wilson 1977:i).

In the same vein, resources in "marginal" archaeological areas can be quite important. King and Casebier's (1976) research in the east Mojave Desert indicated that human adaptation in the area may have been similar to that in parts of central Mexico during the time when agricultural economies were evolving, and data from the desert may aid in studying the causes of the development and spread of farming. Similarly, research into the role of water as a factor in population density and distribution can be done effectively in such desert areas (King and Casebier 1976). Here, again, it seems clear that the full value of the resources can be assessed only when a full set of research questions has been formulated.

Values to Other Sciences

Having mentioned some applications of archaeological data to research in the social sciences, we now examine archaeology's contributions to the natural sciences and technology as a criterion of significance. Even though archaeology often benefits from interdisciplinary research, and the applications of botany, physics, geology, and other sciences to archaeology are well known, we stress the need to explore possible archaeological dividends for natural sciences and technology when evaluating the worth of cultural resources.

Archaeological remains provide data on the operation of natural and cultural systems over long timespans. Because long-range trends, discovered archaeologically, permit a better understanding of environmental change than would be possible otherwise, archaeological deposits are significant banks of vital data for many disciplines (Dixon 1977). For instance, long-range climatic fluctuations can be traced by using pollen, faunal remains, tree rings, and other evidence from cultural sites. A knowledge of such fluctuations can lead to reliable climatic projections, which, in turn, may form the basis for enlightened land management.

In this regard, Ford has shown how those planning to settle and exploit marginal environments can learn a great deal from prehistoric adaptive strategies in such regions as deserts:

> For example, Evenari, Shanan, and Tadmore . . . observed in Israel that many parts of the Negev had supported substantial populations in ancient times. Their inquiries led to the establishment of a deductive model to test hypotheses related to water control and agricultural production. They demonstrated that utilization of rainfall runoff from large sections of land would produce a bounteous harvest. Through knowledge derived from archaeological data, planners can now establish communities in the desert with an awareness of distinctive spatial patterns that will preserve ample land for comparable runoff control. Such knowledge will have further universal applicability as fossil water supplies diminish or become prohibitively costly [1973:90].

In another situation, the botanist G. W. Dimbleby wanted to learn why certain heathlands and moorlands in Britain seemed almost lethal to trees. He identified the soil—a leached and acidic podzol overlying a zone of hardpan—as the problem. At first it was believed that this podzol was the inevitable result of interaction between the land and climate. However, a different explanation came to the fore when excavations under one of the prehistoric barrows in the area showed that the original soil was not a podzol. Pollen in the "preserved" soil indicated that an oak woodland had dominated the surrounding country when the barrow was raised. It was subsequently learned that the poor soils of today are the direct result of forest clearing by earlier societies to facilitate cultivation.

Furthermore, we know now, that if left alone the vegetation and soil will gradually return towards the more fertile condition which previously existed. But the real point of this story lies in the fact that, unbeknown to me, archaeologists already had the relevant information. . . [Had this information been available], it would have made a big difference to what was being taught as the fundamental principles of soil genesis, and I, working in an applied field, would have been saved a great deal of time in working out for myself the principles which I should have been applying [Dimbleby 1965; cf. Wilson 1976:284–285].

Another practical application of archaeology developed when an American utility company was looking into the possible siting of a nuclear power plant on a coastal terrace about 20 meters above the Pacific Ocean. As a safety consideration (as well as an economic one), the firm needed to know whether a tsunami (tidal wave) was likely to affect the terrace. Shell from a sand-dune midden on the terrace yielded ^{14}C dates of ~3400–1800 B.C., establishing that the terrace had been relatively stable and unaffected by tsunami activity for at least 5000 years. The lesson here and in the foregoing examples is that

by their strategic locations and the evidence of past environmental characteristics preserved in them, it is possible for archaeological sites to be the only sources of data available to resolve completely different kinds of problems, often with highly practical applications [Dixon 1977:283; emphasis in original].

Other examples of archaeology's role in the advancement of science come to mind readily. Human remains from archaeological sites on every continent have been studied to shed light on paleopathology, paleoepidemiology, and the evolution of medical practices (Brothwell and Sandison 1967; Majno 1975). Studies of coastal archaeological sites have added to our knowledge of Pleistocene and Recent patterns and rates of sea level fluctuation (Atwater and Hedel 1976; Lajoie 1972; Wright 1971). In the lower Mississippi Valley, Paleo-Indian and Archaic deposits have helped geologists to establish minimal ages for the formation of alluvial surfaces (Saucier 1974). Information on paleotemperatures, fish distributions, life history, predation, and catastrophic events can be gained from the analysis of fish remains from archaeological contexts (Casteel 1976; Fitch 1969). And archaeology can be used to test and amplify models of paleoenvironmental change developed in other sciences (Moratto *et al.* n.d.). The list could be extended almost indefinitely.

When we contemplate the potential worth of archaeological data to science and technology, the resources assume staggering importance as reservoirs of useful knowledge. Since we cannot predict the future needs of archaeology, much less those of other disciplines, a strong case can be made for the enlightened stewardship of the nation's cultural resources.

However, as McMillan *et al.* have pointed out, this realization presents the CRM archaeologist with a dilemma:

> all sites have potential significance relative to present or future research questions but not all sites can be preserved. A compromise solution is to attempt, using a regional perspective . . . to preserve or investigate a *representative* sample of the potentially affected resource base. Representative means a sample characterizing as accurately as possible the full range of variability of the cultural resources [1977:32].

Because the future trajectory of scientific research cannot be predicted, it would be very hazardous to assert that any given cultural property might not someday yield important data (Lipe and Grady 1975). As Dixon has remarked:

> It makes good sense to search out purposefully other significance criteria in addition to those which are either standard operating procedure or specifically designed to serve the archaeologist's own research interest. The more good reasons for support, the more support there should be [1977:280].

Moreover, deliberations of scientific significance in a CRM context are leading to a better appreciation of the very essence of archaeology— matching cultural resources with research questions. Through research efforts, the acquisition of archaeological data adds to the sum of human knowledge, thereby enriching the global culture and improving man's capacity for understanding and solving problems. In the words of Clark, "the significance of world prehistory is the contribution it is able to make to widening the perspectives of history in accord with the needs of today" [1970:40].

Ethnic Significance

A cultural resource that holds religious, mythological, spiritual, or other symbolic importance for a discrete group of people is said to be ethnically significant. This kind of value often transcends the others, but there are also many cases where ethnic and historical or public significance are the same (say, when a society's heritage is enriched through the archaeological discovery of ancestral lifeways). In circumstances where acculturation was severe and traditional lore has been forgotten, archaeology may provide the only access to the patrimony of an ethnic group (Moratto and Kelly 1977).

Beyond illuminating the historical significance of cultural resources, historic archaeology is contributing to the appreciation of American history and the enhancement of a national identity—ethnic identity on a national level, as it were:

In the Far West, for example, several years of excavation have added important data to any discussion as to the landing site of Francis Drake on the coast of California. . . . On a broader scale there are archaeological views of California mission life, including uneven acculturation rates for men and women. . . . In the East, Harrington's (1957) classic study of Washington's Fort Necessity has added the exact size and ground plan to an incomplete historical record, while Deetz (1973) . . . has proposed a tripartite evolution for all of New England society: Stuart yeoman (1620–1660, a localized Angloamerican (1660–1760), and a Georgian (1760–1830). His scheme is based on different aspects of material culture, especially gravestone designs and ceramics, and it is of interest that the American Revolution had little impact on these styles [Schuyler 1976:29].

Many ethnic groups—American Indians, Asian–Americans, Chicanos, Blacks, and Appalachian Whites—have been so excluded from written histories and traditional concepts of national identity that their cultural past is often preserved more in the earth than in documents. Archaeologists are beginning to fill out the picture by investigating such sites as Black slave cabins in the Southeast; a Black oystering settlement on Staten Island; "Chinatowns" and Chinese railroad camps in the West; and various settlements of non-Angloamerican immigrants. Clearly, many types of cultural properties hold ethnic significance as sources of identity and inspiration for America's pluralist society (Schuyler 1976).

Some cultural resources entail another dimension of ethnic significance. Data from habitation sites have been used to reconstruct the aboriginal territories and land-use patterns of certain Indian groups for purposes of the land-claims cases (Heizer and Kroeber 1976). Archaeological and ethnographic testimony proved instrumental in the decision to compensate (however poorly) Indian groups for lands taken from them in the nineteenth century.

We agree with Cummins (1977) that CRM can and should be more concerned with ethnic significance than it has been in the past. But a problem is that most laws governing cultural resources are biased toward Euroamerican belief systems and concepts of history. As Miller (1975) has noted, it is fairly easy to study properties of potential significance if the belief system of the evaluator is simply a specialized version of the cultural values associated historically with the property being studied; however, it is very difficult to apply "completely" different cultural values (for example, those of American Indians) in such assessments.

We suggest that the best way to approach this problem is to involve the Indians (or other groups) directly in appraisals of ethnic significance. This implies, of course, that the Indians and archaeologists can develop effective mutual communication.

To achieve this kind of relationship and understanding it is logical to begin at the point where both the Native American and the archaeologist agree on the importance of the preservation and protection of cultural heritage, even though their respective purposes and methods may differ [Johnson 1977:91].

Sensitivity to ethnic values in the course of CRM studies will add another dimension to the worth of cultural properties in the eyes of decision makers (thereby improving the chances of preserving the resources), and it should enhance the relationship between archaeologists and the ethnic communities with which they interact (Johnson 1977).

A dividend of ethnic participation in archaeological assessments is the knowledge that ethnic groups can bring to bear on at least three levels:

> First, there is the *practical level*, where, for example, Tolowa Indians and Ngatatjara Aborigines were able to direct the archaeologist to useful sites and to describe the current or recent uses of these sites. . . . Second, there is the level of *specific interpretation* (e.g., the reconstruction of a house and the interpretation of projectile points from a northwestern California site). . . . Finally, there is the level of *general interpretation*, where broad syntheses of cultural adaptation are attempted [Gould 1977:167–168].

As a final point, scientific and other values may be so intertwined with ethnic significance that cultural resources may be significant even when the group that produced them cannot preserve them, becomes indifferent, or ceases to exist. Pondering why we should save such cultural achievements, Kroeber (1972:xii) concluded that "it is the future of our own world culture that the preservation of these values can enrich, and our ultimate understandings grow wider as well as deeper thereby."

In sum, to be ethnically significant a cultural property "must have at least a potential role to play in the maintenance of a community's integrity, in the maintenance of some group's sense of place and cultural value, or in the advancement of human knowledge" [King *et al.* 1977:96].

Public Significance

The term public significance refers to those benefits that accrue to a society through the wise stewardship of its archaeological resources. Archaeology provides an engrossing educational medium at several levels; it affords economic benefits to the community from tourism, formal educational programs, and the funding of local research projects; and it enriches the community through the acquisition and interpretation of sites and materials for public edification and enjoyment (McGimsey 1972; Scovill *et al.* 1972). Archaeological resources, as part of the total environment, also have aesthetic qualities that may contribute to the "wilderness experience" without being developed or otherwise interpreted (McMillan *et al.* 1977).

Archaeologists have enjoyed a high degree of public interest in their field for many years. One rough measure of the public interest today is represented by the visitation levels at various archaeological units of the National Park System. Using attendance figures, Green (n.d.:7) has shown that "the public interest in prehistoric resources and the demand for visits to prehistoric sites is growing, and at a faster rate than the demand for the recreational services of the parks generally."

Because the support for archaeology is largely dependent on national priorities and values, maintenance of public goodwill is necessary for the survival of the discipline and continued support of CRM studies. Perhaps if the public significance of cultural resources were highlighted more effectively, the profession could diminish its fear that "unless archaeologists find ways to make their research increasingly relevant to the modern world, the modern world will find itself increasingly capable of getting along without archaeologists" [Fritz and Plog 1970:412].

Unfortunately, archaeology is now under fire by certain journalists and public officials. The State Historic Preservation Officer (SHPO) of one Eastern state has opined that troubling with resources significant only for the information that they contain is too much of a burden for governmental agencies (King 1977). In 1976, with reference to excavation of sites jeopardized by Interstate Highway 88, the *New York Daily News* alleged that "arrowhead collectors" were being allowed to stop construction; in 1977, the *Kansas City Times* led off a misinformed critique of CRM archaeology with the statement, "Encouraged by federal law, state statute, bureaucracy, and the environmental fad, academically trained archaeologists have discovered that one man's trash is another man's treasure"; and a 1977 article entitled "Federal Follies" in the *Sunday News* (New York) sarcastically queried, "Would you believe that construction of a $1.6 billion sewer project in Suffolk County has been delayed for at least six months while archaeologists dig around for Indian arrowheads?" !

The media coverage of such miscreant views can only foster adverse public opinions of archaeology. To some extent, the negative impressions might yield to a more realistic public image of archaeology if the profession would use the media more effectively to report its activities and findings. The media problem, however, is only one aspect of a more pervasive issue. With a few notable exceptions, archaeologists fail to communicate the relevance of their work to the general public.

> A vast number of that same public knows precious little about archaeology or its results, much less how it might have some applicability to their own lives, over and above the level of pure curiosity. . . . It is incumbent on the profession to inform these people, both individually and collectively, about archaeology and why they should be concerned with it [Woodbury and McGimsey 1977:84].

Yet it is evident that archaeological research and public interest in cultural resources go hand in hand. Indeed, the public significance of a cultural property often increases directly as its research potential is realized. Similarly, the public good is served, as archaeologists acquire information of value for land-use planning and other practical applications. Clearly, the maintenance of archaeological programs in America depends on the full and explicit realization of the public significance of cultural resources.

Legal Aspects of Significance

We turn now to the complex and increasingly controversial legal aspects of archaeological significance. Certain federal, state, and local laws and policies provide a structure for evaluating cultural properties and for developing resource management plans. Although these laws and policies do not create legal significance as a "real" category akin to, say, scientific or ethnic significance, they do convery a real legal status to cultural resources, and they establish formal procedures for dealing with cultural resources in the administrative context.

At the federal level, there are several laws and one executive order that form the basis for compliance actions and professional input. Relevant here are Executive Order 11593 ("The Protection and Enhancement of the Cultural Environment," 1971); the Reservoir Salvage Act of 1960 as amended by the Archaeological and Historical Preservation Act (AHPA) of 1974; the Historic Sites Act (HSA) of 1935 and its companion, the Historic Sites Preservation Act (HSPA) of 1966; the Act for the Preservation of American Antiquities (APAA) of 1906; and the National Environmental Policy Act (NEPA) of 1969. These are discussed at length by King *et al.* (1977), McGimsey (1972), and Moratto (1977a).

In addition to these laws, we have the *Code of Federal Regulations* (CFR)—rules with the force of law promulgated by executive agencies for the clarification and implementation of the laws. Several recent titles of the CFR include references to "significant data," "scientific data," and "historical values." Most of the rules discussed below are presently (June, 1977) in draft form and subject to change, but they show current administrative ideas regarding the concept of significance.

Title 36 CFR 66 (*Recovery of Scientific, Prehistoric, Historic, and Archaeological Data: Methods, Standards and Reporting Requirements*), which establishes standards for the conduct of data recovery activities pursuant to the AHPA (King *et al.* 1977:52), defines "significant data" as those that can be used to answer research questions of disciplines engaged in the study of "human behavior, thought, or history" [36 CFR 66.1 (15)].

The same title makes a distinction between "scientific data" and data from prehistory, history, and archaeology.

A companion title, 36 CFR 65 (*Recovery of Scientific, Prehistoric, Historic, and Archaeological Data: Procedures for Coordination and Notification*), contains a similar definition of "significant data," but "scientific data" are those data "provided by sciences other than archaeology, history, and architecture" [36 CFR 65.2 (10)]. The importance of these definitions lies in the fact that 36 CFR 65 regulates the flow information from federal agencies to the Secretary of the Interior with regard to activities that may affect archaeological or historical data, and specifies that data recovery programs under the AHPA can be undertaken only after completing the planning process required by the NEPA, the NHPA, and EO 11593 (King *et al.* 1977:51).

Another regulation, 36 CFR 64 (*Criteria and Procedures for the Identification of Historic Properties*), clarifies the responsibilities of federal agencies set forth in EO 11593 by formalizing procedures for the identification of properties that may qualify for the National Register of Historic Places (NRHP). This title defines "cultural resources" as all phenomena of "cultural value" to the nation, a state, a locality, a community, or a group of people, and the term includes historic properties, social institutions, traditions, folkways, and properties that have lost their integrity but are still deemed "valuable" by society or a part of it. "Historic values" are defined as those attributes that make a property eligible to the NRNP, including but not limited to the four criteria of the NRNP listed below. This title also considers two aspects of resource evaluation—data within the resource location and its social importance—and suggests that measures of significance be formulated as research questions.

In general, 36 CFR 64–66 do not precisely define archaeological significance, but each part does address the concept of significance and its applications to federal compliance actions.

Other important rules are 36 CFR 60 (*National Register of Historic Places: Criteria for Statewide Historic Surveys and Plans*) and 36 CFR 800 (*Procedures for the Protection of Historic and Cultural Properties*). The latter, issued by the Advisory Council on Historic Preservation, presents the legal measures of significance most relevant to CRM studies:

> The quality of significance in American history, architecture, archaeology, and culture is present in districts, sites, buildings, structures, and objects of State and local importance that possess integrity of location, design, setting, materials, workmanship, feeling and association, and:
> (1) That are associated with events that have made a significant contribution to the broad patterns of our history; or

(2) That are associated with the lives of persons significant in our past; or

(3) That embody the distinctive characteristics of a type, period, method of construction, or that represent the work of a master, or that possess high artistic values, or that represent a significant and distinguishable entity whose components may lack distinction; or

(4) *That have yielded, or may be likely to yield, information important to prehistory or history* [36 CFR 800.10; emphasis added].

This definition of significance is the one that determines the eligibility of cultural resources for inclusion on the NRHP, and it is a key measure of such resources in the environmental impact evaluation process.

Archaeologists during the past few years have generally focused on criterion 4 as a standard of significance. While recognizing that the criterion of information potential may be applied to nearly all archaeological sites, we suggest a broader application of all four criteria.

Many cultural resources "embody the distinctive characteristics of a . . . period, method of construction, or . . . represent a significant and distinguishable entity." Also, resources such as petroglyph or pictograph panels may "possess high artistic values." While calling for a wider use of the NRHP criteria, we would point out that many other landmark or inventory systems have also set forth measures of the significance of cultural properties (Kelly 1974).

There is considerable misunderstanding as to the function of the NRHP. On the one hand, some individuals and federal agencies view and use the Register as a planning device:

The National Register is the pivot upon which historic preservation in the United States turns. Properties that qualify for the Register are the subject matter of historic preservation, and they are eligible for preservation, enhancement, and salvage. If they do not qualify, they are not worth worrying about. The bluntness of this pivot is one of the major sources of trouble for historic preservation [King *et al.* 1977:95].

The Register was not meant to be an "honor roll" of places of national significance. . . . Its primary function is as a planning document, and as an "authoritative guide to be used by Federal, State, and local governments, private groups, and citizens to identify the Nation's cultural resources and to indicate what properties should be considered for protection from destruction or impairment" [*Federal Register* 41 (28):5905] [Klein 1977:1].

A different position is taken by at least one senior official of the Advisory Council on Historic Preservation:

(We) need to develop a method for judging the relative significance of archaeological sites. The present criteria used by the National Register are too general. . . . The language (of Criterion 4) invites the interpretation that all archaeological sites are eligible for listing in the National Register of Historic Places. The Federal System, as it is presently organized, cannot tolerate such an assumption [McDermott 1977:58].

We feel that these positions can be reconciled. Properties that qualify for the NRHP need not be on the Register to receive due consideration and protection under the law. The concept of the Register as a "complete" list of significant properties is unworkable; what is important is the *process* of determining eligibility. This process requires the identification and evaluation of significant values, and it permits communication among members of the profession, the Advisory Council, and the SHPOs. In this context, the evaluators need to identify as many aspects of significance as possible so that the full range of impacts can be forecast and the appropriate management action can be planned. Finally, we see the wide latitude of interpretations possible under the language of the Register criteria as necessary and useful. After all, the idea is not to legislate in precise terms what is significant; rather, what we need and have are general guidelines by which current professional evaluations of significance can be advanced on a resource-by-resource basis.

Monetary Significance

Although monetary assessments seem at first glance to run against traditional archaeological values, estimating the potential economic worth of cultural resources is one way to evaluate their significance for CRM purposes. This may be a dangerous method, however, to the extent that scientific, ethnic, or other measures of importance are neglected in favor of cost–benefit ratios or dollar–data comparisons. We feel strongly that monetary significance should be used for preservationist, not exploitative, goals.

In one hypothetical situation involving the mutually exclusive use of a location for the development of a power-generating plant as contrasted with the establishment of a public preserve containing cultural resources, Green (n.d.:18) has shown that "for a period of 50 years (the life of the power plant) the estimate of the monetary benefits of the cultural facility greatly exceeds those of the power plant." We hasten to add that the conversion of archaeological sites to public preserves is only one way to manage them, and we do not mean to imply that preservation for public interpretation is either advisable or feasible for most cultural resources.

When financial assessments are required in CRM, one approach is to calculate the cost of "total data recovery" from the resources to be affected by a project:

> [This figure] should be calculated by a competent professional archaeologist as the amount of funds required to recover all significant data (cultural and environmental) using the most current methodology, technology, and theory available. The cultural inventory should provide the factual basis for this estimate [Scovill *et al.* 1972:21–22].

A basic problem is that cultural information per se cannot be converted to dollars and cents. And, although it may be possible to calculate data recovery costs based on current methods, etc., it is never possible actually to recover all the data potentially available, partly because the destruction of some kinds of information is an unavoidable result of collecting other kinds. Another difficulty, of course, is that new theory, better research designs, and more sophisticated methods will come with the future, and this means that we cannot presently evision what the "total data" potentials of a given site might be, much less arrive at the estimated cost of recovery (Moratto and Kelly 1977). The problem was clearly articulated by House and Schiffer:

> The significance of a body of archaeological resources depends on the research questions to which they relate. Even if it were possible to assign a dollar value to research questions, because the range of questions, and hence significance, is an open-ended quality of an archaeological resource base, a fixed estimate of present-day monetary value could never be an adequate index to its future scientific and historical significance [1975:181].

We concur with House and Schiffer (1975:182) that scientific and historical significance is not convertible into monetary values, and that placing a dollar value on cultural resources has no basis in archaeological theory. Nonetheless, financial evaluations—however poorly they may represent truly significant qualities—may be *useful*. It is feasible to compute the costs of retrieving all the data possible with contemporary methods and research interests, and this is one way to grasp the magnitude of the cultural data loss that might be caused by a project. Such estimates of "total data recovery" costs may be used in project cost–benefit analyses. In some instances the anticipated costs of archaeological mitigation may be high enough to offset calculated gains, and the planned project may be scrapped. More often, when the decision has been made to proceed with a project, archaeologists may use monetary assessments as a strong basis for negotiating mitigative programs.

Although we have argued that calculating the monetary value of cultural resources has utility in certain planning contexts, we strongly agree with Raab and Klinger (1977) that financial realities are to be considered only after the significance of the resources has been established by using other criteria. Cost–benefit comparisons are not substitutes for evaluations of significance, but such comparisons do add another dimension to the value of cultural resources in planning contexts. Fortunately, current trends appear to be moving away from cost–benefit ratios and toward the "least adverse alternative" approach as the primary means of evaluating projects (Grady 1977).

SPECIOUS CRITERIA

Just as there are valid criteria for assessing significance, there are specious measures of cultural worth. We trouble ourselves with some of these here because they are being applied in cultural resource evaluations, and because we feel that these "standards" have no place in archaeological usage.

Egocentrism

At least one archaeologist has evaluated prehistoric remains in terms of the question, "Would I spend my time on this site if I were doing it at my own expense?" The Office of Archaeology and Historic Preservation (OAHP), National Park Service, has responded admirably to this approach: "The answer to such a question would presumably depend not only on the particular archaeologist's research interests but also his or her economic condition, the convenience of the site, the difficulty of excavation, and other factors totally unrelated to its research potential" (OAHP 1976). To this rebuttal, we would add that "spending one's time on a site," as a criterion of worth, fails to consider public, ethnic, or other aspects of significance as discussed earlier in this paper.

Sensationalism

This approach is concerned with the spectacular: Ancient sites are inherently valuable, and the older, the better; large sites are worth more than small ones; sites with rich artifact yields are more impressive than "poor" sites; and so on. Schiffer and Gumerman (1977a) show that such qualities better reflect newsworthiness than archaeological significance. Along the same lines, Hickman (1977) observed that local communities tend to preserve only the attractive, famous, locally unique, visually outstanding, earliest, and biggest historical properties. This illustrates a partial conflict, or at least different foci, between measures of public and scientific significance. Nonetheless, an exclusive concern with superlatives is antithetical to a full and balanced understanding of the cultural past, and it may skew appraisals of significance in the direction of that which is exceptional rather than that which is representative. The bottom line for CRM is not that spectacular properties are inherently less worthy, but that scientific potentials and other qualities must also figure in the significance equation.

The Vintner's Myth

It is often said that recent historic sites, particularly sites less than 50 years old, are insignificant and generally do not qualify for the NRHP. This view seems to assume that historic sites, like certain fine wines, mellow and improve with age. Age therefore becomes an index of significance. We would argue that information potential and symbolic values are valid criteria of significance; age per se is virtually irrelevant. In an excellent paper on the eligibility of twentieth-century sites for the National Register, Klein (1977) provides examples of the data potentials of modern sites. In one case, the New York University Archaeological Field School excavated Bum's Shelter in southern Illinois. The upper 10–20 cm of the deposit in the rock shelter was found to contain numerous artifacts dating from the 1920s and 1930s, and the remains of hearths containing material from the same period. It was learned from local residents that Bum's Shelter had been the site of a ''hobo jungle.''

> A preliminary analysis of the material from the shelter revealed several things, including a relatively specialized and sophisticated adaptive strategy being utilized by the twentieth-century inhabitants of the site. Large quantities of coal were apparently being stolen from the railroad for use in heating and cooking fires. The presence of a large number of railroad spikes may indicate the use of abandoned railroad ties for a multitude of purposes. Initial analysis of a large sample of faunal remains has revealed the presence of both wild and domestic species. This may indicate that hunting played a much larger role in the subsistence strategy of hobos than had previously been thought. The multitude of tin can and bottle fragments may indicate that pilferage of freight cars was also a key component [Klein 1977:5].

Since the hobos have received very little serious attention in social science literature, sites such as Bum's Shelter should be viewed as valuable sources of information about a distinct subculture, which has almost totally disappeared, and which has almost no written history of its own (Klein 1977).

In another instance, Hickman used historic records to postulate social and economic interactions that took place during the early to mid-twentieth century at William Keys' Desert Queen Ranch, now in Joshua Tree National Monument. The analytic concept of social network was used in conjunction with a model from exchange theory in order to predict how developments in the surrounding area could have affected behavior at the ranch. This gave a basis for evaluating how the ranch could be used to test theory-based assumptions about regional and local sociocultural change (Hickman 1977, n.d.).

Klein (1977) has discussed a twentieth-century site that provided data on a little known and nearly vanished lifeway of an American subculture, and Hickman (1977) has shown how modern sites may yield valuable information for testing anthropological propositions. The point is that sites of any age may be significant if they contain information.

Familiarity

A strange but often recited view holds that resources of a "well-known type" are generally less significant than relatively unknown ones. This is a spurious contention on several counts. First, familiarity is always defined with respect to particular research interests, and these change through time. Second, "well-known" resources may permit the answering of complex research questions *because* they are well known—that is, because fundamental aspects of their cultural record have already been worked out. To illustrate, King (1976) was able to investigate the evolution of the social organization of Indians who lived for 3000 years in a small California valley; the study was possible largely because the basic prehistory of the locality had been reconstructed during five seasons' of earlier work by King and the senior author (Moratto 1972). The lesson here is that knowledge is a relative thing, and "well-known" sites may be more or less significant than their "poorly known" counterparts, depending on the research context of the evaluation. Lastly, we would point out that well-studied resources are readily amenable to public interpretation, and, in this sense, the public significance of a resource may increase as its scientific potential is realized and more data become available.

RANKING CULTURAL RESOURCES

Thompson recently observed:

> Under the present system, we have no reasonably objective way to set priorities when the funds available are inadequate. . . . We cannot carry out our proper role as guardians of our archaeological heritage until we develop a better system. Nor can we stand aside and wait for others, such as planners and decision makers, to make the judgment of significance for us. Archaeologists must carry out these evaluations using procedures consistent with sound archaeological principles [1977:5].

Clearly the profession must find ways to translate sound evaluations of significance into recommendations for planning purposes. Unfortunately, some investigators have met this challenge with simple schemes to rank cultural resources in a way that not only reflects a misunderstanding of the concept of significance but also may establish some devastating precedents for cultural resource management (Iroquois Research Institute 1978).

One archaeologist–planner recommends that sites be ranked into "critical," "major," and "minor" categories according to their currently perceived information potential. No other criteria of significance are accommodated by this tripartite scheme. Another archaeologist, in his environmental impact studies, regularly segregates sites into four levels of significance: (1) "potential National Register sites" (e.g., very large pueblos); (2) "significant sites" (e.g., pueblos of 6–20 rooms); (3) "sites of lesser significance" (e.g., pueblos of about 5 rooms); and (4) "sites of minor significance" (e.g., sherd scatters or isolated structures). The explicit purpose of such ranking schemes is to permit compromises with developers—that is, to trade off or relinquish "minor" resources so that "major" ones can be spared. We fully appreciate the need for reasonable management practices; however, we cannot endorse any model of re-source prioritization that depends on a single criterion (such as the size of a pueblo) or that establishes a priori that all resources can be packaged into three (or four) echelons of significance.

Another approach to ranking cultural properties was suggested by Bell and Gettys (n.d.). In their evaluation of various proposed waterway projects in Arkansas, Bell and Gettys developed a series of 18 "factors," each of which was believed to represent some aspect of significance. The factors comprised a mixed bag—the size, depth, type, and uniqueness of sites, along with estimated costs of doing survey and salvage work along each alternate route, etc. The factors were weighted, and the summed numerical values were then used to rank each project in terms of the quantitative magnitude of its anticipated adverse effect (Bell and Gettys n.d.).

In a thoughtful criticism of this system, Schiffer and Gumerman (1977a) note that there is no reason to believe that size or depth of the sites will relate to information potential or any other measures of significance; indeed, from the perspective of settlement systems analysis, the smallest site in a region may offer as many data as the largest. We would add that the costs of survey and salvage work have no logical bearing on the actual significance of cultural remains. One site may return great quantities of data for a modest price; in another case the cost–benefit ratio may be reversed. As we have emphasized already, such financial factors ought to be evaluated only after significance has been determined by using other criteria.

Using an approach similar to that of Bell and Gettys, Thompson (1977) suggested 20 categories of information—chronology, ethnic identity, sociocultural processes, potential for public interpretation, etc.—to be used for evaluating and prioritizing archaeological resources. Many of Thompson's categories are useful, and we concur with his use of multiple professional criteria for resource assessments. Nonetheless, we are not entirely comfortable with his suggestions about prioritizing cultural resources.

The problem here lies more with the concept of ranking than with the particular schemes designed to cope with it. Ranking cultural properties, as a response to developers' needs, is a planning device basically incompatible with archaeological ideals. We are asked to generate simple models (ranked lists) from complex realities (diverse cultural resources) for the ultimate purpose of destroying some resources and preserving others.

This situation has caused a dilemma for archaeologists. On the one hand, it seems clear that cultural resources cannot be ranked because of the complex and polythetic nature of their significance; rank ordering by any given measure of significance will crosscut prioritizations based on other criteria. On the other hand, land managers often want some properties to be set apart as more significant than others (Schiffer and Gumerman 1977a). Some planners confuse ranking sites with ranking management actions, equating "high" and "low" significance with designs for protection and destruction respectively. Lamentably, at least some "researchers" have fallen into the same trap by writing off as "insignificant" hundreds of archaeological sites for which preservation was deemed inconvenient by a project sponsor (Iroquois Research Institute 1978). Cultural resource prioritization is thus an issue of utmost concern today. The critical problems are *how* the significance of properties will be assessed and how significance determinations will figure in the management equation. Our thoughts on this matter are summarized below.

SUMMARY AND CONCLUSIONS

We have emphasized that there are many standards of significance applicable to cultural resources. These vary according to the qualities of the resources, the context of the assessment, and the perspectives of the evaluator. A given property may entail public, historical, ethnic, or scientific significance, or some combination of these. Additionally, legal and monetary considerations will emerge as CRM actions are deliberated. Because of the many possible standards, reviewers need to make explicit their criteria for assessing the individual and relative worth of given resources. We suggest that multiple criteria be applied in any evaluation of cultural resources and in any effort to prioritize them.

The concept of significance is so complex that a formulated or cookbook approach to resource assessment is out of the question. There can be no substitute for professional expertise in determining significance and designing actions based on significance. Beyond professional competency, the archaeologist must have adequate information (such as data from test excavations) about the property being evaluated. In most cases, both regional and site-specific research designs will provide the necessary framework for evaluating significance, and many assessments will be interdisciplinary efforts: Unless the archaeologists ask, they may have no idea of the potential value of their resources to other sciences.

Archaeologists need to go beyond the *process* of evaluating significance and to examine the larger *context* within which the evaluations are manipulated. Although significance appraisals are central to CRM planning, management decisions often represent a compromise to suit the needs of developers and planners. Archaeologists seldom actually make the decisions that directly affect cultural properties, nor do they presently influence most of the high-level policies that will ultimately affect the resources. We therefore see present CRM actions, including significance assessments, as a mid-range strategy. The discipline needs a grand strategy to deal with cultural resources so as to maximize their data return and benefits to society. We envision a national policy for the optimum long-term use of cultural resources—a policy by which specific management plans can be evaluated. Currently archaeological properties are indicated, tried, and sentenced in the courts of sewer and highway projects. It would make far more sense to design CRM actions according to national policies for the optimum use of cultural and other nonrenewable resources.

Toward this end, archaeological information must be gathered from dusty shelves and actively applied to solve modern problems. Consider the implications of this statement, written with regard to energy policies:

> Our leaders must seriously analyze the past activities of our nation to determine the events that have produced our present crisis. We suggest that the root cause of our difficulties is the nation's belief that infinite economic growth is both good and possible. We suggest that another cause is infatuation with quick answers that ignore long-range effects [Christiansen and Clack 1976:578].

In this light, archaeology has a particularly important role to play in the development of national policies for land use and resource exploitation. No other discipline controls so much real and potential data on long-term man–environment relationships. With this immense potential in mind, we must abandon the paradigm that treats cultural remains as victims of progress, and shift to a paradigm that envisions the resources as indispensible banks of data for land-use planning and related contemporary developments.

We can illustrate why archaeological input is critical in land-use planning, especially where long-term projections are needed. The adaptation of the Pacific states depends on vast quantities of water for irrigation, industrial and domestic use, and power generation. Enormous reservoirs and canals, a multi-billion dollar agribusiness, and a population of 30 million people are operating on the assumption that historic climatic conditions, especially precipitation levels, are "normal." Recently, data from archaeology, palynology, dendroclimatology, and allied sciences have shown that this assumption is doubtful. The data indicate that the Far West experienced repeated cycles of climatic change during the past 10,000 years, and that the changes were of sufficient magnitude to greatly affect former cultures (Moratto *et al.* n.d.). The climate now appears to be shifting from a 600-year period of relatively high moisture to an interval of dry conditions. To the extent that projections based on a long archaeological and climatic record may prove valid, the region seems destined for a sustained future—possibly centuries—of drought.

Needless to say, data bearing on such momentous concerns should be embodied in national and regional planning. But how can this be done? How can the full social and scientific potentials of archaeological data be realized and not be sacrificed to the trivial gods of highways and dams? We think the answer lies in the active (as opposed to reactive) participation of archaeologists in policymaking and planning. Archaeological data and their applications must become known to a wider circle of scientists, government officials, planners, and developers. Archaeologists must become tuned in to policy development and planning at the conceptual stage and to remain actively involved through the design and implementation stages. Instead of laboring *in vacuo* to save cultural resources endangered by a planned reservoir, archaeologists should ask whether long-term climatic projections justify the reservoir in the first place. Before scrambling to design a CRM plan in response to an impending sewer project, archaeologists should question whether the population growth to be induced by the sewer is wise in light of the cultural record.

In a word, archaeology must broaden its horizons and develop mechanisms to implant its data into such varied frameworks as the national energy policy, the biosphere reserve program (Franklin 1977), proposals to develop new units in the Park, Forest, Wilderness, and Wild and Scenic River systems, and plans for neighborhood conservation actions.

New levels of archaeological significance will emerge as fresh applications of cultural resource data to modern problems are discovered. In sum, archaeology must evolve to participate more fully in the alliance of science and society for mutual benefit:

> To achieve a truly holistic or ecosystemic approach, . . . disciplines in the natural, social, and political sciences . . . must emerge to new hitherto unrecognized and unresearched levels of thinking and action [Odum 1977:1292].

REFERENCES

Atwater, B. F., and C. W. Hedel
1976 Distribution of seed plants with respect to tide levels and water salinity in the natural tidal marshes of the northern San Francisco Bay estuary. *U. S. Geological Survey Open File Report* No. 76-389.

Bell, R. E., and M. Gettys
n.d. A consideration of the archaeological and historical resources involved in the Mid-Ark project. Manuscript, on deposit, Arkansas Archaeological Survey, Fayetteville.

Birely, R.
1977 A frontier post in Roman Britain. *Scientific American* **236**(2):38–46.

Brothwell, D., and A. T. Sandison (editors)
1967 *Diseases in antiquity*. Springfield, Ill.: Thomas.

Casteel, R. W.
1976 *Fish remains in archaeology*. New York: Academic Press.

Christiansen, B., and T. H. Clack, Jr.
1976 A Western perspective on energy: A plea for rational energy planning. *Science* **194**:578–584.

Clark, G.
1970 *Aspects of prehistory*. Berkeley: University of California Press.

Cummins, G. T.
1977 Ethnic group, site, and society: The concept of ethnic significance of cultural resources. Manuscript on deposit, Arizona State Museum Library, Tucson.

Deetz, J.
1973 Ceramics from Plymouth, 1635–1835. In *Ceramics in America*, edited by I. M. G. Quimby. Charlottesville: University of Virginia Press. Pp. 15–40.
1977 *In small things forgotten*. Garden City: Anchor Press, Doubleday.

Dimbleby, G. W.
1965 Inaugural lecture. Institute of Archaeology, London University.

Dixon, K. A.
1977 Applications of archaeological resources: Broadening the basis of significance. In *Conservation archaeology: A guide for cultural resource management studies*, edited by M. B. Schiffer and G. J. Gumerman. New York: Academic Press. Pp. 277–290.

Fitch, J. E.
1969 Fossil records of certain schooling fishes of the California current system. *California Marine Commission Report* **13**:71–80.

Ford, R. I.
1973 Archaeology serving humanity. In *Research and theory in current archaeology*, edited by C. L. Redman. New York: Wiley. Pp. 83–93.

Franklin, J. E.
1977 The biosphere reserve program in the United States. *Science* **195**:262–267.

Fritz, J., and F. Plog
1970 The nature of archaeological explanation. *American Antiquity* **35**(4):405–412.

Glassow, M. A.
1977 Issues in evaluating the significance of archaeological resources. *American Antiquity* **42**(3):413–420.

Glassow, M. A., L. W. Spanne, and J. Quilter
    1976   *Evaluation of archaeological sites on Vandenberg Air Force Base, Santa Barbara County, California: Final Report.* Santa Barbara: University of California.
Gould, R. A.
    1977   The archaeologist as ethnographer. In *Horizons of anthropology*, edited by S. Tax and L. Freeman (2nd ed.). Chicago: Aldine. Pp. 151–170.
Grady, M. A.
    1977   Significance evaluation and the Orme Reservoir project. In *Conservation archaeology: A guide for cultural resource management studies*, edited by M. B. Schiffer and G. J. Gumerman. New York: Academic Press. Pp. 259–267.
Green, E. L.
    n.d.   Is this site worth saving? New arguments for the preservation of cultural resources. Manuscript on deposit, Southern Region, U. S. Forest Service, Atlanta.
Harrington, J. C.
    1957   New light on Washington's Fort Necessity. Richmond, Va.: Eastern National Park and Monument Association.
Heizer, R. F., and A. L. Kroeber
    1976   For sale: California at 47 cents per acre. *The Journal of California Anthropology* **3**(2):38–65.
Hickman, P. P.
    1977   Problems of significance: Two case studies. In *Conservation archaeology: A guide for cultural resource management studies*, edited by M. B. Schiffer and G. J. Gumerman. New York: Academic Press. Pp. 269–275.
    n.d.   Country nodes: An anthropological evaluation of William Keys' Desert Queen Ranch, Joshua Tree National Monument, California. Manuscript on deposit, Western Archaeological Center, U. S. National Park Service, Tucson.
House, J. H., and M. B. Schiffer
    1975   Significance of the archaeological resources of the Cache River Basin. *Arkansas Archaeological Survey Research Series* **8**:163–186.
Iroquois Research Institute
    1978   Management plan for cultural resources for New Melones Lake Recreation Area. Report to the Sacramento District, U.S. Army Corps of Engineers, Sacramento.
Johnson, E. (compiler)
    1977   Archaeology and Native Americans. In *The management of archaeological resources: The Airlie House report*, edited by C. R. McGimsey, III and H. A. Davis. Washington, D. C.: Society for American Archaeology. Pp. 90–96.
Kelly, R. E.
    1974   An archaeologist looks at landmark programs. *California Historian* **21**(1):6–7.
King, C. D., and D. G. Casebier
    1976   *Background to historic and prehistoric resources of the east Mojave Desert region.* Riverside, Calif.: U.S. Bureau of Land Management.
King, T. F.
    1974   The evolution of status ascription around San Francisco Bay. *Ballena Press Anthropological Papers* **2**:35–53.
    1976   Political differentiation among hunter-gatherers: An archaeological test. Unpublished Ph.D. dissertation, Department of Anthropology, University of California, Riverside.

1977   Open letter to New York Archaeological Council members and others regarding state historic preservation policies and actions in New York. March 5, Washington, D.C. On deposit, New York Archaeological Council, Buffalo.

King, T. F., and P. P. Hickman
1973   *The southern Santa Clara Valley, California: A general plan for archaeology* (Special Publication). San Francisco: A. E. Treganza Anthropology Museum.

King, T. F., P. P. Hickman, and G. Berg
1977   *Anthropology and historic preservation: Caring for culture's clutter.* New York: Academic Press.

Klein, J. I.
1977   20th century archaeological sites: Are they eligible for the National Register? Paper presented at the annual meeting of the Society for Historical Archaeology, Ottawa.

Kroeber, A. L.
1972   More Mojave myths. *University of California Anthropological Records* **27**.

Lajoie, K.
1972   *Ancient shorelines and sea levels of the San Francisco Bay region.* Menlo Park: U. S. Geological Survey (Map).

Lipe, W. D.
1974   A conservation model for American archaeology. *The Kiva* **39**(3/4):213–245.

Lipe, W. D., and M. A. Grady
1975   The problem of significance. Manuscript on deposit, Washington State University, Pullman, and Southern Methodist University, Dallas. (A revised version of this paper was subsequently included in the compilation by McMillan *et al.*, 1977.)

Lipe. W. D., and A. J. Lindsay, Jr. (editors)
1974   Proceedings of the 1974 Cultural Resources Management Conference, Federal Center, Denver, Colorado. *Museum of Northern Arizona Technical Series* **14**:1–231.

McDermott, J. D.
1977   Problems in the protection and preservation of archaeological resources. *Advisory Council Report* **5**(2/3):57–61. (Special Issue.)

McGimsey, C. R., III
1972   *Public archaeology.* New York: Seminar Press.

McGimsey, C. R., III, and H. A. Davis (editors)
1977   *The management of archaeological resources: The Airlie House report.* Washington, D. C.: Society for American Archaeology.

McMillan, B., M. Grady, and W. Lipe (compilers)
1977   Cultural resource management. In *The Management of archaeological resources: The Airlie House report*, edited by C. R. McGimsey, III and H. A. Davis. Washington, D. C.: Society for American Archaeology. Pp. 25–63.

MacNeish, R. S., and D. S. Byers (general editors)
1967   *The prehistory of the Tehuacan Valley.* Austin: University of Texas Press.
1976

Majno, G.
1975   *The healing hand: Man and wound in the ancient world.* Cambridge, Mass.: Harvard University Press.

May, R. V.
1976   The threshhold of significance: Semantic conflicts between land developers, environmental planners, and archaeologists. *The Artifact* **14**(2):33–40.

Meighan, C. W.
 1974 Hints on national site nomination: Registration of archaeological sites and historic monuments. *Society for California Archaeology Newsletter* **8**(6):3, 5, 7.
Miller, D. S.
 1975 *A report on the significance of certain properties associated with traditional ideological beliefs and practices of northwestern California Indians.* San Francisco: California Region, U. S. Forest Service, San Francisco.
Moratto, M. J.
 1972 A study of prehistory in the southern Sierra Nevada foothills, California. Unpublished Ph.D. dissertation, Department of Anthropology, University of Oregon, Eugene.
 1975 On the concept of archaeological significance. Paper presented at the annual northern California sectional meeting of the Society for California Archaeology, Fresno.
 1977a A consideration of law in archaeology. In *The management of archaeological resources: The Airlie House report,* edited by C. R. McGimsey, III and H. A. Davis. Washington, D. C.: Society for American Archaeology. Pp. 8–24.
 1977b Research prospects: New Melones archaeological project. In *Conservation archaeology: A guide for cultural resource management studies,* edited by M. B. Schiffer and G. J. Gumerman. New York: Academic Press. Pp. 401–411.
Moratto, M. J., and R. E. Kelly
 1977 Significance in archaeology. *The Kiva* **42**(2):193–202.
Moratto, M. J., T. F. King, and W. B. Woolfenden
 n.d.   Archaeology and climate in California. Manuscript on deposit, Idaho Panhandle National Forests, Coeur d'Alene.
National Register of Historic Places (NRHP)
 1977 *How to complete National Register forms.* Washington, D. C.: Office of Archaeology and Historic Preservation.
Odum, E. P.
 1977 The emergence of ecology as a new integrating discipline. *Science* **195**:1289–1293.
Office of Archeology and Historic Preservation (OAHP)
 1976 Letter critique of a specious criterion for evaluating archaeological significance. Letter on deposit, Office of Archeology and Historic Preservation, Heritage Conservation and Recreation Service, Washington, D. C.
Raab, L. M., and T. C. Klinger
 1977 A critical appraisal of "significance" in contract archaeology. *American Antiquity* **42**(4):629–634.
Saucier, R. T.
 1974 Quaternary geology of the lower Mississippi alluvial valley. *Arkansas Archaeological Survey Research Series* **6**.
Schiffer, M. B., and G. J. Gumerman
 1977a Assessing significance. In *Conservation archaeology: A guide for cultural resource management studies,* edited by M. B. Schiffer and G. J. Gumerman. New York: Academic Press. Pp. 239–247.
 1977b Mitigation. In *Conservation archaeology: A guide for cultural resource management studies,* edited by M. B. Schiffer and G. J. Gumerman. New York: Academic Press. Pp. 321–330.
 1977c (editors) *Conservation archaeology: A guide for cultural resource management studies.* New York: Academic Press.

Schiffer, M. B., and J. H. House
   1975   (assemblers) The Cache River archaeological project. *Arkansas Archaeological Survey Research Series* **8.**
   1977a   An approach to assessing scientific significance. In *Conservation archaeology: A guide to cultural resource management studies*, edited by M. B. Schiffer and G. J. Gumerman. New York: Academic Press. Pp. 249–257.
   1977b   Cultural resource management and archaeological research: The Cache project. *Current Anthropology* **18**(1):43–68.
Schuyler, R.
   1976   Images of America: The contribution of historical archaeology to national identity. *Southwestern Lore* **42**(4):27–39.
Scovill, D., G. Gordon, and K. Anderson
   1972   *Guidelines for the preparation of statements of environmental impact on archaeological resources.* Tucson: Western Archaeological Center, U. S. National Park Service.
Talmage, V., O. Chesler, and staff of Interagency Archeological Services
   1977   *The importance of small, surface, and disturbed sites as sources of significant archeological data.* Washington, D. C.: Interagency Archeological Services, National Park Service.
Thompson, R. H.
   1977   Letter to C. Silvestro, Chairman, Advisory Council on Historic Preservation, regarding the status of federal programs in archaeological and historic preservation and recommendations to improve it. University of Arizona, Tucson.
Wilson, D.
   1976   *The new archaeology.* New York: Meridian.
Wilson, R.
   1977   Foreward. In *The importance of small, surface, and disturbed sites as sources of significant archeological data*, by V. Talmage, O. Cheslter *et al.* Washington, D. C.: Interagency Archeological Services, National Park Service. Pp. i–ii.
Woodbury, N., and C. R. McGimsey, III
   1977   The crisis in communication. In *The management of archaeological resources: The Airlie House report*, edited by C. R. McGimsey, III and H. A. Davis. Washington, D. C.: Society for American Archaeology. Pp. 78–89.
Wright, R. H.
   1971   Map showing locations of samples dated by radiocarbon methods in the San Francisco Bay region. *U. S. Geological Survey Miscellaneous Field Studies Map* MF-317.

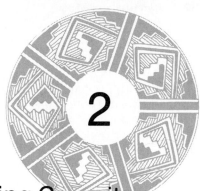

The Concept of Carrying Capacity
in the Study of Culture Process

MICHAEL A. GLASSOW

The concept of carrying capacity has come to be one of the foundation stones of modern cultural ecology, as its prominence in Hardesty's text attests (Hardesty 1977:195–211). In fact, Brush (1975) argues that the concept is a crucial element in what he calls the "New Ecology" paradigm because of its close relation with the concepts of homeostasis and ecological regulation. Although Brush may have overemphasized the importance of the concept in cultural ecological studies (Vayda 1976), it is obvious that the carrying capacity concept is fundamental to many studies of population–environment relationships.

The concept appears to have gained much of its popularity in anthropology over the last 20 years as a result of Birdsell's (1953) study of the relationship between rainfall and Australian aboriginal population density and a somewhat earlier commentary by Bartholomew and Birdsell (1953:488), which argued for the importance of searching for limiting factors in accounting for hunter–gatherer population densities. Explicit use of the concept, particularly with regard to the estimation of the carrying capacity of agrarian adaptations, appears to begin with Carneiro's (1960) and Conklin's (1959) studies of shifting cultivators. One may also perceive the influence of Meggers' (1954) study of "environmental limitations" on cultural development. Although she did not refer to carrying capacity, the various reactions to her study resulted in attempts by others to evaluate the "agricultural potential" of specific regions and

ADVANCES IN ARCHAEOLOGICAL METHOD AND THEORY, VOL. 1

to isolate limiting factors that affect the growth of population and ultimately cultural development—two subjects closely related to the carrying capacity concept (e.g., Coe 1957:332–335; Cowgill and Hutchinson 1963). More recently, social scientists in other disciplines have influenced anthropological use of the concept (e.g., Allan 1949, 1965; Boserup 1965). In particular, Boserup's use of the concept in her study of agricultural growth has stimulated anthropologists to evaluate her model, or the theory implied by it, against their own data (Spooner 1972; Bartlett 1976).

My objectives in this study will be to investigate the place of the concept in contemporary ecological research, to evaluate its role in the explanations of cultural change and evolution, and to propose a theoretical model, which may be seen as an alternative to that using or implying the concept of carrying capacity. Although I shall be defending the concept against criticisms (Brush 1975; Hayden 1975), I shall also be pointing out certain inadequacies in the theoretical models of cultural development that use the concept. I shall *not* be concerned with population pressure models that apply the concept in explanations of cultural change. Recent criticisms (Bronson 1972, 1975; Cowgill 1975a,b) have been leveled primarily against the simplistic or exclusive use of such models rather than against the models themselves. A defense of these criticisms would be beyond the scope of this chapter.

DEFINITIONS AND USES OF THE CARRYING CAPACITY CONCEPT

In defining carrying capacity, it is first necessary to realize that the term has been used in two quite different senses: as an abstract concept in theoretical constructions, and as a measure of specific aspects of the relationship between a particular human population and its environment. Although scholars critical of the concept do make this distinction (Brush 1975:802; Hayden 1975:11), the full implications of this distinction are not fully appreciated. Various texts in biological ecology present carrying capacity as primarily a theoretical concept. In one sense of the term, it refers to the upper asymptote of a sigmoid growth curve—a particular characteristic of a graphical model. In a more popular sense, it is the "upper level, beyond which no major increase [in population size] can occur" (Odum 1959:183), a definition close to that in other texts (Ricklefs 1973:504, 507; Kormondy 1976:79). Many of the classic examples of *measures* of carrying capacity to which these texts refer are either measures of the growth to an equilibrium population size of simple organisms under highly controlled laboratory conditions or are not really measures at all, being instead inductive inferences based on observation of growth curves of natural population (Ricklefs 1973:509; Kormondy 1976:111–112). Nevertheless, the concept as a measure is widely used in such applied fields of biological ecology as wildlife and livestock management. Significantly, however, the theoretical biologists do not seem to be as concerned as are the theoretical anthropologists with the problems associated with the empirical application of the concept.

Anthropological definitions of the concept range from simple to complex. Zubrow has proposed a relatively simple definition comparable to those presented by biological ecologists: "the maximum number of organisms or amounts of biomass which can maintain itself indefinitely in an area, in other words, a homeostatic equilibrium point" (1971:128, 1975:15). More complex definitions include at least one qualifier: Carrying capacity must refer to a particular form of land use (Street 1969) or, to put it another way, to a given level of cultural development (Cook 1972:25). More complex definitions specify that carrying capacity refer to (a) a particular form of land use, or level of cultural development, (b) specific environmental circumstances, and (c) a level of exploitation such that resources are not depleted (Allan 1965:469; Street 1969:104; Cook 1972:25; Brush 1975:806). The addition of these qualifications to the general definition reflect the efforts of anthropologists to measure carrying capacity in the field. That is, anthropologists have realized that a measuring technique developed for one region and cultural adaptation is not necessarily applicable to another (Brookfield and Brown 1963:113; Bayless-Smith 1974:262).

A number of different approaches to the measurement of carrying capacity have been developed, many of which have been summarized by Hardesty (1977:199–203). The approaches to the estimation of carrying capacity of environments in which agricultural adaptations are practiced have generally been concerned with estimating the total amount of arable land in a given region and dividing this value by the amount of land required under a given agricultural system by the average individual. This approach normally requires that information be available regarding agricultural productivity per unit of land, the food value represented by a unit of agricultural production, and the proportion of the diet consisting of agricultural products. Moreover, since this approach has been applied primarily to environments in which swidden agriculture is practiced, the length of the fallow period must also be included in the equation. The different formulas using this approach to measurement are all very similar and have been summarized by Brush (1975:800–801). Brookfield and Brown (1963:108–113) present a useful elaboration of the approach, which takes into account several different land types, each with a different productivity, and Bayliss-Smith (1974:285) employs a formula specific to taro cultivation on Pacific atolls (for which a fallow period factor is unnecessary).

Zubrow's measures of prehistoric agricultural carrying capacities of different microhabitats in the Hay Hollow Valley, Arizona, depart from the above approach. His 1971 study begins with an estimation of the biomass production for each of six microhabitats in his study area, using "somewhat arbitrarily" data presented by Odum (1959:403). He then assumes a 2500-kcal individual daily nutritional requirement and a 5% consumption rate of the biomass production to calculate the number of people who could be supported within the area of each microhabitat. Although Zubrow (1975:86) emphasizes that this procedure is best followed only for relative ordering of the microhabitat carrying capacities, it is unclear how he used Odum's data and how he made his calculations of carrying capacities. In his 1975 study, Zubrow adds a modification to his original procedure, which involves replacing values derived from Odum with values derived from field data reflecting floral and faunal productivities and standing crops in each of the microhabitats. Again, his objective is simply to rank the microhabitats rather than to produce absolute carrying capacity estimates.

Casteel's (1972) two models for estimating maximum hunter–gatherer carrying capacities bear some resemblance to Zubrow's approach. Casteel's "specific" model is based on the net primary production of different types of ecosystems, the trophic level at which the human population articulates with the ecosystem, a 0.5% consumption rate (instead of Zubrow's 5%), and several aspects of human settlement patterns, including the number of days per year of exploitation, the number of ecosystems exploited, and the area in each actually utilized. Modifications of the basic model are made for instances in which food resources are obtained from aquatic environments or through trade. Casteel's "general" model uses basically the same approach, differing only in its dependence on less information about settlement patterns.

Shawcross (1967) has presented a much more specific and specialized measure of carrying capacity in comparison with either Zubrow's or Casteel's in that he is concerned with estimating the carrying capacity of only one resource within his study area. He estimates the maximum human population size that could be supported by the shellfish available in a New Zealand harbor. This estimate was calculated by first collecting a probability sample of shellfish in a portion of the harbor in order to estimate the total size of the shellfish population. The calorific value of this shellfish population was then estimated, and this was divided by the individual daily calorific requirement of humans to yield the number of person–days of available shellfish food. This value was then converted into the number of people who could be supported for a given period of time or, conversely, the amount of time required to exploit the shellfish by a given number of people.

Shawcross (1970) refined his technique in a subsequent study by considering ethnographic and other information on the proportion of the aboriginal New Zealand population that collected shellfish, the number of days during which shellfish were collected per year, and the "productive efficiency" (the proportion of the total resource abundance actually collected). After gaining some confidence in the technique by applying it to another region for which the historic Maori population size was known, he used his technique to estimate the total Maori population of New Zealand, assuming in the process that the population was at carrying capacity.

An approach to estimating the carrying capacity of hunter–gatherers that is roughly similar to Shawcross' has been proposed by Jochim (1976:70–72). His measure assumes that one does or can know the proportional contribution in kilocalories of each food resource in an aboriginal diet, as well as the density or abundance of each resource. For each resource, the number of kilocalories available for consumption per 100 km² is calculated, and this figure is divided by the proportion that this resource contributes to the total annual diet. The quotient of this division is the total kilocalories available for human consumption in the region if this resource is being exploited in the prescribed proportion. The "maximum supportable population" would be equal to this value divided by the annual individual human kilocalorie requirement. The actual carrying capacity, according to Jochim, would be the lowest maximum supportable population size among the resources for which these values were obtained, taking into account harvesting efficiency.

In summarizing the above discussion, the different approaches to the estimation of carrying capacity may be classified in several ways. Casteel's, Jochim's, and Shawcross' approaches apply to hunter–gatherers and refer to the abundance of wild food resources, whereas Zubrow's and the several approaches developed for swidden agriculturalists refer to the abundance and productivity of agricultural lands. The approaches may also be grouped in terms of their specificity. Casteel, Shawcross, and Zubrow estimate "theoretical" carrying capacities with only indirect reference to particular adaptations; the rest of the estimates are tied to particular kinds of adaptation. Finally, the approaches may be grouped in terms of their applications. Shawcross was interested in estimating carrying capacity more or less as a population measure. Zubrow believed that his estimates reflected the degree of "marginality" of different habitats.

All the others wished to ascertain the difference between actual population sizes and those that could, theoretically, be supported in given regions.

CRITICISMS OF CARRYING CAPACITY MEASURES

All these approaches to the measurement of carrying capacity have certain shortcomings, some more serious than others. I present here those already identified, as well as others that are obvious to me.

Street (1969) has argued that the several estimates of carrying capacity for agrarian populations have neglected to give enough attention to the dynamic aspects of carrying capacity—that is, to the fact that carrying capacity is affected by changing agricultural practices and soil fertility. Following Boserup (1965), he argues that agricultural techniques—for instance, level of agricultural intensification—may be relatively fluid in a given region, requiring that careful attention be given to defining what agricultural practices pertain to a given estimate of carrying capacity. Moreover, Street points out that assumptions about the rate of soil depletion, which affect such factors as length of fallow period, have not been supported by adequate empirical data. Brush (1975:807–809) repeats many of these criticisms. He especially emphasizes the difficulties in coping with the complexity of factors that impinge on the variables that must be measured in producing an estimate of carrying capacity.

Zubrow's approach to estimating carrying capacity suffers from two major flaws. In the first place, there is no justification for assuming that either Odum's or his own data in any way reflect the agricultural potential of the microhabitats in his study area. He appears to assume that modern floral and faunal standing crops or productivities reflect prehistoric agricultural potential—a dangerous assumption, especially since fields were probably located in comparatively small and specialized portions of the microhabitats, and irrigation and perhaps other water control techniques were used by prehistoric farmers in this region. Consequently, his ranking of the microhabitats in terms of potential could conceivably be the reverse of his expectations. Second, because the *area* of each microhabitat strongly influences his measures of carrying capacity, Zubrow is unjustified in asserting that his carrying capacity rankings reflect the relative "marginality" of the microhabitats for agricultural pursuits. Because of these flaws, Zubrow's approach does not yield confident estimates of carrying capacity for agricultural adaptations.

Castecl's approach seems adequate if only a comparatively rough approximation is necessary. The principal shortcoming of his two models is that they are concerned with estimating some sort of ultimate carrying capacity for any hunter–gatherer adaptation within a given trophic level. That is, his approach does not compensate for the fact that different hunter–gatherer adaptations at a given trophic level in a given region would each be associated with a different carrying capacity. Moreover, his use of a constant consumption rate across different environments, along with his neglect of what resources are actually exploited by a given population, would appear to jeopardize his estimates of how much below carrying capacity a given population is.

The approach used by Jochim is one of the more rigorous, especially since it is based ultimately on a variety of detailed environmental information and a set of economic assumptions about the nature of hunter–gatherer adaptations. Unfortunately, his approach does not take into consideration the fact that hunter–gatherer carrying capacities may be determined primarily by the seasonal availability or abundance of certain resources rather than their simple densities. Nevertheless, he does provide in his study information on the seasonality of resources, so his measure could be revised by applying his formula to each season (or month, in the case of his data). The carrying capacity would then be the lowest value in the "maximum supportable population" matrix thus produced.

A few general conclusions may be drawn from these critiques of specific approaches to the estimation of carrying capacity. First, any measure used to estimate the population size that a given habitat can support in order to compare it with the actual population size found in the habitat should ideally take into consideration a number of specifics regarding (a) what resources are exploited and what are their abundances, (b) how the resources are exploited, (c) the degree of dependence on each resource, and (d) the viability of the resources under different levels of exploitation. These strictures mean that Casteel's and Zubrow's approaches do not have much utility, since neither is concerned with identifying specific resources exploited or the exploitive technologies used. Second, carrying capacity measures may be seen as existing on different levels of abstraction from reality. While many of the formulas for estimating the carrying capacity of swidden agriculturalists may be reduced to one basic formula, the values for each of the variables in the formula will differ from one application to the next, and different kinds of elaborations of the basic formula will have to be added to order to take into consideration such factors as diversity in land fertility and agricultural practices. This may be true also with regard to Jochim's measure of carrying capacity for hunter–gatherer adaptations, which, with some refinement, could be said to involve the use of a "basic" formula that would be modified in various ways with each empirical application. Finally, there is considerable room for improvement in the specific empirical measures themselves and also in the quality of data that are collected in the course of applying the measures.

A DEFENSE OF THE CARRYING CAPACITY CONCEPT

Brush (1975) and Hayden (1975) have gone beyond simply criticizing particular approaches to the estimation of carrying capacity to argue that the measures will never be refined to a point where we can have much confidence in them, and as a result the concept itself must be discarded. I believe that this position is unjustified, and I shall attempt to demonstrate that the critics of the carrying capacity concept fail to realize that our present difficulty with obtaining accurate measurements is no reason to reject the concept from its role in theoretical constructions.

Of the two critics, Brush appears more moderate. He points to many of the inadequacies of the various attempts to measure carrying capacity as indicating that the concept is untestable (1975:806) and that the value of the concept has been "essentially descriptive and heuristic" (1975:809). Elsewhere, in defending his views on the "New Ecology" paradigm, he asserts that a "crucial task for ecological anthropologists" is to determine "how we are to retain the concept of ecosystem as a practical model, and yet do away with the concept of carrying capacity" (1976:646).

Hayden goes even further in disparaging the concept by asserting that it "has been inadequate to the theoretical and field framework and has proven nonoperational as a measure," and he argues that "it should be replaced by more realistic concepts and measures" (1975:11). Like Brush, he states that it is impossible or nearly impossible to calculate such environmental variables as the amount of potential food resource available to a population or the degree and rate of environmental degradation, and that the calculation of the amount of food that could be obtained by a given technology is nearly unachievable. In addition, he quite correctly points out that the carrying capacity concept fails to take into consideration that there are not only annual cycles of lean seasons to which a population must adjust but also a number of longer-term cycles of lean periods with intervals in the order of 10, 25, or 200 years. In light of these longer-term cycles, he poses the question: "Must one then say that all groups experiencing frequent, intermediate or rare famine and mortality are really over their carrying capacity?" (1975:14).

Hayden points out that populations will regulate their numbers at some level at which shorter-term cycles of resource depletion will have no appreciable effect on mortality rates but will not regulate numbers in light of longer-term cycles—usually characterized by more drastic reductions in resources—because of the great energy expenditures required to maintain the knowledge of these. To Hayden, the important questions concern what cycles of resource depletion will affect population numbers and what factors determine which cycles these are for particular kinds of cultural systems. As a replacement for the carrying capacity measure, he proposes what he calls the Resource Over-Exploitation or Roe rate, which is the "recurrence interval in which varying intensities of shortages occur," given a particular population density and technology (1975:18).

I would certainly agree with Brush and Hayden that the various measures of carrying capacity, or at least their applications, leave much to be desired. However, there is no reason to discard a concept simply because of the inadequacies of current quantitative techniques. What Hayden sees as the "shortcomings" and Brush as the "weakness" of the concept are certainly not insurmountable. It is possible, at least in principle, to hold technology constant and to specify and measure the abundance of the resources upon which a population depends. The fact that these variables are not always measured as accurately as we would like only reflects the minimal concern that has so far been given to the development of quantitative techniques of measurement rather than the degree to which these variables can be operationalized. In other words, whereas Brush and Hayden seem to assume that techniques of ecological measurement will never improve, I would argue that there is considerable potential for refinement.

I would further argue that Hayden's Resource Over-Exploitation rate should not be viewed as an alternative to the carrying capacity concept. The objectives of these two measures are really quite different. On the one hand, the estimation of carrying capacity has normally had the purpose of estimating the maximum population that a given region can sustain, if one assumes that a particular set of resources are being exploited with a given technology. On the other hand, Hayden's rate is not concerned with this at all and instead has the purpose of isolating the effects of temporal variability in environment on human populations. The calculation of his rate leaves unanswered the question of what the difference is between a given level of resource exploitation and the amounts of the resources that are actually available in the environment. This difference would have to be known if we are to discover the factors that determine which cycles of resource depletion actually affect population. From one point of view, Hayden is really only expanding the concept of carrying capacity to accommodate that fact that environment is not constant from year to year. Thus, a more accurate estimate of carrying capacity would include a determination of the resource depletion cycle to which a population is adjusted.

Hayden's and, to some extent, Brush's criticisms reflect the current trends in processual anthropology. Whereas earlier interests in population–environment relationships tended to be concerned with static or equilibrium conditions, the interests of the last decade or so have focused on "disequilibrium" conditions in which population and environment are perceived as varying through time. Consequently, Hayden and Brush have seen the concept of carrying capacity, with its built-in equilibrium assumptions, as somehow inadequate for current needs.

POPULATION PRESSURE THEORY AND CARRYING CAPACITY

Much of the current interest in the concept of carrying capacity is in the context of research into the relationship between population growth and cultural change and evolution. The basic argument of this research is that, under conditions of population pressure on resources, a group will be forced to change its subsistence strategy in some way so that a greater population density can be supported within a region with particular environmental characteristics. Those adhering to the basic thesis popularized by Boserup (1965) argue further that such changes in subsistence generally result in greater energy (labor) costs per unit of food production. This argument has been applied primarily in the context of proposing explanations for the origin of agriculture and the development of agricultural technology. To wit, it is proposed that, when population size increases (as a result of internal fecundity or immigration) to the point where the carrying capacity of specific resources is reached in terms of a particular subsistence technology, there will be a shift to a modified set of subsistence resources or subsistence technology (Binford 1968:332; Flannery 1969:80; Harner 1970:69; Smith and Young 1972:33). A comprehensive treatment of population pressure theory is presented by Smith (1972) and Smith and Young (1972) and does not need to be repeated here.

In developing population pressure models using the carrying capacity concept, the importance of specifying carrying capacity in terms of a particular set of resources and technology is quite evident. Moreover, even though these models are concerned with cultural change or "process," the concept retains its "static" quality—that is, it refers to an unchanging value or limit. In some of the more elaborate population pressure models (e.g., Smith and Young 1972:28–49), several different carrying capacities would have to be specified, each referring to a different level of development in subsistence strategy.

Problems arise, however, in using the concept in models that treat both population growth and aspects of subsistence change (for example, agricultural intensification) as continuous processes with no discernible plateaus of stability. One could justifiably argue that a population is always at carrying capacity under these conditions. Nevertheless, from a theoretical standpoint, such models would imply that a static carrying capacity could be measured at any temporal point through the course of the developmental process, and test implications of these processual models would probably specify that such measurements be taken.

An important assumption of current population pressure models using the carrying capacity concept is that a population will practice a resource exploitation strategy that will involve as little energy expenditure as possible in producing a per capita sustenance. As a corollary, an increase in population density will result in an increase in energy expenditure, which will be manifest in a number of possible ways—for instance, labor intensification, elaboration of technology, increases in resource storage, or expansion of transportation networks. Thus, resource exploitation becomes less efficient and more costly with population growth. In constructing population pressure models, therefore, close attention must be given to the economic factors of resource exploitation strategies.

Is it possible to develop a population pressure model that includes the economic implications just mentioned but does not require the inclusion, implicitly or explicitly, of the carrying capacity concept? I would argue that this is certainly possible. This model (or constellation of models) would suggest that a change from one subsistence strategy to another under population pressure is the result *not* of reaching carrying capacity of certain resources but of reaching a point at which a continuation of the old strategy would be more costly than a specific alternative strategy.

As an example, let us suppose that a growing population has been exploiting a particular resource, designated A, and that concomitant with population growth the cost per unit of production of this resource has been increasing. The increasing cost might be observed as increasing labor involved in ranging greater distances from a camp to obtain an adequate supply of the resource. A point would be reached where this cost would become higher than the cost of exploiting an alternative resource, designated B. That is, although resource B was more costly than resource A at lower population densities, it became less costly at higher population densities. At the point where the cost reversal occurred, resource B would begin to be exploited, and resource A would be exploited only to the extent that it would be no more expensive than resource B. The elements of the model are illustrated in Figure 2.1.

What makes this population pressure model different from one involving the carrying capacity concept is that the addition of the new resource may take place long before the carrying capacity of the old resource is reached. It is the relative costs of alternative resources, not their carrying capacities, that are relevant to understanding cultural development. Although the example focused on change in a resource repertoire, it may also apply to change in the technology used to exploit a given resource. For instance, A and B in the illustration may refer to hoe versus plow agriculture.

The model may take a number of different forms. Another obvious possibility involves economy of scale, wherein the cost curve of resource B is descending with population growth. This possibility is illustrated in Figure 2.2. In this particular version of the model, the cost of exploitation of resource B (or use of B technology) decreases for a while after the intersection of the curves, even though the curve eventually reverses direction. This version implies that resource A (or A technology) would be largely abandoned after the cost intersection and that the change to B would be relatively sudden over a comparatively large area. The inception of irrigation in place of floodwater farming may, in some regions of the world, conform to this version.

To refine both this theoretical model that I have so briefly presented and the model using the carrying capacity concept would require that much

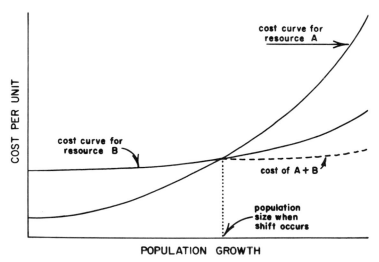

Figure 2.1. Comparison of costs of resources A and B.

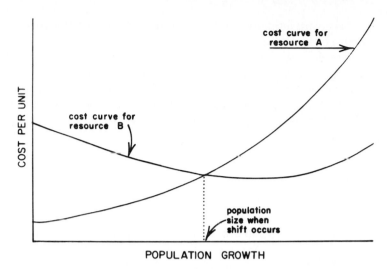

Figure 2.2. Comparison of costs of resources A and B, with B showing economy of scale.

more attention be given to the economics of resource exploitation. I do not wish to enter into a lengthy discussion of the problems of measuring "cost," but some comments are necessary in light of misunderstandings that have entered the literature. In the first place, cost is not meant to refer only to human labor expenditures directly concerned with subsistence (or, more generally, commodity) production. The labor necessary to manufacture and maintain tools and facilities used in the production or storage of resources must also be included. Moreover, other forms of energy expenditure beyond human labor—for instance, fuel expenditures, the labor of draft animals, and, more indirectly, fodder for the latter— must be considered. In view of the fact that all these different kinds of energy expenditures must be included in constructing a cost equation, great care is necessary in making cost comparisons between different subsistence strategies. Barlett's (1976) criticism of some of Bronson's (1972) calculations of costs of different agricultural practices illustrates this problem.

It should also be noted that the models do not presently include any assumptions about *how* costs are calculated and compared. The least-effort principle implies that maximum efficiency in energy utilization would always be sought. But, as some scholars have pointed out (Bronson 1972:200, Jochim 1976:24), cost should also include a security factor. That is, relatively less efficiency might be tolerated in selecting one resource or technology over another if relatively greater security or dependability is obtained. There are actually a number of different assumptions regarding how comparisons are made between two or more strategies, each based on a different decision-making criterion. Jochim (1976:6) has described those that appear to have some relevance to anthropology. Of the several he summarized, he favors (for his purposes) the "satisficer" criterion—one that appears to have gained some popularity among geographers and biological ecologists as well (Rapport and Turner 1977:372; Haggett 1965:26.

As they stand, the two models also assume that a population has perfect and total information about the resources in its environment and is able to use this information with complete effectiveness in calculating and comparing costs of exploiting different resources. Although this is a common assumption of microeconomic models, there is in reality considerable potential error in cost evaluation (which, incidentally, the satisficer criterion takes into consideration). Moreover, social scientists might argue over the magnitude of error and the length of time that an error might be perpetuated. My own opinion on the subject is that an inverse relationship probably exists between the magnitude of error in cost evaluation and the length of time the error is perpetuated. If the focus of analysis is on short time spans of perhaps only a few generations, there is possibly considerable "noise" that must be factored out in attempting to test the models. However, if the focus is on substantially longer time spans, the potential for clearly observing patterns predicted by the models should be much higher.

Under what circumstances would each of the two models—the carrying capacity model and the cost comparison model—apply? This question is not easily answered at present, but I suspect that the cost comparison model may have wider application than the carrying capacity model simply because human populations do have the capability of evaluating one resource exploitation strategy against another and because knowledge of alternative resource strategies often predates their actual incorporation. Generally speaking, the carrying capacity model might apply primarily to situations in which environmental change or population growth is relatively rapid, whereas the cost comparison model would apply to circumstances of relatively slow population growth or environmental change.

The question also arises as to how one would determine which of the models applies to a given instance in which population growth has been demonstrated to be correlated with a shift to a more costly resource exploitation strategy. The most effective avenue of investigation would consider whether the shift in strategy occurred *before* the carrying capacities of the resources exploited earlier were reached. A weaker test would involve comparisons of the costs of earlier and later strategies to determine whether they were approximately equal at the time of the shift. The carrying capacity model does not imply this prediction, although it does not exclude it either.

SUMMARY

The concept of carrying capacity has had a rugged life in anthropology, being promoted by some scholars and maligned by others. The suffering the concept has undergone in the hands of anthropologists results from the great responsibilities they have imposed upon it. On the one hand, anthropologists want it to be an abstract theoretical concept; on the other, they wish it to be an empirical measure that can be estimated with considerable accuracy. Presently, it seems most comfortable as a theoretical concept, but the history of its use is testimony to its potential as a measure. In this regard, the criticisms of Hayden and Brush are not justifications for expelling the concept from anthropology; instead, they have really only offered suggestions as to how it might be made into a more sensitive measure. One might say that the theoretical meaning of the concept has served to goad anthropologists into developing and improving quantitative measures of population and environmental variables. Considering the recency of such attempts, it is little wonder that empirical estimates of carrying capacity are still rather crude.

The use of the concept as a component in population pressure theory is perhaps its most important role in anthropology. Yet, as I have argued, population pressure theory may be subdivided into at least two lower-level alternative theories: one using the carrying capacity concept, and the other concerned with comparisons between the costs of resources and technologies. Both alternatives could benefit from closer attention given to economics, since both are concerned with predicting that successive strategies involve increased costs. Fortunately, economic theory in general is beginning to have a significant impact on ecological studies. Hardesty recognizes the importance not only of conventional economic anthropological perspectives in cultural ecology (1977: 81–87) but also of microeconomic theory that has recently been borrowed by biological ecologists (1977:60–62; see also Rapport and Turner 1977, for a summary of these applications).

My emphasis on the role of economic factors in population pressure theory implies that even more problems must be confronted in conceiving empirical tests than if we were concerned only with estimating carrying capacity. But anthropologists must come to realize that this is a sign of a healthy science. The development of theory should always overreach the capacities of currently available empirical measures. How else are we to know the directions in which to aim our research?

ACKNOWLEDGMENTS

I wish to thank Steven Craig, Michael Jochim, Phillip Walker, and Larry Wilcoxon for their helpful comments on an earlier version of this paper. The editorial comments of an anonymous reviewer are also appreciated.

REFERENCES

Allan, W.
  1949   Studies in African land usage in northern Rhodesia. *Rhodes Livingstone Papers* No. 15.
  1965   *The African husbandman*. Edinburgh: Oliver & Boyd.
Barlett, P. F.
  1976   Labor efficiency and the mechanism of agricultural evolution. *Journal of Anthropological Research* **32**:124–140.
Bartholomew, G. A., and J. B. Birdsell
  1953   Ecology and the protohominids. *American Anthropologist* **55**:481–498.
Bayliss-Smith, T.
  1974   Constraints on population growth: The case of the Polynesian outlier atolls in the precontact period. *Human Ecology* **2**:259–295.
Binford, L. R.
  1968   Post-Pleistocene adaptations: In *New perspectives in archaeology*, edited by S. R. and L. R. Binford. Chicago: Aldine. Pp. 313–341.
Birdsell, J. B.
  1953   Some environmental and cultural factors influencing the structuring of Australian aboriginal populations. *American Naturalist* **87**:171–207.
Boserup, E.
  1965   *The conditions of agricultural growth: The economics of agrarian change under pressure*. Chicago: Aldine.
Bronson, B.
  1972   Farm labor and the evolution of food production: In *Population growth: Anthropological implications*, edited by B. Spooner. Cambridge, Mass.: MIT Press. Pp. 190–218.
  1975   The earliest farming: Demography as cause and consequence. In *Population, ecology and social evolution*, edited by S. Polgar. The Hague: Mouton. Pp. 53–78.
Brookfield, H., and P. Brown
  1963   *Struggle for land*. London: Oxford University Press.
Brush, S. B.
  1975   The concept of carrying capacity for systems of shifting cultivation. *American Anthropologist* **77**:799–811.
  1976   Reply to Vayda. *American Anthropologist* **78**:646–647.

Carneiro, R. L.
  1960 Slash-and-burn agriculture: A closer look at its implications for settlement
        patterns: In *Men and cultures: Selected papers of the fifth International Con-
        gress of Anthropological and Ethnological Sciences*, edited by A. F. C. Wal-
        lace. Philadelphia: University of Pennsylvania Press. Pp. 229–234.
Casteel, R. W.
  1972 Two static models for hunter-gatherers: A first approximation. *World Ar-
        chaeology* **3:**19–40.
Coe, W. R.
  1957 Environmental limitation on Maya culture: A re-examination. *American An-
        thropologist* **59:**328–335.
Conklin, H.
  1959 Population-land balance under systems of tropical forest agriculture. *Proceed-
        ings of the Ninth Pacific Congress of the Pacific Science Association, 1957* **7:**63.
Cook, S. F.
  1972 Prehistoric demography. *Addison-Wesley Modular Publications* No. 16.
Cowgill, G. L.
  1975a On causes and consequences of ancient and modern population changes. *Amer-
        ican Anthropologist* **77:**505–525.
  1975b Population pressure as a non-explanation. In Population studies in archaeology
        and biological anthropological anthropology: A symposium, edited by A. C.
        Swedlund. *Society for American Archaeology, Memoirs* **30:**127–131.
Cowgill, U. M., and G. E. Hutchinson
  1963 Ecological and geochemical archaeology in the southern Maya lowlands.
        Southwestern Journal of Anthropology **19:**267–286.
Flannery, K. V.
  1969 Origins and ecological effects of early domestication in Iran and the Middle
        East. In *The domestication of plants and animals*, edited by P. J. Ucko and G.
        W. Dimbleby. Chicago: Aldine. Pp. 73–100.
Haggett, P.
  1965 *Locational analysis in human geography*. London: Arnold.
Hardesty, D. L.
  1977 *Ecological anthropology*. New York: Wiley.
Harner, M. J.
  1970 Population pressure and the social evolution of agriculturalists. *Southwestern
        Journal of Anthropology* **26:**67–86.
Hayden, B.
  1975 The carrying capacity dilemma: An alternate approach. In Population studies
        in archaeology and biological anthropology: A symposium, edited by A. C.
        Swedlund. *Society for American Archaeology, Memoirs* **30:**11–21.
Jochim, M. A.
  1976 *Hunter-gatherer subsistence and settlement, a predictive model*. New York:
        Academic Press.
Kormondy, E. J.
  1976 *Concepts of ecology* (2nd ed.). Englewood Cliffs, N.J.: Prentice-Hall.
Meggers, B. J.
  1954 Environmental limitations on the development of culture. *American An-
        thropologist* **56:**801–824.
Odum, E. P.
  1959 *Fundamentals of ecology*. Philadelphia and London: Saunders.

Rapport, D. J., and J. E. Turner
    1977   Economic models in ecology. *Science* **195**:367–373.
Ricklefs, R. E.
    1973   *Ecology*. Newton, Mass.: Chiron Press.
Shawcross, W.
    1967   An evaluation of the theoretical capacity of a New Zealand harbor to carry a
           human population. *Tane* **13**:3–11.
    1970   Ethnographic economics and the study of population in prehistoric New Zea-
           land, viewed through archaeology. *Mankind* **7**:279–291.
Smith, P. E. L.
    1972   Changes in population pressure in archaeological explanation. *World Archaeol-
           ogy* **3**:5–18.
Smith, P. E. L., and T. C. Young, Jr.
    1972   The evolution of early agriculture and culture in greater Mesopotamia: A trial
           model. In *Population growth: Anthropological implications*, edited by B.
           Spooner. Cambridge, Mass.: MIT Press. Pp. 1–59.
Spooner, B. (editor)
    1972   *Population growth: Anthropological implications*. Cambridge, Mass.: MIT
           Press.
Street, J.
    1969   An evaluation of the concept of carrying capacity. *Professional Geographer*
           21:104–107.
Vayda, A. P.
    1976   On the "New Ecology" paradigm. *American Anthropologist* **78**:645–646.
Zubrow, E. B. W.
    1971   Carrying capacity and dynamic equilibrium in the prehistoric Southwest. *Amer-
           ican Antiquity* **36**:127–138.
    1975   *Prehistoric carrying capacity: A model*. Menlo Park, California: Cummings
           Publishing Company.

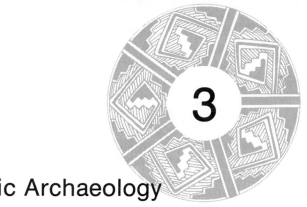

Demographic Archaeology

FEKRI A. HASSAN

DEMOGRAPHIC ARCHAEOLOGY

There has been a definite shift for two decades within archaeology from an obsession with material remains to a healthier concern with past peoples and their behavior. One of the distinctive manifestations of this concern is the growing emphasis on estimating the size, density, and growth rates of archaeological human populations and, more important, the budding but extremely promising attempts to clarify the role of human populations and their demographic dynamics in culture change. It is my aim in this chapter to point out and discuss briefly some of the salient and contemporary approaches in these directions. I chose ''demographic archaeology'' to emphasize the archaeological focus of the subject matter and to avoid confusing what archaeologists do with what demographers are concerned with. Demographic archaeology is an analytical and interpretative approach within archaeology. It addresses the key problems of the role of demographic variables in cultural processes throughout the archaeological past.

This chapter consists of two parts: The first deals with the methods employed in determining the size, density, and growth rate of human populations; the second deals with the use of demographic variables in archaeological explanation. The first part will be helpful in obtaining and evaluating demographic estimates in archaeology, and in designing archaeological research for gathering demographic information. The second part should illustrate the theoretical significance of demographic analysis

ADVANCES IN ARCHAEOLOGICAL METHOD AND THEORY, VOL. 1

in interpreting the archaeological record. These two parts are complementary. The first is primarily methodological, the second theoretical. Demographic investigation in archaeology should not be viewed merely as a means of generating estimates of demographic variables. Such estimates provide the data required for formulating and testing hypotheses about the relationship between demography and subsistence, settlement, social organization, and other aspects of cultural systems (Jochim 1976; Wilmsen 1973; Wobst 1975; Keene 1977).

Explanations in archaeology invoking demographic causality, discussed in the second part, reflect my own theoretical stance in the field. I believe that demographic variables play a critical role in cultural systems, but I do not go as far as to claim that they are invariably the prime movers of cultural evolution. I am disturbed by the frequent reference in archaeological models to population growth at the expense of other demographic variables, such as population size, age and sex structure, spatial population movements, and fertility/mortality patterns.

The majority of the demographic methods in archaeology are concerned with the estimation of population size. The range of methods is impressive and is a tribute to the ingenuity of archaeologists. It is not difficult to criticize most of them (Petersen 1975), but it more difficult to formulate totally acceptable methods. My review of the methods employed outlines their basic structure and provides critical comments as deemed appropriate.

The estimates of population size often refer to the size of a residential unit or a regional group. In many cases, the size may be compared with ecological potentials to test balance between the population in food resources or to monitor the pattern of population growth by estimating the population size at successive points in time.

The ecological parameters of an environment may also be examined in order to determine the probable number of people that may be supported.

The size of a population, its density, and growth rate are the subject of most demographic methods in archaeology. This is reflected in my treatment of the section on methodology. I should like to emphasize, however, the need for identifying and evaluating the role of population controls and for estimating the frequency of demographic flux.

Demographic methods in archaeology are not restricted to those undertaken in the course of archaeological surveys or excavations. In fact, the greatest potentials lie in modeling and simulation. Also, demographic studies of human populations from an anthropological perspective (e.g., Nag 1962; Howell 1977) are highly instructive. The reader who will be lost in the plethora of field and laboratory methods in the first section should try to keep his calm and view these methods within the analytical framework entailed in the theoretical discussion of the second section. At present, there is a considerable lag between method and theory in demographic archaeology. The reader should seize upon this opportunity and examine the possibilities for testing hypotheses and quantifying variables.

Hard evidence from excavation pits and broken sherds, soft data from simulation runs, observations on the demography of contemporary small populations, comparison with wolf packs and other animals, and mathematical models by demographers are some of the resources at the disposal of archaeologists who strive toward elucidating the significance of birth and death in the fabric of human survival and welfare.

I have made an attempt to list as many pertinent references as possible, but the list is by no means complete. Additional references of general anthropological focus may be found in Baker and Sanders (1972), Weiss (1976), Polgar (1972), and Marshall *et al.* (1972).

PART I: DEMOGRAPHIC METHODS IN ARCHAEOLOGY

The sources of demographic information in archaeology are varied, consisting of (*a*) human skeletal remains, (*b*) settlements, (*c*) artifacts, (*d*) food remains, (*e*) the ecological potentials of human habitat, and (*f*) historical and ethnohistoric records. At present, the scarcity of archaeological data pertinent to demographic analysis is frustrating and obstructive. Archaeological surveys and excavations have usually been undertaken with little or no concern for their demographic implications. Thus, even when the demographic data are available, they are usually incomplete, inadequate, or unreliable. There is a definite need for survey and excavation designs that are likely to produce the kinds of information appropriate for demographic analysis. I shall discuss the various methods used in demographic archaeology.

Palaeodemography

The study of human skeletal remains as a tool for demographic inferences is commonly referred to as *palaeodemography* (Acsádi and Nemeskéri 1957; Angel 1969b; Brothwell 1971; Kozhin 1973). It is a relatively recent development (Swedlund and Armelagos 1976), which holds great promise for archaeological inferences. Palaeodemography was pioneered by Vallois (1937), Angel (1947), and Weidenreich (1939).

The first step in palaeodemographic analysis is the determination of the age and sex of the individuals buried at a site. An average age at death may then be determined, and some aspects of the population structure, such as the ratio of males to females or the frequency of old adults, may be examined (Howells 1960; Vallois 1960).

A more sophisticated approach utilizes the *life table*, which represents the mortality history from birth to death of a *cohort*—that is, a group of people born at the same time (Acsádi and Nemeskéri 1970; Weiss 1972a). From the life table, the life expectancy at various ages can be determined. Other vital statistics can also be generated from the life tables. Life tables, however, should be tested independently by cultural and ecological data, since the tables represent a hypothetical construct (Moore *et al.* 1975).

One of the theoretical drawbacks of the life tables lies in assuming that the skeletal collection from a site represents a single population without any migration and with constant age-specific death and birth rates—that is, a stable population. This situation does not often correspond to the demographic flux characteristic of many archaeological populations (Angel 1969a). However, the assumption of a stable population is widely recognized by demographers as a simplifying assumption (Moore *et al.* 1975:57).

Sampling, sexing, and aging problems (Howells 1960; Génoves 1969a, Acsádi and Nemeskéri 1970; Acsádi *et al.* 1974; Lovejoy 1971; Massat 1971, 1973a,b; Weiss 1972b; Ward and Weiss 1976) are an additional nuisance in constructing life tables. Mathematical smoothing and gradua-tion of data may remedy these problems (Weiss 1973), except when the sample is exceedingly deficient or overstocked in a certain age group. It is interesting to note here that infant underrepresentation, which occurs frequently in archaeological samples, has little effect on the estimation of the probability of dying and life expectancy outside the infant age group. However, the effect on the survivorship curve (Figure 3.1) is very strong (Moore *et al.* 1975).

Perhaps one of the major contributions of palaeodemographic analysis was the introduction of *Model Life Tables* (Acsádi and Nemeskéri 1970; Weiss 1973). These tables (Table 3.1) are based on data from several populations thus minimizing the statistical and cultural anomalies evident in many archaeological samples. They are of tremendous benefit in the construction of demographic models in archaeological analysis. An appli-cation of these tables to investigate the spatial relations of hunting–gathering bands was attempted by Wobst (1975).

Wobst (1975) constructed a simulation model in which bands inhabited territories of hexagonal shape. Several variables were manipulated so that they would influence the size of the mating network. Among these vari-ables were age-specific fertility and mortality, obtained from Model Life Tables. His conclusions indicate that a spatial network of one or two tiers of hexagonal spatial units provides the minimum equilibrium size. If the

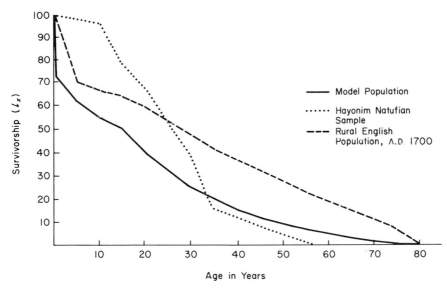

Figure 3.1. Survivorship curves, showing the number of survivors at a certain age starting with 100 persons, for (a) population in Model Table, (b) rural English population, A.D. 1700 (Cox 1970), and (c) Natufian skeletal sample from Hayonim Cave (Bar Yosef and Goren 1973). Note the effect of lack of infants in the Natufian sample on the shape of the curve. In the Model population approximately 55 persons survive to be 10 years old. The Natufian sample indicates that 96 persons survived to that age. Considering the high rate of infant mortality among hunter–gatherers, as shown by the Model Table curve, this high survivorship is unrealistic. Note also that survivorship for adults in the rural English population, A.D. 1700, is higher than that shown by the data from the Model Table.

bands were of 25 people each, the network would consist of 175 to 475 persons.

Palaeodemographic data on human populations at various stages of cultural evolution have significant implications for understanding the changes in the mortality and fertility patterns of past human groups as related to changing life conditions and human biology. The summaries by Acsádi and Nemeskéri (1970) and Weiss (1973) are very useful in showing definite trends of change in life expectancy of adults. In general, the life expectancy is far below that of modern man in industrialized societies. However, the life span (maximum possible length of life) does not seem to have been much different, perhaps with the exception of the Australopithecines, as indicated by the survival of many individuals to what we consider old age today. Infant and maternal mortality as well as death from accidents and diseases was apparently considerably higher in prehistoric times than at present (Brothwell 1971).

TABLE 3.1

Model Mortality Table (I_{15} = 50%; E_{15} = 20 years)[a,b]

Age (years)	q_x	I_x	L_x	T_x	E_x
0	.2670	100.0	83	1896	19.0
1	.1600	73.3	262	1813	24.7
5	.1100	61.6	291	1551	25.2
10	.0876	54.8	262	1260	23.0
15	.1905	50.0	226	998	20.0
20	.1970	40.5	182	773	19.1
25	.2038	32.5	145	591	18.2
30	.2108	25.9	115	445	17.2
35	.2180	20.4	91	330	16.2
40	.2254	16.0	71	240	15.0
45	.2330	12.4	54	169	13.7
50	.2409	9.5	42	115	12.1
55	.2812	7.2	31	73	10.2
60	.3646	5.2	21	42	8.1
65	.4546	3.3	13	21	6.4
70	.5738	1.8	6	8	4.6
75	1.0000	.8	2	2	2.5
80	.0000	0	0	0	0

[a]From Weiss (1973).
[b]q_x = probability of death at age x; I_x = survivors of exact age x; L_x = total number of years lived by survivors between ages x and $x + 1$; T_x = total number of years that can be lived after exact age x until all have died; E_x = life expectancy at age x.

Acsádi and Nemeskéri (1970) provide an excellent synthesis and a great deal of original material on the palaeodemography of prehistoric populations. More recent studies include those by Mann (1974, 1975) and McKinley (1971), Angel (1971a,b, 1972a,b), Greene and Armelagos (1972), Swedlund and Armelagos (1969), Green et al. (1974), Blakely (1971), and Brothwell (1972). Ubelaker (1974) presents one of the most interesting cases of palaeodemographic analysis of ossuary skeletal samples. His study focuses on Late Woodland material from the Tidewater Potomac in southern Maryland. Ubelaker derived an estimate for the length of time represented by the ossuaries and for the regional population size, which he used to test Mooney's (1925) estimate of the size of the aboriginal population. Ubelaker's figure was four times that of Mooney's.

The relationship between palaeodemography and prehistoric ecology is quite intimate. Angel (1968, 1969a, 1972b) explored the ecological aspects of palaeodemography in the Eastern Mediterranean region from the Upper Palaeolithic to the Classic Period. His findings emphasize the role of the shift in the economic base and diet as well as the proximity of settlements to mosquito-infested marshlands. The Neolithic pattern of settlements near open water or marshland facilitated the spread of falciparum malaria. Thalassemic anemia developed as a response to this malaria. The influence of this load of disease and decrease in meat protein intake on adult longevity was negative (Angel 1972b:97–98).

Palaeopathology, the study of disease in prehistoric and ancient populations (Swedlund and Armelagos 1976:42), is an area that should not be overlooked in demographic archaeology. It provides information that can be used to infer some aspects of the ecological setting, the magnitude and pattern of physical activities, and intergroup violence. Changes in disease patterns from 350 B.C. to A.D. 1400 in Nubia were investigated by Armelagos (1969), who demonstrated, for example, that there is an increase in the percentages of arthritic lesions in later (Christian) populations, which may be in part due to increased longevity. The study also shows an increase in osteoporosis (decrease in skeletal mass) with age.

Settlement Data and Population Size

Demographic inferences in archaeology have frequently been drawn from settlement data. These inferences usually concern determination of the number of residents at a site, regional group size, population density, and regional population growth rates.

Several methods are employed to estimate the number of residents at a site. They are usually based on one or more of the following settlement attributes: (*a*) dwelling (or floor) space; (*b*) site area; (*c*) number of dwellings per site; (*d*) number of rooms per dwelling or site; (*e*) number of persons per room; (*f*) volume of site deposits; and (*g*) number of hearths.

Dwelling Space

The size of the dwelling space has been used extensively for groups with permanent residential quarters. From a study of the relationship between the roofed floor area of the largest settlements of the social units investigated and the number of inhabitants in 18 societies from different geographical areas of the world, Naroll (1962) concluded that each person requires an average of about 10 m² of the habitation space. This rule of thumb is a simplification of the following logarithmic relationship:

$$\text{Habitation area} = 21.7 \times \text{population}^{0.84195}$$

Binford *et al.* (1970:84–87), in a study of the Hatchery West site, noted that an application of Naroll's formula provided a very low population estimate, which is improbable on the basis of number of houses and pits at that site. LeBlanc (1971) comments on the inadequacy of the data used by Naroll to generate his formula. With additional data, he showed that the standard deviations of floor areas among family units are large, reducing the reliability of using floor area to determine population size. LeBlanc (1971) further suggests that it will be necessary to collect information on roofed areas and walled space to obtain a better estimate of population size.

Soudsky (1962, 1964, 1969), in dealing with longhouses from Poland, took into consideration the various uses of space within such structures. Only 67% of the total space was taken for living quarters. The rest was used for storage space and as a lobby. Four hearths in the living area indicated that the living space was shared by four families. According to this method, which was applied by Milisauskas (1972) to Linear culture longhouses at Olszanica Bl, Poland, each family requires about 5 m of the length of living space in a house.

Casselberry (1974), in a survey of multifamily dwellings where a single, large, enclosed space is used by several families (based on ethnographic data from eight different cultures), concludes that the population of a multifamily dwelling is a number roughly equal to one-sixth of the floor area, as measured in square meters. Casselberry (1974) checked his method against Soudsky's as applied by Milisauskas (1972). The results of the two methods were similar.

The relationship between population and floor space has been the subject of intensive investigation by Cook and co-workers (Cook and Treganza 1950; Cook and Heizer 1965, 1968), using ethnographic data from California. Their findings were summarized by Cook (1972b), who also provided further information from other parts of the United States. Cook (1972b:15) observes that single-family dwellings in northern and southern California are close to 11.1 m² (120 ft²). Given a family of 6 persons, this amounts to 1.86 m² (20 ft²) per person. Cook (1972b:15) also notes that in the Southwest the single-family dwelling is larger (27.9 m²). Houses larger than 32.5 m² and up to 45.5 m² with no interior partition are inhabited by larger families, between 7 and 9 persons. Houses with a floor area greater than about 50 m² (500 ft²) are most likely multifamily dwelling houses. For such houses, with no walled-off spaces or rooms, the first 6 persons require 13.92 m² (120 ft²)—that is, 2.32 m² (20 ft²) per person. Each additional person requires 9.29 m² (100 ft²).

Sites with multichambered houses pose some problems. It is necessary (a) to have a good estimate of the number of rooms, (b) to determine how many rooms belong to a single family, (c) to determine which rooms were used for "habitation" versus storage or reception, (d) to determine the family size, and, for sites such as the pueblos of the American Southwest, (e) to find out how many dwelling rooms were occupied at one time, and (f) to have an estimate of the duration of occupation.

Plog (1975), in a discussion of demographic inferences in southwestern prehistory, points out these problems and emphasizes the necessity for systematic regional surveys when regional population estimates are desired.

Hill (1970), Longacre (1976), and Plog (1975) provide excellent examples of how some of the problems may be handled. Hill (1970) took (*a*) the number of rooms at Broken K Pueblo, (*b*) an estimate of 2.8 persons per room (obtained from ethnographic data), and (*c*) a factor of 22% of abandoned rooms to arrive at a population estimate of 193 persons. Hill (1970) also estimated the number of households, by three different methods. In the first, he used the number of fire pits (previously discussed by Chang 1958). In the second method, he used the number of household "living" rooms. In the third method, he used the number of storage rooms, since it is assumed that there is one storage room per household. There was a remarkable similarity in the number of households estimated by the three methods. The first method yielded an estimate of 25 households, the second and third methods 26 households each. Using a mean of 6.1 persons per household from ethnographic observations on the Hopi, Hill (1970) obtained a population size estimate of 120 persons. Hill also employed Naroll's (1962) and Cook and Heizer's (1965) formula for living space to arrive at estimates of 55 persons by the first method and 182 by the second. Hill suggests that the method based on the number of households is likely to be more reliable than the other two methods, since it implies what he perceived as a reasonable living space area of 4.55 m² per person. This figure also implies 1.7 persons per room.

Longacre (1976), in an interesting study of the population dynamics at Grasshopper Pueblo, took an estimate of 2.8 persons per room and a factor of 25% for abandoned rooms to arrive at estimates of the population size at the site, at various stages of its growth. Although Hill's household method indicates 1.7 persons per room, the floor space of the rooms at Grasshopper Pueblo was larger than that of the rooms at Broken K Pueblo, which led Longacre to choose the figure of 2.8 persons per room obtained from ethnographic data.

Plog's (1975) work is based on a systematic survey of the Hay Hollow Valley. The number of rooms in a site was estimated by analogy to excavated sites from the Upper Little Colorado. This provided the following relationship:

Number of pueblo rooms = 0.1 × (area of the rubble mound in m²) + 4.0

The number of dwellings in a site was estimated from the proportion of dwelling and nondwelling units found in excavated pueblos elsewhere in the Southwest. Plog (1975) also assumes that a site has a developmental history. At its period of maximum occupancy, about 78% of the dwelling units will be occupied. At 50-year intervals before and after the peak period of occupancy, the number of dwellings occupied is half that of the next or previous period, respectively.

Hill (1970) used an average of 6.1 persons per household for his calculations on the basis of ethnographic data. Outside the Southwest, the size of the household is usually placed at 5–6 persons for nuclear families (Steward 1937; Braidwood and Reed 1957; Butzer 1959; Cook and Heizer 1965; Fairservis 1967; Haviland 1969, 1972; Parsons 1971; Blanton 1972; Winter 1972). This figure is based primarily on ethnographic observations. Extended families vary considerably in size, and the area of floor space should be used to indicate the number of inhabitants per dwelling for houses greater than 30 m² in floor space.

Site Area

The use of the whole site area including dwelling and interdwelling space has been attempted for Kalahari hunting and gathering campsites by Wiessner (1974). The results obtained by Wiessner indicate that for a group of 10 persons an average of about 5.9 m² of campsite area would be required for each person. For a larger group of 25 persons, the area per person increases to 10.2 m². It is uncertain how this relationship would hold for populations greater than 25 persons.

In the ancient Near East the number of inhabitants of villages and towns were estimated by means of the formula

$$\text{Number of inhabitants} = \text{constant} \times \text{site area}$$

where the constant is the number of persons per unit of site area determined from modern villages and towns in the area under investigation, or from other archaeological sites. Frankfort (1950) measured house sizes, estimated the number of people per house, and counted the number of houses per acre, to arrive at an estimate of 120–200 persons per acre— that is, 297–494 persons per hectare, or 20–34 m² per person. He compared this estimate with the number of persons per acre in Aleppo and Damascus, which he calculated at 160. Braidwood and Reed (1957) took the size of the population that lives now on the mound of Erbil to arrive at an estimate of 213 persons per acre (19 m² per person) of town area. Renfrew (1972b) suggested that the population in the late Bronze Age in the Aegean was probably not so dense as in a Sumerian town. Accordingly, he uses an estimate of 300 persons per hectare (30 m² per person). For the Neolithic period he used a figure of 200 persons per hectare (50 m² per person).

In Mesoamerica, Parsons (1971) and Blanton (1972) have both employed site area to arrive at the size of rural and urban settlements, using a constant range of persons per hectare obtained from modern villages and towns. The density of debris was used to suggest whether the "small" or large end of the range applies. In the Southwest, Hack (1942) took the length of a site to arrive at an estimate of units of population. For example, a site 10 yards long is equivalent to 2 population units, and a site 20 yards long equals 5 units.

The poor correlation between site area and residential population size does not seem to provide a firm basis for demographic estimates (Marcus 1976:82). Cook and Heizer (1965) have shown that in California sites ranging in size from 370 to 9200 m² may have the same average number of 30 persons.

Volume of Site Deposits

Estimates of the residential population size may also be obtained from the volume of site deposits if the volume per unit of occupation—for example, a hut—is known. Ammerman *et al.* (1976) have utilized this method to estimate population size at Ali Kosh, Iran. With a value of 20 m³ for the volume of a single house compacted into the site, which has a volume of 15,000 m³, the number of houses at one time can be calculated, if the life expectancy of a house and the period of site occupation are known. The following formula is used:

$$N = (V \times T)/(H \times P)$$

where N is the number of houses at one time, T the life expectancy of a house, V the volume of the site, P the time duration of site occupation, and H the compacted volume of a house. The number of houses may then be multiplied by the number of persons per house to arrive at an estimate of the resident population at one time during the period of occupation. Thus, given 20 m³ for the compacted volume of a house, 15 years for house life expectancy, 750 years of continuous site occupation, and 15,000 m³ of site deposits, the number of houses at one time would be $(15,000 \times 15)/(20 \times 750) = 15$ houses. If there were 5 persons per house, the number of site residents at one time would have been $15 \times 5 = 75$ persons.

Regional Population Estimates

Regional population size can be obtained by summing the population size estimates for sites located in the area under investigation. When it is impossible to study all sites, a sampling strategy should be devised to ensure that extrapolations from the sites used to provide population determinations are reliable (Plog 1975).

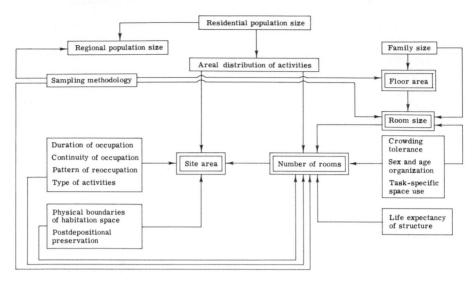

Figure 3.2. Variables that might influence reconstruction of demographic parameters from settlement data.

An Overview

The various methods mentioned above are underlain by different assumptions, often implicit, about the causal relationship between population and various settlement parameters—for example, floor space, number of rooms, and volume of site deposited. Orcutt (1974), in a study on population size estimates for the Chevelon region of Arizona, made a comparison between population size estimates derived from various settlement methods and ran regression analyses among settlement variables. The population estimates differed in magnitude, but showed a similar trend. The highest correlation was observed between the number of rooms and floor space as might be expected.

Orcutt (1974) also provides a commendable attempt to clarify the reasons for the difficulties in determining population size from settlement data. Plog (1975) also discusses some of these reasons. Figure 3.2 presents a model, based on Orcutt's and Plog's lists of variables and other variables, showing the sources of interference that must be considered to obtain better population estimates. For example, the duration of a site, its history of occupation (continued versus interrupted period of net occupation), occupation pattern (seasonal, permanent, periodic, incidental), specificity of activity (workshop, base camp, quarry, etc.), physical boundaries, and so on, should be determined for each specific site before an estimate of population size is attempted.

Artifact Remains and Population Size

Artifacts can be also used to provide a rough estimate of population size at a site. Potsherds were used by Cook (1972a) for this purpose. He relied upon ethnographic data to estimate the ratio of sherd weight to volume on a site and the turnover rate of pottery to arrive at estimates of the population size at Pecos Pueblo, the George C. Davis site, Snaketown, and the S-U site, using published reports on the number of sherds in these sites.

Turner and Lofgren (1966), in a study of museum collections from several sites in northeastern Arizona, estimated family size from the ratio of the volume of the family cooking pot to that of eating bowls used by individual persons. They arrived at an estimate of 5.3 persons for the mean family size of all ceramic "vessel periods" (*sic*) and a range from 4.5 to 7.0 persons. They used this result to estimate population size.

McMichael (1960) attempted to estimate the *relative* population size by determining what he called the Use Intensity Index (*UII*), which he derives from the following formula:

$$UII = 1 - n(D/P)$$

where *n* is the number of sites in a region of a specific period of *P* years' duration, and *D* is the relative density of all kinds of artifacts at an occurrence measured on a scale from 1 to 3.

Schwartz (1956) used potsherds of the early periods of the Cohonina in the southwestern corner of the Colorado Plateau in northwestern Arizona to determine population size. Painted pottery previously dated by dendrochronology was used to determine the time range of individual sites. The time range of each site was divided into 25-year periods called "habitation units." The number of sites occupied during each of the 25 periods throughout the total time span were counted. The frequency of habitation units was considered an indication of population size.

Food Remains and Population Size

Theoretically, the resident population of a site can be estimated if the mass of food consumed at the site at one time can be determined, assuming a specific rate of food consumption per person. This can be done for a single food item or for all food remains combined. Estimates based on food remains have mainly been made for both coastal and midden sites (Cook 1946; Ascher 1959; Shawcross 1967) and for inland sites (Clark 1954, 1972; Meighan 1959; Müller-Beck 1961; Perkins and Daly 1968; Evans and Renfrew 1968; Wheat 1972; Phillips 1972).

Ascher's study, a good example of this approach, is based on estimating the total amount of protein in grams contributed by mussels in the site, divided by the protein intake from mussels per person for the length of the period of site occupancy. Starting with the volume of a site (V), the resident population at one time (RP) can be estimated from the proportion of mussel shells (f) in the site, the density of mussel shell (d), the weight of mussel meat per gram of mussel shell (m), the weight of protein per gram of mussel meat (p), the number of years of site occupancy (T) and (n) the protein intake per person of mussel protein per year (n), from the following formula:

$$RP = \frac{fVdmp}{nT}$$

The values assigned to these variables were criticized by Glassow (1967).

The method developed by Müller-Beck (1961) and used by Phillips (1972:45–46) consists in multiplying the minimum number of individuals of each species by the average weight of edible meat. Totaling the amounts of edible meat from all species at the site provides an estimate of the total edible meat (M). The population size can then be obtained by dividing this total by the requirements per person of meat per day (R), times the net period of site occupation (T):

$$\text{Population size} = \frac{M}{R \times T}$$

Some of the factors that should be considered if reliable estimates of population size based on food remains are to be obtained include the following:

1. Method used to estimate amount, volume, and weight of food remains. Microarchaeological techniques are highly recommended for best results (e.g., Lubell *et al.* 1976).
2. Sampling design. The sampling strategy should ensure that the values from excavated area(s) are representative of the whole site.
3. Loss of food remains as a result of the activity of scavengers or other means of destruction.
4. The proportion of food remains deposited at the site relative to the total amount of food procured, which depends on the food processing technology and food management. Only parts of a catch may be brought to the site for consumption.
5. Net period of site occupation, which is a function of average number of days per year spent at the site and net number of annual occupations at the site during the total period of occupation.
6. Number of sites inhabited by a single group. This is important in estimating regional population size.

7. Adequacy of regional sampling design, in estimates of regional population size.

Other methodological factors include the reliability of ethnographic analogy in determining food requirements per person, the percentage of edible portion, and the nutritional content of foods, when calories or protein values are used for estimating population size.

Ecological Potentials and Population Density:
I. Hunter–Gatherers

Various methods have been developed to determine the probable population density and population size of hunter–gatherers (population size = population density × area) from ecological data. These methods employ various parameters of the ecosystem to arrive at the population estimates. The parameters include rainfall; yield of resources per unit area (resource indexes); primary productivity (productivity of green plants); and available yield to man (amount of resources that can be extracted without disrupting the biotic potential of the resources). I shall discuss briefly these various methods.

Rainfall

One of the pioneering attempts to relate ecological potential to population density was undertaken by Birdsell (1953) on the Australian Aboriginal tribal groups. From a series of 409 tribes, he chose 123 tribes. Those were the tribes that depended on local rainfall in as much as rainfall is a determinant of food resources. For these tribes a correlation coefficient of 0.81 was obtained between rainfall in inches (S) and population density in persons per square mile (D). The equation that expresses the relationship is

$$D = \frac{0.0703037}{X^{-1.58451}}$$

Birdsell (1975) reinvestigated this relationship by expanding his sample to 164 tribes and experimenting with 65 environmental variables. Seven of these variables had a correlation coefficient greater than 0.80, and 11 had a coefficient ranging from 0.70 to 0.80. It was found that among these variables *median* rainfall was one of the best indicators for population density. Data on 99 tribes located where 40% of the annual rainfall is precipitated in the winter provided a coefficient of correlation as high as 0.87. Birdsell (1975:36) also reports that one of his students (M. Vorkapich) analyzed a series of Shoshoni tribes in the Great Basin of the United States. The curve obtained from population density plotted against rainfall was similar to that of the Australian Aborigines. Martin and Read (1973), working with data on some African hunters and gatherers, obtained a similar curve, but with higher values for population density. The implications for archaeological inference are promising. Operationally, one of the difficulties would lie in arriving at reliable estimates of rainfall in palaeoclimatic regimes, but studies such as those by Butzer and Hansen (1968) can be used with confidence. Theoretically, it is risky to base the estimates of prehistoric populations on mathematical relationships established for different cultural groups. Some of the nonecological variables determining population density are discussed by Hassan (1975).

Resource Indexes and Population Density

Baumhoff (1963) took a different approach based on index values for various food resources in California. A resource index is the estimated yield of that resource per unit area. The indexes were calculated for acorn, game, and fish. Baumhoff computed the indexes for the tribes in the Klamath Trinity Basin and Upper Sacramento Valley and correlated the indexes with the population density of the tribes. He found a mathematical relationship expressed by the formula

$$\text{Population density} = 3 \text{ (acorn index)} + 2 \text{ (game index)} + 3 \text{ (fish index)} - 210$$

Application of this method in archaeology will depend largely on the degree of success in determining the resource potential of past environments.

Primary Productivity

Casteel (1972) attempted to provide an ecological model for estimating the population density of hunter–gatherers from the net primary productivity of terrestrial biomes. The model is based on (a) percentage removed from net productivity, (b) trophic levels of consumption, (c) rate of consumption per person per year, and (d) the schedule of the annual subsistence cycle. The total amount of calories available per unit of area to people from various biomes within their catchment territory during a year's period is divided by the calorific requirements per person per year to arrive at a maximum population density. A factor is used to reduce this maximum population density to that of probable population density.

Casteel's results are not encouraging, because in a given biome people subsist at various trophic levels. The most serious problem with the model is the absence of any empirical basis for a specific rate of extraction from net productivity. Casteel uses a figure of 0.5% based on a figure mentioned by Odum (1971:17). For hunter–gatherers this figure seems to be highly inflated. Deevey (1951), for example, suggests a figure of 0.1% for human populations in general.

Available Yield to Man

Hassan (1974b, n. d.a) has devised a model for estimating population density of hunter–gatherers using (*a*) resource potentials, (*b*) extraction efficiency levels, and (*c*) rates of consumption. The general model is expressed by the formula

$$PD = \frac{[\Sigma_{i=1} F_i N_i]}{L}$$

where *PD* is the population density in persons per square kilometer. F_i is the amount of kilograms of the ith food item per square kilometer available to man, which equals the optimum yield to man Y_i from that food item per square kilometer multiplied by a constant. N_i is the nutritional content in calories, grams, or milligrams or other nutritional units elements (protein, food energy, a specific vitamin or mineral, etc.) per kilogram of edible portion of the ith food item. *L* is the average consumption requirement per capita of the nutritional element as in N_i.

This formula can be simplified using food energy in calories, percentage of meat in diet by weight, 2700 cal/kg of meat, 1500 cal/kg for plant food, a rate of exploitation of animal biomass of 5% per year, a consumption of 8×10^5 calories per person per year, and a constant (*X*) of 0.126 (details and explanation of these figures are given in Hassan n.d.a). The Eastern Hadza, as reported by Woodburn (1968), provided an estimate of 0.20 person/km², compared with the ethnographic record of 0.16 person/km². For the Caribou Eskimo, I obtained a population density of 0.0073 person/km², which compares well with 0.010 person/km² for the Asiagmiut (Burch 1972), who are primarily caribou hunters.

Estimation of regional population size for caribou hunters on the basis of resource potentials has also been attempted by Thompson (1966) for the Chipewyan. Thompson's population estimate is based on (*a*) the number of caribou required for feeding and for hide per tent per year, (*b*) the proportional dependency on caribou in the subsistence economy, (*c*) the biomass of caribou, and (*d*) the number of persons per tent.

An Overview

The difficulties in applying ecological models, such as those discussed above, to estimate population density of hunter–gatherers are theoretical as well as methodological. Among major methodological difficulties are the problems of reconstructing the environments of the past and of determining the subsistence base of the population. Proper archaeological investigations and palaeoecological studies can minimize this difficulty, however. In the Nile Valley, for example, changes in subsistence base and ecological conditions have been documented well enough to allow an application of the ecological model of population estimates (Hassan 1974b).

Hayden (1975) has also pointed out the difficulty in determining the amount of potential food available to man given a certain level of technological efficiency. Hayden, in addition, recognizes the difference between carrying capacity as the maximum number of people who can be supported in a region and the actual size of the human populations at any one time. Seasonal scarcity and periodic shortage of resources usually set the upper limit for population size.

Casteel (1972) and Hassan (1974b, n.d.a) estimate the probable actual population size as a percentage of the carrying capacity. According to ethnographic observations, however, this percentage is highly variable (Birdsell 1953:487–488; Lee and DeVore 1968; Sahlins 1972).

These problems are serious when subtle variations are sought, but for crude determinations and for differentiation between groups in dissimilar environments, the ecological methods may not be altogether useless. Moreover, rough estimates of maximum population size that can be supported by certain resources at a given level of food extraction are quite important in simulating changes in technology or food resources and culture change.

Ecological Potentials and Population Density:
II. Cultivators

Estimates of population size or density for swidden agricultural groups have been attempted by Carneiro (1960), Conklin (1959), Cowgill (1962), Allan (1965), Gourou (1966), Rappaport (1968), and Cook (1972b), among others. The most direct approach consists in estimating population size P from (a) total acreage available A_t; (b) number of acres required to support one family A_f, and (c) family size n (Cowgill 1962):

$$P = n(A_t/A_f)$$

Another approach is based on estimating population size from total yield of a specific crop—for example, corn—and the rate of consumption of that crop per person per year. Cook (1972b) used this approach to estimate Maya population size (P) as follows:

$$P = \frac{Y(A_t - A_u)}{C}$$

where A_t is total area in acres; A_u, uninhabitable or uncultivable acreage; Y, the annual yield of crop per acre in pounds; and C, the annual consumption of crop M in pounds per person. Unfortunately, this formula does not allow for the land that must lie fallow. For example, if the fallowing period was 10 years and the life expectancy of a swidden is 2.5 years, only one-fifth of the cultivable land will be used at any one time. One must also allow for allocation of a part of the crop for seeds, fodder, taxes, and rent, and for loss during processing and storage. Other sources of food should also be taken into consideration. Turner (1974), for example, indicates that the prehistoric Lowland Maya were not limited to slash-and-burn food production. He reports raised fields and terraces under intensive agriculture allowing for 150 persons/km².

Estimation of regional population size and density of communities subsisting on irrigation farming is quite similar to that for swidden agriculture with the exception of the absence of a rotating fallow system. Hassan (n.d.c) estimates a population density between 3.3 and 6 persons/km² for Predynastic Egypt on the basis of the area of accessible and cultivable land at the edge of the floodplain, a single cropping of wheat and barley, 10% of annual yield for seeds, 15% for trade, and 10% for spoilage, and allowing for 40% below average annual yield to offset the effects of droughts and overflooding. Under different agricultural systems, allowance may be made for multiple cropping, use of fertilizers, type of cultigens, and so forth.

Estimation of maximum population size that can be supported by agricultural production has been attempted by Zubrow (1971) for the Hay Hollow Valley in the Southwest United States by a different method, based on the amounts of dry biomass of agriculture in arid areas and a consumption rate of 5% of total produced biomass. Unfortunately, Zubrow does not provide any justification for the 5% rate of consumption. There is also no mention of the kinds of resources the biomass of which is used in the calculations.

Historical Records and Population Estimates

Estimations of the size of regional population using a direct historical approach and allowing for changes in population size such as depopulation have been repeatedly attempted, especially for the New World aboriginal populations. This subject has been investigated extensively by Dobyns (1966, 1976 with bibliography).

Case Studies

Reconstructions of regional population sizes and growth trends are numerous. Some of the best examples include those by MacNeish (1970) for the Tehuacan Valley of Mexico (see also Byers 1967); Blanton (1972) on the Ixtapalapa Peninsula; Sanders (1972) for various regions in Mesoamerica; Plog (1975) for the Hay Hollow Valley, Southwest United States; Adams (1965) and Adams and Nissen (1972) for Mesopotamia; and Renfrew (1972a,b) for the Aegean.

Determination of the Rate of Population Growth

Population growth has recently become a central issue in many archaeological models of culture change, yet only a few studies have addressed the problem of determining population growth rates. Carneiro and Hilse (1966) provided an estimate of 0.1% for annual growth rate during the Neolithic on the basis of a guess-estimate of the number of the inhabitants of the Near East at the beginning of the Neolithic (50,000–100,000 persons) and about 1–12 million persons at about 4000 B.C. These figures indicate a probable rate of population growth between 0.08 and 0.12% per year. Barringer (1966), in a comment on Carneiro and Hilse's paper, suggested a higher rate of 0.15–0.25%. But Hassan (1973) used the data obtained by Hole et al. (1969) from Deh Luran to arrive at an estimate of 0.08% during the period of dry farming and 0.12% for the period of irrigation farming. A lower rate of 0.03% was estimated for the period preceding the Neolithic and 0.024% for the period immediately following the Neolithic. The average for the Neolithic period was estimated at 0.1%. This figure compares well with that of Carneiro and Hilse (1966) and with other estimates made by Hassan (1973) on population growth at Kaminaljuyu based on settlement data by Sanders (1974), which comes to 0.1% for the period from the Middle Formative to the Middle Classic times. Cowgill (1975a:511–512), using data from many parts of the world, also comes to the conclusion that rates between 0.1 and 0.2% are common for overall regional trends spanning a millennium or more. Freedman and Berelson (1974) also report an average of less than 0.1% from 8000 B.C. to about A.D. 1500.

The average rate of population growth during the Palaeolithic is exceedingly low by comparison with that of the Neolithic; Polgar (1972) provides an estimate of 0.003%, and calculations based on data by Keyfitz (1966) give an estimate of 0.0015% (Hassan 1973). Also, Coale (1974:43) presents information indicating a rate of 0.0015%. Acsádi et al. (1974) suggest that a rate of 0.002% probably characterizes the average rate of growth during the Palaeolithic. I have calculated average growth rates for the major stages of the Palaeolithic (see Table 3.2). These figures range from 0.00007 to 0.011% per year. Frejka (1973) noted that until A.D. 1700 the human population grew at an average rate of 0.002% per year.

The rise of civilizations seems to have been associated with relatively rapid rates of population increase. The growth rate from the late Uruk period to the late Dynastic period in southern Mesopotamia (Hassan n.d.b; original data from Adams and Nissen 1972) is slightly less than 0.5%. At Ixtapalapa, Mexico, two periods of rapid population increase from 1200 B.C. to A.D. 1520 are characterized by annual growth rates of 0.59% and 0.39% (Hassan 1973; original data from Blanton 1972). At Kaminaljuyu, Guatemala, the annual growth rate from about 800–500 B.C. to about A.D. 500–700 is 0.1% on the average (Hassan 1973; original data from Sanders 1974).

Estimation of the annual rate of population growth (r) in the above cases was determined from an initial population N_0 at time 0 and a population N_t at time t using the equation $N = N_0 e^{rt}$. This equation can be also expressed as $\log N_t = \log N_0 + t(1 + r)$, which is the formula used by Carneiro and Hilse (1966:120). It is also the same as $N_t = N_0 (1 + r)^t$, used by Cowgill (1975a:521).

It should be emphasized that the rates mentioned above are *averages*. Growth rates of local populations must have fluctuated in response, for example, to various magnitudes of population controls and random (stochastic) change (Ammerman 1975; Bronson 1975).

PART II: DEMOGRAPHIC MODELS AND EXPLANATION IN ARCHAEOLOGY

The archaeological literature over the last decade shows an upsurge of interest in demographic variables as influential forces of culture change. One of the pioneer papers which focused the attention of the archaeological community on the probable role of demographic variables is Binford's "Post-Pleistocene Adaptations." The controversial work of the economist Ester Boserup (1965) on the causal role of "population pressure" in culture change also provoked a flurry of responses (Sheffer 1971; Smith 1972; Sherratt 1972; Spooner 1972; Spooner and Netting 1972; Renfrew 1972b, 1973; Hassan 1974b; Bronson 1975; Cowgill 1975a,b) and stimulated numerous studies on "population pressure" and cultural evolution (Smith and Young 1972; Young 1972; Moseley 1972; Cohen 1975; Pearlman 1976). The role of population pressure in culture change was also explored by Harner (1970), whereas Dumond (1965) examined the reciprocal relationship between population growth and cultural change. Adams (1960), as well as Sanders and Price (1968), provides stimulating studies of the relationship between population dynamics and urbanization.

Although interest in demographic variables in archaeology, including population pressure, is by no means limited to the last decade (Childe 1936; Steward 1949; White 1949; Birdsell 1957), the contemporary concern for the role of demography in culture change and human evolution is unprecedented. Cursory reference to demographic variables is now replaced with systematic and sophisticated treatments, and contributions from demographers have started to appear (Durand 1972; Petersen 1975).

Carrying Capacity, Population Growth, and Population Pressure

One of the central themes of current demographic explanations in archaeology is the dynamic relationship between population size, population growth, and carrying capacity (Birdsell 1958, 1971; Carneiro 1970; Skellam 1971; Zubrow 1971, 1974, 1975; Sherratt 1972; Wilkinson 1972; Hayden 1975; Brush 1975; Dumond 1976). It is a theme that is intimately related to population pressure, and it has proved to be one of the most provocative concepts in contemporary archaeology.

Population Growth

Population growth defines the changes in population size over time through birth, death, and migration. Demographers have devised several measures of population growth (see, e.g., Pressat 1972). One of the most widely used measures is the population growth rate, r. It is a measurement of the change in the total number of people and can be determined from the following equation:

$$N_t = N_0\, e^{rt}$$

where N_t is the population size after a time period t, starting with population size N_0. The base of natural logarithms e is approximately equal to 2.718. In this case, r may assume any value, and the growth of a population is exponential. If one assumes that the growth rate of a population diminishes in proportion to the increase in population size, the growth pattern is referred to as logistic. This type of growth is expressed by the following equation (Odum 1959:185; Pressat 1972:470):

$$\frac{dN}{dt} = \frac{(K - N)}{K}$$

where K is the maximum population size possible, and dN/dt is the rate of population growth.

The logistic curve is an S-shaped or sigmoid curve that describes an initial slow increase in population, followed by a rapid increase, and terminating in a progressively slackening of population growth. Many populations in ecological systems grow in a logistic fashion, but deviations from this growth pattern are quite common.

Ammerman *et al.* (1976) fitted a logistic curve of growth to population estimates from the Lower Diyala and Warka regions in Mesopotomia. Eighmy (n.d.), in a study of population growth based on the cumulative increase in the number of logs used in constructing house roofs in the American Southwest, finds a good fit between the cumulative number of logs and a logistic curve for thirteen sites. The study is founded on the assumption that the addition of logs to the house roofs, which can be dated by dendrochronology, is a function of population increase. Although this assumption implies other ancillary assumptions, the pattern of logistic growth revealed in the changes in the cumulative increase of cutting dates may be indeed a reflection of population changes. Further testing by other independent measures of population changes, as well as of the implications of various rates of growth from a cultural and ecological perspective, is required.

Logistic patterns of population growth are also shown by Hassan (1973) and Renfrew (1972b). This should come as no surprise, since a particular environment can support only a certain maximum number of people at a given level of food-getting efficiency. This maximum number may be referred to as "carrying capacity." This upper limit for population growth is calculated so that it represents the maximum number of people that can be supported on a long-term basis—that is, without degrading or damaging the ecological network (Odum 1971:125). The *biotic potential* of a species—the maximum rate of population growth, which is usually very high—thus is rarely fulfilled. The slowing of population growth after an initial spurt may be induced by competition, predation, or reduction of food supply per person. In human populations, lowered levels of nutrition may lead to an increase in mortality, especially of the young, and reduction of fertility (Dumond 1975:714). When the number of individuals begins to exceed available food supply at the subsistence level, the population size dwindles as morbidity and mortality set in.

Population Controls

It has been observed that many animal populations seldom reach carrying capacity, but regulate their numbers at lower levels by curious procedures, which are often difficult to explain (Wynne-Edwards 1961, 1965; Hoagland 1966, Turk *et al.* 1975:51). Among human populations the practice of population control in one form or another is universal. The reproductive sequence may be interrupted at any stage, from the delay or prevention of mating to infanticide.

Population controls among nonindustrial populations are discussed by Krzywicki (1934), Lorimer (1954), Nag (1962), Stott (1962), Devereaux (1967), Benedict (1972), Hinshaw et al. (1972), Weiss (1972a), Howell (1973), Schrire and Steiger (1973, 1974), and Acker and Townsend (1975). Among prehistoric populations, the practice of population controls has been suggested by Birdsell (1968), Hayden (1972), Divale (1972), and Nurge (1973) from archaeological evidence. The practice of population controls during prehistoric times must be inferred from the exceedingly slow rate of population growth during the Palaeolithic period. Polgar (1972) and Hassan (1973) provide estimates well below 0.001% for the average annual rate of increase during the Palaeolithic.

It would be ridiculous to interpret this as indicating steady and even infinitesimal growth rate for all Palaeolithic human groups at all times. It would be equally absurd to infer that the human populations were recklessly uncontrolled, repeatedly overpopulating their habitat, to be reduced in number by starvation and death. The latter view of a sequence of events is so disruptive that cultural traditions would not likely have developed. Moreover, such a view is inconsistent with ethnographic observations of hunting–gathering and agricultural populations. Population growth during the Pleistocene was most likely regulated by cultural procedures (Dumond 1975:715). I believe that some of these controls were inadvertently induced by practices that were not intended to reduce fertility—for example, child-spacing to minimize risk to mothers and interference with female work schedule (Hassan 1973, n.d.a). Automatic biological controls affecting birth-spacing among prehistoric populations have also been suggested. It has been argued that lactation suppresses ovulation and thus prolongs the intervals between births (Newman 1972; Katz 1972; Skolnick and Cannings 1972). Howell (1976), on the other hand, suggests that the effect of lactation on ovulation is related to body fat. In hunting–gathering societies, occasional food scarcity reduces the food storage and thus may be responsible for a low level of fertility (Howell 1976:32). However, the effect of cultural practices often associated with lactation, such as mating taboos, may be responsible for the reduction of fertility during lactation (Skolnick and Cannings 1972).

Even with population controls, (a) stochastic (random) fluctuations in population size, (b) unpredictable changes in weather, (c) incidence of fires, (d) decimation of game animals by disease, or (e) floods may induce a drastic reduction in the amount of food available per person. Under these conditions, severe measures for immediate relief may be undertaken. Infanticide, senilicide, homicide, and warfare may occur under these circumstances. "Civilized" people in Europe between 1750 and 1850, according to Langer (1972), had recourse to infanticide as a check on population growth. A sudden and catastrophic ecological event may also lead to extreme depopulation. Hassan (1972) demonstrated that extraordinarily high Nile floods and severe aridity occurring simultaneously at 10,000 B.C. were of such magnitude that the number of settlements was reduced sharply. Other concomitant changes included a change in subsistence and settlement strategy.

Carrying Capacity in Human Ecology

Street (1969), Hayden (1972), Brush (1975), and Little and Morren (1976:22, 42) are critical of the application of the concept of carrying capacity in anthropology. Their criticisms may be summarized as follows:

1. It is difficult to calculate accurately the amount of potential food in an area.
2. Technological efficiency determines the level of food extraction–production.
3. The maximum number of people is limited by the period of the year when resources are least abundant (Liebig's rule of the minimum).
4. Since negative fluctuations in the abundance of resources in a generation or a century are likely to affect the maximum number of peoples, which "leanest" period should be considered in estimating carrying capacity?
5. Estimation of carrying capacity from energy output of the environment does not take into consideration the limiting factor of key nutrients, such as high-quality protein [see also Bender (1971) on Carneiro (1956)].

Although I am not exactly enchanted with the concept of carrying capacity (Hassan 1974a:209), I think it would be a mistake to do without it altogether. After all, there is only a certain maximum number of people that can be adequately supported at any one time in a region, given certain environmental potentials and a specific regime of food procurement and technology. The high correlation between environmental parameters and population density for hunter–gatherers and agricultural groups at their specific levels of food-getting capabilities, which has been repeatedly demonstrated (Birdsell 1953, 1975; Baumhoff 1963; Hassan n.d.a; Bayliss-Smith 1974), argues for an orderly relationship between actual population size and the maximum number of people who can be supported in a given environment at a certain level of food-getting efficiency. The above-mentioned criticisms of carrying capacity refer to methodological problems, which are undoubtedly serious but not insurmountable.

The difficulty with the use of carrying capacity as a concept in human ecology stems from the fact that in animal ecology it refers strictly to environmental potentials (Thomlinson 1965:66). However, this should not obscure the influence of cultural factors in the case of the human populations. These factors may be listed as follows:

1. Mode of subsistence:
    a. Extraction: hunting, gathering, fishing, fowling, etc.
    b. Production: agriculture, pastoralism
    c. Trade and exchange
    d. Mixed: combination of one or more of the above
2. Food procurement strategy: scheduling of annual economic cycle, intensity of food-getting activity, size of task forces, etc.
3. Tactics, methods, and techniques of food procurement: fertilization, stalking game, trapping, spearing, etc.
4. Methods and procedures of food processing: preparation of food for consumption
5. Consumption habits
6. Storage
7. Communal management of food: sharing, redistribution, etc.

Environmental factors affecting carrying capacity include the following aspects of edible food resources: (a) kinds; (b) yield to man; (c) seasonal availability; (d) spatial distribution; (e) periodic scarcity with a span of 50–100 years; and (f) content of limiting nutrients.

It may be readily observed that there may indeed be difficulties in providing an accurate estimate of carrying capacity, but this should not deter us from attempting to achieve as close an approximation of carrying capacity as might be obtained or as might be needed for a given research question. In addition, the concept is of great heuristic value in discussing population pressure as a prime mover of culture change. Little and Morren (1976:22) criticize the concept of carrying capacity, yet they use population pressure (1976:26) as an explanatory variable when this term can make sense only by comparing actual population size with carrying capacity (Smith 1972:7).

Population Pressure versus Economic–Demographic Equilibrium

The relationship between resources and population size is much more complicated than we are led to believe by those who advocate the primacy of population pressure as a major cause of cultural evolution. One of the major weaknesses of the population pressure concept lies in confusing population increase with population pressure. An increase in population size does not necessarily imply that the resources are being depleted and that famine is around the corner. Indeed, the contrary may be true in some cases. For example, the "optimum economic population size" (Sauvy 1969) under agricultural conditions is much higher than that for hunter–gatherers because more people can obtain a higher yield per person when practicing agriculture. Naturally, beyond a certain size, the yield per person will start to decrease. It is that turning point that marks the optimum economic population size. For hunters and gatherers the optimum economic population size seldom exceeds 50 persons.

Another major difficulty in the population pressure concept lies in equating population increase in one region with local intrinsic population growth. Migrations and population redistribution (Adams and Nissen 1972), especially during periods of urbanization, can lead to an increase in population size without any pronounced change in the annual rate of population growth.

The more serious problem with population pressure lies in overlooking the fact that the balance between resources and population can be disturbed by the deterioration of the resources themselves. Also, an existing equilibrium between population and resources may be shifted toward a new state as a result of the need for new resources that were not exploited before (Hassan 1974a). This could occur without any change in population size or resource availability. Thus it is advisable to drop the term population pressure and to discuss people–land relationship in terms of economic–demographic equilibrium.

Economic–demographic equilibrium (*EDE*) is a function of the ratio of population size at one time (P_i) and carrying capacity (*C*):

$$EDE = f(P_i/C)$$

The carrying capacity should perhaps be calculated over the span of three generations—or approximately 60 years. I chose three generations because decisions by people depend on their own knowledge and that of their elders. Although knowledge is also transmitted through many generations in lore, books, etc., the span of three generations (children, adults, and older adults) is adequate for practical purposes. It should be noted that, in estimating carrying capacity, the levels of consumption (*SL*) of various exploitable resources should be determined (see Hassan's model on determining population density from "available yield to man," p. 65):

$$C = f(RP/SL)$$

where *RP* refers to the productive potentials of exploited resources available for human consumption (these include nonsubsistence resources).

From these two formulas, we can derive the following:

$$EDE = f(P_iSL/RP)$$

It is apparent from this formula that in some cases an increase in population, a rise in the levels of consumption, or a reduction in resource availability may cause economic–demographic stress. At any year, the magnitude of stress is a function of the deviation from a hypothetical state of equilibrium.

It should be noted here that, in calculating the magnitude of stress, stochastic fluctuations in population, as discussed by Ammerman (1975), are considered.

Levels of Carrying Capacity and Culture Change

It is necessary at this stage to note that human populations are observed to subsist at levels below their carrying capacity, maintaining their numbers at a level that is 20–60% of the maximum population size possible (Birdsell 1957, 1968; Washburn 1968; Lee and DeVore 1968; Sahlins 1972; Casteel 1973). This is a successful response to periodic, unpredictable fluctuations in the available yield to man of the utilizable resources (Harpending and Bertram 1975). I shall refer to this population size as optimum carrying capacity (C_o), in the sense that it is "optimum" for human survival. An intermediate population size between the maximum and the optimum will be referred to as the critical carrying capacity (C_c). Population size of C_o will hardly experience any severe to catastrophic stress, whereas a population size of the magnitude C_c is likely to experience severe or extreme stress once every 10 or 20 years. At maximum population size the likelihood of severe stress is very high.

The above formulations are essential to assessing the model of population pressure as a causal variable of paramount importance. This model is essentially a starvation model under which change occurs as people, having increased disproportionately in number relative to carrying capacity, are driven to achieve a technological leap. The inadequacy of this model has been argued by Hassan (1974a) and Cowgill (1975b:129). Empirical evidence, as Cowgill (1975b:127) points out, does not support the assumption that human populations normally propagate their numbers until severe food shortages are experienced. As noted above, there is usually a buffer zone between actual population size (P_i) and carrying capacity (C). A population of the optimum size (C_o) can meet the occasional periods of stress by exploiting areas that are left as reserve areas, by expanding their food base to include items that have been previously minimized, or perhaps by intensifying their catch of animal game. Many other alternatives exist; these may be listed under the following categories:

1. Transformation of subsistence base: for example, from generalized hunting to specialized hunting or vice versa, or from hunting to herding, etc.
2. Expansion of resources utilized
3. Intensification of resource exploitation under existing technology and food-getting system
4. Reorganization of food procurement strategy: change of seasonal scheduling of activity, expansion of task forces, etc.
5. Development of storage–preservation technology
6. Conservation and change of consumption habits
7. Integration of regional resources through food exchange

Under very severe stress, infanticide or senilicide might be employed to reduce population size. This practice might then be institutionalized. Another measure of population control would be that of emigration if it is at all feasible (Hassan 1973).

I would thus contend that a population at an optimum size has sufficient time to accept and integrate social or economic changes if the standard of living begins to drop. By contrast, a population at a critical or maximum level has barely any time whatsoever. Cultural changes are not overnight events, and starvation or catastrophic models are hardly adequate for explaining such changes. First, innovations must occur; second, they should be compatible with the existing cultural system; and third, they must be integrated within that system.

In light of this discussion, I shall now consider (a) demographic models and prehistoric hunter–gatherers, (b) demographic models of agricultural origins, and finally (c) demographic variables and the origins of civilization.

Demographic Models and Prehistoric Hunter–Gatherers

Braidwood and Reed (1957), using several examples of modern hunter–gatherers, provided estimates of population density at various developmental levels of subsistence. These figures were utilized by Deevey (1960) to obtain estimates for world population size during prehistoric times. Taking a broader sample of ethnographic data and archaeological information on population density in different parts of the world and the size of world area occupied by humans during successive developmental stages, I (Hassan n.d.a) arrived at the world population figures and population growth rates shown on Table 3.2.

Although these figures are only gross approximations, they do reflect, at least qualitatively, an exceedingly slow rate of population increase. Certainly population increase must have proceeded at a higher rate at times. At other times, depopulation may have occurred. Wide differences may also have existed between contiguous groups (Ammerman 1975).

The slow average world growth rate during the Pleistocene reflects the limits of carrying capacity under a hunting and gathering mode of subsistence. It should be noted, in addition, that a hunting–gathering economy has a very low growth potential, unlike an agricultural or industrial economy. Regional populations of hunter–gatherers in general must remain relatively small, except where the productivity of resources is abnormally high. The population density for modern hunter–gatherers is characteristically low. For the majority of these groups the density ranges from 0.01 to 1 person/km². The size of bands is also uniformly low, with a modal range from 20 to 50 persons (Martin 1972; Wobst 1974). Hunter-gatherers are also characterized by a great deal of flexibility in their group composition and size (Netting 1971; Lee 1972a; Martin 1972).

These demographic characteristics have significant implications for the continuation of cultural traditions, for technological and stylistic innovations, for diffusion, and for the rates of culture change (Yellen and Harpending 1972; Ammerman 1975). It should be emphasized that there is a wide range of variability in the density, group size, and demographic mobility of hunter–gatherers. It would be a terrible mistake to model all hunter–gatherers after the Eskimos or the Bushmen. The variability of group size and growth rate is in part a result of different cultural norms, but it is also in a large part a function of the environmental parameters of the human habitats. The most important of these parameters from a

TABLE 3.2

Prehistoric World Population Size and Growth Rates

Period	Populated world (area in x10⁶ km²)	Population density (persons/km²)	Approximate world population size at end of period (x10⁶ persons)	Probable population growth rate per year
Epipalaeolithic/Mesolithic	75	.115	8.0–9.0	.0033%
Upper Palaeolithic	60	.100	6.0	.0110%
Middle Palaeolithic	40	.030	1.2	.0054%
Lower Palaeolithic	30	.025	.8	.00007%

demographic perspective are (*a*) kinds of exploitable resources; (*b*) spatial aggregation or dispersion of resources; (*c*) diversity of resources; (*d*) productivity per unit of area; (*e*) seasonal availability; and (*f*) short-term fluctuations. These factors are discussed by Jochim (1976) and Hassan (n.d.a) in more detail.

Sparse and scarce resources are not likely to support highly mobile small groups. The shuffling of individuals and exogamy for economic and biological reasons (Wobst 1974, 1975, 1976) would enhance the interchange of cultural traits, producing a homogenization of cultures over large areas (Yellen and Harpending 1972:251). When there is an abundance of concentrated resources with little or no violent short-term fluctuation, large population units may develop, and endogamy becomes possible. Consequently, demographic flux would be minimized and regional differentiation would ensue. On the other hand, if environmental fluctuations are frequent and violent, the social isolating mechanisms would break down, allowing for demographic flux. Under these conditions the rate of cultural change would be greatest because regional differentiation would foster the emergence of innovations, and the demographic flux would ensure that they get disseminated, stimulating further change, and so on (Isaac 1972).

Ammerman (1975) has suggested that stochastic population fluctuations during the Pleistocene could have led to migrations, which would have promoted the diffusion of stylistic innovations. Although this must be considered as a possibility, it should be viewed only as one of other demographic processes responsible for diffusion. Even without any population fluctuations, the flexbility of band composition or exogamy would seem to have promoted the transmission of ideas and artifacts across group boundaries. It may be recalled that the fluctuations in environmental potentials or population, or both, might induce a rearrangement of the population within its existing boundaries (internal migration), or it might lead to out-migration. However, this is not a deterministic relationship, since other alternatives do exist.

During the terminal Pleistocene, there seems to have been a considerable degree of cultural differentiation and acceleration of the rate of change. Isaac (1972) has suggested that this may have been a result of increasing population density leading to the development of social boundaries, which enhanced regional differentiation. However, this does not explain the increase in the rate of culture change, nor does it explain the reasons for the population increase, which led to high population density (Smith 1972:9). I do not think that there was a rapid population increase during the terminal Pleistocene leading to abnormally high densities. There seems to have been, however, a gradual, but not steady, rise in population growth rate throughout the Pleistocene, which may be related to greater human mastery of the environment and to biological and cultural improvements.

By the end of the Upper Palaeolithic the world population had climbed to about 6 million persons. Although this may seem an insignificant number when compared with the size of the modern world population, it is about 30% of the world's carrying capacity under a hunting–gathering economy where three-quarters of the effective biome areas were exploited (Hassan n.d.a). At 30% of the total carrying capacity, stress conditions would have been minimal, since the population would, in essence, be living well below maximum carrying capacity. However, if the transition from the Last Glacial to the Post-Glacial conditions was associated with climatic oscillations and fluctuations, these would have led to frequent changes in the abundance, seasonality, and availability of food resources. These fluctuations would have promoted migrations, further population controls, and innovations. Both isolation and flux would have alternated, leading to an unprecedented acceleration of change through a high rate of information flow. The unpredictability of resources may also have led to the expansion of the subsistence base to include minor resources such as small animal game or wild cereals, which were previously underemphasized in the diet because of their relatively high cost of extraction and the high cost of processing of cereals. The emphasis on more predictable riverine and coastal resources is another feature of the Mesolithic–Epipalaeolithic that fits this model. The emergence of "Mesolithic economy" and Flannery's (1969) "broad spectrum adaptation" may thus have been a response to frequent and perhaps violent fluctuations in food resources during the terminal Pleistocene–Holocene climatic transition, coupled with the condition of near demographic saturation during the terminal Pleistocene.

It should be noted that progressively worsening conditions of environmental fluctuations would not expose a population of "optimum" size to starvation or decimation. Such conditions would reduce carrying capacity so that the actual population size would approximate that of the critical carrying capacity. The population thus would still be buffered against extreme stress. Cultural groups would start to feel the crunch of resource shortage without being destroyed. Over the span of centuries and a few millennia, cultural changes resulting from an initial slight shift of emphasis of subsistence would accumulate, and by trend-amplifying mechanisms (Flannery 1968) could precipitate major changes in the cultural system.

Transcontinental dispersal of hunter–gatherers leading to the peopling of Australia and the New World occurred during the Late Pleistocene. Birdsell (1957) and Martin (1973) envision rapid waves of migrants sweeping over the newly discovered territory, expanding at annual growth rates of 3.4–3.6%, equivalent to doubling every generation. According to Martin (1973), the waves advanced at a rate of 16–25 km per year. Similarly Birdsell (1957) assumes a rate of 10–25 km. The rate of population growth used by both Birdsell (1957) and Martin (1973) is unrealistically high. At the most, the rate could not have been higher than 0.5–1% (Cowgill 1975a,b). This would mean the rate of annual geographic expansion was far less than previously postulated.

Demographic Models and Agricultural Origins

The question of agricultural origins remains one of the most controversial problems in archaeology. Demographic causality is perhaps the most prominent recent contribution to this stubborn problem. Binford (1968) suggested that a shift toward greater exploitation of aquatic resources during the terminal Pleistocene, brought about probably as a result of worldwide changes in sea level, led to a rapid increase in population size. This increase was a result of a reduction in the daily mobility of females, which had the effect of reducing the selectivity for population controls. Differences in the ecological setting of continuous groups would have led to differential rates of population growth and varying degrees of sedentariness. Optimal areas would have favored a greater degree of sedentariness and a higher rate of increase. Excess population would have had to emigrate to marginal zones, where, under the exigencies of scarcity of food, incipient cultivation would have been developed. A similar model was proposed by Flannery (1969) and Wright (1971) for the Near East. Although this model has been met with what Flannery (1973:284) has referred to as "frightening acceptance," it is not only "unproven and highly speculative," as Flannery (1973:284) has later remarked, but it suffers also from numerous theoretical inadequacies.

The major theoretical drawback in this model lies in assuming that agriculture was first introduced by people who were refugees, and by recipient groups who became so overcrowded with newcomers that they had to resort to agriculture. This ignores the sociology of immigration and the cultural controls regulating the movement of people among cultural groups.

It is also not clear why population controls were not imposed to check the threatening increase in population. Sedentariness is not a viable explanation for population increase (Hassan 1973), despite the repeated mention in the literature of the effect of sedentariness on reducing the period of child-spacing (Sussman 1972; Lee 1972b; Dumond 1975). Moreover, the model is incongruent with the greater rate of population increase in "marginal" habitats in the Levant (Flannery 1973:284), the delay of agricultural origins in the marginal areas around the Nile Valley (Hassan 1976b), the lack of evidence for coastal or riverine adaptation in the Near East during the Epipalaeolithic, and the delay in the development of agriculture in the Nile Valley where riverine adaptation is a distinct feature of the late Palaeolithic (Wendorf and Schild 1976). In addition, Mesolithic adaptation in Europe with an emphasis on riverine and coastal resources did not lead to the development of agriculture.

There is no need to discuss similar models such as the one proposed by Cohen (1975) for agricultural origins on the coast of Peru and later for the whole world (Cohen 1977). Polgar (1975:6–7) has already noted that Cohen's estimates indicate population growth rates of 0.01% from about 10,000 B.C. to the beginning of first settled villages, which is hardly a rapid rate of increase. Bronson (1975) has also dealt in detail with the failure of monocausal population pressure models in explaining agricultural origins. He remarks, in agreement with the model of environmental and population fluctuations discussed above, that, because of the ubiquity of random changes, extreme fluctuations must have been experienced repeatedly by many human populations in prehistoric times. It may be noted here that, if population growth had not been controlled, agriculture would probably have been invented by the Australopithecines. Two individuals would have taken only about 15,000 years at an annual growth rate of 0.1% to populate the earth to the terminal Pleistocene world population size (about 8 million persons).

The role of demographic variables in the transformation of the economic conditions of humanity from hunting and gathering to agriculture should not be minimized on account of the inadequacy of the population pressure models and should not be taken as a basis for rejecting the role of demographic variables altogether. The model of economic–demographic equilibrium should be used judiciously, and consideration must be paid to population aggregation, optimum economic population size, the relationship between dietary changes, nutrition, and the fertility–mortality regime, and the "economic cost" of children.

I have examined the transition from hunting–gathering to food production in the Levant in light of the systemic relationship between population, economy, political organization, and communal management (Hassan 1977a). I have argued that the climatic fluctuations accompanying the shift from the Pleistocene to the Holocene exerted a significant influence on the unpredictability of some resources and the availability of others. Such conditions were overcome by expanding the subsistence base to include those resources that were previously less desirable because of their taste or high cost of extraction and processing. Such resources include small game, rodents, snails, and wild cereals. The unprecedented availability of wild cereals in great abundance at the close of the Pleistocene, as Wright (1976) has argued, may have been an additional factor in adding wheat and barley to the menu.

Increasing dependence on wild cereals, which led to the inception of sedentariness and the enlargement of local population units during the Epipalaeolithic, set in motion numerous changes in settlement, intergroup social and economic relations, political organization, and communal management, which led through complex interactions, feedback relations, and trend amplification to the adoption of agriculture (Hassan 1977a).

Agriculture was not a deliberate choice or a sudden undertaking, but rather a gradual process initiated by emphasizing the harvesting of wild cereals, with no technological innovations of any note at the initial stages. The economic potentials of cereal exploitation, such as storability, high yield, high protein content, and transportability, as well as the peculiarities of its growth and maturation—for example, short harvesting period and brittle rachis in the wild species (Zohary 1969:57–58)—seem to have "invited" certain responses, which led eventually to agriculture (for details, see Hassan 1977a).

The nutritional problems associated with a diet emphasizing wild cereals may also have led to certain changes. For example, the need for supplementing cereals with sources of high-quality protein may have favored cultivation of legumes and the domestication of animals (Hassan 1976a).

One of the major elements of agricultural origins, which seems to be often overlooked, is the translocation of settlements to take advantage of large areas with high ground moisture (Vita-Finzi 1969). Such areas would have minimized the unpredictability of wild cereals, and would have been excellent for growing legumes.

Demographic Models and the Origins of Civilization

The emergence of civilizations in various parts of the world is a spectacular event in the history of humanity. Within a short time span—in comparison with the long journey through the Pleistocene—following the inception of agricultural production, complex political organization, cities, monumental art, and sophisticated religion emerged. The human condition was irrevocably transformed, and a new world order was established.

There is abundant evidence for a rapid increase in the world population size during the Neolithic. The world population climbed from about 8–9 million persons to 50–100 million persons (Brothwell 1971, Deevey 1960).

Various estimates of the average population growth rates in different parts of the world indicate that 0.1% per year is a reasonable figure (see p. 68). Periods of maxium increase were probably characterized by rates that may have reached 0.5–1%.

The increase in population size in the formative stages of the development of civilizations has been highlighted by Young (1972) and Gibson (1973) as the "prime mover" and the most influential causal factor in urbanization. Carneiro (1970) also argued that mounting population pressure within circumscribed areas was instrumental in the emergence of the state. The role of demographic variables in the development of civilization has been treated by many anthropologists (Adams 1966; Adams and Nissen 1972; Sanders and Price 1968; Dumond 1972; Sanders 1974; Hassan 1974a).

According to Young (1972), population increase in Greater Mesopotamia pressured people from the highland zone into southern Mesopotamia, where irrigation was "discovered." Colonization of arable land continued as a means of absorbing excess population until the arable land was completely colonized. Continuing population increase led to further colonization of marginal areas, but in times and in certain circumstances the productivity of the marginal areas declined and conflict between communities began. Consequently, a "balling" of the population into cities for protection and greater organization ensued.

Gibson's model (1973) closely parallels that of Young. According to Gibson, an initial population movement into southern Mesopotamia was followed by low-order irrigation and basic trade. Population increase followed, leading to the colonization of more land, and an intensification of trade and increasing complexity of social relations. As the population continued to grow, agriculture also was intensified. But as the population increased to the point where no more land was available for expansion, settlements grew in size until a point of diminishing return was reached. At this point the settlements disintegrated into small units. These units practiced intensive agriculture, and the population resumed its increase with further agricultural intensification associated with social differentiation, competition for goods, and warfare. Finally, the upper strata succeeded in exploiting the rural manpower, and urban centers emerged.

These two models are reminiscent of the models formulated by Steward (1949), White (1949), and Childe (1936), except that these two models place the greatest emphasis on population increase and population pressure as independent variables, whereas the previous models consider these variables to be closely interrelated with economic variables. Steward's model is perhaps the closest to that of Young and Gibson, since he viewed population increase as a cause for budding off and geographic expansion, irrigation, agricultural intensification, and warfare. White emphasized the potentials of agricultural technology and their implications for economic growth and social differentiation. White, however, viewed the growth of villages into towns and towns into cities, as well as the change from tribes to nations, as partially a result of population increase. Childe (1936) linked population increase to the success of agrarian economy. But, according to Childe, trade, craft specialization, and social differentiation were the causal variables in urbanization and the emergence of civilization.

Sanders and Price (1968:230–232) argued that population growth (meaning increase) is a principal mechanism in the origin of the state, because it leads ultimately to competition and periodic conflicts, which eventually results in the emergence of a state organization to regulate conflict.

Carneiro (1970) has suggested that population increase coupled with geographically circumscribed agricultural land was responsible for the emergence of state political organizations. Villages multiplied and grew in size until the agricultural carrying capacity was reached. Then fighting for scarce resources began. The defeated were subjugated, and warfare continued until the whole region was unified into a kingdom. The warriors who distinguished themselves in battle became in time the administrators and central political figures who welded "an assorted collection of petty states into a single integrated and centralized political unit."

Sanders (1974) takes a different view of the role of population increase. He suggests that in Mesoamerica the growth in population size necessitated the development of a complex pattern of social organization. Surrounding groups served as a barrier against fissioning. The development of economic symbiosis and trade, in addition to the emergence of complex social organization, led ultimately to the emergence of the state.

Adams (1972) suggested that in Mesopotamia rapid population increase could have promoted conflict for scarce resources such as irrigation water, which led to social stratification and militarism and ultimately to the walled city–state. Adams' remarks suggest that population increase in urban areas might have resulted from population redistribution, and that immigration might have been more responsible for population increase than intrinsic population growth.

Dumond (1972) indicated that the evolution from an egalitarian society to a state level of political organization was governed *initially* by population pressure. Population pressure led to the emergence of formalized leadership to protect ownership rights and the distribution of goods. Continued population increase led to the segmentation of the population into numerous groups, each with its top-ranking elite. The elite, drawn together by common interests, allied themselves into a ruling class. This class monopolized coercion and legalized that monopoly, thus making the transition to a state society.

Although the above models stress the role of "rapid" population increase and population pressure, the excess of people relative to available food resources cannot be viewed by itself as the major cause for the origin of the state and the city. I have already discussed some of the problems involved in the population pressure models; I shall now summarize these problems, adding some more. I hope that this will be sufficient to turn our attention to other variables and to consider demographic variables from a broader perspective:

1. Human population growth is regulated by natural and cultural checks. Disruptive, excessive population increase leading to serious economic problems must be viewed as an exception rather than the rule. Uncontrolled, excessive population increase is inconsistent with both biological and cultural norms (Cowgill 1975a,b; Weiss 1976)

2. An imbalance between the number of people and the carrying capacity of their habitat may be no more a function of excessive population increase than of (a) deteriorating resources, (b) an increase in the demands for one or more of the exploited resources, or (c) the rise of demands for new resources (Hassan 1974a; Bronson 1975).

3. Impoverished people suffering from malnutrition are not likely to wage wars that they probably will lose. Prosperous groups with growing demands are apt to expand and annex more territories (Hassan 1974a; Cowgill 1975a,b)

4. The coincidence of population increase and culture change implies neither a precondition of population pressure nor a causal relationship between the two.

5. Although the rate of increase during the Neolithic was higher than that during the Palaeolithic, it is well below the explosive rates of the modern world.

6. There is no evidence for excessive population pressure in the archaeological record. The evidence often cited is inferential, and the argument thus begs the question.

Demographic variables were by no means insignificant during the formative stages of the development of the world civilizations. I am convinced (Hassan n.d.b) that some of the key demographic variables include (a) the emergence of large, permanent population concentrations promoted by the benefits of a higher "optimum economic population size" under agricultural conditions, (b) the decrease in the ratio of food producers to nonproducers (administrators, craftspeople, traders, etc.), and (c) the frequent movement of people among settlements and the impact of growing urban centers on "deruralization" (Hassan n.d.b). I am equally convinced (Hassan 1977b, n.d.b) that nondemographic factors were of great significance in the development of civilization. These non-demographic factors include (*a*) the differential viability of agricultural communities and (*b*) economic uncertainty, which led to regional integration of the economy through food exchange and trade, and the rise of a high-ranking managerial and administrative personnel.

Although I realize that one of the functions of scientific explanation is to provide a comprehensible, simplified, and economic account of events, I do not believe that explanations of changes in complex and dynamic systems with numerous, interrelated variables can be framed adequately within the constraints of a single, omnipotent cause. True, at times we may find that a change in a key variable may precipitate a dramatic change in the system, but to single this variable out and to disregard the attendant transformation provides only an incomplete and biased explanation. In addition, explanations are almost worthless if they do not clarify the processes by which a variable influences the system and *causes* change. For example, what caused a "rapid" population increase? Changes in diet and nutrition, demand for labor force, compensation for high infant mortality, reduction of long-range mobility, increase in life expectancy, or changes in the intensity of population controls? What was the rate of increase, how did it affect the growth of settlements, how had that increase been perceived by the people, and why would they decide to curb the growth or opt for agricultural intensification or warfare?

There is also a definite danger in using a novel and yet untested hypothesis without supporting evidence and without checking its theoretical validity or compatibility with what we already know about cultural and biological systems.

CONCLUDING REMARKS

Demographic archaeology is one of the exciting developments in contemporary archaeology. We can no longer ignore the relationship between population and culture. Questions of human ecology and adaptation, which are central to many of the more recent discussions in archaeology, cannot be answered adequately without examining the role of demographic variables.

Many of the demographic models recently advanced in archaeology to explain some of the major events in the human past have centered on the concept of population pressure. However, the theoretical weakness of this concept is becoming obvious, leading to a more critical and reserved view of the role of uncontrolled population increase.

The construction of demographic models for explanatory purposes in archaeology should not be attempted without taking into consideration the various demographic factors that influence age- and sex-specific fertility and mortality and without considering some of the basic demographic concepts on population structure (for example, age pyramid, dependency ratio, sex ratio) and migration.

With an adequate knowledge of demographic theory, the archaeologist must seek to better his methodology to obtain the demographic information that is essential for formulating hypotheses and testing them. Palaeodemographic investigation is a source of significant information on ancient populations, and a great deal of attention should be devoted to perfecting its techniques and developing its unique potentials. Palaeopathology can provide information on the causes of death and can thus contribute significantly to assessing the impact of ecological factors on mortality.

Determination of population size, density, and growth rates from archaeological data is hazardous, and "though the difficulties in the way of reaching even approximately accurate answers are formidable it is certain that we cannot afford to let slip any opportunity of gaining information on this point" (Clark 1969:244–245).

Demographic information can be gleaned from many different kinds of archaeological data (Figure 3.3). This is indeed fortunate, since demographic estimates should be derived by various methods and cross-checked to ensure their reliability. Even though accurate estimates may not be possible, crude and rough estimates are much better than pure guessing and idle speculation; as Cook has remarked (cited in Dobyns 1976), one uses such estimates and learns something, or abjures such data and learns nothing.

Although demographic archaeology is still in its first stages of development, it has already proved its worth as an archaeological endeavor. It has provided information on the life expectancy of prehistoric populations, rates of population growth during the Palaeolithic and the Neolithic, maternal mortality, average local and regional size of hunting–gathering populations, and levels of population density under various economic conditions. It has also exploded the myth that prehistoric man was always on the verge of extinction and has provided a realistic estimate of the true magnitude of the "rapid" rate of population increase following the adoption of agriculture. The field of demographic archaeology is a promising one, but we may strangle it by demanding too much from the existing meager and fragile data base, or by glossing over its methodological

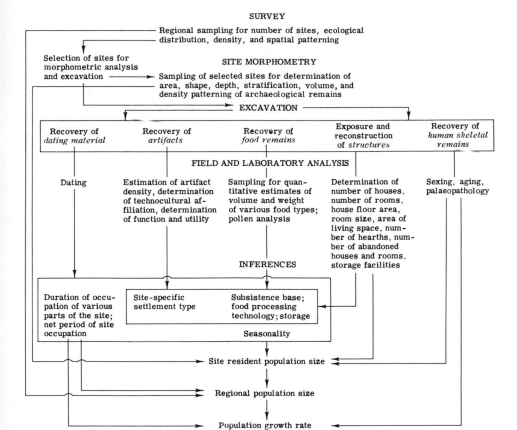

Figure 3.3. Archaeological sources of demographic information and analytical sequence of demographic investigation in archaeology.

problems. Instead, we must move forward to improve our methodology and clear away the theoretical problems that have clouded some of the first attempts to use demography in archaeological explanations.

ACKNOWLEDGMENTS

I am thankful to many individuals with whom, over the years, I have enjoyed many discussions on demographic archaeology. Dr. William D. Lipe read the manuscript and made many useful remarks. His generous assistance is most appreciated.

I should like to dedicate this paper to the memory of Professor Sherburne F. Cook and to Professor Lawrence J. Angel. Their pioneering work in demographic archaeology and palaeodemography, respectively, deserves at this juncture our gratitude and highest esteem.

REFERENCES

Acker, C., and P. K. Townsend
1975 Demographic models and female infanticide. *Man* 10(3):469–470.
Acsádi, G., and J. Nemeskéri
1957 Palaodemographische probleme am beispiel des fruhmittelalterichen graber-feldes von halimba cseres, kom. veszpreml ungarn. *Homo* 8:133–147.
1970 *History of human life span and mortality.* Budapest: Akademai Kiado.
Acsádi, G., J. Nemeskéri *et al.*
1974 History of human life span and mortality: A book review. *Current Anthropology* 15(4):495–507.
Adams, R. McC.
1960 Early civilizations, subsistence, and environment. In *City invincible,* edited by C. H. Kraeling and R. McC. Adams. Chicago: University of Chicago Press.
1965 *Land behind Baghdad: A history of settlement on the Diyala Plains.* Chicago: University of Chicago Press.
1966 *The evolution of urban society: Early Mesopotamia and pre-hispanic Mexico.* Chicago: Aldine.
1972 Demography and the urban "revolution" in lowland Mesopotamia. In *Population growth: Anthropological implications,* edited by B. Spooner. Cambridge, Mass.: MIT Press. Pp. 60–63.
Adams, R. McC., and H. J. Nissen
1972 *The Uruk countryside: The natural setting of urban societies.* Chicago: University of Chicago Press.
Allan, W.
1965 *The African husbandman.* New York: Barnes & Noble.
Ammerman, A. J.
1975 Late Pleistocene population alternatives. *Human Ecology* 3(4):219–233.
Ammerman, A. J., L. L. Cavalli-Sforza, and D. K. Wagener
1976 Toward the estimation of population growth in Old World prehistory. In *Demographic anthropology,* edited by E. B. W. Zubrow. Albuquerque: University of New Mexico Press. Pp. 27–61.
Angel, J. L.
1947 The length of life in ancient Greece. *Journal of Gerontology* 2:18–24.
1968 Ecological aspects of palaeodemography. In *The skeletal biology of earlier human populations,* edited by D. R. Brothwell. *Symposia for the Study of Human Biology* 8:263–270.
1969a Paleodemography and evolution. *American Journal of Physical Anthropology* 31:343–353.
1969b The bases of paleodemography. *American Journal of Physical Anthropology* 30(3):427–438.
1971a Early Neolithic skeletons from Catal Huyuk: Demography and pathology. *Anatolian Studies* 21:77–98.
1971b *Lerna* (Vol. 2): *The people of Lerna. Analysis of a prehistoric Aegean population.* Princeton, N.J: American School of Classical Studies at Athens and Smithsonian Institution Press.
1972a Biological relations of Egyptian and eastern Mediterranean populations during Pre-dynastic and Dynastic times. *Journal of Human Evolution* 1:307–313.
1972b Ecology and population in the eastern Mediterranean. *World Archaeology* 4:88–105.

Armelagos, G. J.
    1969   Disease in ancient Nubia. *Science* **163:**162–259.
Ascher, R.
    1959   A prehistoric population estimate using midden analysis and two population models. *Southwestern Journal of Anthropology* **15:**168–178.
Barringer, B.
    1966   Neolithic growth rates. *American Anthropologist* **68**(5):1253.
Bar Yosef, O., and N. Goren
    1973   Natufian remains in Hayonim Cave. *Paleorient* **1:**49–68.
Baumhoff, M. A.
    1963   Ecological determinants of aboriginal California populations. *University of California Publications in American Archaeology and Ethnology* **49**(2):155–236.
Bayliss-Smith, T.
    1974   Constraints on population growth: The case of the Polynesian outlier atolls in the Precontact period. *Human Ecology* **2**(4):259–295.
Bender, D. R.
    1971   Population and productivity in tropical forest bush fallow agriculture. In *Culture and population: A collection of current studies,* edited by S. Polgar. Chapel Hill: University of North Carolina, Carolina Population Center and Cambridge, Mass.: Schenkman Publishing. Pp. 32–45.
Benedict, B.
    1972   Social regulation of fertility. In *The structure of human populations,* edited by G. A. Harrison and A. J. Boyce. London and New York: Oxford University Press (Clarendon). Pp. 73–89.
Binford, L. R.
    1968   Post-Pleistocene adaptations. In *New perspectives in archeology,* edited by S. R. Binford and L. R. Binford, Chicago: Aldine. Pp. 313–341.
Binford, L. R., S. R. Binford, R. Whallon, and M. A. Hardin
    1970   Archaeology at Hatchery West. *Society for American Archaeology, Memoirs* **24**.
Birdsell, J. B.
    1953   Some environmental and cultural factors influencing the structuring of Australian populations. *American Naturalist* **87:**171–207.
    1957   Some population problems involving Pleistocene man. *Cold Spring Harbor Symposia on Quantitative Biology* **22:**47–69.
    1958   On population structure in generalized hunting and collecting populations. *Evolution* **12:**189–205.
    1968   Some predictions for the Pleistocene based on equilibrium systems among recent hunter-gatherers. In *Man the hunter,* edited by R. B. Lee and I. DeVore. Chicago: Aldine. Pp. 229–240.
    1971   Ecology, spacing mechanisms, and adaptive behavior in aboriginal land tenure. In *Land tenure in the Pacific,* edited by R. Crocombe. London and New York: Oxford University Press. Pp. 334–361.
    1975   A preliminary report on new research on man-land relations in aboriginal Australia. In Population studies in archaeology and biological anthropology: A symposium, edited by A. C. Swedlund. *Society for American Archaeology, Memoirs* **30:**34–37.
Blakely, R. L.
    1971   Comparison of the mortality profiles of Archaic and Middle Mississippian skeletal populations. *American Journal of Physical anthropology* 34(1):43–53.

Blanton, R. E.
  1972 Prehispanic adaptation in the Ixtapalapa region, Mexico. *Science* **175**:1317–1326.
Boserup, E.
  1965 *The conditions of agricultural growth.* Chicago: Aldine.
Braidwood, R. J., and C. A. Reed
  1957 The achievement and early consequences of food-production: A consideration of the archeological and natural-historical evidence. *Cold Spring Harbor Symposia on Quantitative Biology* **22**:19–31.
Bronson, B.
  1975 The earliest farming: Demography as cause and consequence. In *Population, ecology and social evolution,* edited by S. Polgar. The Hague: Mouton. Pp. 53–78.
Brothwell, D. R.
  1971 Palaeodemography. In *Biological aspects of demography,* edited by W. Brass. London: Taylor & Francis. Pp. 111–130.
  1972 Palaeodemography and earlier British populations. *World Archaeology* **4**:75–87.
Brush, S. B.
  1975 The concept of carrying capacity for systems of shifting cultivation. *American Anthropologist* **77**(4):799–811.
Burch, E. S., Jr.
  1972 The caribou/wild reindeer as a human resource. *American Antiquity* **37**(3):339–368.
Butzer, K. W.
  1959 Environment and human ecology in Egypt during Predynastic and early Dynastic times. *Extrait du Bulletin de la Société de Géographie d'Egypte* **32**:43–87.
Butzer, K. W., and C. L. Hansen
  1968 *Desert and river in Nubia: Geomorphology and prehistoric environments at the Aswan Reservoir.* Madison: University of Wisconsin Press.
Byers, D. S. (general editor)
  1967 *The prehistory of the Tehuacan Valley (5 vols.).* Austin: University of Texas Press.
Carneiro, R. L.
  1960 Slash-and-burn agriculture: A closer look at its implications for settlement patterns. In *Men and cultures: Selected papers from the Fifth International Congress of Anthropological and Ethnological Sciences,* edited by A. F. C. Wallace. Philadelphia: University of Pennsylvania Press. Pp. 131–145.
  1970 A theory of the origin of the state. *Science* **169**:733–738.
Carneiro, R. L., and D. F. Hilse
  1966 On determining the probable rate of population growth during the Neolithic. *American Anthropologist* **68**(1):179–181.
Casselberry, S. E.
  1974 Further refinement of formulae for determining population from floor area. *World Archaeology* **6**(1):118–122.
Casteel, R. W.
  1972 Two static maximum population-density models for hunter-gatherers: A first approximation. *World Archaeology* **4**:19–40.
  1973 The relationship between population size and carrying capacity in a sample of North American hunter-gatherers. Paper circulated at the meeting of the Ninth International Congress of Anthropological and Ethnological Sciences, Chicago.

Chang, K. C.
 1958 Study of the Neolithic social groupings: Examples from the New World. *American Anthropologist* **60**:298–334.
Childe, V. G.
 1936 *Man makes himself.* New York: New American Library. (Revised edition, 1951.)
Clark, G.
 1954 *Excavations at Star Carr.* London and New York: Cambridge University Press.
 1969 *Archaeology and society.* New York: Barnes & Noble.
 1972 Star Carr: A case study in bioarchaeology. *Addison-Wesley Modular Publications* 10.
Coale, A. J.
 1974 The history of the human population. *Scientific American* **231**(3):41–51.
Cohen, M. N.
 1975 Population pressure and the origins of agriculture: An archaeological example from the coast of Peru. In *Population, ecology, and social evolution,* edited by S. Polgar. The Hague: Mouton. Pp. 79–121.
 1977 *The food crisis in prehistory.* New Haven: Yale University Press.
Conklin, H.
 1959 Population-land balance under systems of tropical forest agriculture. *Proceedings of the Ninth Pacific Science Congress of the Pacific Science Association, 1957* **7**:63.
Cook, S. F.
 1946 A reconsideration of shellmounds with respect to population and nutrition. *American Antiquity* **12**:51–53.
 1972a Can pottery residues be used as an index to population? *Contribution of the University of California Archaeological Research Facility* No. 14, 17–40.
 1972b Prehistoric demography. *McCaleb Module in Anthropology.* Reading, Mass.: Addison-Wesley.
Cook, S. F., and R. F. Heizer
 1965 The quantitative approach to the relation between population and settlement size. *Contribution of the University of California Archaeological Research Facility* No. 64.
 1968 Relationships among houses, settlement areas, and population in aboriginal California. In *Settlement archaeology,* edited by K.C. Chang. Palo Alto, Calif.: National Press. Pp. 79–116.
Cook, S. F., and A. E. Treganza
 1950 The quantitative investigation of Indian mounds. *University of California Publications in American Archaeology and Ethnology* **40**:223–262.
Cowgill, G. L.
 1975a On causes and consequences of ancient and modern population changes. *American Anthropologist* **77**(3):505–525.
 1975b Population pressure as a non-explanation. In Population studies in archaeology and biological anthropology: A symposium, edited by A. Swedlund. *Society for American Archaeology, Memoirs* **30**:127–131.
Cowgill, U. M.
 1962 An agricultural study of the southern Maya Lowlands. *American Anthropologist* **64**:273–286.
Cox, P. R.
 1970 *Demography.* London and New York: Cambridge University Press.

Deevey, E. S., Jr.
  1951   Recent textbooks of human ecology. *Ecology* **32**(2):347–351.
  1960   The human population. *Scientific American* **203**:195–204.
Devereaux, G.
  1967   *A study of abortion in primitive societies.* New York: Julian Press.
Divale, W. T.
  1972   Systemic population control in the Middle and Upper Palaeolithic: Inferences based on contemporary hunter-gatherers. *World Archaeology* **4**(2):222–237.
Dobyns, H. F.
  1966   Estimating aboriginal American population: An appraisal of techniques with a new hemispheric estimate. *Current Anthropology* **7**(4):395–416.
  1976   *Native American historical demography. A critical bibliography.* Bloomington: Indiana University Press.
Dumond, D. E.
  1965   Population growth and cultural change. *Southwestern Journal of Anthropology* **21**:302–324.
  1972   Population growth and political centralization. In *Population growth: Anthropological implications,* edited by B. Spooner. Cambridge, Mass.: MIT Press. Pp. 286–310.
  1975   The limitation of human population: A natural history. *Science* **187**:713–721.
  1976   Review of *Prehistoric carrying capacity: A model,* by E. B. W. Zubrow. *American Anthropologist* **78**:710–711.
Durand, J. D.
  1972   The viewpoint of historical demography. In *Population growth: Anthropological implications,* edited by B. Spooner. Cambridge, Mass.: MIT Press. Pp. 370–374.
Eighmy, J. L.
  n.d.   Logistic trends in the Southwest population growth. Manuscript on deposit with author.
Evans, J. D., and C. Renfrew
  1968   *Excavations at Saliagos near Antiparos.* London: Thames & Hudson.
Fairservis, W. A.
  1967   The origin, character, and decline of an early civilization. *American Museum Novitiates* No. 2302, 1–48.
Flannery, K. V.
  1969   Origins and ecological effects of early domestication in Iran and the Near East. In *Domestication and exploitation of plants and animals,* edited by P. J. Ucko and G. W. Dimbleby. Chicago: Aldine. Pp. 73–100.
  1973   The origins of agriculture. *Annual Review of Anthropology* **2**:271–310.
Frankfort, H.
  1950   Town planning in ancient Mesopotamia. *Town Planning Review* **21**:98–115.
Freedman, R., and B. Berelson
  1974   The human population. *Scientific American* **231**(3):31–39.
Frejka, T.
  1973   The prospects for a stationary world population. *Scientific American* **228**:(3):15–23.
Génoves, S.
  1969a Estimation of age and mortality. In *Science in archaeology,* edited by D. Brothwell and E. Higgs, New York: Praeger. Pp. 342–352.
  1969b Sex determination in earlier man. In *Science in archaeology,* edited by D. Brothwell and E. Higgs, New York: Praeger. Pp. 429–439.

Gibson, McG.
  1973 Population shift and the rise of Mesopotamian civilization. In *The explanation of culture change*, edited by C. Renfrew. London: Duckworth. Pp. 447–463.
Glassow, M. A.
  1967 Considerations in estimating prehistoric California coastal populations. *American Antiquity* **32**:354–359.
Gourou, P.
  1966 *The tropical world* (4th ed.). New York: Ronald Press.
Green, S., S. Green, and G. J. Armelagos
  1974 Settlement and mortality of the Christian site (1050–1300 A.D.) of Meinarti (Sudan). *Journal of Human Evolution* **3**:297–316.
Greene, D. L., and G. Armelagos
  1972 The Wadi Halfa Mesolithic population. *University of Massachusetts, Department of Anthropology, Research Report* No. 11.
Hack, J. T.
  1942 The changing physical environment of the Hopi Indians of Arizona. *Papers of the Peabody Museum of American Archaeology and Ethnology, Harvard University* **35**(1).
Harner, M. J.
  1970 Population pressure and the social evolution of agriculturalists. *Southwestern Journal of Anthropology* **26**:67–86.
Harpending, H., and J. Bertram
  1975 Human population dynamics in archaeological time: Some simple models. In Population studies in archaeology and biological anthropology: A symposium, edited by A. C. Swedlund. *Society for American Archaeology, Memoirs* **30**: 82–91.
Hassan, F. A.
  1972 Population dynamics and the beginning of domestication in the Nile Valley. Paper presented at the 71st annual meeting of the American Anthropological Association, Toronto (mimeographed).
  1973 On mechanisms of population growth during the Neolithic. *Current Anthropology* **14**(5):535–540.
  1974a Population growth and cultural evolution. *Reviews in Anthropology* **2**: 205–212.
  1974b *The archaeology of the Dishna Plain, Egypt* (Paper No. 59). Cairo: Geological Survey of Egypt.
  1975 Determinants of the size, density, and growth rate of hunting-gathering populations. In *Population, ecology, and social evolution*, edited by S. Polgar. The Hague: Mouton. Pp. 27–52.
  1976a Diet, nutrition, and agricultural origins in the Near East. In *Origine de l'élevage et de la domestication*, edited by E. Higgs. Pp. 227–247. Paris: Union Internationale des sciences Prehistoriques et protohistoriques.
  1976b Prehistoric studies of the Siwa Oasis region, preliminary report, 1975 season. *Nyame Akuma*, Newsletter of African Archaeology, Department of Archaeology, University of Calgary, Calgary.
  1977a The dynamics of agricultural origins in Palestine: A theoretical model. In *Agricultural origins*, edited by C. Reed. The Hague: Mouton.
  1977b The origins of the Egyptian civilization: A working model. *Conference on Current Research in Anthropology at Washington State University, Pullman, Program and Abstracts*.
  n.d.a Demographic archaeology of hunter-gatherers, 290 pp. Manuscript on deposit with author.

n.d.b Demographic variables and early urbanization in southern Mesopotamia. Paper presented at the Cambridge Archaeology Seminar, Massachusetts Institute of Technology, Cambridge, 1975.

n.d.c The Predynastic of Egypt: A cultural ecology, 55 pp. Manuscript on deposit with author.

Haviland, W. A.
1969 A new population estimate for Tikal, Guatemala. *American Antiquity* **34**:429–432.
1972 Family size, prehistoric population estimates and the ancient Maya. *American Antiquity* **37**(1):135–139.

Hayden, B.
1972 Population control among hunger-gatherers. *World Archaeology* **4**(2):205–221.
1975 The carrying capacity dilemma. In Population studies in archaeology and biological anthropology: A symposium, edited by A. C. Swedlund. *Society for American Archaeology, Memoirs* **30**:11–21.

Hill, J. N.
1970 *Broken K Pueblo. University of Arizona, Anthropological Papers* No. 18.

Hinshaw, R., P. Pyeatt, and J.-P. Habicht
1972 Environmental effects on child spacing and population increase in Highland Guatemala. *Current Anthropology* **13**(2):216–230.

Hoagland, H.
1966 Cybernetics of population control. In *Human ecology: Collected readings,* edited by J. B. Bresler. Reading, Mass.: Addison-Wesley. Pp. 151–159.

Hole, F., K. V. Flannery, and J. A. Neely
1969 Prehistory and human ecology of the Deh Luran Plain. An early village sequence from Khuzistan, Iran. *Memoirs of the Museum of Anthropology, University of Michigan* No. 1.

Howell, N.
1973 The feasibility of demographic studies in "anthropological" population. In *Methods and theories of anthropological genetics,* edited by M. H. Crawford and P. I. Workman. Albuquerque: University of New Mexico Press. Pp. 249–262.
1976 Toward a uniformitarian theory of human paleodemography. In *The demographic evolution of human populations,* edited by R. H. Ward and K. M. Weiss, New York: Academic Press. Pp. 25–40.
1977 The population of the Dobe area Kung. In *Kalahari hunter–gatherers,* edited by R. B. Lee and I. DeVore. Cambridge, Mass.: Harvard University Press.

Howells, W. W.
1960 Estimating population numbers through archaeological and skeletal remains. In The application of quantitative methods in archaeology, edited by R. F. Heizer and S. F. Cook. *Viking Fund Publication in Anthropology* No. 28, 158–180.

Isaac, G. L.
1972 Early phases of human behaviour: Models in Lower Palaeolithic archaeology. In *Models in archaeology,* edited by D. L. Clarke. London: Methuen. Pp. 167–199.

Jochim, M. A.
1976 *Hunter-gatherer subsistence and settlement: A predictive model.* New York: Academic Press.

Katz, S. H.
1972 Biological factors in population control. In *Population growth: Anthropological*

implications, edited by B. Spooner. Cambridge, Mass.: MIT Press. Pp. 351–369.

Keene, A. S.
1977   Economic optimization models and the study of hunter-gatherer subsistence settlement systems. Paper presented at the 42nd Annual Meeting of the Society for American Archaeology, April 30, 1977, New Orleans (mimeographed).

Keyfitz, N.
1966   How many people have lived on the earth? *Demography* **3:**581–582.

Kozhin, P. M.
1973   Archaeological sources for paleodemographic reconstructions. Paper circulated at the meeting of the Ninth International Congress of Anthropological and Ethnological Sciences, Chicago.

Krzywicki, L.
1934   *Primitive Society and its vital statistics.* Macmillan: London.

Langer, W. L.
1972   Checks on population growth: 1750–1850. *Scientific American* **226**(2):92–99.

LeBlanc, S.
1971   An addition to Naroll's suggested floor area and settlement population relationship. *American Antiquity* **36**(2):210–211.

Lee, R. B.
1972a   Kung spatial organization: An ecological and historical perspective. *Human Ecology* **1**(2):125–147.
1972b   Population growth and the beginnings of sedentary life among the !Kung Bushmen. In *Population growth: Anthropological implications,* edited by B. Spooner. Cambridge, Mass.: MIT Press. Pp. 327–350.

Lee, R. B., and I. DeVore
1968   What hunters do for a living, or how to make out on scarce resources. In *Man the hunter,* edited by R. B. Lee and I. DeVore. Chicago: Aldine. Pp. 30–48.

Little, M. A., and G. E. B. Morren, Jr.
1976   *Ecology, energetics, and human variability.* Dubuque: W. C. Brown.

Longacre, W. A.
1976   Population dynamics at the Grasshopper Pueblo, Arizona. In *Demographic anthropology,* edited by E. B. W. Zubrow. Albuquerque: University of New Mexico Press. Pp. 169–184.

Lorimer, F., (ed.)
1954   *Culture and human fertility. Paris: UNESCO.*

Lovejoy, C. O.
1971   Methods for the detection of census error in palaeodemography. *American Anthropologist* **73:**101–109.

Lubell, D., F. A. Hassan, A. Gautier, and J.-L. Ballais
1976   The Capsian escargotieres. *Science* **191:**910–920.

McKinley, K.
1971   Survivorship in gracile and robust australopithecines: A demographic comparison and a proposed birth model. *American Journal of Physical Anthropology* **34**(3):417–426.

McMichael, E. V.
1960   Towards the estimation of prehistoric populations. *Indiana Academy of Sciences, Proceedings* **69:**78–82.

MacNeish, R. S.
1970   Social implications of changes in population and settlement pattern of the 12,000 years of prehistory in the Tehuacan Valley of Mexico. In *Population and*

economics, edited by P. Deprez. Winnipeg: University of Manitoba Press. Pp. 215–250.

Mann, A. E.
  1974   Australopithecine demographic patterns. Paper presented at the Conference on African Hominidae of the Plio-Pleistocene: Evidence, problems, and strategies, Wenner-Gren Foundation for Anthropological Research, Stockholm.
  1975   Some paleodemographic aspects of the South African Australopithecines. *University of Pennsylvania Publications in Anthropology* No. 1.

Marcus, J.
  1976   The size of the early Mesoamerican village. In *The early Mesoamerican village,* edited by K. V. Flannery. New York: Academic Press. Pp. 79–90.

Marshall, J. F., S. Morris, and S. Polgar
  1972   Culture and natality: A preliminary classified bibliography. *Current Anthropology* **13**:268–277.

Martin, C. R., and D. W. Read
  1973   The relation of mean annual rainfall to population density for some African hunters and gatherers. *California Anthropologist* **3**:1–10.

Martin, J. F.
  1972   On the estimation of the sizes of local groups in a hunting-gathering environment. *American Anthropologist* **75**(5):1448–1468.

Martin, P. S.
  1973   The discovery of America. *Science* **179**:969–974.

Massat, C.
  1971   Erreurs systématiques dans la détermination de l'âge par les sutures craniennes. *Bulletin et Mémoires de la Société d' Anthropologie, Paris* **12**:85–105.
  1973a   Influence du sexe et de l'âge sur la conservation des os humains. In *L'homme, hier et aujourd'hui.* Paris: Editions Cujas. Pp. 333–343.
  1973b   La démographie des populations inhumées: Essai de paléodemographie. *Homme* **13**:95–131.

Meighan, C. W.
  1959   The Little Harbor Site, Catalina Island. An example of ecological interpretation in archaeology. *American Antiquity* **24**(4):383–405.

Milisauskas, S.
  1972   An analysis of linear culture longhouses at Olszanica B1, Poland. *World Archaeology* **4**(7):57–74.

Mooney, J.
  1925   The aboriginal population of America north of Mexico. *Smithsonian Miscellaneous Collections* **80**(7).

Moore, J. A., A. C. Swedlund, and G. J. Armelagos
  1975   The use of life tables in paleodemography. In Population studies in archaeology and biological anthropology: A symposium, edited by A. Swedlund. *Society for American Archaeology, Memoirs* **30**:57–70.

Moseley, M. E.
  1972   Subsistence and demography: An example of interaction from prehistoric Peru. *Southwestern Journal of Anthropology* **28**(1):25–50.

Müller-Beck, H.
  1961   Prehistoric Swiss Lake dwellers. *Scientific American* **205**(6):138–147.

Nag, M.
  1962   *Factors affecting fertility in nonindustrial societies: A cross-cultural study.* New Haven, Conn.: Human Relations Area Files Press.

Naroll, R.
1962   Floor area and settlement population. *American Antiquity* **27**:587–589.
Netting, R. McC.
1971   *The ecological approach in cultural study.* Reading, Mass.: Addison-Wesley.
Newman, L.
1972   Birth control: An anthropological view. *Addison-Wesley Modular Publication* 27.
Nurge, E.
1973   Abortion in the Pleistocene. Paper circulated at the meeting of the Ninth International Congress of Anthropological and Ethnological Sciences, Chicago.
Odum, E. P.
1959   *Fundamentals of ecology.* Philadelphia: Saunders.
Odum, H. T.
1971   *Environment, power and society.* New York: Wiley.
Orcutt, J. D.
1974   The measurement of prehistoric population size: The Chevelon region of Arizona. Unpublished M. A. thesis, Department of Anthropology, University of California, Los Angeles.
Parsons, J. R.
1971   *Prehistoric settlement patterns in the Texcoco region, Mexico* (Memoirs No. 3). Ann Arbor: University of Michigan, Museum of Anthropology.
Pearlman, S. R.
1976   Factors in the transition to agriculture. *American Anthropological Association, Abstracts of the 75th Annual Meeting,* p. 52.
Perkins, D., Jr., and P. Daly
1968   A hunter's village in Neolithic Turkey. *Scientific American* **219**(5):96–106.
Petersen, W.
1975   A demographer's view of prehistoric demography. *Current Anthropology* **16**(2):227–246.
Phillips, P.
1972   Population, economy and society in the Chassey-Cortaillod-Lagozza cultures. *World Archaeology* **4**(1):41–56.
Plog, F.
1975   Demographic studies in Southwestern prehistory. In Population studies in archaeology and biological anthropology: A symposium, edited by A. C. Swedlund. *Society for American Archaeology, Memoirs* **30**:94–103.
Polgar, S.
1972   Population history and population policies from an anthropological perspective. *Current Anthropology* **13**:203–211, 260–262.
1975   Population, evolution, and theoretical paradigms, In *Population, ecology, and social evolution,* edited by S. Polgar. The Hague: Mouton. Pp. 1–25.
Pressat, R.
1972   *Demographic analysis* (translated by J. Matras). Chicago: Aldine.
Rappaport, R. A.
1968   *Pigs for the ancestors: Ritual in the ecology of a New Guinea people.* New Haven, Conn.: Yale University Press.
Renfrew, C.
1972a Patterns of population growth in the prehistoric Aegean. In *Man, settlement and urbanism,* edited by P. J. Ucko, R. Tringham, and G. W. Dimbleby. London: Duckworth. Pp. 383–399.

1972b *The emergence of civilization.* London: Methuen.
1973 Population and culture change. *Science* **182**:46.
Sahlins, M.
1972 *Stone age economics.* Chicago: Aldine-Atherton.
Sanders, W. T.
1972 Population, agricultural history, and societal evolution in Mesoamerica. In *Population growth: Anthropological implications,* edited by B. Spooner, Cambridge, Mass.: MIT Press. Pp. 101–153.
1974 Chiefdom to state: Political evolution at Kaminaljuyu, Guatemala. In *Reconstructing complex societies: An archaeological colloquium,* edited by C. B. Moore. *Bulletin of the American Schools of Oriental Research, Supplement* No. 20, 97–113.
Sanders, W. T., and B. J. Price
1968 *Mesoamerica: The evolution of a civilization.* New York: Random House.
Sauvy, A.
1969 *General theory of population.* New York: Basic Books.
Schrire, C., and W. L. Steiger
1973 Population control among hunter-gatherers. *Centre de Recherches Mathématique, Université de Montréal* Tech. Rep. No. 351, 9 pp.
1974 A matter of life and death: An investigation into the practice of female infanticide in the Arctic. *Man* **9**:161–184.
Schwartz, D. W.
1956 Demographic changes in the early periods of Cohonina prehistory. *Prehistoric settlement patterns in the New World. Viking Fund Publications in Anthropology* No. 23.
Shawcross, W.
1967 An investigation of prehistoric diet and economy on a coastal site at Galatea Bay, New Zealand. *Proceedings of the Prehistoric Society* **33**:107–131.
Sheffer, C.
1971 Review of the conditions of agricultural growth (Ester Boserup). *American Antiquity* **36**:337–379.
Sherratt, A. G.
1972 Socio-economic and demographic models for the Neolithic and Bronze Ages of Europe. In *Models in archaeology,* edited by D. Clarke. London: Methuen. Pp. 479–542.
Skellam, J. G.
1971 Human population dynamics considered from an ecological standpoint. In *Biological aspects of demography,* edited by W. Brass. London: Taylor & Francis. Pp. 131–146.
Skolnick, M. H., and C. C. Cannings
1972 Natural regulation of numbers in primitive human populations. *Nature (London)* **239**:287–288.
Smith, P. E. L.
1972 Changes in population pressure in archaeological explanation. *World Archaeology* **4**:5–18.
Smith, P. E. L., and T. C. Young, Jr.
1972 The evolution of early agriculture and culture in greater Mesopotamia: A trial model. In *Population growth: Anthropological implications,* edited by B. Spooner. Cambridge, Mass.: MIT Press. Pp. 1–59.
Soudsky, B.
1962 The Neolithic site of Bylany. *Antiquity* **36**:190–200.

1964 Sozialökonomische Geschichte des älteren Neolithikumus in Mitteleuropa. *Aus der Ur-und Frühgeschichte* **2**:62–81.
1969 Étude de la maison néolithique. *Slovenská Archeólogic* **17**:5–96.
Spooner, B. (editor)
1972 *Population growth: Anthropological implications.* Cambridge, Mass.: MIT Press.
Spooner, B. and R. Netting
1972 Boserup in the context of anthropology. *Peasant Studies Newsletter* Pp. 154–159.
Steward, J. H.
1937 Ecological aspects of southwestern society. *Anthropos* **32**:87–104.
1949 Cultural causality and law: A trial formulation of the development of early civilizations. *Bobbs-Merrill Reprint in Social Sciences* No. A216. (Reprinted from *American Anthropologist* **51**.)
Stott, D. H.
1962 Cultural and natural checks on population growth. In *Environment and cultural behavior: Ecological studies in cultural anthropology,* edited by A. P. Vayda. Garden City, N. Y. Natural History Press. Pp. 90–115.
Street, J.
1969 An evaluation of the concept of carrying capacity. *Professional Geographer* **21**:104–107.
Sussman, R. W.
1972 Child transport, family size, and increase in human population during the Neolithic. *Current Anthropology* **13**:258–259.
Swedlund, A. C., and G. J. Armelagos
1969 Une recherche en Paleo-demographie: La Nubie Soudanaise. *Annales Économies-Sociétiés Civilizations* **6**.
1976 *Demographic anthropology.* Dubuque: W. C. Brown.
Thomlinson, R.
1965 *Population dynamics.* New York: Random House.
Thompson, H. P.
1966 A technique using anthropological and biological data. *Current Anthropology* **7**:417–424.
Turk, J., J. T. Wittes, R. Wittes, and A. Turk
1975 *Ecosystems, energy, population.* Philadelphia: Saunders.
Turner, B. L., II
1974 Prehistoric intensive agriculture in the Mayan Lowlands. *Science* **185**:118–124.
Turner, C. G., and L. Lofgren
1966 Household size of prehistoric western Pueblo Indians. *Southwestern Journal of Anthropology* **22**(1):117–132.
Ubelaker, D. H.
1974 *Reconstruction of demographic profiles from ossuary skeletal samples: A case study from the Tidewater Potomac* (Smithsonian Contributions to Anthropology, No. 18). Washington, D. C.: Smithsonian Institution Press.
Vallois, H.V.
1937 La durée de la vie chez l'homme fossile. *Anthropologie* **47**: 499–532.
1960 Vital statistics in prehistoric population as determined from archaeological data. In *The application of quantitative methods in archaeology,* edited by R. F. Heizer and S. F. Cook. *Viking Fund Publication in Anthropology* No. 28, 186–222.

Vita-Finzi, C.
  1969 Geological opportunism. In *The domestication and exploitation of plants and animals*, edited by P. J. Ucko and G. W. Dimbleby. Chicago: Aldine, Pp. 31–34.
Ward, R. H., and K. M. Weiss
  1976 The demographic evolution of human populations. In *The demographic evolution of human populations*, edited by R. H. Ward and K. M. Weiss, New York: Academic Press, Pp. 1–24.
Washburn, S. L.
  1968 The central Eskimo: A marginal case. In *Man the hunter*, edited by R. B. Lee and I. De Vore. Chicago: Aldine. Pp. 83–85.
Weidenreich, F.
  1939 The duration of life of fossil man in China and the pathological lesions found in his skeleton. *Chinese Medical Journal* **55**:34–44.
Weiss, K. M.
  1972a A general measure of human population growth regulation. *American Journal of Physical Anthropology* **37**:337–344.
  1972b On the systematic bias in skeletal sexing. *American Journal of Physical Anthropology* **37**:239–250.
  1973 Demographic models for anthropology. *Society for American Archaeology, Memoirs* **27**.
  1976 Demographic theory and anthropological inference. *Annual Review of Anthropology* **5**:351–381.
Wendorf, F., and R. Schild
  1976 *Prehistory of the Nile Valley*. New York: Academic Press.
Wheat, J. B.
  1972 The Olsen-Chubbuck site: A Paleo-Indian bison kill. *Society for American Archaeology, Memoirs* **26**.
White, L.
  1949 *The science of culture*. New York: Grove Press.
Wiessner, P.
  1974 A functional estimator of population from floor area. *American Antiquity* **39**(2):343–350.
Wilkinson, P. F.
  1972 Ecosystem models and demographic hypotheses: Predation and prehistory in North America. In *Models in archaeology*, edited by D. L. Clarke. London: Methuen. Pp. 543–576.
Winter, M. C.
  1972 *Tierras Largas: A formative community in the valley of Oaxaca, Mexico*. Unpublished Ph.D. dissertation, Department of Anthropology, University of Arizona, Tucson.
Wobst, H. M.
  1974 Boundary conditions for paleolithic social systems: A simulation approach. *American Antiquity* **39**(2):147–178.
  1975 The demography of finite populations and the origins of the incest taboo. In Population studies in archaeology and biological anthropology: A symposium, edited by A. C. Swedlund. *Society for American Archaeology, Memoirs* **30**:74–81.
  1976 Locational relationships in paleolithic society. In *The demographic evolution of human populations*, edited by R. H. Ward and K. M. Weiss. New York: Academic Press. Pp. 49–58.

Woodburn, J.
1968 An introduction to Hadza ecology. In *Man the hunter,* edited by R. B. Lee and I. DeVore. Chicago: Aldine. Pp. 49–55.
Wright, G. A.
1971 Origins of food production in southwestern Asia: A survey of ideas. *Current Anthropology* **12**(4/5):447–477.
Wright, H. E., Jr.
1976 The environmental setting for plant domestication in the Near East. *Science* **194**:385–389.
Wynne-Edwards, V. C.
1961 Population control in animals. *Scientific American* **211**(2):68–74.
1965 Self-regulating systems in population of animals. *Science* **147**:1543–1548.
Yellen, J., and H. Harpending
1972 Hunter-gatherer populations and archaeological inference. *World Archaeology* **4**(2):245–253.
Young, C. T.
1972 Population densities and early Mesopotamian urbanism. In *Man, settlement, and urbanism,* edited by P. J. Ucko. London: Duckworth. Pp. 827–842.
Zohary, D.
1969 The progenitors of wheat and barley in relation to domestication and agricultural dispersal in the Old World. In *The domestication and exploitation of plants and animals,* edited by P. J. Ucko and G. W. Dimbleby. Chicago: Aldine. Pp. 47–66.
Zubrow, E. B. W.
1971 Carrying capacity and dynamic equilibrium in the prehistoric Southwest. *American Antiquity* **36**(2):127–138.
1974 *Population, contact, and climate in the New Mexican Pueblos* (Anthropological Papers of the University of Arizona, No. 24). Tucson: University of Arizona Press.
1975 *Prehistoric carrying capacity: A model.* Menlo Park, N.J.: Cummings.

Mortuary Practices and the Study of Prehistoric Social Systems

JOSEPH A. TAINTER

There are a variety of ways in which a review might be written. Organization of research in a chronological framework is one possibility; discussion of substantive results of research would be another. The present review will follow a different course. In a field in which the literature detailing substantive results has proliferated considerably, a review organized chronologically, or as a listing of research results, might become tedious. More important, such approaches might not yield a clear picture of the strengths and weaknesses of the concepts and analytical methods underlying research. This review is primarily oriented toward a discussion of these latter topics. Among the points to be discussed are the extent to which different concepts of the social significance of mortuary remains, and the analytical methods that derive from these concepts, may be expected to augment our ability to study social variation and change. If the archaeological study of mortuary practices does not ultimately contribute to the general anthropological study of social change, then our research may ultimately prove to be of limited interest. This review is, then, not concerned so much with the past accomplishments of mortuary studies, as with the present and the future. With these points in mind, it is hoped that the present review will show that the study of mortuary practices currently aspires to increasingly objective and quantitative methods of analysis, to concepts that are increasingly sensitive to the recognition of how mortuary remains may reflect social phenomena, and to explicit

ADVANCES IN ARCHAEOLOGICAL METHOD AND THEORY, VOL. 1

evaluation of concepts and methods by reference to ethnographic mortuary systems.

MORTUARY PRACTICES: BASIC CONCEPTS

The conceptual framework that underlies the use of mortuary data for social inference has been set forth by Saxe (1970) and Binford (1971). Saxe's approach uses elements of anthropological role theory developed by Goodenough (1965). Goodenough has developed a set of terms defining elements of social interaction that have archaeological implications.

Goodenough's term *social identity* corresponds to what otherwise might be called a social status. Examples of social identities might be chief or commoner, professor or student, mother or mother's brothers' daughter, and the like. When two or more identities engage in a proper social relationship, this is termed an *identity relationship*. The parties to a social relationship do not usually interact in terms of only one social identity at a time. An individual might manifest the identities of faculty advisor, friend, and coauthor, all in the course of a single interaction. Not all identities that a person could manifest are appropriate for each interaction. The composite of several social identities selected as appropriate for a given interaction is termed the individual's *social persona* for the interaction.

The kind of social persona that a person may manifest for an interaction will be determined by the organizational characteristics of the social system. Hence, a set of social personae will reflect, and contain information about, the organizing principles of a particular society (Saxe 1970:7). Knowledge of this fact is useful for archaeological inference. In societies organized on differing levels of complexity, social identities will vary as to the number of identity relationships that it is possible for them to have. In egalitarian societies infants will have few social identities, whereas adults will have acquired many. Drawing on this principle, Saxe (1970:8) points out that, if archaeologists find infants buried in a manner indicating a social persona larger than that possessed by some adults, a principle of social ranking by birth is probably indicated.

With this array of concepts derived from role theory, Saxe proceeds to formulate a comprehensive approach to the analysis of mortuary data. We shall have occasion to discuss Saxe's work at many points in this review.

Ethnographic confirmation for concepts relating to mortuary practices is crucial for archaeology. Saxe (1970) and other practitioners (Tainter 1975b; Goldstein 1976; Vehik 1975) have devoted considerable effort to this area. But perhaps the most important survey of ethnographic mortuary procedures is that of Binford (1971). In this case the word "important'' is used not simply because Binford has consulted a substantial body of ethnographic literature, but also because the results of his survey confirm beyond serious contention the argument (still rated skeptically by some) that variability in mortuary practices must be understood in terms of variability in the form and organization of social systems, not in terms of normative modes of behavior.

Binford set out to test the following two propositions: (1) that "there should be a high degree of isomorphism between (a) the complexity of the status structure in a socio-cultural system and (b) the complexity of mortuary ceremonialism as regards differentiated treatment of persons occupying different status positions," and (2) that "there should be a strong correspondence between the nature of the dimensional characteristics serving as the basis for differential mortuary treatment and the expected criteria employed for status differentiation among societies arranged on a scale from simple to complex" (1971:18–19). Rephrasing this last proposition, Binford argues that in an ethnographic survey we should find that among egalitarian hunters and gatherers age and sex should commonly serve as bases for mortuary distinction, whereas among more complex societies of agriculturalists social position (varying independently of age, sex, and subgroup affiliation) should more frequently be the basis for distinctions in mortuary treatment.

Binford acknowledges that his ethnographic sample is not ideally structured and suffers some operational problems. For example, since it was not possible to directly measure social complexity from the ethnographic literature, this was done indirectly by noting means of subsistence. Binford bases this procedure on the "generally accepted correlation between forms of subsistence production and societal complexity" (1971:18). Subsistence mode was grouped into four categories: hunters and gatherers, shifting agriculturalists, settled agriculturalists, and pastoralists.

Despite this problem the results obtained were meaningful. Binford considered the following points to be satisfactorily demonstrated.

> 1. The specific dimensions of the social persona commonly given recognition in differentiated mortuary ritual vary significantly with the organizational complexity of the society as measured by different forms of subsistence practice.
> 2. The number of dimensions of the social persona commonly given recognition in mortuary rituals varies significantly with the organizational complexity of the society, as measured by different forms of subsistence practice.
> 3. The forms, which differentiations in mortuary ritual take, vary significantly with the dimensions of the social persona symbolized [1971:23].

Binford concludes: "These findings permit the generalization that the form and structure which characterizes the mortuary practices of any society are conditioned by the form and complexity of the organizational characteristics of the society itself'' (1971:23).

PROBLEMS IN THE INTERPRETATION OF MORTUARY REMAINS

In a discussion which suggested that archaeologists should be cautious in the interpretation of mortuary remains, Ucko (1969:273) noted a case which he referred to as "an archaeologist's nightmare." The Ashanti follow a general rule that an interred body should not face the village. But some Ashanti say that immediately after burial the body turns itself around to face the village. Some, but not all, Ashanti cope with this dilemma by placing the body facing the village, knowing that it will turn itself around to the correct orientation.

The game of "archaeologist's nightmare" is an easy one to play with ethnographic data. Consider the following example from western Australia.

> The Lyne River people have a unique custom of dividing the bones of adults into three bundles. The arms, shins, hands, shoulder-blades, collar-bone, and ribs are placed in one. The thighs, feet, hips, spine, and teeth are bestowed in a second. The knee-caps, breast-bone, top of spine, and jaw are assigned to the third. One bundle is taken to the pool where the deceased was first "found" as a spirit child by his or her father. Another bundle is interred at the place the deceased's umbilical cord is buried. The third is taken by a mother's brother to the place where the man was initiated or the women rubbed with charcoal after birth. A man's skull is put under the stone which commemorates his first killing of a kangaroo. A woman's skull is carried to the place where she first crawled [Davidson 1949].

There are many possible reactions to such ethnographic cases. Perhaps the easiest would be to simply shake our heads, mutter something unrepeatable, and conclude that interpretation of mortuary remains is impossible. Such a reaction is, unfortunately, not unknown in the archaeological profession. The goal of any science, however, is to make sense out of seeming chaos, to find the common factors linking apparent diversity. None of the persons whose work is reviewed in this chapter have ever claimed, or implied, that the analysis of mortuary remains is simple, straightforward, or *easy*. The diversity of approaches that have been developed for mortuary analysis clearly indicate the contrary. If the factors conditioning mortuary ritual, and its archaeological preservation, are complex, this circumstance should not be thought of as a detriment, but rather as an opportunity. To suggest that complexity of mortuary ritual renders burial data inscrutable is to suggest that we ignore an opportunity to understand a major component of the archaeological record.

Any listing of ethnographic "archaeologist's nightmares" will clearly indicate that the form of a mortuary ritual is a complex interplay of ritual, social, and environmental factors. The archaeological transformation of mortuary remains adds yet another level of uncertainty to attempts at modeling past societies. The literature reviewed in this chapter concentrates on the social dimensions of mortuary practices. Perhaps one criticism to be voiced is that the other factors that condition mortuary practices ought to be treated as systematically as have social dimensions. For those archaeologists who are primarily concerned with the nature of past societies, the advantage of systematic treatment of the ritual and environmental aspects of mortuary practices would be the potential for discriminating, in archaeological data, those variables that genuinely reflect social factors. To a degree, this can be accomplished within the state of our present knowledge, but not to a sufficient degree as to warrant complacency that the problem has been solved.

The archaeological transformation of mortuary ritual provides further nightmares. All archaeologists with anthropological training are familiar with examples of people who bury their dead in trees, in rivers, at sea, and so forth. Although there are sound reasons (to be discussed shortly) for believing archaeological remains to reliably reflect the social information communicated through mortuary ritual, nevertheless the archaeological recovery of mortuary remains clearly presents a sampling problem. Attempts to characterize prehistoric societies from mortuary remains require that we obtain information about all kinds of burial practiced in a society. This is obviously impossible in many cases. Rather than find this a discouraging limitation, we might see it as a genuine opportunity. There may well be patterns in the extent to which mortuary remains are not recoverable archaeologically. Similarly, it may be possible to obtain positive information from such negative conditions as absence of burials. For example, the extent to which certain age or sex classes are absent from an archaeological mortuary population may reflect significant social factors. We shall see later in this review that such a negative condition as the absence of formal cemeteries is a very informative characteristic.

In short, the complexity of mortuary ritual, and the problems of archaeological analysis, should be viewed as opportunities rather than detriments. Such a view does not imply that analysis of mortuary remains may be considered a simple procedure. There are good reasons to believe that common factors condition the social dimensions of mortuary ritual in varying cultural contexts. However, these common factors are of a highly abstract nature; their archaeological application will vary with each case being considered. Thus, the concepts to be discussed here should not be taken as a tool kit for archaeological interpretation, but rather as a base for deriving interpretive principles appropriate for each individual case.

THE SIGNIFICANCE OF MORTUARY DATA

To evaluate the usefulness of mortuary data for social modeling, two criteria may be discussed. These are the range of social information that may be derived from mortuary remains, and the reliability of burial data as indicators of social phenomena.

In his discussion of the archaeological application of role theory, Saxe (1970:6) noted that the occasion of death will involve an interaction between the deceased person and many of the persons with whom he or she had engaged in identity relationships during life. It can be seen then that death and mortuary ritual call forth a fuller representation of an individual's various social identities than does any occasion during life. Hence, the archaeological record of mortuary ritual should contain a greater range of information about the social identities present in a past society than does any other category of information. Additionally, since individuals acquire social identities by virtue of membership in the structural parts or components of a social system, mortuary ritual will simultaneously convey information about the nature of a past society. Indeed, to the extent to which a mortuary population contains individuals who held membership in the various components of a society, that mortuary population can be expected to reflect the structure of the extinct society (Tainter 1977b:70). There does not appear to be any other category of archaeological data for which this claim might be so confidently advanced.

Given that mortuary ritual has such potential for extensive representation of social phenomena, we must consider whether archaeological mortuary remains will reliably reflect the information conveyed through mortuary ritual. This, of course, is the question continuously raised by the skeptics and critics of social modeling. Deriving an answer to this question will involve a discussion of topics that will figure prominently in later sections of this review.

Much of Saxe's work deals with the application of formal analysis to mortuary data, an approach pioneered by Brown in the middle 1960s (but not published until 1971). Formal analysis is a technique used to evaluate and display the combinations of mortuary attributes found in a mortuary domain. Such combinations of attributes are often displayed as a branching diagram, or key, as shown in Figure 4.1.

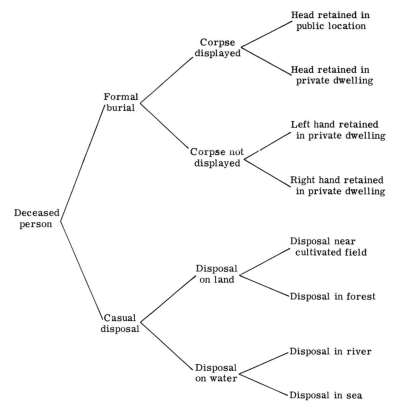

Figure 4.1. Key diagram of a perfect tree.

The key in Figure 4.1 is a perfect tree. A perfect tree is an absolutely redundant structure in that the decision made at any one contrast set (for example, whether the person merits formal or casual treatment) automatically prescribes the choices available in subsequent contrast sets. Thus, if a person is to be disposed of casually, the question of whether the corpse should be publicly displayed is inapplicable. Instead, the next choice to be prescribed is whether the disposal should be on land on on water. Similarly, disposal in a forest redundantly emphasizes the fact that disposal was on land, and was carried out casually.

In polar contrast to a perfect tree is a perfect paradigm. In a perfect paradigm all attributes are independent. Choice of one attribute does not prescribe or limit subsequent contrast sets. Hence, the redundancy is zero. A perfect paradigm is illustrated in Figure 4.2.

Techniques for measuring whether a key represents a tree or a paradigm are available fron the field of information theory. In a situation

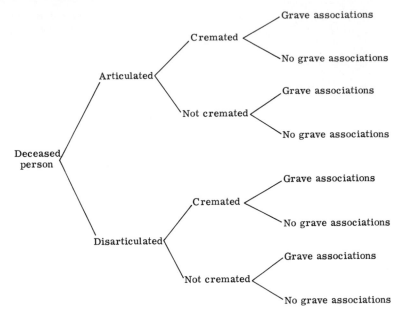

Figure 4.2. Key diagram of a perfect paradigm.

of complete nonredundancy, all attributes combine with all others; there is complete randomness in organization. In information theory, this is a situation of maximum entropy. In a state of high redundancy, the combinations of attributes are highly determined; there is high organization and low entropy. So to determine whether a key represents a tree or a paradigm we measure its degree of entropy.

In a situation of maximum entropy all attributes will combine randomly with all others. If the number of possible combinations (termed *significata*) is denoted as S, then the situation of complete randomness will be expressed as

$$S = C_a \times C_b \times \cdots C\infty$$

where C represents the number of different values each attribute may take. (In Figures 4.1 and 4.2, there are two values for each attribute, with the exception of the attribute Deceased person.) The value S will indicate the maximum number of possible burial modes and might be referred to as S_{max}.

The amount of information in S_{max} can be measured as

$$E = \log_2 S_{max}$$

Here E will represent the maximum entropy possible in a key.

To measure actual entropy we tabulate the number of burial modes (or significata) actually observed. This will be referred to as S_{actual}. The entropy of S_{actual} will be

$$e = \log_2 S_{actual}$$

where e is a measure of actual entropy.

Relative entropy (RE) is measured as

$$RE = e/E$$

And conversely, to measure redundancy (R) we apply the formula

$$R = 1 - RE$$

For a perfect paradigm R will equal zero, whereas for a perfect tree it will have a value of 1 (Saxe 1970:102–107).

There are many implications of Saxe's application of information theory to mortuary remains. For the moment we shall consider only the following (Tainter 1975b:107–109).

Mortuary ritual is basically a communication system in which certain symbols are employed to convey information about the status of the deceased. As in any communication system, the messages generated through mortuary ritual are subject to noise, which may induce errors or distortion, or inject extraneous material into a message. Since noise can alter the meaning or significance of a message, it is necessary for reliable communication to develop codes that allow transmission of information in the presence of noise. This is accomplished by building redundancy into the code (Shannon 1949:75).

As we have seen, where some symbols are used jointly to designate a number of disposal types (as in a paradigm), the redundancy is low. And where each set of symbols pertains exclusively to only a single burial type (as in a tree), redundancy is high. In the former situation, archaeological identification of socially distinctive individuals will be difficult, because certain symbols will pertain to a variety of burial modes. In situations of high redundancy the opposite will be true. More important for our present purposes, where redundancy among the symbols employed in mortuary ritual is high, the reliability of the archaeological record will be high. This is so because the elements of mortuary ritual that are preserved in the archaeological record will redundantly reaffirm the same message that was conveyed by nonpreservable elements of the ritual. Hence, the archaeological loss of certain aspects of mortuary ritual will, in situations of high redundancy, not result in loss of information about the social characteristics of the deceased individuals.

Using the equations detailed above, Saxe investigated the amount of redundancy in three ethnographic mortuary domains (Ashanti, Bontoc Igorot, and Kapauku Papuans). Although his sample was small, the results obtained were meaningful. Saxe (1970:230) found redundancy values of .764 (Kapauku Papuans), .834 (Ashanti), and .88 (Bontoc Igorot). These values are consistently high, indicating tree-like keys, and suggesting that mortuary ritual as a communication system *may* universally employ a highly redundant code. This finding suggests a high degree of reliability for the archaeological record in respect to the information communicated through disposal of the dead.

THE USE OF SOCIAL TYPOLOGIES IN MORTUARY STUDIES

One of the basic problems in the study of prehistoric societies has been the development of scales on which archaeological societies may be placed for comparative purposes. The scales most frequently used are derived from ethnology, primarily from the work of Service (1962) and Fried (1967). [Service has since retracted his typology (1971:156–157), although many archaeologists continue to employ it.] These scales aspire to an ordinal level of measurement in that a societal typology is developed in which kinds of societies are ranked according to increasing degrees of structural complexity and increasing numbers of mechanisms for organizing populations.

The use of evolutionary typologies as analogues for archaeological societies has dominated mortuary studies. Some examples will suffice to illustrate the types of conclusions usually derived when evolutionary typologies are employed.

> . . . data from the cemetery at Rincon suggest . . . an egalitarian society [Stickel 1968:227].
> . . . the Mrn-27 cemetery seems most likely to reflect a society in which ascribed rank was an important element of the social structure [King 1970:22].
> . . . social stratification . . . existed among the Northern Chumash at least as early as 500 A.D. [Tainter 1971:16].
> The mortuary patterning of the CCo-308 Middle Horizon components is consistent with the patterning predicted for egalitarian societies [while the Late Horizon witnesses] the emergence of a rank society in Fried's sense [Fredrickson 1974:62,64].
> [The mortuary patterns at Spiro] fulfill some of the requirements of an adaptive level of organization called a chiefdomship [Brown 1971:102].
> It is suggested that a chiefdom model should continue to be employed in research involving the Dallas archaeological culture [Hatch 1974:251].
> [The Moundville Phase mortuary data fulfill] the expectations of hypotheses which have as their premises that the Moundville Phase was a ranked society [Peebles 1974:191].

This listing could continue much further, but the point has certainly been made that the archaeological study of the social dimensions of mortuary practices has been overwhelmingly dependent on evolutionary typologies. This being the case, it is appropriate to devote some discussion to the logic and the limitations of this approach.

The ethnologists who have developed evolutionary typologies have largely conceptualized social variables as dichotomous, and have utilized such dichotomies as the basis for abstracting societal "types." Typical of evolutionary typologies are statements such as the following:

> Band society, out of which tribes grew, was egalitarian [Service 1962:114].
> Leadership is personal—charismatic—and for special purposes only in tribal society [Service 1962:114].
> Tribes are integrated by pan-tribal sodalities, but chiefdoms are not, though, like bands, they may have a few minor sodalities for limited purposes [Service 1962:165].
> Apart from age and sex, there is little significant division of labor [in rank societies] [Fried 1967:129].
> A stratified society is one in which members of the same sex and equivalent age status do not have equal access to the basic resources that sustain life [Fried 1967:186].

It is combinations of such dichotomous attributes that are used to define societal typologies. Given that categories of societies are conceptualized as combinations of discrete attributes, it would follow that the means by which a newly discovered society (whether ethnographic or archaeological) can be assigned to a proper evolutionary slot is by a process of keying the society, on its various dichotomous attributes, until the final combination of elements indicates its appropriate designation.

Leaving aside the question of whether social characteristics can indeed be considered discrete attributes, we shall consider the archaeological application of these principles. If prehistoric societies are to be assigned to an evolutionary slot by means of an identifying key, then the archaeologist should proceed to the analysis of data with a list of criteria for identifying each dichotomous attribute that contributes to the keying procedure. Such a process is logically intrinsic to evolutionism, but is not consistently applied. Instead, archaeologists working within an evolutionary framework regularly abridge this keying procedure by identifying only a limited number of social characteristics, most often rank differences, and from these inferring the appropriate typological designation for the society in question. The implicit assumption in this approach must be that the dichotomous attributes defining societal types are so strongly associated, and so highly redundant, that identification of one implies all the others, as well as the abstracted societal form they collectively designate. This assumption has never been subjected to rigorous testing, and so must be viewed with caution.

One recent archaeological study that has avoided the pitfall of determining a typological designation for a prehistoric society on the basis of only one or two social variables is Renfrew's (1973) evaluation of social organization in neolithic Wessex. Renfrew proposes that the large earthworks and monuments that typify the later portions of this time period reflect the existence of chiefdoms. To test this hypothesis, Renfrew abstracts from the formulations of Service (1962) and Sahlins (1968) twenty defining characteristics of chiefdoms. He lists these as follows:

(1) a ranked society
(2) the redistribution of produce organized by the chief
(3) greater population density
(4) increase in the total numbers of the society
(5) increase in the size of individual residence groups
(6) greater productivity
(7) more clearly defined territorial boundaries or borders
(8) a more integrated society with a greater number of sociocentric statuses
(9) centres which coordinate social and religious as well as economic activity
(10) frequent ceremonies and rituals serving wide social purposes
(11) rise of priesthood
(12) relation to a total environmental situation favouring specialization in production (and hence redistribution)—i.e. to some ecological diversity
(13) specialization, not only regional or ecological but also through the pooling of individual skills in large cooperative endeavors.
(14) organization and deployment of public labor, sometimes for agricultural work (e.g. irrigation) and/or for building temples, temple mounds, or pyramids
(15) improvement in craft specialization
(16) potential for territorial expansion—associated with the 'rise and fall' of chiefdoms
(17) reduction of internal strife
(18) pervasive inequality of persons or groups in the society associated with permanent leadership, effective in fields other than the economic
(19) distinctive dress or ornament for those of high status
(20) no true government to back up decisions by legalized force [Renfrew 1973:543].

Armed with these indicators, Renfrew proceeds with an analysis of the neolithic Wessex archaeological data, eventually concluding that the documented or inferred presence of the majority of these characteristics indicates the existence of chiefdoms.

Renfrew's analysis is satisfying in many ways, including not only its relative completeness but the explicitly stated recognition that the chiefdom concept is a catchall that lacks specificity. Indeed, Renfrew suggests that the chiefdom analogue "will have to make way for, or be refined to yield, subtler and less inclusive concepts" (1973:557). This realization is refreshing, but some disturbing aspects of Renfrew's analysis remain. Most serious is his handling of the list of chiefdom characteristics. Although many linkages can be discerned among these twenty attributes, the reader is still left with the impression that Renfrew regards a chiefdom not as an adaptive system, but as a list of traits. Renfrew seems to advocate what might be termed the *checklist* approach to social modeling.

In a subsequent work, Renfrew has accepted his own challenge to substitute for the chiefdom analogue "subtler and less inclusive concepts." His solution is to subdivide the category of chiefdom into two varieties: *group-oriented chiefdoms* (chiefdoms with little evidence of differential access to wealth, but considerable evidence of communal labor), and *individualizing chiefdoms* (chiefdoms that display material indications of ranking, but only a minimum of monumental construction) (Renfrew 1974:74). Renfrew is careful to point out that this is not intended to be an exercise in typology. Yet it is not hard to envision what the outcome of this approach might be. Taken to its logical conclusion, this solution to deriving "subtler and less inclusive concepts" will bring us an endless proliferation of new pigeonholes in the evolutionary typologies, as each archaeologist discovers that his or her prehistoric chiefdom was not quite like all the others. And ultimately the literature may become filled with endless debates concerning whether this or that set of archaeological data reflects Chiefdom Type 32a or Chiefdom Type 32b! Clearly the development of "subtler and less inclusive concepts" will lead nowhere as long as such concepts focus on the proliferation of new *labels* to apply to prehistoric societies. To concentrate our research effort worrying over what to *call* a past society is a waste of that effort. If one of our objectives is to study social variation and change, then we should concentrate on the development of truly quantitative scales for measuring social characteristics. Such quantitative methods have been developed and will be discussed shortly.

CLASSIFICATION OF MORTUARY DATA

Certainly basic to any analysis of mortuary data is the problem of classification. The purpose of classifying mortuary data is to isolate clusters of burials, which can be interpreted as socially distinctive. The use of formal analysis (Brown 1971; Saxe 1970) for this purpose has been discussed previously. Saxe has taken the techniques of formal analysis and developed a system of interrelated hypotheses concerning the social dimensions of mortuary practices. Among these hypotheses are the following.

> The Components of a Given Disposal Domain Cooperate in a Partitioning of the Universe, the Resultant Combinations Representing Different Social Personae [Saxe 1970:65].

Putting it in other words, Saxe postulates that each burial type represents a different social persona.

> Within a Given Domain Personae of Lesser Social Significance Tend to Manifest Fewer Positive Components in Their Significata Relative to Others, and Conversely [Saxe 1970:69].

The reasoning behind this last hypothesis is that social personae of higher significance will engage larger numbers of persons in identity relationships (usually status obligations) than will personae of lesser significance. These identity relationships will be symbolized in mortuary ritual, and reflected as positive components (or in other words, positive attributes) in the burial domain. Hence, personae of higher significance will display more positive components. Parenthetically, it might be added that in his ethnographic survey Saxe found support for the former hypothesis, whereas the latter tested ambiguously.

These hypotheses clearly underscore the potential of formal analysis. It will be useful to evaluate how the technique has actually been applied to archaeological materials.

Following Brown's exposition of the use of formal analysis (original paper 1966, published 1971), the technique was applied to several archaeological data sets in California (Stickel 1968; Decker 1969; Finnerty *et al.* 1970; T. King 1970) and was used in one case involving the lower Snake River region in southeastern Washington (Rodeffer 1973). Viewed from the perspective of Saxe's work, several of these studies display a common problem. When applied to archaeological data, formal keys tend to focus the classification process on variables that reflect idiosyncratic variations peculiar to individual burials. The resultant classifications often yield burial types represented by only one individual each. When formal classification procedures isolate individual burials, it is difficult to gain information concerning the structure and the organizing principles of social systems. Social positions that existed in past societies can be identified archaeologically by isolating sets of burials manifesting similar social personae, not by keying out individual burials.

These negative results do not imply that formal analysis may not be used archaeologically, or that Saxe's hypotheses may not be operationalized. The mortuary attributes used in a formal classification should be selected carefully. The criterion for selection must be that such attributes display common variance.

As an alternative to formal analysis, mortuary data might be classified through the use of multivariate statistical techniques. Such techniques are ideally suited for the task of isolating sets of interrelated variables that display common variance. Unfortunately, when different kinds of multivariate procedures are applied to the same set of mortuary data, the results obtained may vary widely. This review is perhaps not the proper place to discuss the nuances of multivariate statistics, so we shall restrict ourselves to citing the results of an experiment in classifying mortuary data using a variety of statistical procedures (Tainter 1975a). The results of this experiment seemed to indicate that polythetic classification procedures (Clarke 1968:37) are not entirely suitable for mortuary data because the clusters derived through these procedures are not satisfactorily homogeneous. In a set of experimental classifications polythetic techniques yielded clusters of burials containing members of several rank grades. An alternative set of techniques are available, known as monothetic–divisive procedures. These procedures progressively subdivide a population in such a way that the resulting subgroups, at each hierarchical level, are maximally homogeneous. A stopping rule is applied to halt the subdivisive process at the proper point. Of the various algorithms available for deriving the hierarchical arrangement of attributes on which the population is divided, two of the most common are various functions of chi-square (Whallon 1972) and the information statistic (Peebles 1972). In a test using Middle Woodland mortuary data the latter statistic gave superior results (Tainter 1975a), and it has proved useful in analysis of a large variety of archaeological data sets (Peebles 1972, 1974; Tainter 1975b; T. King 1976; Goldstein 1976).

SELECTION OF DATA FOR MORTUARY STUDIES

The selection of categories of archaeological data for use in mortuary studies must be based on the variety of means by which social positions are symbolized in mortuary treatment. Many archaeological studies have neglected the diversity of symbolic forms which may be employed in mortuary ritual, and have assumed instead that the most significant information may be derived from one data class: grave associations. As a result, a rather elaborate interpretive framework has been built around the study of grave associations. Initiated by Binford (1962), this framework has been elaborated by Stickel (1968). Stickel's goal was to develop criteria for determining whether a set of mortuary data reflect a society that was egalitarian or ranked. For an egalitarian society, Stickel (1968:217) proposed that grave associations should reflect the following characteristics:

1. A predominance of artifacts that served primarily in the technological sphere
2. Status symbols of the sort attainable by individual achievement

3. Within such status groups as exist, grave associations that distribute differentially among individuals rather than groups
4. Noninheritance of status symbols, potentially signified by inclusion of status symbols in graves

In contrast, among the members of a society characterized by class ranking, grave associations should pattern in a contrasting fashion (Stickel 1968:217), as follows:

1. Increased frequency of status symbols
2. Possession of specific status symbols by groups
3. Considerable individual variation in mortuary associations
4. Inheritance of status symbols

Applying these concepts to the 1700 B.C. southern California Rincon cemetery, Stickel (1968:227) concluded that the mortuary remains reflected an egalitarian society.

Stickel's paper proved to be a stimulus for research into the social organization of California hunter–gatherers. Subsequent studies documented the evolution of complex, ranked social systems in several areas of California beginning about 2000 B.P. (T. King 1970, 1974, 1976; Tainter 1971; Fredrickson 1974). Such complex social systems, unusual for hunter–gatherers, are clearly documented in the ethnographic literature, as well as in the archaeological record. Late prehistoric cemeteries, for example, seem to reflect the ethnographic situation of differentially ranked kinship groups (King 1969; Finnerty et al. 1970).

Despite the florescence of productive research stimulated by Stickel's paper, some nagging questions about this approach remain. Much of Stickel's framework boils down to a distinction between differentiation in quantity of grave associations and differentiation in quality. In an egalitarian society there will be few structural status positions that need to be symbolized through exotic material items. Thus, grave associations in such a society will be restricted, as Stickel proposes, to differentiations in quantity of items. Differentiation of burials in terms of quality or type of status markers will be minimal, since few status positions exist that require use of such markers. In a ranked society there are more structural status positions, and there exists a corresponding need for more kinds of material items to denote status distinctions. In addition to differentiation in quantity of items, deceased members of a ranked society should also be distinguished in terms of the kinds of status markers placed in the grave. Of course, both egalitarian and ranked societies will be characterized by burial differentiation in *both* quantity and quality of material associations. But it is to be expected that in egalitarian mortuary populations differentiation in quality or type of grave association will be less pronounced than in a ranked population.

There are ethnographic data that create doubts about archaeological use of the concepts presented above. The northern California Modoc practiced cremation of their dead. In addition to the corpse, the clothing and personal possessions of the deceased were placed on the pyre to be consumed. Rarely, though, were valuable items lost in this way. Any individual attending the ceremony might remove an object from the pyre and replace it with a quantity of shell beads, or perhaps render some service such as fire-tending (Ray 1963:116–117). For the archaeological record the consequences of such actions are significant. In the case of the Modoc the material items accompanying the deceased person are initially differentiated in terms of type and quality of materials. In Stickel's framework (as interpreted here) this would seemingly indicate a ranked society. Yet such evidence of ranking would apparently not make its way into the archaeological record. Instead, the initial distinction in type and quality of grave associations is ultimately collapsed to mere differentiation in *quantity* of shell beads, an archaeological characteristic that might be interpreted as reflecting egalitarianism!

Many archaeological studies have paralleled Stickel's approach by relying on grave associations as the sole or primary class of data for deriving social inferences (in addition to the studies cited above, see Winters 1968; Larson 1971; Peebles 1971, 1974; Hatch 1974; Rathje 1970, 1973; Autry 1974; Baker 1974; Clark 1969; Randsborg 1974, 1975; Rothschild 1973; Shennan 1975). In most cases in which other variables enter the analysis (type of interment facility, location of grave, etc.), these characteristics are not used as independent sources of information, or used in conjunction with grave associations to derive social information. Instead, grave associations are consistently treated as the major information source, with other categories of mortuary data treated in a wholly subsidiary fashion.

There is no logical or empirical basis for this approach. Mortuary ritual is a process of *symbolizing*. The nature of a symbol is such that the relationship between the form of the symbol and its referent is arbitrary, or, at most, expedient. Given this, there is no intrinsic reason why social distinctions must be symbolized by mortuary associations. Indeed, in a recent survey of ethnographic mortuary systems (Tainter 1974: 125), it was found that the use of material inclusions to signify status distinctions was a decidedly minor practice, *used in less than 5% of all cases* (*n* = 93). This result alone suggests that the extensive reliance archaeologists place on grave associations is likely to be inappropriate.

We are left then with the question, On which dimensions of mortuary ritual should archaeologists concentrate their analysis? To answer this question directly would essentially entail listing all dimensions of mortuary ritual that have ever been observed, either archaeologically or ethnographically. Such a list would not only be ponderous, but, without a valid interpretive framework for each such dimension, it would be meaningless. Instead, the next section of this review will concentrate on a discussion of mortuary variables that seem most suitable for comparative analysis.

MORTUARY STUDIES: CROSS-CULTURAL PERSPECTIVES

If the study of past social systems is ever to aspire to the study of social process, then archaeologists must develop the ability to model prehistoric societies in ways that yield comparable results. Two of the factors involved in the development of comparable social models are explicit consideration of the dimensions of a social system that are being investigated, and the development of cross-culturally valid criteria for isolating and measuring these dimensions.

Any social system is differentiated along a number of dimensions. Archaeologists dealing with past societies generally neglect this crucial consideration, deriving only those social inferences that are most easily obtained from a set of data, rather than specifying in advance which social dimension is the objective of the study. Blau provides a characterization of the concept of dimensions of differentiation:

> A dimension of differentiation is any criterion on the basis of which the members of an organization are formally divided into positions, . . . or into ranks, . . . or into subunits . . . . A structural component is either a distinct official status . . . or a subunit in the organization. . . . The term differentiation refers to the number of structural components that are formally distinguished in terms of any *one* criterion [1970:203–204; emphasis in original].

Failure to consider the important concept of dimensions of differentiation has led archaeologists to derive an impressive array of information about past societies, but has rarely led to the production of information that is *comparable*. Thus, where archaeologists working in one region of the Southwest infer the existence of uxorilocal residence units (Longacre 1970; Hill 1970), an archaeologist working nearby discovers a society with hereditary ranking (Clark 1969:82–83). Investigators wishing to study social variation and change in these adjacent regions are left at a loss.

Given that we should be explicit about the dimensions of a social system we are attempting to model, we must tackle the more difficult question, How may comparable social information be derived from mortuary data? The means by which social differentiation among the dead is symbolized at burial varies considerably, even among groups living in geographical proximity (Kroeber 1927). The problem confronting the archaeologist has, for this reason, been the lack of ability to develop general principles for interpreting mortuary remains that could be applied cross-culturally. This lack of generalizing power has produced a situation where nearly every set of mortuary data must be approached with a unique strategy for social inference. And yet we have seen that at least one attempt to produce an objective, cross-culturally valid strategy for mortuary analysis (Stickel 1968) contained unforeseen shortcomings. We may ask, then, if it is feasible or conceptually realistic to search for analytical frameworks intended to produce comparable information.

At present, two social dimensions have been singled out for the development of comparable analytical frameworks. These are (*a*) descent group differentiation and (*b*) rank differentiation. Treating the first characteristic, Saxe proposed the following hypothesis:

> To the Degree that Corporate Group Rights to Use and/or Control Crucial but Restricted Resources are Attained and/or Legitimized by Means of Lineal Descent from the Dead (i.e., Lineal Ties to Ancestors), Such Groups Will Maintain Formal Disposal Areas for the Exclusive Disposal of Their Dead, and Conversely [1970:119].

Saxe's hypothesis is provocative, for it helps account for a number of questions that have long puzzled archaeologists. The factors determining whether burials are present or absent in a particular location, or, if present, whether they are clustered, dispersed, randomly distributed, or associated with certain types of features, such as houses, are undoubtedly multiple. Saxe's hypothesis suggests that much of the variation in burial distribution may be accounted for by social factors, and that we may use such distributional variations to gain certain types of social information. More specifically, Saxe's hypothesis offers an opportunity to derive comparable information concerning the number and nature of corporate decent groups making up prehistoric communities.

Saxe initially tested this hypothesis against his sample of three ethnographic societies and found consistent confirmation. More recently, Goldstein (1976) has tested this hypothesis on a more extensive sample of thirty cases. The results of this test seem to indicate (*a*) that the presence of formal disposal areas is consistently associated with corporate groups practicing lineal descent and (*b*) that most, though not all, such groups use formal disposal areas. Thus, the presence of formal disposal areas will strongly indicate that the archaeologist has isolated individual corporate groups, and the absence of formal cemeteries will suggest, with a probability that is high but less than unity, the absence of social groups of this sort. This last interpretive ambiguity must be kept in mind.

Two recent applications of Saxe's hypothesis have shown its usefulness. Goldstein (1976) has found the concept useful in elucidating the significance of the spatial organization of two Mississippian cemeteries in the Illinois Valley. In the Kaloko cemetery, located in the Hawaiian Islands, the spatial organization of the cemetery appears to be hierarchically arranged (Tainter 1976). The entire Kaloko community was organized as a single corporate unit, reflected in the fact that the region contains a single temple, and is physically separated from adjacent settlements by unoccupied zones and boundary cairns (Tainter and Cordy 1977). Ethnographically, such settlements corporately held the land on which they were situated. Hence, it is not surprising that Kaloko contains but a single, formal cemetery. At the same time though, both the cemetery and the community were subdivided into smaller units. There appear to have been a total of four residential units at Kaloko, each of which maintained a separate agricultural area seemingly for its exclusive use. This subdivision of the larger community into smaller corporate groups is reflected in a similar subdivision in the cemetery. Within the larger disposal area there are a number of subareas that are discrete and bounded. Each of these subareas in the cemetery may correspond to one of the residential groups of the community, or, alternatively, two or more cemetery groups may have been linked to form a single residential unit. This second alternative is indicated by the fact that, although there are only four residential units, the cemetery seems to contain at least nine corporate descent groups (Tainter 1976).

Coupling Saxe's hypothesis with some hindsight allows us to see the significance of distributional patterns observed in earlier mortuary studies. Chumash cemeteries along the southern California coast, between about 2000 B.P. and the historic period, seem to contain evidence of at least two differentially ranked descent groups: a higher ranking one in the western part of the cemetery, and a lower ranking group in the eastern segment (L. King 1969; Tainter 1971). Viewed from the perspective of Saxe's hypothesis, and with archaeological and ethnographic knowledge about social ranking in native California, these patterns might have been anticipated. More recently, T. King (1976) emphasized locational considerations to demonstrate the existence of politically differentiated communities of hunters and gatherers about 2000 B.P. in the southern Sierra foothills of Califronia.

The analysis of social ranking similarly benefits from objective and cross-culturally valid criteria for analysis. We have previously discussed the use of formal analysis for classifying the components, or attributes, or mortuary domains. From the use of formal analysis Saxe has developed the following hypothesis

Within a Given Domain Personae of Lesser Social Significance Tend to Manifest Fewer Positive Components in Their Significata Relative to Others, and Conversely [1970:69].

The reasoning behind this hypothesis was discussed in the section of this chapter dealing with the classification of mortuary data. Although the logic behind the hypothesis is consistent, ethnographic testing proved dubious (Saxe 1970:226–227). In operational terms, we have already seen that the archaeological use of formal analysis tends to focus the classification on idiosyncratic attributes, producing keys that isolate individual burials.

An alternative approach to isolating rank distinctions is derived from Binford's (1971:17, 21) observation that the form of a mortuary ritual will be determined by, among other factors, the size and composition of the social aggregate recognizing obligatory status responsibilities to the deceased. Binford proposes that such a larger array of duty–status relationships (which is characteristic of persons of high rank) will entitle the deceased to a larger amount of corporate involvement in the act of interment, and to a larger degree of disruption of normal community activities for the mortuary ritual. Expanding on this, Tainter (1973) has suggested that both the amount of corporate involvement and the degree of activity disruption will positively correspond to the amount of energy (or labor) expended in the mortuary act. Directionally, higher social rank of a deceased individual will correspond to greater amounts of corporate involvement and activity disruption, and this should result in the expenditure of greater amounts of energy in the interment ritual. Energy expenditure should in turn be reflected in such features of burial as size and elaborateness of the interment facility, method of handling and disposal of the corpse, and the nature of grave associations. Reversing this reasoning, when sets of mortuary data cluster into distinctive levels of energy expenditure, this occurrence will signify distinctive levels of social involvement in the mortuary act, and will reflexively indicate distinctive grades or levels of ranking.

The use of energy expenditure for determining rank grading may provide a solution to some dilemmas encountered by archaeologists. Energy expenditure allows the analysis of rank patterns in situations where grave associations are not present. Indeed, the energy expenditure argument was first formulated for the analysis of a cemetery where the primary dimensions of variation were the size and elaborateness of the interment facility (Tainter 1973). Energy expenditure provides a preferable alternative to interpretive frameworks that focus on only one dimension of mortuary ritual, such as grave associations. In the case of the Modoc, we observed that an initial contrast in the type and quality of items associated with individuals was transformed into a situation where the archaeological record would reflect only quantitative contrasts in grave associations. Such a situation confounds the interpretive framework specified by Stickel (1968). The use of energy expenditure as the analytical criterion would solve this dilemma, for rank differences would still be apparent if the archaeological record of Modoc mortuary practices were viewed from this perspective.

The proposition linking energy expenditure in mortuary ritual to the rank of the deceased has been tested on an extensive ethnographic sample. In a set of 103 ethnographic cases, the energy expenditure argument was not contradicted once (Tainter 1975b). A selection of examples from these ethnographic cases will illustrate the kinds of energy expenditure contrasts that are consistently found in the literature.

Complexity of Body Treatment

Selecting an example to illustrate variations in the complexity of body treatment is difficult, but only because so many cases might be cited. Among the Salinan Indians, near San Antonio Mission, California, "the most distinguished dead were cremated, while persons of no particular importance were merely buried" (Mason 1912:167). A Papuan group in the Fly River region buried commoners in a sewn mat. In contrast, a chief, a chief's only child, or a respected person would be exposed on a wooden platform, the skull removed, decorated, and placed in a specially erected building, and the other bones collected and buried (Riley 1925:166, 170). Ngadju–Dayak communities of Borneo practice a type of secondary burial associated with considerable economic expenditures. Only the economically more successful households are able to afford this ritual (Miles 1965).

Construction and Placement of the Interment Facility

Two interesting examples illustrate energy expenditure contrasts in these variables. Among the Padju Epat Ma'anyan Dayaks, the final resting place for the bones of a deceased individual is in the *tambak,* an ornately carved box used by the bilateral descendants of the person who founded it. The establishment of a new *tambak* is an expensive affair, but such an act symbolizes the attainment of an almost unique social and economic status by the founder. When an individual achieves such a social and economic level that he wishes to disassociate himself from his natal group, he commissions the construction of a new *tambak* to be used by himself and by his decendants (Hudson 1966). In the Morobe District of New Guinea, the body of a deceased individual was ordinarily placed in the ground and allowed to decompose for a period of five months. After that time, the skeletal remains were taken to a cliff face where they were interred. The amount of energy expended in disposing of the remains in the cliff varied with the status of the deceased. Children and women were left at the foot of the cliff, or placed on lower ledges. Important men were placed on higher ledges, and the remains of the highest ranking members of the community were carried to the highest ledges of the cliff (McWilliam 1936).

Extent and Duration of Ritual Mortuary Behavior

Two missionaries' accounts of early Hawaiian mortuary practices, both dating to the same time period, clearly illustrate how differences in rank may be reflected in the extent and duration of ritual mortuary behavior, and correspondingly in energy expenditure. The two accounts relate mortuary procedures for community outcasts, and for persons of chiefly rank. These two social classes represent the extremes of the Hawaiian rank system. In the early 1820s, Charles S. Stewart noted that social outcasts (including those with physical abnormalities) were often simply left where they fell, or, if necessary, were removed from the living area of the community. Stewart described one example of such a means of disposal (quoted in Bowen 1961:74).

> An instance recently came to our knowledge in which a poor wretch thus perished within sight of our dwelling, after having lain uncovered for days and nights in the open air, most of the time, pleading in vain to his family, still within the hearing of his voice, for a drink of water! And when he was dead, his body, instead of being buried, was merely drawn so far into the bushes, as to prevent the offense that would have arisen from the corpse, and left a prey to the dogs who prowl through the district in the night!

Ellis described a starkly contrasting level of social involvement on the death of a local chief on the Island of Hawaii.

> . . . the whole neighborhood exhibited a scene of confusion, wickedness, and cruelty, seldom witnessed in the most barbarous society. The people ran to and fro without their clothes, appearing and acting more like demons than human beings; every vice was practised, and almost every species of crime was perpetrated. Houses were burnt, property plundered, even murder sometimes committed, and the gratification of every base and savage feeling sought without restraint [1969:177].

Two additional categories of energy expenditure that have been recorded ethnographically are material contributions to the ritual, and human sacrifice. Ethnographic examples of these will not be detailed at this point, since the Modoc might be cited as an example of the former category, and the latter is relatively unambiguous.

The ethnographic literature seems to indicate clearly, then, that energy expenditure in mortuary ritual is directly related to rank grading. As is often the case, however, the archaeological application of this idea is not without ambiguity. One major problem is measuring energy expenditure, and determining what constitutes a meaningful energy contrast in types of burial. At present, measurement of energy expenditure can only be accomplished on an ordinal scale with burials ranked by greater or less (apparent) energy expenditure. In some cases decisions concerning ordinal ranking are difficult to arrive at. A second, and potentially more important, problem is the extent to which archaeologically apparent distinctions in energy expenditure always reflect rank differences. The ethnographic literature provides numerous examples of mortuary practices that might appear archaeologically as energy expenditure variations, but in fact are not. The ossuary burials of the Huron are a case in point. Among the Huron, the bones of deceased individuals were periodically gathered and placed in a communal cemetery. Most ossuary interments had the flesh removed from the bones, but this was not done to individuals who died shortly before the reburial ceremony (Bushnell 1920:74–75). Archaeologically, a Huron ossuary would then display both articulated and disarticulated individuals, a contrast that might be mistakenly interpreted as a variation in energy expenditure.

Such an ethnographic example underscores a caution suggested previously. Although it is possible to develop abstract generalizations concerning mortuary practices, archaeological application of such generalizations will always require careful study of individual data sets. With careful scrutiny it should be possible to isolate many of the archaeological contrasts in energy expenditure that do not reflect rank differences. Ubelaker (1974), for example, has properly noted that degree of skeletal articulation in a Maryland ossuary probably reflects the amount of time that passed between death and ossuary interment (as among the Huron). With careful application the energy expenditure perspective does offer a cross-culturally valid criterion for deriving comparable information about rank differentiation in varying contexts. Its usefullness is ultimately illustrated by the number of archaeological studies in which it has been employed (Buikstra 1972; Brown 1973; Tainter 1973, 1975a,b, 1976, 1977a,b; Tainter and Cordy 1977; T. King 1976; Peebles 1974).

QUANTITATIVE MODELING

Ultimately, our goal in studying past societies must be to monitor and explain variation and change. Such a goal presupposes that we possess a scale against which social variables may be measured. In archaeological studies the scales used for this purpose have largely consisted of evolutionary typologies. Previously, we found reason to doubt whether such typologies are really suitable for this purpose. Fortunately, there are sophisticated and sensitive alternatives to evolutionary typologies. As in some earlier sections of this review, we find two basic approaches to quantitative modeling: one based on formal analysis, the other linked to the evaluation of energy expenditure.

In developing his comprehensive approach to the analysis of mortuary practices, Saxe proposed the following hypotheses:

> The More Paradigmatic the Attributes Evidenced in the Key Structure of the Domain, the Less Complex and More Egalitarian the Social Organization. Conversely, the More Tree-Like the Attributes, the More Complex and the Less Egalitarian the Social Organization [1970:75].

> The Simpler a Sociocultural System the Greater Will Be the Tendency for There To Be a Linear Relationship Between Number of Components in Significata, Number of Contrast Sets Necessary To Define Them, and the Social Significance of the Significata; and Conversely [1970:112].

The former hypothesis is based on the application of information theory to key structures. We have already discussed this application, as well as the procedure for measuring the extent to which any given key represents a tree or a paradigm. It is timely at this point to recall one of Saxe's previous hypotheses: that persons of higher social significance manifest more positive components (positive attributes) in their disposal domains than do less significant persons. If this is so, then not all attributes would be equally applicable to all burial modes as would be the case in a perfect paradigm (see Figures 4.1 and 4.2). Furthermore, persons of greater social significance should evidence more and more kinds of mortuary treatment that are not applicable to less significant persons. Hence, as social complexity increases, the mortuary domain should become less paradigmatic.

This hypothesis indicates a quantitative measure for social complexity. Ethnologically, Saxe (1970:230–231) could not find demonstrable support for it, most likely because of incomplete ethnographic reporting. Archaeologically, the information measures for mortuary keys have been applied by Thomas King (1976) to data from the Buchanan Reservoir, located in the southern Sierra foothills of California. The resulting measures indicated highly tree-like structures. For comparative purposes, King computed the same measures for keys of Late Woodland mortuary systems from the Illinois Valley (Tainter 1975b). The results of this application are of uncertain significance, for in both archaeological cases the keys were produced through statistical techniques designed to minimize the degree of entropy in the resulting classification.

The latter hypothesis is complex (Saxe 1970:112–118). It uses two scales: the Depth of Persona (D) scale and the Contrast (C) scale. The first is based on the number of positive attributes in a given disposal type. For any disposal type it is measured as the ratio of the number of positive attributes in a disposal mode (n) over the number in the disposal mode that has the highest number (n_{max}). Thus, $D = n/n_{max}$. The C scale is based on the number of contrast sets necessary to define a disposal type. In this case, $C = n/n_{max}$, where n contrast sets are required to define a given burial mode, and n_{max} is the maximum number required by any disposal type in the domain.

A disposal type that is unique for all its components is characterized by maximal redundancy. It will require only one contrast set to differentiate it. For reasons already discussed, such a disposal type would signify a persona of high social significance. In this case, the lower the value on the C scale, the more discrete will be the burial type.

On the other hand, a burial mode that requires many contrast sets to differentiate it will reflect a social persona sharing many social characteristics with other personae. Social distinctiveness in such a case is graded continuously, reflecting insignificant social status. In an egalitarian society such continuous grading will cause a linear relationship between the C and D scales. As the social significance of the deceased increases, so will the number of positive attributes in the disposal domain, and so also will the number of contrast sets necessary to define such a disposal mode.

In contrast, more complex societies will display graded, rather than continuous, levels of ranking. In such societies mortuary practices will exhibit multiple, redundant attributes restricted to persons of distinctive status. Given such redundancy, the number of contrast sets necessary to define disposal classes will be lower. Such societies will have mortuary domains characterized by several social strata, each of which may, in its mortuary domain, show a linear relationship between the C and D scales. However, between strata the relationship will not be linear, since in each higher stratum the number of contrast sets needed to differentiate burial modes will be lower than in the previous lower stratum. Hence, a measure of the degree of linearity in the relationship between the C and D scales provides a quantification of the degree of complexity of the social system. Ethnographic testing of this hypothesis proved promising (Saxe 1970:231–233), but it has not been applied archaeologically.

Another approach to quantitative analysis of past societies utilizes the perspective of systems theory (Tainter 1975b, 1977a, b; Tainter and Cordy 1977). Viewing prehistoric societies in a systems perspective suggests that our goal is to model such societies as complex, integrated entities. Such a goal entails a considerable shift in the types of social dimensions for which information is sought. Most archaeological studies concentrate on familiar dimensions such as residence or ranking. A consideration of prehistoric societies as *systems* requires a shift to a higher level of abstraction. A system simply cannot be characterized merely by describing the attributes of its parts. A system is a holistic entity the characteristics of which are not equivalent to the summed characteristics of its individual parts (von Bertalanffy 1968:55). To characterize a social *system* we must isolate and measure social dimensions that reflect the constituent parts of a system, as well as the patterned relationships among these parts. Such abstract, composite dimensions are the *structure* and the *organization* of social systems. The structure of a system is meant to indicate the number, nature, and arrangement of its articulated components and subsystems (Miller 1965:209, 218), whereas organization is most basically defined as the constraints imposed on the ranges of behavior which may possibly be pursued by the elements of a system (Rothstein 1958:34–36).

This perspective suggests four social dimensions for which information is to be sought. These are the degree of structural differentiation, the nature of structural differentiation, the amount or degree of organization, and the nature of organization. The degree of structural differentiation and of organization are quantitative variables, and must be modeled as such.

For archaeological analysis, we can isolate two dimensions of structural differentiation that are of general significance. These might be termed the vertical and the horizontal dimensions. The first refers to the structure of rank grading in a society. The horizontal dimension encompasses structural components that equate on identical hierarchical levels. Examples of the latter might include sodalities, certain types of coresident descent units, task groups, territorial bands, and the like.

In terms of structural differentiation along the horizontal dimension, we have seen how the spatial organization of mortuary remains can reveal the existence of corporate descent groups. Yet there are many components of the horizontal dimension for which such universal criteria for analysis have not been developed. The study of the vertical dimension presents fewer ambiguities. Levels of ranking may be confidently isolated as distinctive levels of energy expenditure (Tainter 1975b; cf. Randsborg 1974). As Blau (1970:203–204) has noted, such levels of ranking may be viewed as structural components of a social system. The number of such rank levels will mark the degree of structural differentiation along the vertical dimension.

The analysis of vertical differentiation allows the indirect measurement of the total structural complexity of a social system. In an analysis of structural differentiation on contemporary organizations Blau (1970) found that the size of an organization correlated strongly with both its degree of vertical differentiation and its degree of horizontal differentiation. Blau noted that this finding is not limited by the function of an organization. Hence, the observation can be considered applicable to prehistoric as well as to contemporary social systems. This finding is significant for archaeological research. The strength of the observed correlations (see Blau 1970) suggests that any one of these characteristics of a social system may be used to monitor not only itself, but the state of the other two as well. Structural differentiation along the vertical dimension can thus serve as an index of the total structural complexity of past social systems.

The measurement of organization is a more complex matter. Organization has been defined as constraint on behavior (Rothstein 1958:34–36). Thus, the measurement of organization must be approached through the measurement of behavioral constraint. The field that provides techniques for the measurement of organization is information theory.

The central concepts of information theory that are of use to us are entropy (disorder, disorganization, randomness), and its converse, organization. An additional concept is statistical equilibrium. In communication theory this would refer to a situation where, in a set of messages, all messages have an equal probability of transmission. A situation of statistical equilibrium corresponds to a condition of entropy. In statistical equilibrium the occurrence of any specific message is unpredictable, and thus the maximum information may be obtained when a particular message is sent. Hence, information and entropy are quantities that covary (Weaver 1949; Goldman 1953; Theil 1967; Young 1971).

To illustrate the archaeological use of these concepts, consider some hypothetical social system structurally differentiated into a number of components. In the total absence of *any* organizational constraints the process by which individuals acquire membership in the components would be purely random. Such a random process will ultimately result in a situation where the proportion of the population selecting affiliation with each component would be a fraction equal to $1/N$, where N is the number of components. Such a proportional distribution corresponds to a situation of statistical equilibrium, and so to a condition of entropy.

But of course no social situation lacks constraints of one form or another. To the extent that either social or demographic pressures limit freedom to acquire membership in certain components (such as those of high status), there is constraint and thus organization. In the presence of such constraints, the proportion of the population affiliating with certain components will depart from a condition of statistical equilibrium. It is precisely such departures from equilibrium that the mathematical techniques of information theory may be used to measure (Tainter 1975b, 1977a, b; Tainter and Cordy 1977).

Shannon's (1949:50–51) formula for measuring information may be transformed in a number of ways. For our purposes the formula may be given as

$$H = \sum_{i=1}^{N} p_i \log_2 1/p_i$$

where H is the entropy (information) of a set of probabilities, and p_i is the probability of occurrence of the ith message (or the ith structural component). This information measure ranges from 0.0 (no entropy) to $\log_2 N$ when all messages or components are equally probable (maximum entropy, referred to as $H_{\max}$).

Rothstein (1958:36) has suggested that organization be measured as the excess of the entropy a system may potentially exhibit ($H_{\max}$), less the entropy it actually does exhibit (H). Gatlin (1972:35–36) refers to this measure as the Divergence from Equiprobability, symbolized as D_1. The formula for organization ($D_1 = H_{\max} - H$) can range from 0.0 (maximum entropy) to a value that converges on $H_{\max}$ (maximum organization).

It is apparent in the calculation of the D_1 measure that the amount of organization a system may potentially exhibit increases with its degree of structural complexity. D_1 is a measure of *amount* of organization. Since the maximum D_1 value may increase with increases in $H_{\max}$, it is useful to calculate the ratio $RD_1 = D_1/H_{\max}$ as a measure of *degree* of organization. Where D_1 assesses the amount of constraint on a population's access to membership in structural components, RD_1 measures how much constraint is imposed relative to the amount that *might* be imposed. The ratio RD_1 will range between 0.0 (maximum relative entropy) and a value that approaches 1.0 (maximum relative organization).

Within the perspective being discussed, the final variable to be measured is rank differentiation. Rank differentiation is considered an important variable to measure because it includes elements of both structure and organization. Levels of ranking may be viewed as structural components of a system, while organization (behavioral constraint) is clearly an element of rank differentiation.

A measure for rank differentiation proposed by Harary (1959:23–25) is useful for mortuary studies. In this measure the status of an individual is based on two interacting factors: the number of persons subordinate to the individual, and the number of rank grades that separate these subordinates from the person of higher status. In a ranked hierarchy, any person P will have n_k subordinates in rank level k (rank levels are numbered downward from any given level, so that the first lower level is 1, the second is 2, etc.). If M is the number of rank levels below P, the status $s(P)$ of person P can be measured by the formula

$$s(P)= \sum_{k=1}^{M} k(n_k)$$

Expressed verbally, the status measure of a person is the number of the individual's immediate subordinates, plus twice the number of their immediate subordinates, plus three times the number of their immediate subordinates, and so forth. Hence, persons at the top of a hierarchy will have a higher status measure if they have a greater number of subordinates and/or if their subordinates are heavily distributed in the bottommost rank levels. The rationale behind this measure is discussed in more detail by Harary (1959) and Tainter (1975b, 1977a, b).

In archaeological analysis it is impossible to determine the precise number of individuals subordinate to a person of paramount rank at any point in time. But it should be possible to determine the number of levels of ranking in a past social system, and to ascertain the number of persons from a total mortuary population who were members of each rank grade. To compute the $s(P)$ measure it is necessary to consider the population of subordinate rank levels as multiples (or fractions) of the number of persons in the paramount rank grade. The formula used for this purpose in N_k/N_1, where N_k refers to the number of persons in rank level $k,$ and N_1 indicates the number in the highest rank level. With this transformation the paramount rank grade is always associated with the value 1.0, and subordinate levels become appropriate multiples (or fractions) of 1.0. The degree of rank differentiation in a hierarchy can then be expressed as the difference between the highest and lowest levels. Since the status of the lowest level is always zero, the degree of rank differentiation can be expressed as $s(1)$, the status measure of the highest level.

It should be clear that the archaeological application of these measures requires complete sets of mortuary data. The use of the measures may be illustrated by reference to a set of Middle Woodland (ca. 150 B.C.–A.D. 400) burials from mounds situated on the western bluffs of the Illinois Valley. In a set of 512 interments, the following levels of energy expenditure and ranking were observed (Tainter 1975b, 1977a, b).

Level 1: Individuals interred in, or processed through, large, log-roofed tombs, which served as the central feature of most mounds
Level 2: Peripheral burials in smaller, log-covered graves
Level 3: Burials with limestone slab inclusions
Level 4: Individuals buried with locally produced sociotechnic items, most often Hopewell series pottery vessels
Level 5: Interments in simple subfloor graves
Level 6: Individuals placed on accretional mound surfaces.

The distribution of the population among these rank levels is shown in Table 4.1. This table also illustrates the calculation of the entropy measure for this system. The Middle Woodland rank system displays an entropy of 1.8354 bits. H_{max} for six rank levels is 2.58496 bits, and so the measure of amount of organization (D_1) is (2.58496 − 1.8354) .7496. The degree of organization (RD_1) amounts to (.7496/2.58496) .29. The measure of rank differentiation is shown in Table 4.2. For this Middle Woodland system, $s(1)$ amounts to 13.671.

Such quantitative measures are most meaningful when used for the assessment of variation and change. In two such applications these measures have yielded excellent results. In a study of Woodland social change in west-central Illinois during the period A.D. 200–800 there appeared a general decrease in the structural complexity of social systems between the Middle and Late Woodland (A.D. 400–900) periods. Also evident are two contrasting quantitative trends: (a) a decrease in both organization (amount and degree) and rank differentiation in the *early* Late Woodland period; and (b) a corresponding increase in these variables during *later* Late Woodland, just prior to the emergence of the truly complex social systems characteristic of the Mississippian period. The pattern of social change evidenced by the quantitative measures is significant, not only for the information it discloses, but also because it parallels and is confirmed by nonquantitative assessments (Tainter 1975b, 1977a, b). It might be added at this point that, if evolutionary typologies had been used in this study, both Middle and Late Woodland systems would have been characterized as ranked societies (in Fried's terminology). Thus, no social change between the Middle and Late Woodland periods would have been evident. The pattern of social change that *was* observed was evident only because of the use of quantitative measures.

In a second study these measures have been applied to two contem-

TABLE 4.1

Entropy of Middle Woodland Rank System

Rank level	p	$\log_2 1/p$	$p \log_2 1/p$
1	.205	2.28630	.4687
2	.131	2.93236	.3841
3	.025	5.32193	.1330
4	.011	6.50635	.0716
5	.544	.878321	.4778
6	.084	3.57347	.3002
			$\Sigma = 1.8354$

TABLE 4.2

Middle Woodland Rank Differentiation

Rank level	N	N_k/N_1	$s(1)$
1	91	1.000	13.671
2	58	.637	
3	11	.121	
4	5	.055	
5	241	2.648	
6	37	.407	

poraneous prehistoric social systems from the Island of Hawaii. One of these (Kaloko) displays a complex rank hierarchy evidenced by both mortuary data and settlement patterns. The other (Anaehoomalu) displays a very truncated rank hierarchy with no persons of the highest rank grades. Quantitative analysis corroborates these qualitative conclusions, and indicates that Kaloko was characterized by greater structural complexity, organization, and rank differentiation (Tainter and Cordy 1977).

A comparative study that applies the quantitative methods developed by Saxe (1970) and Tainter (1975b) to the same data sets would be a useful step in furthering mortuary studies.

MORTUARY PRACTICES: CONCLUDING EVALUATIONS

This discussion of the social dimensions of mortuary practices leads to a set of conclusions and recommendations for future archaeological research. Perhaps most basic is the recommendation that investigators be explicit about which dimensions of a social system are to be monitored in a given study. (It does not need to be emphasized that this suggestion applies to all studies of past societies, whether dependent on mortuary data or not.) Along with the recognition that social dimensions of interest should be explicitly stated goes the responsibility to model these dimensions in a manner that will allow the study of social variation and change. The minimum requirement entailed by this consideration is that social dimensions be modeled by criteria that are objective and cross-culturally valid. For mortuary practices two analytical criteria have been developed that fulfill these requirements. These are the spatial distribution of mortuary remains, a variable that contains information relating to corporate group differentiation, and energy expenditure, an indicator of rank grading. A second consideration in the study of variation and change is that social dimensions be measured on true interval or ratio scales. The nominal categories that are characteristic of evolutionary typologies are simply not sensitive enough to yield the kinds of information we need for the study of social change. Two approaches to quantitative modeling of past social systems have been developed (Saxe 1970; Tainter 1975b). Such quantitative measurement of social variables must become a central goal in the study of mortuary practices.

REFERENCES

Autry, W.
    1974   Analysis of Post-Formative burial practices: Valley of Oaxaca, Mexico. Paper presented at the 1974 Annual Meeting of the Society for American Archaeology, Washington, D.C.

Baker, B. L.
    1974   Statistical analysis of Maya mortuary data: A re-evaluation of the relative importance of males and females at Altar de Sacrificios. Paper presented at the 1974 Annual Meeting of the American Anthropological Association, Mexico City.

Binford, L. R.
    1962   Archaeology as anthropology. *American Antiquity* **28**:217–225.
    1971   Mortuary practices: Their study and their potential. In Approaches to the social dimensions of mortuary practices, edited by J. A. Brown. *Society for American Archaeology, Memoirs* **25**:6–29.

Blau, P. M.
    1970   A formal theory of differentiation in organizations. *American Sociological Review* **35**:201–218.

Bowen, R. N.
    1961   Hawaiian disposal of the dead. Unpublished M.A. thesis, Department of Anthropology, University of Hawaii, Honolulu.

Brown, J. A.
    1971   The dimensions of status in the burials at Spiro. In Approaches to the social dimensions of mortuary practices, edited by J. A. Brown. *Society for American Archaeology, Memoirs* **25**:92–112.
    1973   Cultural evolution and the rise and fall of Spiro. Paper presented at the 1973 Southeastern Archaeological Conference, Memphis.

Buikstra, J. E.
    1972   Hopewell in the lower Illinois River valley: A regional approach to the study of biological variability and prehistoric mortuary activity. Unpublished Ph.D. dissertation, Department of Anthropology, University of Chicago.

Bushnell, D. I.
    1920   Native cemeteries and forms of burial east of the Mississippi. *Bureau of American Ethnology, Bulletin* No. 71.

Clark, G.
    1969   A preliminary analysis of burial clusters at the Grasshopper site, east-central Arizona. *The Kiva* **35**:57–86.

Clarke, D. L.
  1968 *Analytical archaeology*. London: Methuen.
Davidson, D. S.
  1949 Disposal of the dead in western Australia. *Proceedings of the American Philosophical Society* **93**:71–97.
Decker, D. A.
  1969 Early archaeology on Catalina Island: Potential and problems. *Archaeological Survey Annual Report (University of California, Los Angeles)* **11**:69–84.
Ellis, W.
  1969 *Polynesian researches: Hawaii*. Tokyo: Tuttle.
Finnerty, P., D. Decker, N. Leonard, III, T. King, C. King, and L. King
  1970 Community structure and trade at Isthmus Cove: A salvage excavation on Catalina Island. *Pacific Coast Archaeological Society Occasional Papers* No. 1.
Fredrickson, D. A.
  1974 Social change in prehistory: A central California example. In ? Antap:California Indian political and economic organization, edited by L. Bean and T. King. *Ballena Press Anthropological Papers* No. 2, 57–73.
Fried, M. H.
  1967 *The evolution of political society, an essay in political anthropology*. New York: Random House.
Gatlin, L. A.
  1972 *Information theory and the living system*. New York: Columbia University Press.
Goldman, S.
  1953 *Information theory*. New York: Dover.
Goldstein, L.
  1976 Spatial structure and social organization: Regional manifestations of Mississippian society. Ph.D. dissertation, Northwestern University. Ann Arbor: University Microfilms.
Goodenough, W. H.
  1965 Rethinking "status" and "role": Toward a general model of the cultural organization of social relationships. In The relevance of models for social anthropology, edited by M. Banton. *A.S.A., Monographs* No. 1, 1–24.
Harary, F.
  1959 Status and contrastatus. *Sociometry* **22**:23–43.
Hatch, J. W.
  1974 Social dimensions of Dallas mortuary patterns. Unpublished M.A. thesis, Department of Anthropology, Pennsylvania State University, University Park.
Hill, J. N.
  1970 Broken K Pueblo: Prehistoric social organization in the American Southwest. *University of Arizona Anthropological Papers* No. 18.
Hudson, A. B.
  1966 Death ceremonies of the Padju Epat Ma'anyan Dayaks. In Borneo writing and related matters, edited by T. Harrison. *Sarawak Museum Journal* **13**(27):341–416. (Special Monograph No. 1).
King, L.
  1969 The Medea Creek cemetery (LAn-243): An investigation of social organization from mortuary practices. *Archaeological Survey Annual Report (University of California, Los Angeles)* **11**:23–68.

King, T. F.
  1970 The dead at Tiburon: Mortuary customs and social organization on northern San Francisco Bay. *Northwestern California Archaeological Society Occasional Papers* No. 2.
  1974 The evolution of status ascription around San Francisco Bay. In ? Antap: California Indian political and economic organization, edited by L. Bean and T. King. *Ballena Press Anthropological Papers* No. 2, 37–53.
  1976 Political differentiation among hunter-gatherers: An archaeological test. Ph.D. dissertation, University of California, Riverside. Ann Arbor: University Microfilms.
Kroeber, A. L.
  1927 Disposal of the dead. *American Anthropologist* **29**:308–315.
Larson, L. H.
  1971 Archaeological implications of social stratification at the Etowah site, Georgia. In Approaches to the social dimensions of mortuary practices, edited by J. A. Brown. *Society for American Archaeology, Memoirs* **25**:58–67.
Longacre, W.
  1970 Archaeology as anthropology: A case study. *University of Arizona Anthropological Papers* No. 17.
McWilliam, N. D.
  1936 Disposal of the dead in the Buang Mountains, Morobe District, Mandated Territory of New Guinea. *Mankind* **2**(2):39–42.
Mason, J. A.
  1912 The ethnology of the Salinan Indians. *University of California Publications in American Archaeology and Ethnology* **10**(4):97–240.
Miles, D.
  1965 Socio-economic aspects of secondary burial. *Oceania* **35**:161–174.
Miller, G.
  1965 Living systems: Basic concepts. *Behavioral Science* **10**:193–237.
Peebles, C. S.
  1971 Moundville and surrounding sites: Some structural considerations of mortuary practices, II. In Approaches to the social dimensions of mortuary practices, edited by J. A. Brown. *Society for American Archaeology, Memoirs* **35**:68–91.
  1972 Monothetic-divisive analysis of the Moundville burials: An initial report. *Newsletter of Computer Archaeology* **8**(2):1–13.
  1974 Moundville: The organization of a prehistoric community and culture. Ph.D. dissertation, University of California, Santa Barbara. Ann Arbor: University Microfilms.
Randsborg, K.
  1974 Social stratification in early Bronze Age Denmark: A study in the regulation of cultural systems. *Praehistorische Zeitschrift* **49**:38–61.
  1975 Social dimensions of early Neolithic Denmark. *Proceedings of the Prehistoric Society* **41**:105–118.
Rathje, W. L.
  1970 Sociopolitical implications of Lowland Maya burials: Methodology and tentative hypotheses. *World Archaeology* **1**:359–374.
  1973 Models for mobile Maya: A variety of constraints. In *The explanation of culture change: Models in prehistory,* edited by C. Renfrew. London: Duckworth. Pp. 731–757.

Ray, V.
  1963 *Primitive pragmatists: The Modoc Indians of Northern California.* Seattle: University of Washington Press.
Service, E. R.
  1962 *Primitive social organization, an evolutionary perspective.* New York: Random House.
  1971 *Cultural evolutionism: Theory in practice.* New York: Holt.
Shannon, C. E.
  1949 The mathematical theory of communication. In *The mathematical theory of communication,* by C. E. Shannon and W. Weaver. Urbana: University of Illinois Press. Pp. 29–125.
Shennan, S.
  1975 The social organization at Branč. *Antiquity* **49:**279–288.
Renfrew, C.
  1973 Monuments, mobilization, and social organization in neolithic Wessex. In *The explanation of culture change: Models in prehistory,* edited by C. Renfrew. London: Duckworth. Pp. 539–558.
  1974 Beyond a subsistence economy: The evolution of social organization in prehistoric Europe. In Reconstructing complex societies, edited by C. Moore. *Bulletin of the American Schools of Oriental Research* No. 20. 69–85. (Supplement)
Riley, E.
  1925 *Among Papuan headhunters.* Philadelphia: Lippincott.
Rodeffer, M. J.
  1973 A classification of burials in the lower Snake River region. *Northwest Anthropological Research Notes* **7:**101–131.
Rothschild, N. A.
  1973 Sex, graves, and status. Paper presented at the 1973 Annual Meeting of the American Anthropological Association, New Orleans.
Rothstein, J.
  1958 *Communication, organization, and science.* Indian Hills, Colo.: Falcon's Wing Press.
Sahlins, M. D.
  1968 *Tribesmen.* Englewood Cliffs. N.J.: Prentice-Hall.
Saxe, A. A.
  1970 Social dimensions of mortuary practices. Ph.D. dissertation, University of Michigan. Ann Arbor: University Microfilms.
Stickel, E. G.
  1968 Status differentiations at the Rincon site. *Archaeological Survey Annual Report (University of California, Los Angeles)* **10:**209–261.
Tainter, J. A.
  1971 Salvage excavations at the Fowler site: Some aspects of the social organization of the northern Chumash. *San Luis Obispo County Archaeological Society Occasional Papers* No. 3.
  1973 The social correlates of mortuary patterning at Kaloko, North Kona, Hawaii. *Archaeology and Physical Anthropology in Oceania* **8:**1–11.
  1974 Analytical approaches to the archaeological study of social change. Department of Anthropology, Northwestern University, Evanston, Illinois (Xerox).
  1975a Social inference and mortuary practices: An experiment in numerical classification. *World Archaeology* **7:**1–15.
  1975b The archaeological study of social change: Woodland systems in west-central

Illinois. Ph.D. dissertation, Northwestern University. Ann Arbor: University Microfilms.

1976   Spatial organisation and social patterning in the Kaloko cemetrery, North Kona, Hawaii. *Archaeology and Physical Anthropology in Oceania* **11:**91–105.

1977a Modeling change in prehistoric social systems. In *For theory building in archaeology,* edited by L. R. Binford. New York: Academic Press. Pp. 327–351.

1977b Woodland social change in west-central Illinois. *Mid-Continental Journal of Archaeology* **2:**67–98.

Tainter, J. A., and R. H. Cordy

1977   An archaeological analysis of social ranking and residence groups in prehistoric Hawaii. *World Archaeology* **9:**95–112.

Theil, H.

1967   *Economics and information theory.* Amsterdam: North-Holland Publishing Co.

Ubelaker, D. H.

1974   Reconstruction of demographic profiles from ossuary skeletal samples: A case study from the tidewater Potomac. *Smithsonian Contributions to Anthropology* No. 18.

Ucko, P. J.

1969   Ethnography and archaeological interpretation of funerary remains. *World Archaeology* **1:**262–280.

Vehik, S.

1975   Sociocultural implications of central European early Bronze Age mortuary practices. Ph.D. dissertation, University of Missouri, Columbia. Ann Arbor: University Microfilms.

von Bertalanffy, L.

1968   *General system theory.* New York: Braziller.

Weaver, W.

1949   Recent contributions to the mathematical theory of communication. In *The mathematical theory of communication,* by C. E. Shannon and W. Weaver. Urbana: University of Illinois Press. Pp. 1–28.

Whallon, R.

1972   A new approach to pottery typology. *American Antiquity* **37:**13–33.

Winters, H.

1968   Value systems and trade cycles in the Late Archaic in the Midwest. In *New perspectives in archeology,* edited by S. Binford and L. Binford. Chicago: Aldine. Pp. 175–222.

Young, J. F.

1971   *Information theory.* New York: Wiley (Interscience).

Social Interaction and Stylistic
Similarity: A Reanalysis*

STEPHEN PLOG

In the 1960s, several archaeologists (Deetz 1965; Hill 1967, 1970a,b; Longacre 1964, 1970; Whallon 1968, 1969) argued that aspects of prehistoric social organization could be inferred through analyses of stylistic variability of prehistoric artifacts. Research carried out by these individuals was considered supportive of this conclusion. In the succeeding years, this topic has been a lively one among archaeologists, with much discussion pro and con. The studies of Deetz, Hill, and Longacre have become archaeological classics, studies that are cited in almost every archaeology text. Many similar studies have been carried out since these analyses were done (Clemen 1976; Connor 1968; Cook 1970; Gerald 1975; Leone 1968; Tuggle 1970; Wiley 1971); at the same time several criticisms have been published (Allen and Richardson 1971; Dumond 1977; Johnson 1972; Stanislawski 1969a,b, 1973).

The goal of this chapter is to evaluate these various positions concerning the proposal that aspects of prehistoric social organization can be inferred through stylistic analysis. The chapter will consist of two parts. First, I shall briefly summarize the assumptions and methods that have been used, and then discuss some of the major problems relating to these areas. The intent of this section will not be to provide answers to the

---

*This is a slightly revised version of a paper entitled "The inference of prehistoric social organization from ceramic design variability," *Michigan Discussions in Anthropology* **1**, 1–47 (1976).

ADVANCES IN ARCHAEOLOGICAL METHOD AND THEORY, VOL. 1

problems but rather to try and pinpoint areas where reasoning or methods have been questionable and, thus, where attention in future studies should be concentrated. In the second part of the study, I shall reanalyze the study of Cronin (1962) and the data from Broken K Pueblo, the Carter Ranch site, and the Hay Hollow Valley on which the studies of Hill (1967, 1970a) and Longacre (1964, 1970) were based. It has been argued that the results of these studies support the proposed relationship between prehistoric social organization and stylistic variability. However, the data and techniques used in these studies have never been reanalyzed in order to verify the original conclusions. It is hoped that this second part of the study will satisfy that need. Thus, this chapter will evaluate the theoretical base, the methods and techniques, and the conclusions of studies that have attempted to infer aspects of prehistoric social organization from stylistic analysis of prehistoric ceramics. In the process, topics that future studies must consider will be delineated.

ASSUMPTIONS AND METHODS

The approaches that have been used in analyzing stylistic variability in order to derive information concerning prehistoric social organization are each dependent on one or more of a set of assumptions concerning the formation of the archeological record (this applies only to analyses of the spatial distribution of stylistic elements within sites), the learning of techniques of ceramic manufacture and decoration, the producers of the pottery, and the causes of the variability in the distribution of stylistic elements. The primary assumptions are as follows:

1. "The spatial distributions of cultural materials are patterned or structured (non-random) and will be so within an archaeological site . . . . These patterns reflect the loci of *patterned behavior* that existed in pre-historic times" (Hill 1970b:19). In Schiffer's (1972a) terms, there is a direct correspondence between archaeological context and systemic context.
2. At a single point in time, variation in the distribution of stylistic elements may be a result of the locations of activities or functions, or a result of the location of social segments, or a result of both (Hill 1970a:16). That is, some stylistic elements may be associated with certain activities, whereas others may be associated with particular social groups (Hill 1970b:20).
3. Techniques of pottery manufacture and decoration were learned before marriage, and were handed down from mother to daughter, or within the framework of a social segment such as a lineage or

residence group. The degree to which designs diffuse between individuals, social segments, or villages is directly proportional to the amount of interaction between the units.

4. Manufacture of ceramics was a female activity.
5. All households made the pottery they used; none was exchanged between households.

Given these assumptions, three different methods of stylistic analysis have been used to draw inferences about prehistoric social organization. The first of these methods has been used by Hill (1970a) and by Longacre (1964, 1970). They have argued that the spatial distributions of female-manufactured ceramic style elements, and of male-manufactured style elements on other artifacts, within a site provide evidence concerning the postmarital residence rule practiced in the community. They propose that, with a matrilocal rule, there should be a nonrandom distribution of ceramic designs within the community because of the channeling of design learning within the localized residence group from generation to generation. On the other hand, if a patrilocal rule is practiced, females are brought into the localized group from other residence groups in the community, or from other communities. This will result in neither spatial nor temporal continuity in the designs painted by women of the residence group, and a random distribution of designs within the community is therefore expected. In contrast, a random distribution of male-manufactured style elements would be expected with a matrilocal residence rule, and a nonrandom distribution with a patrilocal rule. In their analyses of two prehistoric pueblos, Longacre and Hill measured the similarity between design elements in the pueblo rooms, and felt that there was evidence for spatially localized clusters of similar rooms. They argued that these spatial clusters represented matrilocal residence groups.

The measurement of *similarity* between designs in different spatial units has also been extended to the analysis of groups of communities (Longacre 1964; Cook 1970; Tuggle 1970; Wiley 1971). It has been proposed that the level of similarity between the designs in two communities is indicative of the intensity of past interaction between the communities. This is a logical extension of the within-community methodology if interaction is defined as intermarriage. Predominately endogamous communities will have little intermarriage with other villages, so that design traditions will not move between villages, whereas predominately exogamous communities will have a large amount of intermarriage with other villages. The similarity levels between villages cannot always be used to infer residence rules. If it is assumed that high levels of design similarity indicate a large amount of intermarriage between communities, they should be characteristic only of patrilocal villages, since a matrilocal rule results in females remaining in the village. But low similarity levels and little intermarriage between communities could be a result of either a matrilocal, endogamous community or a patrilocal, endogamous community. Both result in all females and therefore all ceramic traditions remaining in the village. Because the ceramic assemblage of the entire community is considered as a whole with this method, the two types of communities cannot be distinguished.

However, the similarity levels between villages have been intrepreted not only in terms of marriage patterns. Rather, the levels have been interpreted also as being indicative of economic or religious cooperation between villages (Longacre 1964:167; Cook 1970:72; Tuggle 1970; Wiley 1971:24). Although this interpretation is not in contradiction with the assumptions listed earlier, it is a shift in emphasis from the interpretation of within-site similarity levels. Little or no discussion has been provided concerning the reasons for the differences in interpretation.

Longacre has summarized both the between-site and the within-site methodologies as follows:

> Social demography and social organization are reflected in the material system. In a society practicing post-marital rules stressing matrilocality, social demography may be mirrored in the ceramic art of the female potters; the smaller and more closely tied the social aggregate, the more details of design would be shared. Augmented by clues from other aspects of the cultural system, differential relative frequencies of designs may suggest the delimitation of various social aggregates: larger social units such as the villages interacting in a relatively large area and producing pottery of the same Variety or Type; groups of villages forming a unit through social interaction along kin-based, religious, and political lines; the village as a social group; and residence groups forming a village [1970:28].

The second method of dealing with prehistoric social organization through stylistic analysis has been used by Connor (1968), Leone (1968), and Whallon (1968); it involves the measurement of the *homogeneity* of classes of ceramic style attributes. They proposed that the degree of homogeneity will be a function primarily of the amount of movement of women between villages. Leone (1968:1150) and Connor (1968) treated the coefficient of homogeneity as a measure of community endogamy. Whallon has proposed that the level of the coefficient is related to post-marital residence on a village level.

> If residence is generally not in the village of the bride, women will move about among several villages, bringing with them all their characteristic techniques and styles of pottery manufacture. Under this hypothesis, the presence in a community of women who have come from several different villages at marriage should create a situation of relative heterogeneity of style. Conversely, a high rate of village matrilocality should be characterized by a greater stylistic homogeneity within each village [1968:229].

It should be noted, however, that village homogeneity could result from an endogamous marriage rule and either a matrilocal or a patrilocal within-village residence rule. Whallon (1968:229) also added that minor fluctuations in the level of homogeneity would be due to variability in the rates of simple intercommunication between communities.

Whallon (1968:236) used this measure in his analysis of ceramic collections from a number of Owasco and Iroquois sites in New York State. His results showed a high level of homogeneity at all the sites, which he felt was congruent with the ethnographically known matrilocal residence of Iroquois groups and with previous evidence of Owasco–Iroquois continuity in social organization. The coefficients also showed an increase through time, which he interpreted as due to a decreasing rate of social contact through time (1968:236). Leone and Connor measured the homogeneity of colors on plainware pottery and of design elements on painted pottery. They interpreted trends in the degree of community endogamy as due to trends in community dependence on agriculture.

A third type of relationship between stylistic attributes and social organization has been proposed by Deetz (1965) and Whallon (1968). This approach does not deal with the frequency of stylistic attributes, but with the *association* between attributes in different style classes.

> Under a matrilocal rule of residence, reinforced by matrilineal descent, one might expect a large degree of consistent patterning of design attributes, since the behavior patterns which produce these configurations would be passed from mother to daughters, and preserved by continuous manufacture in the same household. Furthermore, these attribute configurations would have a degree of mutual exclusion in a community, since each group of women would be responsible for a certain set of patterns differing more or less from those held by other similar groups. Change in the social structure might then bring about a change in the nature of ceramic attribute patterning, if this change in any way tended to disrupt the exclusive nature of the shared behavioral patterns existing under a matrilocal residence rule. Thus an alteration in the residence rule could bring about a reduction in the number of repeated patterns, and ultimately lead to a more random association between the attributes which constitute the total design vocabulary of the culture. This might occur under any stress which would shift residence away from the earlier matrilocal norm [Deetz 1965:2].

Using this aspect of stylistic variability, Deetz (1965:37) attempted to measure the degree of attribute association for three temporal components of an Arikara site. This site was occupied during a time period when historical evidence suggested that the inferred prehistoric Arikara pattern of matrilocal residence was changing, owing to the increasing status of men. In his work with the Owasco–Iroquois ceramics, Whallon (1968:240) altered the interpretation of degrees of attribute association, proposing that it would primarily be a function of the "degree of integration and importance of coresident groups,'' and would secondarily be related to the average size of these groups.

CRITICISMS OF THE ASSUMPTIONS

Several criticisms have been published concerning the assumptions of the methods outlined in the previous section. These criticisms deal primarily with three of the assumptions listed: (*a*) that the spatial patterning of archaeological remains reflect the spatial patterning of past behavior; (*b*) that techniques of pottery manufacture and design were passed down within the social group; and (*c*) that each household manufactured its own pottery.

Spatial Distributions

Both Stanislawski (1969a,b, 1973) and Friedrich (1970) have presented evidence questioning the assumption that the spatial patterning of archaeological remains reflects the spatial patterning of past behavior. Friedrich (1970:340), in her study of a Tarascan village, found that different parts of a broken vessel have different uses, and thus different deposition patterns. Because of this, "the ultimate distribution of a painted element in the village is not merely a function of the location of the artisan who used it in his painting" (1970:340). Stanislawski (1969a,b) found a similar situation in his study of pottery making at the Hopi villages. He notes that both modern and prehistoric sherds may be collected and used in several different ways: for chinking in house walls, for temper for new pottery, as new sources of designs, and for covering unfired pottery in the firing process.

Stanislawski (1973:117–118) also criticizes Longacre's (1970:37) statement that the room fills at the Carter Ranch site resulted from dumping "from rather stable activity areas" as being too simplistic. He cites evidence from studies of two prehistoric sites where more complex deposition patterns are suggested, and adds that "modern ethnographic studies also suggest that within a few years contiguous room units are abandoned, refuse is deposited and fills the rooms, and then the refuse is thrown elsewhere as the rooms are cleared and re-used" (Stanislawski 1973:117–118).

The importance of these problems has also been discussed by Colton and Hargrave (1937:23–25) and particularly by Schiffer (1972a). They clearly must be considered in any type of study dealing with the spatial distributions of artifacts within a site. There is some evidence that considerations such as these may not have been taken into account in at least one of the earlier studies of design distributions within a site—Hill's work at Broken K Pueblo. The evidence is as follows. Hill (1970a:33) argues that more hunting was done during the early occupation period of Broken K, because the early rooms at the site have a larger number (generally more than 55) of animal bones on the room floors than the number of bones (less than 55) on room floors of the later period of occupation. However, a chi-square test shows that there is a significant association at Broken K between rooms with greater than 55 animal bones and rooms with trash deposits above the floor, and between rooms with less than 55 animal bones and rooms without trash above the floor ($\chi^2 = 9.63$, sig. = .01). [Information for the test was taken from Figure 8 (Hill 1970a:31) and Appendix 1 (1970a:111–112). Only rooms in the main room blocks were used in the test.] This suggests that, where bones were numerous on room floors, they were dumped there after the room was abandoned. Since these bones were considered by Hill to have been left on the room floors by the occupants, it would seem that it may not have been possible at Broken K to distinguish debris left by the original occupants from debris thrown into the room after it was abandoned, both of which lay on the floor at the time of excavation. Other evidence, such as the fact that design material from both room floors and fills at the Carter Ranch site suggested the same cluster of rooms in the northern part of the site (Longacre 1970:34–40), is also interesting in this same light. Longacre (1970:40) proposes that this suggests "continuity through time for the occupation of the north cluster of rooms and the associated Kiva I." It seems equally likely that both the fill and the floor material showed the same cluster of rooms because both sets of material were dumped into the rooms after occupation. Colton and Hargrave have previously discussed the problem of whether sherds found on room floors should be considered as contemporaneous with the structure.

> Sherds found upon or almost resting upon the floors are often considered contemporary with the structure. It must be mentioned that small miscellaneous sherds are not habitually seen knocking about floors of occupied pueblos. We cannot assume that this was true in prehistoric times. If datable timbers are recovered dates *cannot* be assigned to miscellaneous sherds found upon or near the floor since these sherds most probably came from the collapsed roof or wall, unless modifying conditions were encountered in the excavation. They must then be considered with the same doubt as "surface sherds" [1937:24].

This discussion clearly indicates that the manner in which the archeological record is formed must be considerd when any analyses of within-site spatial distributions are planned. However, it should not be concluded that, because there are problems in dealing with intrasite distributions, they should not be dealt with; or that, because it is not possible to work with them at one site, it is therefore not possible at all sites. This is one of the real dangers of Stanislawski's implication that the deposition patterns at Carter Ranch *must* be more complex than Longacre has indicated, because evidence from some other sites suggests that depositions patterns there were complex. As Schiffer (1972a:163) has noted, "Archaeologists have gone from the one extreme of viewing a site as spatially and behaviorally undifferentiated rubbish to the other extreme of viewing remains as mostly reflecting their locations of use in past activities. At this point, it appears that neither extreme is often the case." Furthermore, deposition problems can be handled. Both Schiffer (1972a:162) and Colton and Hargrave (1937:25) have noted that deposition patterns will be less complex at smaller sites. They have also noted criteria for determining if pottery found on room floors was left by the occupants of the room (Colton and Hargrave 1937:25; Schiffer 1972b). Thus, before it is concluded that cultural formation processes preclude recognition of past behavior and organization, it is necessary to devise ways for determining what processes operated. It may often be the case that by taking these processes into account more confidence can be placed in various inferences of this sort.

Learning Patterns

Data have been presented recently that also question the assumption that women learn techniques of pottery manufacture and design from other women of their social group. Stanislawski's study of Hopi pottery making has shown that Hopi potters do not necessarily learn ceramic production in this way. He notes that "there are a minimum of four ceramic teaching models in use, three of which involve cross-clan teaching of ceramic techniques, designs, and styles. Modern Hopi–Tewa whiteware, for example, developed about 1925 and is now shared by women of 4 to 5 Tewa and 6 to 7 Hopi clans, stemming from 5 villages and 2 settlement areas and 2 tribal and linguistic groups" (1973:121). Because of this, he concludes that the use of similar design styles does not indicate a common clan or lineage background (1969a:31).

Stanislawski has also criticized Longacre's interpretation of Bunzel's data on pueblo pottery making. Bunzel's statement that "all women state that they learned from their mothers not only the techniques of pottery making, but also the particular designs and style of decoration which they use," was one of the sources noted by Longacre (1964:163, 1970:38) and Hill (1970:57) in support of the validity of their approach. Stanislawski emphasizes that, on the same page of the above quotation, Bunzel also says, "It is therefore of particular importance not that all women mention their mother's teaching, which is natural, but that practically all recognized other sources of inspiration as well" (1929:54). He argues that this information is consistent with the data he obtained (Stanislawski 1973:119).

Several comments should be made about Stanislawski's criticisms. First, his data raise an important issue concerning variability in design learning and design distribution. The isolation of social groups from design distributions in prehistoric sites does not require that potters must learn all the designs they paint from women in their residence group. For example, neither Hill nor Longacre argues that every design will be found only with a particular residence group. Longacre (1964:166) notes that at Carter Ranch roughly 60% of the designs were found throughout the pueblo, whereas only the remaining "sensitive" elements showed definite clustering. And, in their isolation of social groups at Carter Ranch and Broken K, Longacre and Hill relied on the relative frequencies of designs or design factors, rather than simply the presence or absence of the factors in different parts of the pueblo. As noted earlier, Longacre (1964:158, 167) and others (Whallon 1968; Cook 1970:72; Tuggle 1970; Wiley 1971:24) have argued that other factors such as economic or religious ties or simple intercommunication will also result in design transmission between individuals. A more general expression of these ideas is that the amount of design transmission between individuals will be directly proportional to the amount of interaction between them. Because members of a matrilocal residence group should have more interaction with each other than with individuals outside the group, it would be expected that they would share more designs with each other than with individuals outside the group. However, because an individual's interaction is not limited to other individuals in her social group, some design transmission would be expected between social groups of the same village and of different villages. The basis for the interaction could be social, economic, or religious.

At the same time, neither Hill nor Longacre has demonstrated that it is social interaction that accounts for the variability in design distributions which they have found. As noted earlier, Longacre (1970:28) states that village interaction along kin-based, religious, and political lines may produce differential relative frequencies of designs between groups of villages, but for some reason drops the "religious and political lines" from consideration when noting factors causing differential frequencies of designs within villages. This argument does not account for the 60% of the designs that are found in all parts of the Carter Ranch site. It would seem that the important question here is: Given the variability in the distribution of designs, how does one explain it, and how does one isolate the variability that is due to different factors? If one concentrates only on a limited number of "sensitive" elements, how does one know that only social factors account for the distribution, or that the frequencies are not simply a random occurrence? Even a random spatial distribution of designs would result in designs restricted to parts of the pueblo as well as designs distributed throughout the pueblo. Stanislawski does point out some of the possible causes of the variability in design distributions. But simply because there *is* variability does not mean that some of the variability is not a result of social factors, or that the social variability cannot be isolated. Particularly interesting in this regard is Stanislawski's (1969a:31) statement that virtually all the Hopi potters who make whiteware, including those noted earlier that come from different clans and villages, "are related by marriage or descent, and learned from one another."

Finally, use of both Stanislawski's and Bunzel's data should be discussed. It is hard to talk about this evidence without questioning its relevance to the prehistoric situation. The context of Hopi pottery making today is completely different than it was in prehistoric times, and this difference must influence the learning and transmission of design styles. Even in 1929, Bunzel notes that pottery making was "an important and profitable industry" at First Mesa (1929:5) and that "Hopi pottery is made commercially with the greatest economy of time" (1929:56). More to the point, she notes, "Pottery is manufactured for sale to white tourists, and *the Indian potter makes what the trader tells her and the white man wants*" (1929:58; emphasis mine). Furthermore, in describing Nampeyo's innovative efforts in reviving the Sikyatki style, she states:

> There is no doubt that it was Nampeyo and not the traders and ethnologists who was responsible for the revival of the Sikyatki style. Its rapid adoption by other potters was, of course, due to its commercial success, but the complete assimilation and subsequent efflorescence of the style point to something more than commercial expediency in its adoption [1929:83].

These quotes indicate that a major factor influencing what designs are painted on modern Hopi pottery is their ability to sell in the commercial market. It is extremely unlikely that similar market conditions existed prehistorically in the Southwest. Models of design transmission based on modern Hopi should be used by neither Longacre and Hill nor Stanislawski in interpreting the archeological record, without testing the validity of the models using prehistoric data. It should be emphasized that Longacre and Hill's studies have not tested the model they derived from ethnographic data. They have only interpreted archeological data, given the assumption that the model is a valid one.

Exchange

A final assumption that needs to be discussed concerns the manufacture of pottery. As noted above, many previous ceramic design studies have assumed that each household manufactured its own pottery. However, several studies in some areas, such as the American Southwest, have suggested that ceramics were sometimes exchanged in large quantities. For example, Shepard (1939, 1942) and Warren (1969) have demonstrated large-scaled ceramic trade in Chaco Canyon and in the Rio Grande Valley. Furthermore, a study of the relationship of ceramic exchange and design variation in the Chevelon Canyon area of Arizona indicates that a large percentage of the ceramic design variation in that area can probably be explained by the fact that large quantities of painted vessels were imported into the Chevelon area prehistorically (Plog 1977). Chemical and petrographic analysis of ceramics from the Chevelon area and petrographic analysis of pottery from the Carter Ranch site also indicated that some of the pottery included in Longacre's (1970) analysis of ceramic designs from that site was probably imported rather than locally made (Plog 1977). Thus, an increasing amount of evidence suggests that ceramic exchange was a frequent occurrence prehistorically. If it was, spatial variability in the distribution of ceramic designs in many areas may be partially explained by the spatial distribution of trade networks.

CRITICISMS OF THE INTERPRETATIONS

Criticisms of the interpretations of archaeological patterns suggested by design studies can be grouped into two types: (a) those that provide alternative explanations of the patterns, but assume that only a single period of time is being dealt with, and (b) those that argue that the patterns may be due to temporal differences in parts of the data set.

Synchronic Alternatives

Several comments concerning alternative synchronic interpretations have been made by Allen and Richardson (1971). First, they emphasize that individuals may actually have a wide range of residence choices within and outside the rule or structure of the system (1971:46), a point that has also been made by Johnson (1972:370). Because of this, they argue that one cannot infer behavior from rules, and that one must be able to deal with individual residence choices in order to determine a residence pattern. This problem does not seem relevant to the studies of Hill and Longacre, neither of whom were trying to isolate rules and then infer behavior from them (Wilcox 1971:7), but rather were trying to work with the material products of actual behavior and infer behavior. However, Allen and Richardson's point does suggest the low probability of a completely matrilocal community, such as Longacre (1970:46) suggests for Carter Ranch.

A second comment by Allen and Richardson (1971:46, 49) is that ethnographic data suggest that factors other than residence rules, such as economic activities, ownership of property, land-use patterns, and geographic strictures, account for the construction of local aggregates. Johnson (1972:369) has made a similar point in arguing that "patterned distributions of artifacts and site features . . . might also reflect only the existence of localized task groups of a noncorporate sort." These comments emphasize the point made in the previous section concerning the need to demonstrate what factors account for the variability in design distribution patterns.

Finally, Allen and Richardson note that even ethnographers have difficulty in interpreting extant residence patterns and in defining categories such as "matrilocal residence" (1971:44–45; but see the comments of Watson 1977). In addition, they argue that "studies of kinship structures have low information content (even in many ethnographic situations) and because the resulting reconstructions are tenuous, the archeologist would profit by concentrating his efforts elsewhere" (1971:51). However, they do not question archaeologists' abilities to isolate local aggregates through the study of material culture (1971:50). This point is similar to Harris's statement that archaeologists should not think

> that the units which you seek to reconstruct must match the units in social organization which contemporary ethnographers have attempted to tell you exist. . . . The great strength of archeology is that it can deal with groups which are defined by the actual coming together and working together or living together of specific individuals at specific times and places [1968:360].

As Allen and Richardson (1971:50–51) and Hill (1970a:72) have argued, what one calls the local units that are isolated is unimportant; what is important is that much can be learned about cultural variability and change by studying the changing composition of these groups through time.

In addition to the possibility that spatial clusters of ceramic designs may be a product of organizational units other than residence or descent groups, they may also be a result of functional differences between separate areas of a site, as noted above. While this possibility has been explicitly recognized (Hill 1970a:16), little attempt has been made in previous design studies to test this hypothesis. For example, designs frequencies were not tabulated separately for different vessel forms, but rather were recorded for all forms as a group (Plog 1977; Watson 1977). However, ethnographic studies have suggested that different vessel forms, such as bowls, jars, and pitchers, and different parts of a single vessel, such as the body and neck of a jar, are sometimes painted with different designs (Friedrich 1970:334–335; Bunzel 1929:16). Some studies of prehistoric materials have also shown this to be true (Amsden 1936; Rohn 1971:149; Plog 1977:127–129; Watson 1977:388). If vessel form is related to vessel function, and if different functions or different proportions of several functions are carried out in different spatial units, then different frequencies of vessel forms will be found at these spatial units. The level of design similarity between units may thus be affected if different design features are associated with these different vessel forms.

Temporal Control

Control of temporal variability in design frequencies has received little attention in studies using design variation as a social indicator. However, other design studies have suggested that the degree of design similarity between archaeological sites is negatively correlated with the temporal difference in the occupations of the sites. That is, the closer the dates of site occupations, the greater the design similarities between sites. For example, Beals *et al.* (1945:87) state that the study of surface color and finish, rim form, line thickness and spacing, and the smallest design elements "has been highly successful . . . in determining the general chronology of sites." And Colton and Hargrave (1937:17) propose that design styles may be used as time correlation criteria "in a manner similar to the use of index fossils in paleontology."

If design similarities and differences between spatial units can be shown to correlate with temporal differences between these units, then synchronic explanations of the similarities and differences, such as the proposal that they are a result of different intensities of interaction between the populations of the units, are not likely to be valid. If our explanation of variability in the similarity of rooms or sites through space are synchronic ones, we must make sure that the data being analyzed are synchronic. Design studies that attempt synchronic explanation must, therefore, control the dimension of time.

An important topic that must be considered in order to control the temporal dimension is the rate and pattern of design change through time in the prehistoric Southwest. In most recent studies it has been implicitly assumed that design change was not continuous through time but rather that there was relative stability in designs for a period of time, then rapid change, then stability, and so on, as Spaulding (cited in Willey and Phillips 1958:15) has argued. This is shown by the use of pottery types, defined by types of designs, to date sites used in these studies and to assign them to temporal phases. When sites of the same phase are analyzed, however, design similarities and differences are explained not by design change through time but by design diffusion as a result of interaction intensities between sites. This approach assumes that the designs defining pottery types suddenly appear and disappear. Martin and Plog (1973:256–257) have suggested, however, that rates of increase and decrease in the abundance of pottery types vary considerably. Their analysis of Breternitz's tree-ring dates suggested that "different pottery types are adopted at different rates by different populations who are adapting to different environmental conditions" (1973:256).

Studies of rates of design change are thus needed. Earlier design studies have indicated that designs can change greatly within a period of one hundred years. For example, many of the pottery types defined for the Southwest have estimated durations of only one hundred years or less (Colton 1955). Studies have also shown that the degree of design similarity between sites whose average occupation dates (the median of their phase dates) differ by 150–200 years is correlated with the differences in the occupation dates (Tuggle 1970; Plog 1976b).

Recent studies have demonstrated significant changes in design frequencies over even shorter periods of time. A study of design variation between sites in the Chevelon region of Arizona showed statistically significant differences between design attribute state frequencies between two groups of sites whose estimated construction periods, based on tree-ring dates, were 34–66 years apart. This evidence is consistent with other recent studies. Changes in line widths and in other ceramic attributes other than designs have been demonstrated for periods of less than 25 years in the Cibola area of western New Mexico (LeBlanc 1975). In addition, Redman's (1976:35) continuing analysis of design attribute frequencies from the Cibola area has indicated that temporal differences between sites is the primary determinant of intersite similarity in design attribute frequencies. There also appears to be a significant temporal pattern in the changing design attribute frequencies on black-on-white pottery for the periods from A.D. 860 to 970 and from A.D. 1050 to 1150 on Black Mesa in northeastern Arizona (Deutchmann 1976; Klesert 1977).

The above results demonstrate that temporal variability cannot be ignored in design studies, as it has been in many recent design studies that have used design variability to make inferences concerning prehistoric social organization. Studies of groups of sites dating to the same 150- to 200-year period and studies of single sites occupied for even brief periods of time must consider the temporal dimension.

CRITICISMS OF THE METHODS

Two of the most important aspects of design studies have received little attention, either in the original studies or in the reviews. These are: (*a*) the similarity coefficients that have been used and their relationship to sample size, and (*b*) the construction of the design classification.

Similarity Coefficients

One of the most important problems concerning similarity coefficients is their relationship to sample size. Although most studies have ignored this problem, its importance has been shown by Tuggle (1970). Plotting both Brainerd–Robinson and product–moment coefficients (Pearson's *r*) for over 32 sites against sample size, he found that the Brainerd–Robinson coefficients varied directly with sample size below 75–100 design occurrences per site, whereas the product–moment coefficients tended to cluster around zero below this sample size range (Tuggle 1970:80–81).

This conclusion is an important one. If samples sizes of 75–100 design occurrences are required, the intrasite analyses of design distributions, such as Hill's and Longacre's, must simply be forgotten, since samples that large from a room or of a single design are rare. For example, there is only one room floor at Broken K with a sample size in the 75–100 range, and none above this range (Hill 1970a:131). Intersite analyses would still be possible, but the number of sites that could be included would be reduced. This would be particularly true in areas or time periods where site sizes are small, and consequently design samples may be small.

Because of the importance of Tuggle's conclusions, his findings were reexamined with additional data. It seemed possible that Tuggle's analysis might have been affected by other factors. For example, if later time periods have higher interaction rates between sites and higher intersite similarity levels, as Tuggle (1970) has argued, and if the earlier sites, which have lower interaction rates and lower intersite similarity levels, also have smaller samples sizes simply because they are smaller sites than those present in later time periods, one might expect a positive relationship between sample size and similarity levels, which is not directly due to sample size. To minimize this problem, it was decided to treat contemporaneous groups of sites as separate data sets for the test of the hypothesis, when possible. The tests were carried out by using coefficients calculated from data from a group of sites analyzed by Cronin (1962), which were estimated to be roughly contemporaneous. (See the next section for a discussion of these coefficients and the sites involved. The Goesling site was excluded from this analysis.) Other data sets included were three sets of sites from Longacre's (1964) analysis, which are contemporaneous according to his dates; a group of sites from the Valley of Oaxaca, which are not contemporaneous; and a group of sites from the Chevelon Canyon area of Arizona, which probably date to the same 100-year period, approximately A.D. 1150–1250. [See Plog (1976a) for a discussion of the latter two data sets.]

Tuggle does not clearly state whether he plotted the average sample size for each pair against the similarity coefficient, or the maximum or minimum sample size for each pair. The tests done here were carried out by using the minimum and maximum sample size per pair, and the sum of the sample sizes for each pair. The relationship between the similarity levels and sample size was measured by Spearman's rank correlation coefficient.

The tests indicate that, on the whole, there is little relationship between the variables. [See Plog (1976b) for the correlation coefficients and information on the sample sizes for the different data sets.] These results contrast with the conclusions of Tuggle and suggest that the relationship between sample sizes and values of similarity coefficients that Tuggle discovered for his data should not be assumed to apply to all data sets but rather should be evaluated on a case-by-case basis.

Design Classification

Another of the major problems in design studies is choosing a way of constructing the design typology. How does one choose the attributes on which the typology will be based? Few of the authors of past design studies have discussed the criteria used in forming their typology. Hill (1970a:23), for example, simply states that the typology he used was created by feel. Longacre (1964:163) states that "we hoped to isolate the smallest units or elements of design that would be non-consciously selected based upon learning patterns within the social frame," but does not say how one determines what attributes would be nonconsciously selected.

Examination of other studies of Southwestern pottery designs suggests several other aspects of design styles that could be dealt with in addition to the design elements that have been emphasized in works such as Hill's and Longacre's. For instance, Carlson (1970:84–85) discusses field of decoration, focus of decoration, layout, motifs, color pattern, and motif pattern. Beals *et al.* (1945:87–123) and Kidder (Kidder and Amsden 1931; Kidder and Shepard 1936) discuss small attributes such as ticks, dots, and line widths. At the same time, it is often impossible to deal with these other aspects of style when one is dealing with sherds, rather than whole vessels. In working with the designs on black-on-white pottery from the Chevelon Canyon area (Plog 1976a), I found it possible to deal with only one of the aspects of design styles that Carlson discusses—motifs—and with only two of the subvariations of this aspect—motif composition (solid, hatched, negative, or combinations of these) and motif units or elements (frets, scrolls, terraced units, etc.).

One of the problems with the lack of discussion concerning how specific design typologies were created is simply that it makes it impossible to exactly replicate studies such as Hill's or Tuggle's. And, as Amsden (1936:2) notes, "design is very easy to disagree upon." In an experiment, Tuggle (1970:72) had three people analyze the same set of data, and found that "the number of distinct elements and recorded occurrences varied greatly." He also found that correlations between two groups of data he had classified two months apart were lower than correlations within a data set classified at one time (1970:72). This problem raises the question of whether or not completely different conclusions might be reached by two people working separately on the same problem with the same data. For instance, simply combining Longacre's design elements into larger groups, and then recalculating the correlations between rooms, resulted in coefficients whose correlation with the original coefficients was .80. Thus, the two sets of coefficients had only 64% of their variability in common.

A critical question is, then, how does one choose the attributes to be used in design classifications, or how does one know which classifications are reliable descriptions of the design variability? Only two papers have suggested answers to this problem.

The first study that describes a method for evaluating design typologies is Justeson's (1973). Using an information–theoretic approach, he argues that one can evaluate typologies by measuring their coding efficiency.

The degree of efficiency in terms of binary coding is a measure of the relative degree of discrimination within the total system of design elements. The choice of attributes used in any system is assumed to reflect choices between aesthetic, ideological, representational or functional ideas with which these elements are consciously or unconsciously associated by the people who made these choices or by the people for whom they were made. We should expect a high efficiency value, reflecting a high level of discrimination of ideas, in any cultural subsystem [1973:146].

This approach basically places emphasis on the probabilities or frequencies of the elements in the typology. The degree to which a group of elements can be coded efficiently is dependent primarily on the degree to which equiprobable subgroups are yielded at each stage of the binary partition (Singh 1966:34). For equiprobable subgroups to occur, "the probability pattern of the messages (elements) in our repertoire has to be of a rather special kind. Indeed, each probability has to be a fraction like 1/2, 1/4, 1/8, 1/16, and so on" (Singh 1966:34). For example, a typology consisting of two elements, each with a probability of .5; a typology of eight elements, each with a probability of .125; and a typology of three elements, one with a probability of .5, and two with probabilities of .25, are all equal in terms of coding efficiency. Justeson's measure of coding efficiency, h_*, would be equal to 100% for all three typologies. A typology of three elements with probabilities of .6, .2, and .2 gives $h_* = .979$, and a typology of four elements, with probabilities of .7, .1, .1, and .1 gives $h_* = .905$.

I know of no theoretical discussions of typology that suggest that elements or attributes should have probability values of the type that yields maximum coding efficiency. Nor does Justeson make it clear how such probability values show higher degrees of discrimination in a cultural subsystem than do values that do not match these probabilities. Justeson's method does not seem to be a reasonable way of evaluating typologies.

The second study relating to design typologies, by Friedrich (1970), was an ethnographic study of a Tarascan pottery-making village. This study was done to determine "how variation in pottery painting can serve as an indicator of intensity of social interaction between painters" (1970:332). Her analysis suggested three good indicators of interaction: (a) the organization of spatial divisions, (b) the degree and types of subclass variation within configuration classes, and (c) the function of design elements in a configuration (1970:338). However, she rejects all three of these strategies because of problems noted earlier with the ultimate deposition of sherds. She then proposes that interaction between painters could be measured by isolating the products of individual painters, through the study of subdesign element variation, and then grouping the products on the basis of the similarity in the style of painting (1970:340).

However, as was discussed earlier, deposition problems will not always eliminate the possibility of doing intrasite distribution analyses. Also, intersite correlations do not have to deal with intrasite patterns, although there are some deposition problems of concern, such as the degree to which surface samples are representative of subsurface samples. Therefore, Friedrich's three indicators of interaction should not be ignored. In addition, as Watson (1977:390) has argued, more studies such as Friedrich's are needed in order that our choices of design attributes and our methods of design classification can be improved.

In regard to systems of design classification, Friedrich (1970) suggested a hierarchical system of design analysis emphasizing different levels of design organization. Several recent analyses of prehistoric ceramic designs have employed such a hierarchical system (Deutchman 1976; Redman 1976; Klesert 1977; Plog 1977). The latter studies also have explicitly defined the design attributes and attributes states on which the classification was based. I have argued elsewhere that the different design attributes or hierarchical levels employed represent different decisions for the potter made at different points in the process of decorating a vessel (Plog 1977). Many previous design classifications have not recognized the different design attributes as different decisions and have thus analyzed relative frequencies of different design elements that are not alternative choices. The different attribute states must be alternatives that are mutually substitutable for the analyses that are carried out to be meaningful (Plog 1977). These recent design studies have employed design classifications that are more explicitly defined. Therefore, their analyses are more likely to be replicable. In addition, by focusing on the different decorative decisions, they are more likely to describe accurately the variability in the designs painted by the potters.

REANALYSIS OF THE DATA

In the preceding sections, I have discussed problems relating to the assumptions, interpretations, and methodology of studies that have attempted to derive information concerning prehistoric social interaction and organization from stylistic analyses. The problems discussed are found in many of these studies. In this section, I shall deal with three of the studies individually. The three are Cronin's (1962) analysis of designs on pottery types from a group of prehistoric sites in east-central Arizona, Hill's (1967, 1970a) study of ceramic designs at Broken K Pueblo, and Longacre's (1964, 1970) analysis of design frequencies at the Carter Ranch site and at a group of sites in Hay Hollow Valley. As noted earlier, the results of these studies have been cited to support the proposed relationship between prehistoric social interaction and stylistic variability.

Cronin

Cronin analyzed design frequencies on pottery types (Kiatuthlana, Red Mesa, and Snowflake black-on-white) at a group of prehistoric sites in east-central Arizona to determine the relationships between these types through time. Brainerd–Robinson coefficients were calculated between pottery types at each site with the design frequencies used as cases. One conclusion of this study was that "generally speaking there is greater similarity (shared design elements) between types at one site (e.g., Kiatuthlana and Snowflake at Chilcott 1) than between different time levels of one type (e.g., Kiatuthlana at Chilcott 1 and Kiatuthlana at Rim Valley)" (Cronin 1962:109). Binford (1972:201) and Longacre (1964:156) generalized this conclusion, arguing that Cronin had demonstrated greater similarity between types at a single site than between samples of the same type from different sites, and thus deleted the "different time levels" phrase in Cronin's statement.

However, Cronin's (1962:114) data do not support their generalized conclusion strongly. One can test this hypothesis by comparing each of Cronin's Brainerd–Robinson similarity coefficients between designs on different pottery types at a single site with all the intersite Brainerd–Robinson coefficients between designs on the same pottery type, which includes the same site and the same pottery types of the intrasite coefficient. For example, one would compare the similarity coefficient between designs on Kiatuthlana black-on-white and designs on Red Mesa black-on-white at site 1 with the similarity coefficients between designs on Kiatuthlana at site 1 and designs on Kiatuthlana at site 2, site 3, etc., and with the similarity coefficients between designs on Red Mesa at site 1 and designs on Red Mesa at site 2, site 3, etc. One would then repeat the same thing for site 2 and all other sites. The number of coefficients between a single type at different sites that are higher than the coefficients between different types at a single site could then be tabulated.

Using only the Brainerd–Robinson coefficients that Cronin calculated, 15 of the 33 possible comparisons show that the intersite coefficients are higher than the intrasite coefficients. This can be seen from an examination of Table 5.1. However, neither spatial nor temporal variability is taken into account in this comparison. For example, these sites range in time from approximately A.D. 925 to 1225, according to estimates (Martin *et al.* 1962:212–213). To make the kind of social inferences from this study that have been made, one would need to compare intersite and intrasite correlations from sites of the same time period. One cannot expect two samples separated by 300 years to be as similar as two contemporaneous samples, as shown earlier. Furthermore, the sites should be from a relatively small geographic area. I have argued elsewhere (Plog 1976a) that distance should have an effect on the intersite correlations if the inference that the correlations measure interaction is correct. Using sites close together would minimize the effects of distance. The maximum distance

TABLE 5.1

Comparison of Similarity Coefficients for Designs on Different Pottery Types at a Single Site with Similarity Coefficients for Designs on a Single Pottery Type at Different Sites. Coefficients Used Are Those Given in Cronin (1962:112–113).

Site	Intrasite data		Number of intersite similarity coefficients higher than intrasite coefficients		
	Pottery types	Intrasite BR	Type K–K	Type RM–RM	Type S–S
Goesling	K–RM	121.2	0–2	0–1	—
Chilcott 1	K–RM	94.4	0–2	1–2	—
Chilcott 1	K–S	137.6	0–2	—	0–1
Chilcott 1	RM–S	98.0	—	1–2	1–1
Chilcott 2	RM–S	62.4	—	2–2	2–2
Chilcott 3	RM–S	105.6	—	0–2	0–2
Thode	RM–S	63.8	—	2–2	2–2
Rim Valley	K–RM	47.0	0–2	1–1	—
Rim Valley	K–S	97.9	0–2	—	1–1
Rim Valley	RM–S	67.7	—	1–1	1–1
			0–10	8–13	7–10
		Total		15–33	(45.4%)

Chi-square statistic, for departure from random distribution, = .12, significance level = .50. K= Kiatuthlana black-on-white, RM= Red Mesa black-on-white, S= Snowflake black-on-white.

between any pair of Cronin's sites is approximately 29 miles, and the minimum distance is approximately 1 mile or less. [The exact location of the Rhoton site is not given in the report on these sites. It is assumed to be in the area of the Rhoton ranch house, which is near the southwest quadrant of Section 16, Township 12N, Range 25E, according to Longacre's survey notes (Martin *et al.* 1961).]

An additional problem in using Cronin's coefficients concerns her design typology and her use of it in calculating the Brainerd–Robinson coefficients. One of Cronin's 45 design classes is a miscellaneous category, and 15.5% of all designs classified were placed in this category. When Cronin computed the coefficients, she treated this class like the other classes. That is, all designs from the different sites that were in this category were considered to be the same. For the designs to be the same in reality would be an unlikely occurrence. Thus, I would argue that these designs are more likely completely different, and should have been considered so when computing the coefficients. Because the percentage of designs placed in this category at a site ranged from .0% to 33.3%, some of the coefficients would be changed considerably.

Because of this problem, Cronin's coefficients were recalculated with all the sherds in the miscellaneous category considered to be different. [In the original version of this paper (Plog 1976b) product–moment coefficients were also calculated. However, this was probably inappropriate because of the large percentages of designs placed in the miscellaneous category. This design category thus disproportionately determines the value of the product–moment coefficients, whereas it does not have this effect on the Brainerd–Robinson coefficient.] In addition, it was decided to calculate all possible coefficients rather than simply recalculate the sample Cronin dealt with. One problem encountered in calculating the new coefficients should be mentioned. There appear to be some typographical errors in the published data (Cronin 1962:112–113). Two of the site percentages total 94.2% and 110.3%, when they should total to 100%. Although these errors will affect the coefficients, there was no alternative other than to use the figures as given.

A reanalysis of the original problem is shown in Table 5.2. The entire population of coefficients is used. [See Plog (1976b) for the values of the coefficients.] Again, the data do not support the conclusion that designs on different types of pottery at a single site are more similar than designs on a single pottery type at different sites. Slightly less than half of the

TABLE 5.2

Number of Intersite Similarity Coefficients That Are Higher Than the Intrasite Coefficients. Coefficients Are Based on Corrected Data (see text).

	Intrasite pottery types	Number of intersite similarity coefficients higher than intrasite coefficients		
Site		Type K–K	Type RM–RM	Type SF–SF
Goesling	K–RM	0–2	0–6	—
Chilcott 1	K–RM	0–2	0–6	—
Chilcott 1	K–SF	0–2	—	1–5
Chilcott 1	RM–SF	—	3–6	3–5
Chilcott 2	RM–SF	—	4–6	4–5
Chilcott 3	RM–SF	—	0–6	2–5
Thode	RM–SF	—	6–6	5–5
Rim Valley	K–RM	0–2	5–6	—
Rim Valley	K–SF	0–2	—	0–5
Rim Valley	RM–SF	—	4–6	1–5
Rhoton	RM–SF	—	4–6	5–5
		0–10	26–54	21–40
	Total		47–104	(45.2%)

Chi-square statistic for Brainerd–Robinson total= .78, significance level = .25. K= Kiatuthlana black-on-white, RM= Red Mesa black-on-white, SF= Snowflake black-on-white.

comparisons of the Brainerd–Robinson coefficients show that the inter-site coefficients are higher (47 of 104 possible comparisons—45.2%) than the intrasite coefficients.

If only sites with similar occupation dates and restricted to a smaller geographic area are considered, the results are more definitive. The Goesling site is eliminated, since it dates to approximately A.D. 925, whereas the Chilcott sites and the Thode site date to approximately A.D. 1200, and Rim Valley dates to approximately A.D. 1225, according to estimates (Martin *et al.* 1962:212–213). Martin gives no date for the Rhoton site, but Freeman's seriation of the pottery types from these sites seems to indicate that it is similar to the Thode site and the Chilcott sites in period of occupation. He states:

> The Chilcott Ranch site and Rhoton and Thode Ranch sites show much more similarity among themselves than any of them shows to any other site. We seem to have an early site, Goesling, separated widely in time and cultural affiliations from a group of three sites, Rhoton, Chilcott, and Thode. Separated from them by relatively great divergences in sherd collection is the Rim Valley Site [Freeman 1962:93].

The pottery count from the three Chilcott sites were lumped in Freeman's analysis. The Goesling site is also spatially separated from the other sites, approximately 21 miles from the closest site. Rim Valley pueblo is eliminated from the reanalysis because it is also separated spatially from the remaining sites, approximately 20 miles from the closest remaining site. This reduces the maximum distance between any two sites to approximately 13 miles, compared with the original maximum spread of 29 miles.

Considering only the similarity coefficients for the Rhoton, Thode, and Chilcott sites, the comparisons show that coefficients between designs on the same pottery type at different sites tend to be higher than the coefficients between designs on different pottery types at the same site in 29 of 48 cases (60.2%) for the Brainerd–Robinson coefficients. This is shown in Table 5.3.

Thus, designs on different pottery types at a single site are not more similar than designs on a single pottery type at different sites. If only somewhat contemporaneous sites in a limited geographic area are considered, the opposite tends to be true. This same conclusion was also reached by Tuggle (1970:80) on the basis of a smaller sample of sites. One of the critical variables that is not controlled with Cronin's data is trade. Dissimilarity between different types at the same site could result if one pottery type was made at the site and one type was imported, as suggested above. This does seem a possibility here, since data from Breternitz (1966:79, 90, 95) suggest that Snowflake black-on-white is indigenous in the area of the sites used in Cronin's analysis, whereas Red Mesa and

TABLE 5.3

Number of Intersite Similarity Coefficients That Are Higher Than the Intrasite Coefficients. Coefficients Are Based on Corrected Data. Only Those Sites of Roughly the Same Time Period and from a Restricted Geographic Area Are Used.

Site	Intrasite pottery type	Number of intersite similarity coefficients higher than intrasite coefficients	
		Type RM–RM	Type SF–SF
Chilcott 1	K–RM	0–4	—
Chilcott 1	K–SF	—	1–4
Chilcott 1	RM–SF	1–4	3–4
Chilcott 2	RM–SF	3–4	4–4
Chilcott 3	RM–SF	0–4	2–4
Thode	RM–SF	4–4	4–4
Rhoton	RM–SF	3–4	4–4
		11–24	18–24
		Total 29–48	(60.2%)

Chi-square statistic for Brainerd–Robinson total = 1.69, significance level = .10. K = Kiatuthlana black-on-white, RM= Red Mesa black-on-white, SF= Snowflake black-on-white.

Kiatuthlana are indigenous in the area to the northeast of these sites. However, regardless of the trade hypothesis, the reanalysis of Cronin's data suggests that, in measuring design similarities within or between sites, types should be analyzed separately.

Village Interaction and the Carter Ranch Residence Groups

The generalized conclusion that Longacre drew from Cronin's analysis, which has been shown to be incorrect, suggested to him that "the generations of potters at a village tended to utilize a system of designs which through time was relatively conservative. It also indicated that this traditional usage was probably a kin-based phenomena" (Longacre 1970:27). On the basis of this and other arguments, Longacre made the statement quoted earlier in which he proposed the possibility of isolating residence groups within villages and groups of interacting villages, from analyses of design frequencies (1970:27–28).

In an attempt to delimit such groups of interacting villages, Longacre collected surface samples of black-on-white pottery from several "roughly contemporary sites dating about A.D. 1100" in adjacent valleys in east-central Arizona (Longacre 1964:159). After studying the designs on the pottery from these sites, Longacre concluded that

> the relative frequencies of elements were more similar for some groups of sites than for others.
>
> To explain this fact we must turn to the spatial distribution of the sites in our analysis. In terms of element frequencies by site, the sites in the rough southeastern half of the main valley were more similar to one another than to those in the northwestern half. This correlated with the presence of two Great Kivas in the valley. One Great Kiva was at the Carter Ranch Site in the approximate center of the southeastern half of the valley; the other was at LS-228 in the northwestern half (1964:167).

Longacre never published the similarity coefficients that supported this statement, and does not say explicitly whether any were actually calculated. The design frequencies for the sites were published (Martin *et al.* 1964a,1964b), and two sets of similarity coefficients were calculated in order to test the validity of Longacre's conclusions. Brainerd–Robinson and product–moment coefficients were chosen, simply because it seemed likely that, if Longacre did calculate coefficients for his analysis, he used one of these. Unfortunately, a map of the sites used in the study was never published. The location of the sites in terms of section, township, and range, along with short descriptions of the locations has been published in Longacre's survey notes (Martin *et al.* 1960, 1961, 1964b), but these accounts are sometimes conflicting. For example, in the survey notes Longacre states that LS-208 is on a flat next to an arroyo about 100 yards east of the Carter Ranch site (Martin *et al.* 1964b). However, LS-208 is listed as being in Section 33, Township 13N, Range 23E; the Carter Ranch site (LS-155) is listed as being in Section 21, Township 13N, Range 23E (Martin *et al.* 1960, 1961, 1964b). In another case, Longacre states in the survey notes that LS-211 is 1 to 1 1¼ miles due east of the Carter Ranch site (Martin *et al.* 1964b), but in another publication (Longacre 1964:162) he states that it is 3 miles west of the Carter Ranch site. As a result, it was difficult to determine whether a site was closer to LS-228 or to the Carter Ranch site. A map of some of the sites was obtained from records at the Field Museum, but it also conflicted with some of the statements regarding site locations. As a result, the locations that fit the majority of facts were used. For some sites, it was still uncertain whether they were closer to LS-228 or to the Carter Ranch site; this is noted in Table 5.4.

Table 5.4 shows the similarity coefficients for the sites in Longacre's main valley, Hay Hollow Valley, with the Carter Ranch site and LS-228. Longacre does not list the sites he considered to be in the main valley, and it is possible that he might have excluded LS-177 and LS-216. However, they are close to Hay Hollow Wash and have therefore been included in

TABLE 5.4

A Comparison of the Similarity of Design Elements on Sites in Hay Hollow Valley with Two Sites in the Valley with Great Kivas

| Sites in Hay Hollow Valley | Product–moment coefficients | | Brainerd–Robinson coefficients | | Closest site (LS 228 or Carter Ranch) |
	With Carter Ranch	With LS 228	With Carter Ranch	With LS 228	
LS–208	.8846	.9746	86.59	149.14	CR
LS–209	.8455	.9929	72.06	163.85	CR
LS–211	.8903	.7309	127.09	65.28	CR
LS–212	.8537	.8903	83.62	112.41	CR
LS–216	.8029	.7883	96.32	86.91	CR
LS–217	.9075	.8794	97.21	112.70	CR
LS–224	.7609	.7675	74.66	101.17	Uncertain
LS–230	.8114	.6777	81.22	83.85	Uncertain
LS–231	.4640	.3027	65.71	50.80	Uncertain
LS–177	.7871	.6965	96.54	79.93	LS 228
LS–229	.7920	.5893	109.89	77.04	LS 228

the table. An examination of the table shows that the sites in the main valley do not tend to be most similar to the closest site, LS-228 or the Carter Ranch Site, with a great kiva. Three of eight sites follow the expected pattern with the product–moment coefficients, and two of eight sites fit the pattern with the Brainerd–Robinson coefficients. This does not support Longacre's conclusion.

Another conclusion of Longacre's (1964:167) analysis of the sites was that sites in the main valley are more similar to each other than to sites in other valleys. The conclusion was reexamined by comparing the coefficients between sites in the main valley with coefficients between these sites and sites outside the valley. The averages of the similarity coefficients between sites in the main valley were 96.53 for the Brainerd–Robinson coefficients and .7526 for the product–moment coefficient. The corresponding averages for the coefficients between sites in the main valley and sites outside the main valley were 92.86 and .7005. A t-test showed that the difference between the average Brainerd–Robinson coefficients is not statistically significant. The assumptions for such a test of normal distributions and equal variances for the two populations were satisfied. These assumptions were not met for the original product–moment coefficients. The assumptions were satisfied by transforming the coefficients by the function recommended by Bartlett (1947), $\frac{1}{2} \log ([r + 1]/[r - 1])$, and a t-test showed that the difference between the average values is not statistically significant. This does not support Longacre's conclusion. That neither of Longacre's conclusions concerning the similarity between designs at different villages was supported is not surprising, considering the temporal variability among the sites in the sample. As noted earlier, he states that the sites are roughly contemporary, and date to about A.D. 1100. However, the survey notes indicate that the site dates range from A.D. 700 to 1300, and suggest that very few of the sites are completely contemporary with one another.

The second part of Longacre's study consisted of an analysis of design frequencies within the Carter Ranch site. This analysis suggested the existence of two and possibly three matrilocal residence groups at the site. The evidence for these groups was two clusters of rooms with similar designs, one in the northern half of the pueblo (rooms 3, 5, 10, 12, 15, and Kiva I) and one in the southern half of the pueblo (rooms 2, 4, 7, and 8). Longacre also suggested (1970:39) that room 11, which belonged to a group of unexcavated rooms, may represent a third residence group, and may have split off from the southern group, since its designs were most similar to the rooms in this group. These room clusters were established through a multiple regression analysis. Longacre states:

> As the problem progressed, two ways of demonstrating correlations were possible. When the element distribution for one room was quite different in one of the rooms being regressed, a negative correlation was expressed. This, in effect, tells us that the distribution of elements was opposite that of the dependent variable (the room in the regression) . . . . In any one problem, then, two ways of factoring out rooms were possible: (1) a group expressed as positive correlations, (2) a group expressed as negative correlations with respect to the first group, i.e., a group that factors out as behaving oppositely with respect to the first group [1970:39].

One of the main problems with this analysis is the use of multiple regression analysis to isolate groups of rooms with similar design frequencies. Blalock has shown that

> whenever the correlation of two or more independent variables is high, the sampling error of the partial slopes and partial correlations will be quite large. As a result there will be a number of different combinations of regression coefficients, and hence partial correlations, which give almost equally good fittings to the empirical data [1963:233].

The partial correlation coefficients are thus unstable and extremely sensitive to sampling and measurement errors. Blalock's data (1963:235) suggest that intercorrelations of the same level as those between rooms at the Carter Ranch site can cause this problem. Multiple regression analysis thus is not an appropriate technique for isolating clusters of highly correlated variables.

A better method for grouping similar rooms at the Carter Ranch site would be cluster analysis. Several cluster analyses were done for Carter

Ranch based on the simple correlation coefficients calculated from the published design frequencies from Carter Ranch (Martin *et al.* 1964b). It should be noted that the published data give only the design frequencies for the combined fill and floor levels from each room. However, Longacre's analysis placed multiple floors of the same room in the same cluster (1970:39), and his analysis of the designs in the fills showed a cluster of rooms in the northern part of the pueblo, except that room 10 was not included, as it was not used in the analysis because of a small sample size (1970:39–40). A southern cluster was not isolated in the fill analysis, but rooms 2 and 4 were not used because of small sample size (1970:39). Thus, lumping the counts from the floors and fills should not affect the analysis significantly. One of the clustering techniques used as a centroid method (Sokal and Sneath 1963:185–188), and the program was ICLUST, a program written at the University of Michigan. The results are shown in Figure 5.1, with the rooms in Longacre's southern residence group circled. Figure 5.1 suggests that, if room clusters exist at Carter Ranch, they crosscut the groups suggested by Longacre. Single-link and average-link clustering techniques (Sokal and Sneath 1963) also did not support the existence of Longacre's two groups.

Additional evidence for the existence of the two main residence groups at Carter Ranch was the burial data. Longacre (1970:41–45) found evidence for the existence of three burial clusters. One in the northern end of the east trash dump contained burials primarily oriented east–west. A cluster in the center of the midden consisted of burials oriented both

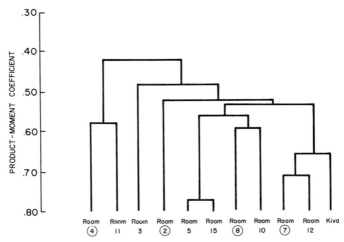

Figure 5.1. Dendrogram from cluster analysis of the Carter Ranch site rooms using design element frequencies.

north–south and east–west, and a cluster in the south had only burials oriented north–south. Longacre's analysis of the designs on the burial vessels suggested that the northern burial cluster was associated with the northern block of rooms in the pueblo, and the southern burial cluster was associated with the southern block of rooms (Longacre 1970:43). According to the published design counts (Martin *et al.* 1964b), however, there are some errors in Longacre's analysis. For instance, he states that designs 15, 85, 139, and 9, which occur with the southern burial vessels, "occur only in south pueblo" (Longacre 1970:44). The published counts show that these designs were not found in any of the rooms in the pueblo; they were found only in the trenches where the burials were. Because of these and other errors, Longacre's table listing the distribution in the pueblo of the designs on burial vessels (1970:44) has been reworked, and is shown in Table 5.5. For each design, the rooms where it was found in the northern and southern room blocks are listed. Rooms that are in the northern and southern room blocks, but which were not used in the multiple regression analysis, and thus were not included in Longacre's social groups, are listed in the table so that there will be no possible misrepresentation of the published data. The additional rooms included are room 16 in the northern room block and rooms 6, 9, 13, and 17 in the southern room block. Room 11 is also included in the table, since Longacre (1970:43) suggests that the residence group which this room represents placed their burials in the southern burial cluster. Again, the reanalysis is not consistent with Longacre's conclusions. Of the 17 designs on the southern burial vessels, 10 are found in the northern room block and 8 in the southern block. A greater percentage of the designs associated with the northern burials are found in the southern cluster, 6 of 7, than the percentage of designs associated with the southern burials that are found in the southern room cluster, 8 of 17. All the burial clusters are associated more strongly with the northern room cluster than with the southern room cluster.

In summary, the evidence relevant to Longacre's isolation of two groups of interacting villages in Hay Hollow Valley, his delineation of a design tradition for the valley as a whole, and his argument for matrilocal residence groups at the Carter Ranch site has been reexamined. The reanalysis suggests that his conclusions must be questioned.

Residence Groups at Broken K Pueblo

From his analysis of the design distributions at Broken K, Hill (1970a) isolated two uxorilocal residence units, labeled Unit I and Unit II; three uxorilocal subdivisions within Unit I, labeled Subunits IA, IB, and IC;

TABLE 5.5

Distribution within the Pueblo of Designs on Burial Vessels at the Carter Ranch Site

Burial cluster	Design element number	Distribution in pueblo		
		North rooms[a]	South rooms	Room 11
I	117	K	None	No
North	19	3,10,12,15,K	4,7,9	No
trash	3	3,K	4	No
	140	3,5,K	7,17	No
	143	15,16,K	8	No
	106	K	7,8	No
	163	3,5,10,12,15,16,K	2,4,6,7,8,9,17	Yes
II	79	10	None	No
Center	127	12,15,K	None	No
trash	32	3,15,K	None	Yes
	71	3,5,K	None	No
	80	3,5,10,K	None	No
	30	3,5,10,15,K	2,6,8	Yes
	24	3,K	4,7,8	Yes
	19	3,10,12,15,K	4,7,9	No
	26	12,15,K	4,7,8	No
	108	3,5,10,12,15,K	4,7,8,9	No
	137	K	8	No
	70	5,10,12,15,K	2,4,7,8,9,13,17	Yes
	136	K	None	No
	114	5,15,K	None	No
	56	3,10,12,15,K	2,7,9	No
III	15	None	None	No
South	85	None	None	No
trash	139	None	None	No
	9	None	None	No
	89	None	8	Yes
	29	3	4	No
	112	5,15,K	8,17	No
	143	15,16,K	8	No
	32	3,15,K	None	Yes
	130	12,K	None	No
	115	None	None	No
	37	K	None	No
	146	None	2	No
	163	3,5,10,12,15,16,K	2,4,6,7,8,9,17	Yes
	50	12,15,K	None	No
	24	3,K	4,7,8	Yes
	35	3,5,15,K	4	No

[a]K = kiva

and two uxorilocal subdivisions within Unit II, labeled Subunits IIA and IIB. Several criticisms can be made of the methods Hill used in isolating these groups.

Hill analyzed the distributions of several stylistic categories in his attempt to delineate residence units and subunits. Many of these stylistic categories were the groups of pottery types and groups of design elements, from the room floors and fills, isolated by factor analysis. In his distribution maps (1970a:60, 61, 65–67, 69) of where these factors occurred in the pueblo, Hill used "percentages of factor composition" to show the relative strength of occurrence of a factor in the pueblo rooms. This is defined as the ratio of the factor scores for one given factor to the total of the positive factor scores for all factors in a given provenience unit (1970a:24). The problem is that Hill was not consistent in his definition of how high the percentage of factor composition had to be to conclude that a given provenience was associated with a given factor. For instance, if 11% of the designs in factors from a room floor were in factor 13, the provenience was colored black on the distribution maps and the factor was considered present in the relevant subunit in Hill's summary table of the distribution of stylistic categories (1970:62, 70). (In general, Hill indicated the presence of significant amounts of a factor in a provenience by coloring the unit black on the map, while rooms with nonsignificant amounts were left white. In some cases, Hill indicated three levels of relative strength by including an intermediate level, indicated on the map by cross-hatching.) On the other hand, with factor 9 for designs in fills, the cutoff point was 61% (1970a:62). That is, a factor composition of 61% is required in a room before it is colored black on the maps, and the factor is considered present in the relevant subunit. Hill gives no reason for the variability in cutoff points. Is it the dividing point in a bimodal distribution of percentages of factor composition? Is it all percentages above the mean, or the top 10% of the percentages? There is no way to know. In the absence of this knowledge, it seems inconsistent to state that in one case a factor must have a factor composition score of 61% to be considered present in a subunit, whereas in another case a factor composition score of 11% is sufficient. This seemingly arbitrary manner in which the cutoff point was determined seems even more arbitrary when one notes that, in six of the eight cases in which Hill includes an intermediate factor composition strength in his distribution maps, one or more of the cross-hatched rooms is an exception to the residence pattern he argues for. Hill gives no reason why he uses the intermediate strength level in some cases and excludes it in others.

A similar point can be made for the manner in which Hill compiled his summary table of the distribution of stylistic categories. In some cases, the occurrence of one room in a residence subunit with a factor composition score above the cutoff point was considered sufficient for the factor to be listed as present for that subunit in the summary table (for example, Figs. A, B, C, and E, p. 60; Figs. D, E, p. 66). In other cases, one room with a factor composition score above the cutoff point in a subunit was not enough for it to be listed in the table (for example, Fig. G, p. 62; Fig. N, p. 65; Fig. B, p. 66; Fig. K, p. 67). Also, in some cases an intermediate score in one room was sufficient for a factor to be considered present in a subunit (Fig. D, p. 60; Fig. C and D, p. 66), and in some cases it was not sufficient for a factor to be considered present (Fig. M, p. 65). In light of these points, Hill's Table 13 (1970a:70) was redone. For the stylistic factors, a minimum factor composition score of 30% was used arbitrarily to indicate the presence of a factor in a room, when possible. Hill does not give the factor composition score for each factor in a provenience, but rather places it within a certain range, such as 0–35%. When the factor composition range for either the low or the intermediate strength levels overlapped the 30% cutoff point—when the range was 0–35% for example—the cutoff point was raised to 36% in order that scores lower than 30% would not be considered indicative of the presence of a factor in a room. When the factor composition range for the highest strength level overlapped the 30% cutoff point—when the range was 25–75% for example—the cutoff point was lowered to 25% in order that the factor could be considered present in some rooms. The cutoff points for the stylistic categories that were not factors, such as gopher bones, remained the same. Also, one room in a subunit with a factor composition score above the cutoff point was considered sufficient to consider the factor present in that subunit. The resulting distribution of stylistic categories is shown in Table 5.6. The stylistic categories used by Hill in the original table are listed above the broken line. Additional stylistic categories, which Hill listed in the appendix (1970a:122–127), are given below the broken line. These are included because, to determine if there is a non-random distribution of a particular class of stylistic elements, all stylistic elements in the class should be considered. The new table shows that 13 of the 28 stylistic categories originally used by Hill crosscut the residence units (Units I and II) he defined. Including all the stylistic categories listed in the table, 24 of 39 crosscut the residence units. The remaining 14 categories are consistent with his original conclusions. This table suggests that there is more variability in the distribution of stylistic categories than Hill's analysis revealed. [See also Lischka's (1975) and Dumond's (1977) comments on Hill's factor analysis of the pottery type and design element frequencies.]

TABLE 5.6

Revised Distribution of Stylistic Categories at Broken K

Stylistic category	Residence units				
	IA	IB	IC	IIA	IIB
Firepits, type IV	x	x	x	x	
Factor 2, pottery types, floors	x	x	x		x
Factor 1, pottery types, floors	x	x	x		
Factor 12, ceramic design, floors	x	x	x	x	
Factor 2, ceramic design, floors			x		
Storage pits, 7 to 15 present	x	x	x		
Factor 13, ceramic design, floors	x	x			
Firepits, type I	x	x			x
Flake choppers, floors	x	x			
Factor 5, ceramic design, floors	x			x	
Factor 4, ceramic design, fills	x				
Prairie-dog bone, floors	x				x
Factor 9, ceramic design, fills	x		x	x	
Factor 6, ceramic design, floors		x			x
Factor 3, pottery types, floors				x	x
Factor 4, pottery types, floors		x		x	x
Factor 1, ceramic design, fills				x	x
Factor 2, ceramic design, fills				x	
Firepits, type III				x	x
Factor 3, ceramic design, floors				x	
Factor 9, ceramic design, floors			x	x	
Mountain-sheep bone, floors				x	
Gopher bone, floors				x	
Firepits, type V		x		x	
Factor 4, ceramic design, floors					x
Factor 3, ceramic design, fills					x
Firepits, type II	x		x		x
Storage pits, none present	x	x	x		x
Factor 5, pottery types, floors	x		x	x	x
Factor 6, pottery types, floors		x			x
Factor 7, pottery types, floors		x		x	
Factor 7, ceramic designs, floors		x		x	
Factor 8, ceramic designs, floors			x	x	x
Factor 10, ceramic designs, floors		x		x	
Factor 11, ceramic designs, floors	x		x		x
Factor 5, ceramic designs, fills	x			x	
Factor 6, ceramic designs, fills	x	x	x		x
Factor 7, ceramic designs, fills	x		x	x	x
Factor 8, ceramic designs, fills	x	x	x	x	

Of course, Hill does not argue that all stylistic categories must fit the residence group patterns. As noted earlier, he proposed (1970a:25) that some factor distributions will reflect activities or temporal differences. However, it has been argued previously that even a random spatial distribution would result in some designs or design factors that occur only in restricted parts of the pueblo. Hill's factor analysis may have indicated nonrandom clusters of designs, but the nonrandomness of the distribution of these designs in space has not been demonstrated. Nor has it been demonstrated, even assuming that there is a nonrandom distribution of stylistic categories, that the variability in the distribution of these categories is due primarily to stylistic differences between Hill's residence units and subunits, and is not due to intrasite stylistic differences which crosscut these groups. The evidence presented in Table 5.6 suggests that Hill's groups are not homogeneous in terms of design frequencies.

The question of the nonrandomness of the factor distributions can be answered by simply calculating a chi-square statistic for the factor frequencies in Hill's two residence units. Using the factor frequencies for the 13 factors for design elements on floors, the chi-square value is 55.13, significant at beyond the .01 level. This can also be done for the factor frequencies for the five subunits. After deleting factors 10, 11, 12, and 13 because the expected frequencies are too low, the chi-square value for the remaining 9 factors is 202.34, and this is also significant at the .01 level. These tests suggest that the distribution of designs within the pueblo is nonrandom. [See Plog (1976b) for the factor frequencies by residence unit and subunit.]

The problem of the homogeneity of the residence units and subunits remains. This was dealt with in two ways. First, one would expect that, if there is less variability in design frequencies within the two residence units than between them, the design frequencies in the subunits of Unit I would be more similar to each other than to the design frequencies in the subunits of Unit II. Such is not the case. Using only those designs in the design factors from the room floors used by Hill in isolating the units and subunits, product–moment and Brainerd–Robinson coefficients were calculated between subunits. This was done by summing the frequencies for all the rooms of a subunit for each design. These similarity coefficients are shown in Table 5.7. With either similarity coefficient, the similarity levels between subunits of different residence units—between IA and IIB, for example—is greater than or equal to the similarity between subunits of the same residence unit—IA and IC, for instance.

If the residence subunits are homogeneous units, one would also expect the rooms of a single subunit to be more similar to each other than to rooms of a different subunit, in terms of design frequencies. To test this,

TABLE 5.7

Similarity Coefficients between Subunits at Broken K, Using the Design Elements from the Floor Factors Used by Hill (1970a:70) in Isolating the Residence Units and Subunits

Subunits	Brainerd–Robinson coefficient	Rank	Product–moment coefficient	Rank
IA–IB	103.51	7	−.0439	6
IA–IC	112.22	3	.1016	8
IB-IC	96.48	8	−.1180	9
IIA–IIB	109.60	4	.0946	4
IA–IIA	127.45	1	.1534	2
IA–IIB	107.25	6	.1635	1
IB–IIA	115.19	2	.1401	3
IB–IIB	87.65	9	.0697	5
IC–IIA	107.94	5	−.0651	7
IC–IIB	81.68	10	−.2366	10

product–moment coefficients were calculated between the design frequencies of all the rooms. For each subunit, the frequency of positive and negative correlations between rooms within the subunit was compared with the frequency of positive and negative correlations between rooms of the two different residence units, and chi-square values were calculated. None of the chi-square values are significant at lower than the .67 level. [See Plog (1976b) for the chi-square values and a frequency table for the product–moment coefficients.] This indicates that the rooms of a subunit are not more similar to each other than they are to rooms of other subunits. It should be noted that only designs in the floor factors used by Hill in isolating the units and subunits were used in calculating the coefficients.

To summarize, the evidence presented suggests that there is a nonrandom distribution of design frequencies at Broken K. However, it also indicates that the rooms in the residence units and subunits are not homogeneous groups in terms of design frequencies, as Hill's analysis suggested. This parallels the conclusion reached earlier concerning Longacre's analysis of the Carter Ranch site. One of the problems with both of these analyses is that designs on separate pottery types were not considered separately, because of the conclusions the authors had drawn from Cronin's study.

CONCLUSIONS

The discussion and analysis presented above demonstrates that there are significant problems with making inferences concerning prehistoric social interaction from ceramic design variability and that conclusions reached in three such studies must be questioned. Evidence that I have presented elsewhere (Plog 1976a, 1977) also supports these conclusions. Thus, one should not simply calculate a similarity coefficient between design frequencies at two sites and assume that it measures interaction and nothing else.

One of the primary research needs in regard to future design studies is better control of the dimensions of time and space. Intrasite analyses must study in detail what Schiffer (1976) has called the formation processes of the archaeological record. The degree of correspondence between archaeological context and systemic context (Schiffer 1972a) must be determined before one can even consider possible relationships between prehistoric social units and nonrandom artifact distributions. In regard to the dimension of time, we need additional studies to measure rates of design change. As noted above, studies (Klesert 1977, Plog 1977) have suggested statistically significant changes in design attributes frequencies within a period of 35 to 75 years in some areas of the world, whereas relatively slow rates of change are indicated for other areas (Plog 1976a).

In addition to these types of studies, we must start to try to explain design variability rather than assume that we know what the explanations are, as the authors of the studies discussed above have done. Other possible explanations of design variability must be tested. For example, I have shown elsewhere (Plog 1977) that design differences between imported and locally made vessels and between different vessel forms are important factors in explaining design variability on ceramics from prehistoric sites in the Chevelon region in Arizona. It is reasonable and necessary in building models to control the effect of other variables by holding them constant. At the same time, as these models are developed, applied, and tested, the effect of other factors must be gradually considered if the model is to be realistic. The studies of Deetz, Longacre, and Hill were pioneering efforts to develop methods of reconstructing prehistoric social organization. However, the models that were originally constructed were never developed past the initial stage either by the initial researchers or by others. Except for a few changes in methods of data analysis, the studies of Gerald (1975) and Clemen (1976) are duplicates of the studies done in the first half of the 1960s. At a time when archaeologists have increasingly recognized the complex nature of cultural systems, it is surprising and unfortunate that many of those studying ceramic designs have often assumed that design variability is not a complex phenomenon and that it can be described and explained very easily.

ACKNOWLEDGMENTS

I should like to thank Kent Flannery, Rex Gerald, James Hill, Fred Plog, Michael Schiffer, Robert Whallon, and particularly Richard Ford for reading and making critical comments on this paper. This research was carried out during my tenure as a National Science Foundation Graduate Fellow. This support is gratefully acknowledged.

REFERENCES

Allen, W. L., and J. B. Richardson, III
    1971   The reconstruction of kinship from archaeological data: The concepts, the methods, and the feasibility. *American Antiquity* **36**:41–53.
Amsden, C.
    1936   An analysis of Hohokam pottery design. *Medallion Papers* No. 23.
Bartlett, M. S.
    1947   The use of transformations. *Biometrics* **3**:39–52.
Beals, R., G. Brainerd, and W. Smith
    1945   Archaeological studies in northeast Arizona. *University of California Publications in American Archaeology and Ethnology* **44**(1).
Binford, L. R.
    1972   *An archeological perspective*. Chicago: Aldine.
Blalock, H. M.
    1963   Correlated independent variables: The problem of multicollinearity. *Social Forces* **42**:233–237.
Breternitz, D.
    1966   An appraisal of tree-ring dated pottery in the Southwest. *University of Arizona, Anthropological Papers*, No. 10.
Bunzel, R.
    1929   *The Pueblo potter, a study of creative imagination in primitive art*. New York: Columbia University Press.
Carlson, R.
    1970   White Mountain Redware: A pottery tradition of east-central Arizona and western New Mexico. *University of Arizona, Anthropological Papers* No. 19.
Clemen, R. T.
    1976   Aspects of prehistoric social organization on Black Mesa. In *Papers on the archaeology of Black Mesa, Arizona*, edited by G. Gumerman and R. Euler. Carbondale: Southern Illinois University Press. Pp. 113–135.
Colton, H. S.
    1955   Pottery types of the Southwest. *Museum of Northern Arizona Ceramic Series* No. 3B.
Colton, H. S., and L. L. Hargrave
    1937   Handbook of northern Arizona pottery wares. *Museum of Northern Arizona Bulletin* No. 11.
Connor, J.
    1968   Economic independence and social interaction: Related variables in culture change. Manuscript on deposit, Department of Anthropology, Field Museum of Natural History, Chicago (Xerox).

Cook, T.
    1970   Social groups and settlement patterns in Basketmaker III. Unpublished M.A. thesis, Department of Anthropology, University of Chicago.

Cronin, C.
    1962   An analysis of pottery design elements, indicating possible relationships between three decorated types. In Chapters in the prehistory of eastern Arizona, I, by P. S. Martin, J. Rinaldo, W. Longacre, C. Cronin, L. Freeman, and J. Schoenwetter. *Fieldiana: Anthropology* **53:**105–114.

Deetz, J.
    1965   The dynamics of stylistic change in Arikara ceramics. *Illinois Studies in Anthropology* No. 4.

Deutchman, H. L.
    1976   Attribute analysis of Toreva phase ceramic design variability. Unpublished M.A. thesis, Department of Anthropology, Southern Illinois University, Carbondale.

Dumond, D. E.
    1977   Science in archaeology: The saints go marching in. *Amerrican Antiquity* **42:**330–349.

Freeman, L.
    1962   Statistical analysis of painted pottery types from Upper Little Colorado drainage. In Chapters in the prehistory of eastern Arizona, I, by P. S. Martin, J. Rinaldo, W. Longacre, C. Cronin, L. Freeman, and J. Schoenwetter. *Fieldiana: Anthropology* **53:**87–104.

Friedrich, M. H.
    1970   Design structure and social interaction: Archaeological implications of an ethnographic analysis. *American Antiquity* **35:**332–343.

Gerald, R. E.
    1975   Drought correlated changes in two prehistoric pueblos communities in southeastern Arizona. Unpublished Ph.D. dissertation, Department of Anthropology, University of Chicago.

Harris, M.
    1968   Comments. In *New perspectives in archeology*, edited by R. Binford and L. R. Binford. Chicago: Aldine. Pp. 359–361.

Hill, J. N.
    1967   Structure, function, and change at Broken K Pueblo. In Chapters in the prehistory of eastern Arizona, III, by P. S. Martin, W. A. Longacre, and J. N. Hill. *Fieldiana: Anthropology* **57:**158–167.
    1970a Broken K Pueblo: Prehistoric social organization in the American Southwest. *University of Arizona, Anthropological Papers* No. 18.
    1970b Prehistoric social organization in the American Southwest: Theory and method. In *Reconstructing prehistoric pueblo social organization*, edited by W. A. Longacre. Albuquerque: University of New Mexico Press. Pp. 11–58.

Johnson, L.
    1972   Problems in "avant garde" archaeology. *American Anthropologist* **74:**366–377.

Justeson, J. J.
    1973   Limitations of archaeological inference: An information-theoretic approach with applications in methodology. *American Antiquity* **38:**131–149.

Kidder, A., and C. Amsden
    1931   *The pottery of Pecos* (Vol. 1). New Haven, Conn.: Yale University Press.

Kidder, A. and A. Shepard
    1936   *The pottery of Pecos* (Vol. 2). New Haven, Conn.: Yale University Press.
Klesert, A. L.
    1977   An analysis of intra-site ceramic design variability. Unpublished M.A. thesis,
           Department of Anthropology, Southern Illinois University, Carbondale.
LeBlanc, S. A.
    1975   Micro-seriation: A method for fine chronological differentiation. *American An-*
           tiquity **40:**22–38.
Leone, M.
    1968   Neolithic economic autonomy and social distance. *Science* **162:**1150–1151.
Lischka, J. J.
    1975   Broken K revisited: A short discussion of factor analysis. *American Antiquity*
           40:220–227.
Longacre, W. A.
    1964   Sociological implications of the ceramic analysis. In Chapters in the prehistory
           of eastern Arizona, II, by P. S. Martin, J. Rinaldo, W. Longacre, L. Freeman,
           J. Brown, R. Hevly, and M. E. Cooley. *Fieldiana: Anthropology* **55:**155–170.
    1970   Archaeology as anthropology: A case study. *University of Arizona, An-*
           thropological Papers No. 17.
Martin, P. S., and F. Plog
    1973   *The archaeology of Arizona.* New York: American Museum of Natural His-
           tory.
Martin, P. S., J. Rinaldo, and W. Longacre
    1960   Documentation for some late Mogollon sites in the upper Little Colorado
           drainage, eastern Arizona. *Archives of Archaeology* No. 6.
    1961   Documentation for prehistoric investigations in the upper Little Colorado
           drainage, eastern Arizona. *Archives of Archaeology* No. 13.
Martin, P. S., J. Rinaldo, W. Longacre, C. Cronin, L. Freeman, and J. Schoenwetter
    1962   Chapters in the prehistory of eastern Arizona, I. *Fieldiana: Anthropology* **53.**
Martin, P. S., J. Rinaldo, W. Longacre, L. Freeman, J. Brown, R. Hevly, and M. E.
           Cooley
    1964a Chapters in the prehistory of eastern Arizona, II. *Fieldiana: Anthropology* **55.**
    1964b Documentation for prehistory of eastern Arizona, II. *Archives of Archaeology*
           No. 24.
Plog, S.
    1976a Measurement of prehistoric interaction between communities. In *The early*
           Mesoamerican village, edited by K. V. Flannery, New York: Academic Press.
           Pp. 255–272.
    1976b The inference of prehistoric social organization from ceramic design variability.
           Michigan Discussions in Anthropology **1:**1–47.
    1977   A multivariate approach to the explanation of ceramic design variation. Unpub-
           lished Ph.D. dissertation, Department of Anthropology, University of Michi-
           gan, Ann Arbor.
Redman, C. L.
    1976   Artifact analysis as a basis for organizational interpretation. Manuscript on
           deposit, Department of Anthropology, State University of New York, Bing-
           hamton (Xerox).
Rohn, A. H.
    1971   Mug House, Mesa Verde National Park, Colorado. *National Park Service*
           Archeological Series No. 7-D.

Schiffer, M. B.
    1972a Archaeological context and systemic context. *American Antiquity* **37**:156–165.
    1972b Cultural formation processes of the archeological record: Preliminary equations. Paper presented at the 71st Annual Meeting of the American Anthropological Association, Toronto.
    1976 *Behavioral archeology*. New York: Academic Press.

Shepard, A.
    1939 Technology of La Plata pottery. In Archaeological studies in the La Plata district, by E. H. Morris. *Carnegie Institution of Washington Publication* No. 519, 249–287.
    1942 Rio Grande glaze paint ware. *Contributions to American Anthropology* No. 39.

Singh, J.
    1966 *Great ideas in information theory, language, and cybernetics*. New York: Dover.

Sokal, R. R., and P. H. A. Sneath
    1963 *Principles of numerical taxonomy*, San Francisco: W. H. Freeman and Co.

Stanislawski, M.
    1969a The ethno-archaeology of Hopi pottery making. *Plateau* **42**:27–33.
    1969b What good is a broken pot? *Southwestern Lore* **35**:11–18.
    1973 Review of Archaeology as anthropology: A case study. *American Antiquity* **38**:117–121.

Tuggle, H. D.
    1970 Prehistoric community relations in east-central Arizona. Unpublished Ph.D. dissertation, Department of Anthropology, University of Arizona, Tucson.

Warren, H.
    1969 Tonque, one pueblo's glaze pottery industry dominated middle Rio Grande commerce. *El Palacio* **76**:36–42.

Watson, P. J.
    1977 Design analysis of painted pottery. *American Antiquity* **42**:381–393.

Whallon, R.
    1968 Investigations of late prehistoric social organization in New York State. In *New perspectives in archeology*, edited by S. R. Binford and L. R. Binford. Chicago: Aldine. Pp. 223–244.
    1969 Reflection of social interaction in Owasco ceramic decoration. *Eastern States Archaeological Federation Bulletins* **27**; **28**:15.

Wilcox, D.
    1971 City blocks post-date hamlets: Developmental cycles at Broken K Pueblo. Manuscript on deposit, Department of Anthropology, University of Arizona, Tucson (Xerox).

Wiley, C.
    1971 Social interaction and economic exchange in the Hay Hollow Valley 900–1200 A.D. Manuscript on deposit, Department of Anthropology, Field Museum of Natural History, Chicago (mimeographed).

Willey, G. R., and P. Phillips
    1958 *Method and theory in American archaeology*. Chicago: University of Chicago Press.

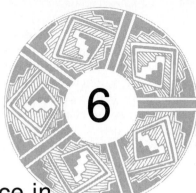

Inference and Evidence in Archaeology: A Discussion of the Conceptual Problems

ALAN P. SULLIVAN

> Since no science can progress without inference, it becomes of critical importance that inference should not proceed along lines which are haphazard or capricious or controlled by unconscious prejudice.
>
> Clyde Kluckhohn

INTRODUCTION

Over the years, countless philosophers and scientists who share Kluck-hohn's attitude have discussed the nature of evidence and the problems related to the justification of claims of knowledge. In archaeology, one frequently encounters comments made in response to claims about the past that seem inadequately justified, given the evidence offered in support of them (e.g., Roberts 1937:3; Haury 1956:10; Sanders and Price 1968:221). The concern is over the uncertain fit or linkage between the claims being advanced and the evidence proffered. Given this situation, two questions naturally arise: (*a*) what is responsible for the uncertainty, and (*b*) how can it be resolved? In addressing these questions, inquiry is directed not at the situation that gave rise to the inferences (the context of discovery) but to an analysis of the arguments put forth for accepting the inferences (context of justification; Salmon 1973:10–13).

ADVANCES IN ARCHAEOLOGICAL METHOD AND THEORY, VOL. 1

In what follows, it is argued that one aspect of the justification process—determining the relevance of evidence offered in support of a conclusion—has received inadequate attention from archaeologists. One of the major problems has been a failure to make a rigorous conceptual distinction between deposits of material remains and the evidence or data that may be generated from them. In addition, the role that archaeological theory should play in maintaining these distinctions has not been appreciated generally, which accounts, in part, for the lack of development of concepts of evidence in archaeology.

The first part of this chapter is a review of the general features of scientific inference and how inference has been discussed by archaeologists. This is followed by an explication of current problems in the following areas: (*a*) the justification of archaeological conclusions, (*b*) concepts of archaeological evidence, and (*c*) the undeveloped relations between archaeological theory and archaeological evidence. The second part of the chapter addresses these problems and attempts to resolve them or at least suggest potential solutions to them.

It is argued that, in order to resolve many of the problems surrounding uncertain links between inference and evidence, archaeologists must develop a rigorous model that specifies how information about the past is transmitted to the present via material remains. The structure of such a model is outlined. It is an attempt to describe some of the processes responsible for producing the material remains that archaeologists manipulate in assembling evidence to support claims about past phenomena.

Also by way of introduction, it should be noted that one of the rationales that prompted this chapter was supplied by the late David Clarke.

> What is currently required is the internal analysis (with external aid) and explicit development of valid principles of archaeological reasoning (archaeological logic), the specification of the general nature and special qualitites of archaeological information (archaeological epistemology) and the careful clarification of archaeological concepts and their limitations (archaeological metaphysics) [1972:238].

The first step in executing Clarke's program of "rethinking" is to develop a firm appreciation for some of the philosophical problems involved in coming to know the past by the examination of archaeological materials. This is followed by a brief account of the nature of scientific inference and by a discussion of some of the problems of inference in archaeology.

Finally, this chapter is not a review and discussion of explanation in archaeology. I have chosen to discuss how archaeologists might proceed in gathering relevant evidence that satisfactorily supports the claims they would like to make about past phenomena. Well-supported conclusions about past phenomena are requisites for attempts at explanation. For, quite clearly, "one does not try to explain something unless one thinks it has occurred" (Scriven 1962:220).

KNOWING THE PAST

From an epistemological viewpoint it would appear legitimate to seek to understand how statements about the past are to be substantiated through the investigation of archaeological materials. At first glance, archaeological science is beset with a major logical and methodological problem. Archaeologists want to acquire firm knowledge of the past. However, the medium for apprehending the past, the archaeological record, is a contemporary phenomenon (Binford 1968b:271; Fritz 1972:137; Malik 1962:506). Although the causes for the production of deposits of material remains lie in the past, observations made on those materials refer to the present. How, then, can observations of contemporary archaeological phenomena be used to inform on the nature of past phenomena?

The severity of the problem has been overstated deliberately as a means of introducing the well-known notion that, whenever an archaeologist attempts to go beyond presenting an observational narrative of the properties of material remains, the end product is referred to as an inference. Archaeologists need not be distressed by this activity, since the business of gaining knowledge of unobservable phenomena in terms of observable phenomena is not peculiar to archaeology, but characterizes science in general (see Platt 1964; Salmon 1966). Thus, the past may be unobservable, but that does not mean it is unknowable (Aron 1958:12; Spaulding 1968:37; Fritz 1972). The important question is whether or not the inferences can be supported. This requires an in-depth examination of the nature of inferring and how it relates to the general tasks of the archaeologist.

INFERENCE AND ARCHAEOLOGY

The process of inferring is essentially a psychological activity (Salmon 1973:8). Inferences may be rendered susceptible to critical scrutiny by transforming them into arguments. Arguments have a basic structure. There is a premise, or a set of premises, and a conclusion. The logical relations that obtain between premises and conclusion describe two different kinds of argument and two kinds of reasoning. When the conclusion is necessitated by the premises, the argument is deductive. When the relation between premises and conclusion is probabilistic, the argument is inductive (see Salmon 1976 for additional useful distinctions between deductive and inductive arguments).

The purpose in drawing these distinctions is not to advocate that archaeology, or more precisely archaeological reasoning, should be deductive (Binford 1968a; Watson *et al.* 1971; Hill 1972) or inductive (Hawkes 1954; Thompson 1958; see also Morwood 1975), but rather to suggest that each type may be appropriate for certain situations. Many archaeologists will recognize that certain activities, such as classification, are characterized by deductive reasoning (e.g., Dunnell 1971). Since most archaeologists, however, seem to be concerned with generating knowledge that goes beyond simple description of archaeological phenomena, they are reasoning inductively. It is precisely because the link between premises and conclusion of an inductive argument admits of probability (Jeffreys 1973:23) that special problems arise when one is examining the degree of support that archaeological data provide for a conclusion about past phenomena (see Concepts of Archaeological Evidence below).

Archaeologists have generated a substantial body of literature related to the topic of archaeological inference. Notions of the role of inference in archaeology have been developed within the context of larger theoretical and synthetic statements (Rouse 1958; Willey and Phillips 1958; Spaulding 1960b; Willey 1966; Deetz 1968b; Trigger 1968; Binford 1968a; Hill 1970b; Isaac 1971; Wilcox 1975; Schiffer 1976), but some archaeologists have discussed inference in a very explicit fashion (Steward and Seltzer 1938; Kluckhohn 1940; Taylor 1948; Ehrich 1950, 1963; M. A. Smith 1955; Thompson 1956, 1958; Longacre 1968; B. Smith 1977; see also R. Watson 1976). At least three themes can be isolated in these and other discussions of archaeological inference. They are (*a*) limitations, (*b*) procedural matters, and (*c*) inference justification. Each theme is now discussed in turn.

Limitations

The limitations of archaeological inference have been viewed as being a function of the refractory nature of archaeological data (Taylor 1948:143; M. A. Smith 1955; Leach 1973:768), inadequate methodological sophistication (Binford 1968a), and incoherent conceptual development (Taylor 1948; Fritz 1972). These concerns for delineating limitations are reflected in the common practice of ranking inferences in terms of how far they supposedly depart from the data used to confirm them (Hawkes 1954:161–162; Thompson 1958:149; Willey and Phillips 1958:4; Piggott 1960:87; Ehrich 1963:19; Chang 1967:12–13).

Unfortunately, the limitations arguments are based on questionable assumptions about how activities become represented by material remains. The conceptual problems involved in providing unambiguous evidence for the existence and nature of ceremonial activities are little different from those related to determining economic or technological activities (*pace* Hawkes 1954). *All* activities are remote, since they occurred in the past. The problem lies in the inadequacies of our theories (and not just our methodologies; see Binford 1968a) to model how information about these different kinds of past activities is transmitted to the present in the form of material remains. A general solution to this problem is proposed below (see A Model of Past Information Transmission).

Procedural Matters

Many archaeologists have been concerned with procedural matters of archaeological inference (e.g., Hill 1970b). Their contributions have centered on arguments specifying the appropriate use of certain domains of information. The papers of Slotkin (1952), MacWhite (1956), Binford (1967), and Dozier (1970), for example, are concerned primarily with stipulating how ethnographic information should be used appropriately in the inferential process. In addition, much attention has been devoted to the development of stage-like schemes that specify how the archaeologist should proceed in making inferences. These schemes differ in terms of whether data collection should precede (Randall-MacIver 1932:8; Deetz 1967) or follow (Taylor 1948; Swartz 1967; Binford 1968a; Fritz and Plog 1970) problem definition, and how archaeological data should be manipulated to produce inferences (Thompson 1958; Longacre 1968; R. Watson 1976).

Clearly, these discussions are concerned with the discovery process (see especially Willey 1953). There is, however, still considerable debate over the existence or necessity of a logic of discovery (pro: Caws 1969; con: Salmon 1973:10–13). This controversy and the fact that investigators may arrive at an inference in a variety of ways (many of which are not susceptible to formal systemization) suggest that archaeologists should be concerned more with how to justify their conclusions and less with how to generate them.

It is fair to state that previous discussions of the limitations of archaeological inference and statements about procedural matters have simply missed the mark. In addition to the drawbacks mentioned above, these discussions have tended to assume that archaeological data (rather than material remains) exist independently of the investigator, that variability of archaeological remains admits of only one interpretation, and that all sites contain remains that can inform on any problem the archaeologist has in mind. Criticisms of these assumptions are developed below (see Concepts of Archaeological Evidence).

The Problem of Justification

The issue of justification arises from the very natural tendency among scientists to be skeptical of research results. There is little doubt that critically oriented skepticism is essential for the advancement of knowledge. To preclude unbridled and unwarranted skepticism, it appears necessary to develop "a set of ideas for assessing when the propositions that archaeologists advance should be deemed verified or usable and when they should not" (Plog 1973:649; see also Wilford 1954:174–175; Lowther 1962).

As stated earlier, the first step in justifying an inference is to transform it into an argument that specifies which statement is the conclusion and which statements are evidence that purportedly support the conclusion (Salmon 1973:1–3). Once the transformation has been accomplished, appropriate systems may be employed to assess the logical relation between premises and conclusion. In the case of deductive arguments, the evaluative principles of deductive logic are well established (e.g., Copi 1961) and invalid arguments can be readily ascertained. Such is not the case, unfortunately, with inductive arguments, since there is still considerable dispute over the structure of an inductive system of logic (Skyrms 1966: 22–51; Salmon 1967). This means that there is more uncertainty in discriminating correct from incorrect inductive arguments. Part of the problem is that the correctness of inductive arguments is dependent to a large extent on the nature of the evidence, especially its relevancy, put forth to support the conclusion (Salmon 1973:82). In addition, since the probability of the conclusion of an inductive argument depends on current knowledge, changes in what is considered current knowledge will modify the relation between premises and conclusion, thus affecting the justification of the conclusion. For these reasons, it is essential "that we give special attention to the precise formulation of the evidence in relation to which we estimate the probability of any proposition" (Kneale 1952:11).

CONCEPTS OF ARCHAEOLOGICAL EVIDENCE

The "precise formulation" of archaeological evidence is an aspect of archaeological epistemology that has received little systematic conceptual development. Although all archaeologists have referred, at one time or another, to the *evidence* for their conclusions, only a few workers have ever explicated the intended referent of the concept and used it consistently (e.g., Haury 1958). In fact, it seems that archaeologists prefer to speak in terms of the *data* for their propositions. For example, Willey (1966:2) has referred to "objects made by men and the ground they were left in or on" as the "primary data of the discipline" (see also Taylor 1948:112; Thompson 1958:2; Longacre 1968:386; Hester 1976:24). The use of the terms data and evidence interchangeably creates no logical problems. Problems do arise, however, when no distinction is made and maintained between material remains and data. Material remains are not data. They are phenomena, which archaeologists manipulate to generate data (Thomas 1976:7; see also Riley 1974:489; Wilmsen 1974:57). Further, material remains exist independently of any type of archaeological activity, whereas archaeological data do not (Bidney 1962:503; *pace* Fritz 1972:137).

Failure to consistently discriminate between material remains and data contributes, in part, to the unsatisfactory justification of many archaeological conclusions. The view that material remains are data (rather than a source of data) is phenomenological (see Willey 1953:361) and suggests that contemporary physical properties of material remains are sufficient to adequately support conclusions about past phenomena. This view of archaeological evidence can lead to difficulties, as the following example illustrates. Early in the history of Southwestern archaeology, it was thought that the inhabitants of cliff-houses were of diminutive stature, given the low height and narrow width of the doorways of their houses. But, it was soon pointed out that an "examination of the human remains found in the cliff-dwellings proves conclusively that the inhabitants of these lofty abodes were people of ordinary size, and that they were no more dwarfs than were the mound-builders giants" (Duff 1904:305). Clearly, doorway morphology can be used to support the conclusion of midget inhabitants of cliff-houses, but it provides only very weak support. This is because of the quite uncertain link—that is, relevant connection—between doorway variability and stature of occupants.

Thus, one of the major problems with the phenomenological concept of archaeological evidence is that it relies heavily on single-interpretation correlates to generate data. Interestingly enough, forty years ago, Steward and Seltzer (1938:9) argued against viewing archaeological phenomena as direct indicators of past phenomena. They suggested that knowledge of the different roles that objects play in different subsistence systems, for example, "may not only contribute to an understanding of culture process, but even modify historic and taxonomic conclusions."

To overcome the inadequacies of the phenomenological concept of data and evidence, it has been suggested that archaeologists select specified sets of material remains that bear on a particular problem (Nelson 1919:115; Collingwood 1939:122; Watson *et al*. 1971:114–120). Accordingly, certain aspects of material remains become data when there is a match between expectations (test implications) and observations. The major difficulties with this view are that strong assumptions are being made about the processes responsible for producing the sample examined by the archaeologist to generate the requisite data. The assumptions are that the patterning of variability in the archaeological record reflects past behavioral patterning (Binford 1962:219; Thompson and Longacre 1966:270; Hill 1970a:15); that there has been little significant postdepositional modification of material remains (Watson *et al*. 1971:113–114; Hill 1972:97); and that all deposits of material remains will yield data about most aspects of past phenomena if the archaeologist is clever enough to discover them (Binford 1968a:23; Hill 1970b:30; Watson *et al*. 1971:114). These assumptions are questionable, since archaeological patterning need have no past behavioral referent (Krause and Thorne 1971; Wilcox 1975; Baldwin 1975; Dumond 1977). A wide variety of processes, not necessarily cataclysmic postdepositional ones, affect the structure of material remains and therefore the nature of the sample the archaeologist manipulates to generate data (Colton and Hargrave 1937:24; Brew 1946:100–101; Wilcox 1975; Schiffer 1976). And finally, "All sites are not amenable to the solution of all problems" (Reid 1975:127), given the diverse nature of the processes responsible for their production.

Although the so-called "problem-oriented" approach is an advance over the phenomenological one, it still is beset with some of the same difficulties as the latter. That is, there are difficulties in pinpointing oversight and error in research design if the requisite remains for generating certain kinds of data needed to support a particular claim about the past are not encountered (Cordell 1977). Does this mean that the requisite remains were never deposited; or that they were deposited but were not available for observation (the sampling dilemma); or that the remains were deposited and available for observation but went unrecorded (for a variety of reasons) by the archaeologist?

The point is that archaeologists will not reduce the uncertainty of the link between conclusions about the past and supportive data if the contemporary properties of archaeological phenomena are accepted uncritically as evidence (Reid *et al*. 1975). All data are archaeological and refer therefore to the present. The problem is, how can data, as present phenomena, be used to support claims about past phenomena? The answer lies in the development of archaeological theory: "Archaeological theory is required precisely because the present archaeological record differs so markedly from the past phenomena archaeologists hope to know" (Fritz 1972:137).

ARCHAEOLOGICAL EVIDENCE AND ARCHAEOLOGICAL THEORY

In order for data to support a conclusion about the past, the material remains from which they are generated must have a past referent—that is, some prearchaeological source of production. Clearly, all deposits have a large set of past referents. This is because material remains are not instantaneously produced nor hermetically sealed. Different factors are constantly affecting the structure of deposits as they are being formed and before they are encountered by the archaeologist. When an archaeologist encounters a deposit of material remains, an innumerable set of properties is present for potential selection as evidence to warrant a particular conclusion about the past. This situation is responsible for the preeminent problem in archaeological methodology— namely, how are present-day properties of material remains to be unambiguously partitioned according to the factors responsible for their production?

It is important to determine the factors responsible for the formation of deposits of material remains because different formation processes can generate sites that have markedly similar properties when encountered by an archaeologist (Cowgill 1977b:972; see also Adams 1973:24–28). For example, two sites may have similar complements of objects incorporated within their respective deposits. If, however, the objects became incorporated as a result of processes associated with differences in activity surface use-life, rate of activity performance, occupation span, etc., the remains are not comparable and cannot be used to answer the same research questions (Wilcox 1976:131; see also Sullivan and Schiffer 1978:169). More correctly, data generated from the two sites are not comparable, even if they were generated from the same properties (for example, sherds per cubic meter), since they represent different past phenomena. As Adams (1968) has shown, interpretational problems arise if different formation factors are not taken into account when assembling data to support a conclusion. In short, similar depositional histories are not entailed by similarity of observable properties (for example, site size, site type).

Clearly, what is required is a theory concerned with the formation of deposits of material remains. The following view is espoused:

Archaeological theory consists of propositions and assumptions regarding the archaeological record itself, its origins, its sources of variability, the determinants of differences and similarities in the formal, spatial, and temporal characteristics of artifacts and features and their interrelationships [Binford and Binford 1968:2; see also Schiffer 1976; Klejn 1977:11].

Since the formation of deposits of material remains is dependent on the nature of different sources of variability, it would seem incumbent on the archaeologist to attempt to enumerate them and seek to understand how they influence the transmission of information about past phenomena ("past" information; see Childe 1956:31–32). Interestingly enough, except for a few notable attempts (Daniels 1972; Fritz 1972; Clarke 1973; Justeson 1973), archaeologists have not attempted a thorough theoretical understanding of how "past" information is transmitted to the present via material remains. This would seem a reasonable prerequisite for developing a more rigorous concept of archaeological evidence, since the more precisely the factors responsible for the production of certain kinds of remains can be delimited, the greater is the likelihood of selecting those properties that are pertinent to the claims being advanced (Thompson 1958:147; Thorne 1969:3–4; Krause and Thorne 1971). To facilitate the selection process, it is argued that a model of past information transmission be coupled with the view of archaeological theory advocated above—that is, a theory of the formation of the archaeological record.

In what follows, the prerequisites of a model of past information transmission are outlined and the virtues and shortcomings of previous work in this area of archaeological epistemology are discussed. The remainder of the chapter is, in effect, an extended argument of how the successful rapproachment between archaeological theory and a model of past information transmission will assist in the identification of relevant data. It should become clear that discussions of certain aspects of the general model, such as the role of sampling in Recovery Theory and classification in Analytic Theory, are not particularly revolutionary. These aspects were included to provide a comprehensive and internally consistent model of all the factors that influence the generation of relevant data by the archaeologist.

A MODEL OF PAST INFORMATION TRANSMISSION

Prerequisites

The present concern is to construct a model that specifies how information about the past is transmitted to the present via material remains. A minimally adequate model must (a) specify those past circumstances surrounding how and where information is likely to be mapped (that is, become represented) onto items, surfaces, and their relations; (b) specify the circumstances affecting the likelihood that the mapped information will be encountered in an archaeological situation; and (c) provide the conceptual tools to partition the properties of material remains in terms of the factors responsible for their production. Three different theories refer to each of the model's adequacy criteria. They are, respectively, Formation Theory, Recovery Theory, and Analytic Theory. The components of Formation Theory will be explicated following a discussion of previous work on information transmission models. Recovery Theory and Analytic Theory will then be discussed in turn.

Models of Past Information Transmission:
Previous Attempts

The most explicit theoretical attempts to model how past information is transmitted to the present are represented by the work of Daniels (1972) and Clarke (1973). These schemes are predicated on a subtractive model of past information transmission (Daniels 1972:203; Clarke 1973:14–17). Both workers envision the essentialy uncontrollable decay of past information as the greatest hindrance in getting to know the past via material remains.

There is, of course, physical attrition of material remains between the time they are deposited and the time they are encountered by an archaeologist. This does not mean, however, that there is a steady and inexorable loss of information. The archaeologist is not limited by having little or no information to work with but, rather, by an overwhelming abundance of information. Again, the selection of relevant information is the pre-eminent problem. A subtractive model of past information transmission depicts only part of the process. It must be supplemented by a model that stresses an information growth relation that is time-dependent (specification of whether the growth mode is linear, exponential, or logistic is beyond the scope of this chapter). This means that, the longer an item, set of items, or surfaces are not observed by the archaeologist, the greater is the probability that a vast and varied amount of information is going to be *added* to the remains, including information related to their disintegration.

Daniels and Clarke disagree on the kind of information being transmitted. Daniels (1972:205, 212) views objects as the link between past and present, and the material from which archaeological data are generated. His model attempts to control for how numbers of artifacts may change between the time they are deposited and the time they are recovered and analyzed. Daniels is assuming that the ability of archaeologists to gain knowledge of the past is directly proportional to the number of representative objects recovered and correctly analyzed. The major problem with such an assumption is that information about the past may be represented by no artifactual material, or several kinds of information may be mapped onto one or more artifacts or facilities (ergo, the frequently used but poorly developed concept of feature).

Clarke's (1973:16–17) scheme overcomes the emphasis on artifactual material by focusing instead on traces, which unfortunately are never defined explicitly. Note that Clarke's position has changed from his earlier one where he stated that archaeology is primarily concerned "with the recovery, systematic description and study of relict *artefacts*" (1968:13; emphasis added). Clarke assumes that the observable properties of material remains are surviving traces and that these traces are unambiguous clues to past human behavior (given the vagaries of bad samples). These assumptions are unwarranted, since observable traces may have a variety of past sources of production, other than purely behavioral factors (see Formation Theory; see also Fritz 1972:143).

These two attempts at modeling the transmission of past information are incomplete. The models do not contribute to the reduction of uncertainty surrounding the production of different kinds of material remains. Undue attention has been paid to the subtractive aspects of past information flow, to the exclusion of considering the significance of additive processes. In terms of information theoretic concepts (Justeson 1973:132–134), Daniels' scheme misconstrued the artifact as both channel and message, leaving the archaeologist to be concerned only with obtaining adequate collections of objects (the channel) rather than obtaining representative samples of traces (the message being transmitted over the channel). While Clarke's scheme correctly characterized the artifact as channel and the trace as the input message, it failed to provide any means for determining how traces needed to support a certain conclusion are to be retrieved and partitioned according to the factors responsible for their production. Although Clarke's approach is more suitable in terms of the present problem, neither model possesses the theoretical apparatus that satisfies the adequacy criteria outlined above. Therefore, the following theories have been developed to refine and supplement these models.

FORMATION THEORY

Formation Theory consists of concepts designed to portray how information, in the form of traces, comes to be represented by items and surfaces (that is, activity surfaces; see Wilcox 1976:121). A trace is defined as an alteration in the physical properties of an object (or the relations between objects) or a surface (or the relations between surfaces) (Ascher 1968:43; Webb *et al.* 1966:35–37; cf. Lipe 1970:84; Isaac 1971:123;

Stjernquist 1971:28). Conjoined with the concept of trace is the concept of trace-production context. This refers to a situation where there is a potential for traces to be mapped onto items and surfaces. The important thing to bear in mind is that trace production is context-dependent (Thorne 1969:3–4; Krause and Thorne 1971:246; see also Taylor 1972). This means that archaeologists can expect only certain kinds of traces to be produced with a certain frequency in a given context, thus influencing the kinds of data an archaeologist can expect to generate from a given sample.

Trace-Production Contexts

At least four trace-production contexts may be distinguished. The contexts are defined on the basis of three variables: H, R, and B. The variable H refers to the situation where an item or surface is in direct physical association with hominids—that is, an object is being manipulated or a surface is being trod upon; R means that an item has not been removed from an activity area or a surface has not fallen into disuse; B refers to a behavioral system whose activities are contributing to the formation of a deposit of material remains during a continuous occupational episode. The values taken by these variables (+ signifies that the definition of the variable has been satisfied;—signifies that the definition of the variable has not been satisfied) and the interaction between them describe the different contexts (Table 6.1; see especially Speth and Johnson 1976:55). Note that the trace-production contexts defined in Table 6.1 do not exhaust all the logical permutations of the variables and their variates. The four contexts do, however, exhaust all possibilities that are not nonsensical. Several examples are presented to clarify the conceptual distinctions between the different contexts and how they affect the transmission of past information.

It should also be noted that the various trace-production contexts refer to *generalized* situations where information is likely to be mapped onto items and surfaces. Theoretically, each trace-production context may be composed of several stages. Traces that pertain to different stages convey

TABLE 6.1

Trace-Production Contexts

Trace-production context	H	R	B
Interactive	+	+	+
Depositional	−	+	+
Discard	−	−	+
Archaeological	−	−	−

information about distinct phenomena. For example, different traces may be mapped as items and surfaces participate in the procurement, transport, manufacture, and use-stages of interactive context (cf. Schiffer 1972:158–162, 1975b). I have chosen not to indicate how different stages affect the transmission of past information because that would expand astronomically this already lengthy discussion. My purpose is simply to examine the complexities involved in determining relevant evidence when the information transmitting properties of trace-production contexts in general are considered.

Interactive Context

In an animal carcass reduction activity, the carcass, the chipped-stone tools involved in dismembering the carcass, and the surface on which the activity takes place are in interactive context. The most obvious context-dependent traces produced in this situation would be the striations, micro-flaking, abrasion, and polish mapped onto the tools and modifications to the bones of the carcass (Thomas 1971).

The traces that are mapped onto living surfaces as a result of the successive habitation of pueblo rooms is another example of interactive context trace-production processes. Whenever an activity is performed within a pueblo room, the surface it occurs on and the items, facilities, energy sources, etc., involved in the execution of the activity are in interactive context. The context-dependent traces that would reflect changes in occupation are modifications to the living surface such as the digging of pits, plastering of floors, sealing of doorways, and the repositioning of hearths (Wilcox 1975).

In the examples that follow, it must be remembered that items or surfaces in depositional discard, or archaeological context have participated, at least once, in interactive context. Otherwise they never would have been involved in a behavioral system.

Depositional Context

There is an interesting statistical generalization that applies to depositional context trace-production processes. That is, prior to discard, most items and surfaces most of the time are in depositional context. The notion underlying this generalization is that all the items and surfaces that pertain to the activities of a human group are not in use simultaneously. This generalization has some direct implications for identifying many of the processes responsible for the production of traces. If it is warranted to assume that, among other things, trace production is time-dependent (that is, the probability that a trace will be mapped onto an item or surface participating in a particular context is directly dependent on the time spent in that context), then many traces are produced rather indirectly in a depositional context situation. Examples include the smoke-blackening found on the undersides of roof beams, corrosion on metal tools, soil deposits that accumulate in back of water-control devices—in short, any trace produced without *direct* human agency (human beings do not physically apply smoke-blackened substances to the undersides of roof beams).

The monitoring of traces produced in depositional context is not the exclusive territory of the archaeologist. The importance of the "at-rest" effect has been recognized by bakers, pharmacologists, librarians, archivists, and vintners. The term *shelf-life* signals the time interval during which physiochemical changes in commodities are not likely to occur. Following the expiration of shelf-life, there is a higher probability that certain kinds of traces, generally of an unfavorable or undesirable nature, will be mapped onto commodities irrespective of human agency (milk that goes sour, grans that rot, etc.).

Discard Context

The trace-production processes that pertain to discard context are difficult to enumerate. A few examples should suffice to indicate the importance of discard context processes in contributing to the variability of material remains. One example is the reduction of discarded sherds into smaller pieces. The context-dependent trace would be a larger number of smaller-sized sherds coming to represent individual vessels. This may occur as a result of additional objects, such as grinding stones, being tossed in on top of the previously discarded sherds.

Another example is represented by the thermal alteration of discarded lithic and ceramic items as a result of their proximity to a suitable firing temperature in discard context. Smoldering trash dumps frequently account for the production of these traces (see Figure 36 in Martin *et al.* 1954:66).

Archaeological Context

There is an important conceptual distinction between discard and archaeological context signaled by the negative value of the B variable. The implication of this negative value is that processes associated with hominid activity performance no longer account for trace production. Only natural processes map traces onto items and surfaces.

There has always been a hint of ambiguity in the concept of archaeological context. The original definition went as follows: "Archaeological context describes materials which have passed through a cultural system, and which are now the objects of investigation of archaeologists" (Schiffer 1972:157). Clearly, the times at which objects and surfaces cease to participate in a behavioral system are not observable, since they are past events. Whether or not the places at which objects and surfaces ceased to participate in a behavioral system correspond to the places where they are encountered by the archaeologist is another question; this depends on the nature and extent of natural formation processes. Thus the statement "Descriptions of the archaeological record, as discovered and perceived by the archaeologist, constitute the archaeological context" (Schiffer 1975a:62) is erroneous. The archaeologist does not perceive the archaeological context of objects and surfaces, since they entered that context in the past. The archaeologist can make observations of the archaeological record (which is, of course, a present phenomena). The particular configuration of the archaeological record at the time it is observed by the archaeologist is called the recovery context (for an example, see Hough 1919:410). A rigorous distinction is thus maintained in this paper between archaeological context (which is a past phenomenon) and recovery context (which is a present phenomenon). The implications of these distinctions have been developed in greater detail elsewhere (Sullivan 1976).

There are many kinds of traces that can be produced in archaeological context. The disintegration of pueblos produces traces related to the reduction in mass of previously discarded materials. For example, as the roof beams of pueblo rooms decay, they may drop onto underlying trash deposits and generate more sherds and lithic fragments. As the entire roof gives way, materials discarded on roof activity surfaces, such as pots and hearths, may be thrown into several alternative locations (Wilcox 1975:155–156). Plaster, murals, and other water-soluble substances may dissolve and be redeposited elsewhere (Beeson 1957). Noncultural materials, like blowsand, may be interjected into already deposited remains (Heindl 1955). Sherds and lithic fragments deposited on the surface of sites may be thermally altered as a result of passing forest fires (Burgh 1960). And, of course, the traces produced by the spatial displacement of abandoned objects by natural forces (Rick 1976; Wood and Johnson, this volume) is an all-too-familiar process.

Factors Affecting Trace Production

The different trace-production contexts described above label sets of circumstances that surround the potential mapping of information onto items and surfaces. However, whether information about past phenomena does get mapped onto items and surfaces is dependent on several factors.

Factor 1: Context Participation (Type and Interval Length). As noted earlier, different kinds of traces pertain to different production contexts. A trace is said to be context-specific if and only if it is mapped onto an item or surface as a result of participating in a particular trace-production context. The likelihood that context-specific traces will be mapped depends on how long (temporal interval) an item or surface is available for mapping. It is not known whether there is a direct or inversely proportional relationship between the interval of context participation and the amount of traces that are mapped. My hunch is that the amount of unambiguous context-specific information mapped varies inversely with the interval of context participation. This is a testable notion, and one that should interest experimental archaeologists. If these relations could be determined, they would be very powerful tools within the domain of Analytic Theory (see below).

Factor 2: Order of Intercontext Movement. The second factor affecting the mapping of traces is the order in which items and surfaces become exposed to different trace-production contexts. This is not unreasonable, given the sequential nature of most activities (Moberg 1971).

At least two kinds of relations characterize the nature of intercontextual movement (see Krause and Thorne 1971 for an excellent problem-solving application of these concepts; cf. Deetz 1968a:35). The first kind is called *commutative*. This relation specifies that the outcome of the interaction between two or more entities is independent of their arrangement (addition and multiplication are good examples). An archaeological example of a commutative relation is represented by Worsaae's Law (Rowe 1962). The order in which individual items are placed in a grave (thus moving from interactive to depositional context) does not affect the end result—that is, the production of a mortuary assemblage.

A *noncommutative* relation obtains when the end result is affected by the arrangement of the variables (subtraction and division are good examples). Archaeological instances would include the reduction of chipped stone (Collins 1975a), the manufacture of ceramic objects (Guthe 1925), and the construction of dwellings (Roberts 1929:10–16; Johnson and Thompson 1963:466–467; Dean 1969:23–26). In fact, most trace-production processes that involve successive modification (addition or deletion) of the properties of materials represent noncommutative relations. The point is that more unambiguous context-specific information is likely to be mapped when the movement of items and surfaces between trace production contexts proceeds noncommutatively. Modern analytic techniques, such as path analysis (Goody 1973), implicational analysis

(Jorgensen 1975), and behavioral chain analysis (Schiffer 1975b; Magers 1975; Stier 1975), are designed to elicit this type of information.

Factor 3: Frequency of Intercontext Movement. It is not only the type and the ordering but the number of trace-production contexts (cf. Webb *et al.* 1966:50) that an item or surface is exposed to that affects the mapping of traces. The frequency of participation in different trace-production contexts affects both the previously mapped traces and the likelihood that further traces will be mapped. Traces mapped in a previous context may remain unaffected (for example, design elements on ceramic objects), be partially modified (for example, the digging of pits through superimposed living surfaces), or be totally obliterated (for example, the decay of vegetal materials in hostile environments) by subsequent mapping. These considerations have particular relevance for inferring how certain processes, like reuse and recycling, affect the formation of archaeological assemblages (for an excellent example see Frison 1968).

Factor 4: Probability of Intercontext Movement. This factor is concerned with determining the probabilities of movement of items and surfaces between different trace-production contexts. If archaeologists knew whether the participation of an item or surface in a particular trace-production context governed the probabilities for movement into another specifiable context, they would have a more powerful framework for understanding how deposits are formed and how information about past phenomena is likely to be encoded in deposits. Consider the following.

The probability that all material remains currently available for archaeological investigation have entered archaeological context is 1 (certainty). The probability that all items and surfaces that have entered archaeological context have also been in interactive context *at least once* is 1 (certainty). However, the probability that all items and surfaces that have entered archaeological context have also been exposed to trace production in depositional context is less than 1. These rather simple probability statements illustrate, nevertheless, that the values for intercontextual movement are not invariable. That is, the relative frequency with which items and surfaces participate in different trace-production contexts is dependent on, and should reflect therefore, variability of past phenomena such as population levels, duration of occupational episodes, and periodicity of occupational episodes (e.g., Cook 1972; Jelinek 1977:19). The development of intercontextual movement probabilities is clearly an area where ethnoarchaeological research could make additional significant contributions (e.g., Pastron 1974).

In addition, our models for understanding how information about past phenomena is transmitted need no longer be portrayed in "black box" fashion (Clarke 1968:59–62; Leach 1973:765; Irwin-Williams 1977). Archaeologists can now go beyond postulating the quantitative relations that obtain between the inputs and outputs of behavioral systems (Flannery 1973). The formulation of intercontextual movement probabilities according to a probability calculus (e.g., Derman *et al.* 1973) should enable archaeologists to determine the inner workings of behavioral systems as reflected in the ways that items and surfaces circulate through different trace-production contexts. Knowledge of this kind has implications for predicting the nature and frequency of traces that the archaeologist can expect to encounter in a recovery context situation (see p. 204 for an example).

Site-Building Processes

As items and surfaces move through the different contexts, the factors discussed above operate in different combinations and with varying intensity, to produce different site-building processes (Binford 1971). Each diagram in Figure 6.1 illustrates a basic site-building process. These site-building processes are the four simplest ones. Items and surfaces may enter and re-enter the same or different contexts a number of different times and in different order (refer to Factors 1–4 above). Each permutation describes a different site-building process.

It would be inadvisable to view the site-building processes as generating different refuse types (Schiffer 1976:27–40). The forcing of all archaeological materials into primary, secondary, and de facto refuse types would only tend to obscure the diversity of site-building processes. For example, for each trace-production context of a single site-building process, materials may be laid down at that location or deposited elsewhere. This possibility would generate at least two distinct refuse types, neither of which conforms to Schiffer's (1972:160–161) original definitions (Sullivan 1976:67–72).

The point of explicating the complex nature of site-building processes is not simply to accentuate the immensity of the archaeologists' task when the time comes to account for site variability. Rather, it is to erect a framework within which archaeologists can begin to define the boundaries of the processes responsible for generating the variability that characterizes archaeological sites and their contents (see Plog 1976). The situation is complicated, of course, by several additional factors. Not all traces survive to be encountered by the archaeologist. In addition, surviving traces do not necessarily represent totally unambiguous sources of past information (Collins 1975b:31), owing to the accumulation of information

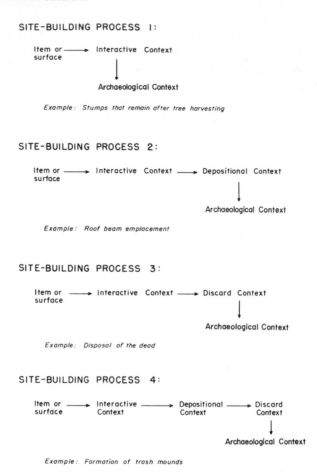

SITE–BUILDING PROCESS 1:

Item or ⟶ Interactive Context
surface

Archaeological Context

Example: Stumps that remain after tree harvesting

SITE–BUILDING PROCESS 2:

Item or ⟶ Interactive Context ⟶ Depositional Context
surface

Archaeological Context

Example: Roof beam emplacement

SITE–BUILDING PROCESS 3:

Item or ⟶ Interactive Context ⟶ Discard Context
surface

Archaeological Context

Example: Disposal of the dead

SITE–BUILDING PROCESS 4:

Item or ⟶ Interactive ⟶ Depositional ⟶ Discard
surface   Context   Context   Context

Archaeological Context

Example: Formation of trash mounds

Figure 6.1. Basic site-building processes.

from a variety of trace-production contexts. Thus, in the process of creating data, the problem for the archaeologist is one of untangling and assigning traces to their appropriate production contexts. Should this task be accomplished successfully, not only will the nature of archaeological sites be rendered more comprehensible, but decisions regarding the selection of properties of depsoits for use as evidence can proceed in a much more informed atmosphere. One of the first steps in this process is to determine the structure of the material remains and evaluate its potential for generating relevant data. Recovery Theory is designed to assist the archaeologist in this task.

RECOVERY THEORY

Recovery Theory is "largely a theory of sampling, field research design and flexible response strategies" (Clarke 1973:16) that enables the archaeologist to make informed decisions prior to and during the manipulation of deposits of material remains. Recovery theoretic concepts are brought into play when archaeologists attempt (*a*) to assess the research potential of archaeological materials and (*b*) to physically acquire representative sets of traces that can be used to support certain claims about the past. These two aspects of recovery theory, which will be discussed separately, are often sequentially related (especially in multistage research projects; Schiffer *et al.* 1978).

It should be noted that Clarke's term for these activities is Retrieval Theory (1973:16). I opt for the term Recovery Theory because, in Clarke's own words, it is a theory designed to link "(3) the sample of that sample (2) which survived to be *recovered*," and "the sample of that sample (3) which was *recovered* by excavation or collection" (1973:16; emphasis added). Further, Clarke's discussion of Retrieval Theory is vague and not developed in detail. The notion of Recovery Theory builds on Clarke's notion of Retrieval Theory but is labeled differently, since it encompasses more concepts and archaeological activities than those cryptically described in his seminal article.

The main value of Recovery Theory is that it enables the archaeologist to approach the intense diversity of recovery context phenomena as systematically as possible. Recovery context is defined as the structure of the archaeological record that exists at the time it is encountered by the archaeologist.

Research Potential

Research potential can be viewed as the degree of probability that the remains under consideration will yield relevant data for a particular problem when subjected to various sorts of archaeological operations. Research potential is determined on the basis of recovery context data and can be acquired in a variety of ways. Using a particular recovery theoretic concept, such as *site,* archaeologists can generate regional site inventories (Ruppé 1966:314). Inventory data coupled with observations of the presence or absence of certain classes of objects (sherds, lithic fragments, bone) can lead to the formulation of site types and the recording of their distribution in terms of local landforms (e.g., Plog 1974). The metrics of sites, such as height of rubble mound (e.g., Kluckhohn 1939b:30) or site size (e.g., Bandelier 1884), are another major source of recovery context data. All these data are useful in establishing the research potential of regions (e.g., Olson 1963), localities (e.g., Haury 1957:2), or sites (e.g., Schiffer and Rathje 1973). Recovery context data obviously assist the archaeologist in determining significance (Moratto and Kelly 1976) and in evaluating the site–research problem match (Reid 1975:127–128).

Also, given a particular problem, these kinds of recovery context data may be used to support statements about the unobservable properties of recovery context phenomena, since, naturally enough, the archaeologist cannot observe the entirety of the archaeological record at once. Examples include parameter estimates of the number of sites in a region (Fuller *et al.* 1976), the probable number of first-story room spaces of masonry pueblos (Plog 1974:88–92), and the depth of sites.

A good example of how this approach can lead to productive results is represented by recent work at a Southwestern cliff-dwelling site called Red Rock House (Reynolds 1975). Information was needed to test a number of hypotheses regarding the architectural correlates of social groups, and changes in their habitations through time. The investigator wanted to retrieve certain context-specific traces indicative of roof construction strategies and architectural growth episodes. These data were obtained efficiently, owing to the archaeologist's knowledge that there was a high probability that traces produced in conjunction with site-building process 2 had survived relatively intact to the present.

The Acquisition of Traces

The second aspect of Recovery Theory consists of methodological concepts that aid the archaeologist in physically acquiring representative sets of traces that have survived to be observed in a recovery context situation (Clarke 1973:16). Sampling strategies (Mueller 1974; Redman 1974), collection and excavation procedures (Redman and Watson 1970; Hester *et al.* 1975), and provenience designation (Schiffer and Reid 1975; Wilcox n.d.) are all methodological concerns whose differential use affects the kinds and quantities of traces, and therefore the nature of the sample, acquired by the archaeologist. The importance of these archaeological activities in initially creating archaeological data is signified by the many cautions that have been issued against their inconstant use (Binford 1975; Cowgill 1975; Wilcox n.d.).

Archaeologists have long been aware that access to past phenomena is always hindered by prevailing recovery context relations (Kluckhohn 1939a:161). The problem centers on the predictable lack of correspondence between samples of material remains and samples of past human behavior (Cowgill 1970; Collins 1975b). One of the major reasons why this "discontinuity" problem has not been resolved satsifactorily, which also accounts for much of the difficulty surrounding the identification of relevant evidence, is that the utility of provenience concepts has not been fully appreciated. Support for this assertion is provided by the common practice of employing an invariable provenience system to monitor a variety of recovery contexts despite the fact that there is a high probability that very different site-building processes produced the deposits. For example, Martin and his associates used arbitrary 20-cm levels to remove the fill from cave sites (Martin *et al.* 1954:24–26) and pit-houses (Martin and Rinaldo 1960:94). The failure to use depositionally significant provenience concepts not only obscures potentially informative recovery context variability (the "homogenization" effect), but inevitably leads to the production of data that refer to a variety of trace-production contexts.

Basically, there are two aspects to the concept of provenience. Each aspect performs a different function in the process of acquiring traces: (*a*) the *documentary* aspect describes the structure of recovery context relations—that is, the position of objects vis-à-vis one another and surfaces (LeBlanc 1976); (*b*) the *interpretive* aspect provides arguments about the operation of the depositional processes responsible for the relationships described by (*a*) (Wilcox n.d.). Data generated in terms of a documentary provenience concept only support conclusions about the nature of present-day recovery spaces rather than past behavioral spaces (Schiffer and Reid 1975). Both aspects of provenience are required, however, to resolve the discontinuity problem. That the application of an expanded concept of provenience can lead to productive results was demonstrated at a Pueblo III site in East-Central Arizona. At that ruin, several construction and abandonment episodes were delineated by using the following logic of provenience relations:

> If trash (a concept defined in the introduction to this paper as the outcome set due to throwing garbage into an abandoned room) occurs above all roofing debris and its associated artifacts in a room space, this relation between the class of roofing debris and that of trash means that the roof had fallen in or collapsed before the trash was deposited. If trash only occurs below all roofing debris, then it must have been deposited while the roof was still intact. From the distribution of different depositional histories of this sort, important inferences about site structure and the relative length of occupation can be deduced [Wilcox 1975:156].

Thus, data generated from materials from these different proveniences, and the relations between the proveniences, inform on different past phenomena because they represent the operation of different site-building processes (Jelinek 1976:23). Further, conclusions supported from these kinds of data are more adequately justified than conclusions supported by data generated only in terms of the documentary aspect of provenience (Wasley 1960:600; Speth and Johnson 1976).

It is hoped that a strong case has been made for the role that the interpretive aspect of provenience plays in understanding the nature and operation of depositional processes, and how those processes impinge upon the acquisition of relevant trace data. However, recovery context data alone are seldom sufficient to substantiate many conclusions. A good example is represented by recent attempts to analyze prehistoric subsistence-settlement systems in the Southwest (Gumerman 1971, 1972; SARG 1974). These studies, and others that rely on some type of distance statistic as a measure of documenting relations between prehistoric communities, are simply monitoring spatial relations between deposits of material remains—that is, recovery context relations. It is not possible to meaningfully discuss variability in prehistoric subsistence-settlement systems without determining the following: "1) absolute contemporaneity between relevant deposits; 2) systemic linkage between relevant deposits; and 3) the boundaries of subsistence settlement systems" (Sullivan and Schiffer 1978:173; see also Gregory 1975). In fact, the relevant trace data needed to support many of the conclusions archaeologists would like to make about subsistence-settlement systems, paleodemography, prehistoric social organization, or chronological relations are available only after recovery context phenomena have been partitioned into context-specific production classes. The tools required to accomplish this task are represented by the concepts and methods of Analytic Theory.

ANALYTIC THEORY

Analytic Theory is "largely a theory of information retrieval, selection, discarding, evaluation, compaction, and decision costs" (Clarke 1973:17). The primary function of Analytic Theory is to provide appropriate methods to partition the properties of archaeological materials according to their context-specific production classes. Archaeologists have long been aware that inadequate attention to this component of the archaeological enterprise can jeopardize efforts to compile relevant data in a systematic and rigorous, but nontrivial, fashion (Steward and Seltzer 1938; Binford 1965; Daniels 1972; Speth and Johnson 1976:43–44). In fact, recognition of the critical nature of analysis has produced considerable controversy over goals and methods (see Hill and Evans 1972 for a comprehensive review). A brief review of some of these controversies is necessary to sort out the questionable assumptions underlying certain analytic theoretic concepts and their applications. It will be argued that these assumptions have interfered with the assembling of relevant data.

There can be no argument with the general goals of classification (one of the major methodological activities of Analytic Theory): (*a*) the organization of observed variability (Hill and Evans 1972:233), (*b*) the facilitation of comparability and communication (Krieger 1960), and (*c*) most important, the generation of relevant data to support conclusions about past phenomena. Whether an archaeologist is simply describing a collection of material or measuring some aspect of variability, typological rules should produce a classification that is consistent and exhaustive (that is, one that unambiguously accommodates the range of observed variability) and is replicable (that is, the set inclusion rules are as free from subjectivity as possible). Problems arise over how these goals are to be realized in a scientific manner.

Attempts to satisfy classificatory adequacy criteria have led to considerable controversy over the nature of the categories used to objectively facilitate the systematization of archaeological phenomena. Much of the controversy has revolved around the epistemological status of two analytic theoretic concepts—the attribute and the type. There are two aspects to these discussions: (*a*) what the types and the attributes represent, and (*b*) what these concepts do (how they function in different analytic activities). It has been asserted that types are elemental units of culture (Krieger 1960:143), represent recurrent sets of attributes (Spaulding 1953:305), characterize classes of materials (Dunnell 1971:157–158), or correspond to patterned human behavior (Watson *et al.* 1971:132). The second aspect of these discussions suggests that types are direct links to understanding a wide range of past phenomena such as historical process (Krieger 1944), emics (Taylor 1973), cognitive processes (Levin 1976), value systems (Gifford 1960), the existence of peoples (Rouse 1965, 1970), and function (Hill 1968; Spaulding 1973), to name only a few of the more common examples.

The point in enumerating these distinctions is to suggest that archaeologists cannot establish *a priori* the connection between the properties of archaeological phenomena and past phenomena (Steward and Seltzer 1938:10). Discussions of the role of classification and typology in Analytic Theory have bypassed the central issue:

> What is noteworthy here is the absence of explicit arguments attempting to demonstrate that a cluster of attributes is a relevant indicator of a particular past use or that the past use is a relevant explanation for the occurrence of the set of attributes [Fritz 1972:143; see also Jelinek 1976:19–20].

In attempting to achieve the general goals of classification mentioned earlier, archaeologists have opted, apparently, for rigor and consistency rather than relevancy in delimiting analytical categories (e.g., Spaulding 1960a, 1971). Consistency and rigor are necessary criteria to be satisfied in order for classifications to be considered adequate (that is, exhaustive and replicable), but it does not follow perforce that they generate relevant data (Krause 1976; Kluckhohn 1939c; see also Cowgill 1977a:328). The utility of classification as a measurement device is seriously compromised if archaeological phenomena (which theoretically represent a variety of past phenomena) are partitioned in terms of a typology whose dimensions crosscut or lump different sources of variability production (in terms of both trace-production contexts and site-building processes; Binford 1965, 1968a:24). The resultant classifications tend not only to obscure potentially informative traces of past phenomena but to generate data that have an uncertain or fictional source of production in the past (Speth and Johnson 1976:50–57; see also Childe 1956:31).

As a potential solution to this problem, Hill and Evans (1972:257) have argued that "by having hypotheses in mind *prior* to type formation, the investigator will not only have the best chance of selecting the relevant attributes, but will also be assured that the types that result are relevant—and he [*sic*] will know ahead of time precisely *how* they are relevant" [emphases in original]. There is an important step missing in this scheme, however. Enumerating potential significata in terms of a particular hypothesis does not entail establishing relevant significata. A step toward establishing relevancy is achieved when the archaeologist assesses the probability that the significata or attributes under consideration would obtain *after* alternate sources of variability had been evaluated and ruled out. This means that specifying which properties of archaeological phenomena are relevant for generating requisite data presupposes that no other (or at least a small enumerable set of) past phenomena could account for those properties. The difficulty of ruling out likely alternatives stems from the fact that different past phenomena may produce markedly similar archaeological phenomena (Plog 1977). The determination of relevant analytic data is clearly a major problem in Analytic Theory. How, precisely, are material remains to be unambiguously partitioned into relevant data sets that support conclusions about past phenomena?

The Partitioning of Traces

It is argued that the use of appropriate analytic theoretic principles, in conjunction with information supplied by recovery context activities (Spaulding 1973; Wilcox 1975, n.d.), greatly increases the investigator's chances of isolating traces that were produced in the same context (and refer, therefore, to the same past phenomena). A considerable body of principles has been systematized to assist archaeologists in partitioning traces mapped onto ceramics in interactive context (Colton 1953; Shepard 1965) and archaeological context (Burgh 1960). Archaeologists interested in supporting conclusions with data generated from lithic analyses can draw on correlates (Schiffer 1974) to assist in partitioning traces mapped onto chipped stone intentionally (Crabtree 1972) or inadvertently (Newcomer 1976) in interactive context, or traces mapped as a result of chipped stone having participated in some other trace-production context (Tringham *et al.* 1974). Similar principles exist for partitioning traces, representing a variety of production contexts, mapped onto adobe structures (Hayden 1957; Wilcox 1977) and occupation surfaces (Haury 1955; Drucker 1972).

When inadequate attention is paid to the processes responsible for trace production, it becomes difficult to determine precisely what phenomena a proposed classification is measuring. This is especially true of conclusions about time relations, which are often based on relative frequencies of ceramic types found at different sites or components of a single site. The relative frequencies reflect differences in sherd counts of the respective pottery types (Ford 1962:37). But sherd counts are recovery context data. As such, they provide quite ambiguous support for chronological conclusions because of the many factors (that is, different trace-production contexts) that contribute to the reduction of vessels into sherds (Pastron 1974). Differences in sherd counts are dependent, at a minimum, on (*a*) the number of whole "parent" vessels of a particular type, (*b*) the number of sherds into which each vessel was reduced, (*c*) the number of sherds of each type recovered, and (*d*) the number of sherds correctly typed (Daniels 1972; Egloff 1973:352). The use of sherd counts as data for quantitative techniques, such as seriation, is likely to produce equivocal results, since the archaeologist has little control over the phenomena being measured. Which of the four factors enumerated above is a seriation ordering? Clearly, a seriation based on relative frequencies of ceramic types may simply be ordering differences in breakage or recovery indices, or both, rather than any sort of time-dependent phenomena (Jelinek 1967:80–84). Although sherd counts have been argued to be relevant evidence for conclusions that did not involve arrangement problems, such as the detection of trampling (McPherron 1967:251–256) or differences in population levels (Cook 1972), their utility as a *sensitive* measure of chronology needs to be reevaluated. Interestingly enough, it has long been argued that a more relevant measure for chronological and other problems is represented by the analytic theoretic concept of *vessel representation*—that is, the number of vessels represented by the sherds of a particular type (Krieger 1949:75–77; Egloff 1973; Doelle 1976:182; see also Baumhoff and Heizer 1959). This concept, along with other measures, especially weight (King 1949:109–115; Solheim 1960; Evans 1973), is more likely to generate relevant data to support conclusions about past phenomena than sherd counts alone (sherd counts, of course, do neatly summarize recovery context information).

CONCLUDING REMARKS

Establishing relevant data to support conclusions about past phenomena is only part of the overall process of generating archaeological knowledge. The relations between facts must be organized coherently. Thus, as Kluckhohn (1940:47) so astutely remarked, "Probably no fact has meaning except within the context of a conceptual scheme." And interestingly enough, since conceptual schemes change, "what is considered evidence to one excavator, or at one time, may not be considered as such for another" (Hole and Heizer 1973:87). The implication is that essentially new or at least different arguments about past phenomena are being advanced that have different probabilities obtaining between the conclusion and the evidence offered in support of it. This dialectic is responsible in part for changing perspectives on persistent archaeological problems (Braidwood 1971; Martin 1971; MacNeish 1974).

Finally, this chapter has attempted to identify some of the processes affecting how information about past phenomena is transmitted to the present via material remains, and to rekindle an appreciation for the priority of archaeological theory in shaping the investigator's notions of how relevant evidence may be assembled. If the arguments developed above are not invalid, it would seem more appropriate to speak in terms of the limitations of our models of trace-production contexts and site-building processes than the "innate" limitations of archaeological phenomena when discussing epistemological matters in archaeological science.

ACKNOWLEDGMENTS

Earlier drafts of this article were revised substantially as a result of comments received from Clara A. Gualtieri, Neal W. Ackerly, Patricia P. Robertson, Stephanie M. Whittlesey, Jeffrey S. Dean, Michael B. Schiffer, David R. Wilcox, Michael W. Graves, Arthur J. Jelinek, R. Gwinn Vivian, and anonymous reviewers. Special thanks are extended to Schiffer, Wilcox, and Graves for their very detailed comments.

REFERENCES

Adams, W. Y.
   1968   Invasion, diffusion, evolution? *Antiquity* **42**:194–215.
   1973   The archaeologist as detective. In *Variation in anthropology: Essays in honor of John C. McGregor,* edited by D. W. Lathrap and J. Douglas. Ann Arbor, Mich.: Braun-Brunfield. Pp. 17–29.

Aron, R.
   1958   Evidence and inference in history. *Daedalus* **87**:11–39.

Ascher, R.
   1968   Time's arrow and the archaeology of a contemporary community. In *Settlement archaeology*, edited by K. C. Chang. Palo Alto, Calif.: National Press Books. Pp. 43–52.

Baldwin, S. J.
   1975   Archaeological reconstruction of social structure: A critical evaluation of two examples from the Southwest. *Western Canadian Journal of Anthropology* **4**:1–22.

Bandelier, A. F.
   1884   Reports by A. F. Bandelier on his investigations in New Mexico during the years 1883–84. *Fifth Annual Report of the Archaeological Institute of America* pp. 55–98.

Baumhoff, M. A. and R. F. Heizer
   1959   Some unexploited possibilities in ceramic analysis. *Southwestern Journal of Anthropology* **15**:308–316.

Beeson, W. J.
   1957   The stages of fill of Room 10 at the Pollock Site. *Plateau* **29**:66–70.

Bidney, D.
   1962   Comments. *Current Anthropology* **3**:503–504.

Binford, L. R.
   1962   Archaeology as anthropology. *American Antiquity* **28**:217–225.
   1965   Archaeological systematics and the study of culture process. *American Antiquity* **31**:203–210.
   1967   Smudge pits and hide smoking: The use of analogy in archaeological reasoning. *American Antiquity* **32**:1–12.
   1968a   Archaeological perspectives. In *New perspectives in archeology,* edited by S. R. and L. R. Binford. Chicago: Aldine. Pp. 5–32.
   1968b   Some comments on historical versus processual archaeology. *Southwestern Journal of Anthropology* **24**:267–275.
   1971   Review of *Reconstructing prehistoric pueblo societies,* edited by W. A. Longacre, University of New Mexico Press, Albuquerque, 1970. *Science* **172**:1225–1226.
   1975   Sampling, judgment and the archaeological record. In *Sampling in archaeology,* edited by J. W. Mueller. Tucson: University of Arizona Press. Pp. 251–257.

Binford, S. R. and L. R. Binford
   1968   Archeological theory and method. In *New perspectives in archeology,* edited by S. R. and L. R. Binford. Chicago: Aldine. Pp. 1–3.

Braidwood, R. J.
   1971   Archeology: The view from Southwestern Asia. *Annual Report of the American Anthropological Association*, 1971 pp. 43–52.

Brew, J. O.
  1946   Archaeology of Alkali Ridge, Southeastern Utah. *Papers of the Peabody Museum* No. 21.
Burgh, R. F.
  1960   Potsherds and forest fires in the pueblo country. *Plateau* **33**:54–56.
Caws, P.
  1969   The structure of discovery. *Science* **166**:1375–1380.
Chang, K. C.
  1967   *Rethinking archaeology.* New York: Random House.
Childe, V. G.
  1956   *Piecing together the past.* New York: Praeger.
Clarke, D. L.
  1968   *Analytical archaeology.* London: Methuen.
  1972   Review of *Explanation in archaeology: An explicitly scientific approach* by Patty Jo Watson, Steven A. LeBlanc, and Charles L. Redman, Columbia University Press, New York. *Antiquity* **46**:237–239.
  1973   Archaeology: The loss of innocence. *Antiquity* **47**:6–18.
Collingwood, R. G.
  1939   *R. G. Collingwood: An autobiography.* London and New York: Oxford University Press.
Collins, M. B.
  1975a   Lithic technology as a means of processual inference. In *Lithic technology, making and using stone tools,* edited by E. Swanson. Chicago: Aldine. Pp. 15–34.
  1975b   Sources of bias in processual data: An appraisal. In *Sampling in archaeology,* edited by J. W. Mueller. Tucson: University of Arizona Press. Pp. 26–32.
Colton, H. S.
  1953   Potsherds. *Museum of Northern Arizona, Bulletin* No. 25.
Colton, H. S., and L. L. Hargrave
  1937   Handbook of northern Arizona pottery wares. *Museum of Northern Arizona, Bulletin* No. 11.
Cook, S.
  1972   Can pottery residues be used as an index to population? *Contributions of the University of California Archaeological Research Facility, Miscellaneous Papers on Archaeology* No. 14.
Copi, I. M.
  1961   *Introduction to logic* (2nd ed.). New York: Macmillan.
Cordell, L. S.
  1977   Late Anasazi farming and hunting strategies: One example of a problem in congruence. *American Antiquity* **42**:449–461.
Cowgill, G. L.
  1970   Some sampling and reliability problems in archaeology. In *Archéologie et calculateurs: Problèmes semiologiques et mathematiques.* (Colloque Internationaux du Centre National de la Récherche Scientifique). Paris: Editions du Centre National de la Récherche Scientifique. Pp. 161–175.
  1975   A selection of samplers: Comments on archaeo-statistics. In *Sampling in archaeology,* edited by J. W. Mueller. Tucson: University of Arizona Press. Pp. 258–274.
  1977a   Albert Spaulding and archaeological method and theory. *American Antiquity* **42**:325–329.

1977b Review of *Spatial analysis in archaeology,* by Ian Hodder and Clive Orton, Cambridge University Press, New York. *Science* **196:**972–973.

Crabtree, D. R.
 1972 An introduction to flintworking. *Idaho State University Museum, Occasional Papers* No. 28.

Daniels, S. G. H.
 1972 Research design models. In *Models in archaeology,* edited by D. L. Clarke. London: Methuen. Pp. 201–229.

Dean, J. S.
 1969 Chronological analysis of Tsegi Phase sites in Northeastern Arizona. *Laboratory. of Tree-Ring Research, Papers* No. 3.

Deetz, J. F.
 1967 *Invitation to archaeology.* Garden City, N.Y.: Natural History Press.
 1968a Cultural patterning as reflected by archaeological materials. In *Settlement archaeology,* edited by K. C. Chang. Palo Alto, Calif.: National Press Books. Pp. 31–42.
 1968b The inference of residence and descent rules from archaeological data. In *New perspectives in archeology,* edited by S. R. and L. R. Binford. Chicago: Aldine. Pp. 41–48.

Derman, C. L., J. Gleser, and I. Olkin
 1973 *A guide to probability theory and application.* New York: Holt.

Doelle, W. H.
 1976 Desert resources and Hohokam subsistence: The Conoco Florence Project. *Arizona State Museum, Cultural Resource Management Section, Archaeological Series* No. 103.

Dozier, E. P.
 1970 Making inferences from the present to the past. In *Reconstructing prehistoric pueblo societies,* edited by W. A. Longacre. Albuquerque: University of New Mexico Press. Pp. 202–213.

Drucker, P.
 1972 Stratigraphy in archaeology: An introduction. *Addison-Wesley Modular Publications in Anthropology* No. 30.

Duff, U. F.
 1904 Some exploded theories concerning southwestern archeology. *American Anthropologist* **6:**303–6.

Dumond, D. E.
 1977 Science in archaeology: The saints go marching in. *American Antiquity* **42:**330–349.

Dunnell, R. C.
 1971 *Systematics in prehistory.* New York: Free Press.

Egloff, B. J.
 1973 A method for counting rim sherds. *American Antiquity* **38:**351–353.

Ehrich, R. W.
 1950 Some reflections on archaeological interpretation. *American Anthropologist* **52**(No. 4, Part 1):468–482.
 1963 Further reflections on archeological interpretation. *American Anthropologist* **65:**16–31.

Evans, J. D.
 1973 Sherd weights and sherd counts—a contribution to the problem of quantifying pottery studies. In *Archaeological theory and practice,* edited by D. E. Strong. New York: Seminar Press. Pp. 131–149.

Flannery, K. V.
1973 Archaeology with a capital S. In *Research and theory in current archeology*, edited by C. L. Redman. New York: Wiley. Pp. 47–58.

Ford, J. A.
1962 A quantitative method for deriving cultural chronology. *Pan American Union, Technical Manual* No. 1.

Frison, G. C.
1968 A functional analysis of certain chipped stone tools. *American Antiquity* **33**:149–155.

Fritz, J. M.
1972 Archaeological systems for indirect observation of the past. In *Contemporary archaeology*, edited by M. P. Leone. Carbondale: Southern Illinois University Press. Pp. 135–157.

Fritz, J. M., and F. T. Plog
1970 The nature of archeological explanation. *American Antiquity* **35**:405–12.

Fuller, S. L., A. E. Rogge, and L. M. Gregonis
1976 The archaeological resources of Orme alternatives: Roosevelt Lake and Horseshoe Reservoir. *Arizona State Museum, Archaeological Series* No. 98.

Gifford, J. C.
1960 The type-variety method of ceramic classification as an indicator of cultural phenomena. *American Antiquity* **25**:341–47.

Goody, J.
1973 Correlation and causal inference: A case study. In *The explanation of culture change: Models in prehistory*, edited by C. Renfrew. Pittsburgh: University of Pittsburgh Press. Pp. 711–716.

Gregory, D. A.
1975 Defining variability in prehistoric settlement morphology. In Chapters in the prehistory of eastern Arizona, IV. *Fieldiana: Anthropology* **65**:40–46.

Gumerman, G. J.
1971 (editor) The distribution of prehistoric population aggregates. *Prescott College, Anthropological Reports* No. 1.
1972 (editor) Proceedings of the Second Annual Meeting of the Southwestern Anthropological Research Group. *Prescott College, Anthropological Reports* No. 3.

Guthe, C. E.
1925 *Pueblo pottery making*. New Haven, Conn.: Yale University Press.

Haury, E. W.
1955 Archaeological stratigraphy. In Geochronology: With special reference to southwestern United States, edited by T. L. Smiley. *University of Arizona, Physical Science Bulletin* No. 26, 126–134.
1956 Speculations on prehistoric settlement patterns in the Southwest. In *Prehistoric settlement patterns in the New World*, edited by G. R. Willey. New York: Wenner-Gren Foundation for Anthropological Research. Pp. 3–10.
1957 An alluvial site on the San Carlos Indian Reservation. *American Antiquity* **23**:2–27.
1958 Evidence at Point of Pines for a prehistoric migration from northern Arizona. In Migrations in New World culture history, edited by R. H. Thompson. *University of Arizona, Social Science Bulletin* No. 27, 1–8.

Hawkes, C.
1954 Archeological theory and method: Some suggestions from the Old World. *American Anthropologist* **56**(No. 2, Part 1):155–168.

Hayden, J. D.
    1957   Excavations, 1940, at University Indian Ruin. *Southwestern Monuments As-sociation, Technical Series* **5.**

Heindl, L. A.
    1955   "Clean Fill" at Point of Pines, Arizona. *The Kiva* **20:**1–8.

Hester, J. J.
    1976   *Introduction to archaeology.* New York: Holt.

Hester, T. R., R. F. Heizer, and J. A. Graham
    1975   *Field methods in archeology.* Palo Alto, Calif.: Mayfield Publishing Co.

Hill, J. N.
    1968   Broken K Pueblo: Patterns of form and function. In *New perspectives in archeology,* edited by S. R. and L. R. Binford. Chicago: Aldine. Pp. 103–142.

    1970a   Broken K Pueblo: Prehistoric social organization in the American Southwest. *University of Arizona, Anthropological Papers* No. 18.

    1970b   Prehistoric social organization in the American Southwest: Theory and method. In *Reconstructing prehistoric pueblo societies,* edited by W. A. Longacre. Albuquerque: University of New Mexico Press. Pp. 11–58.

    1972   The methodological debate in contemporary archaeology: A model. In *Models in archaeology,* edited by D. L. Clarke. London: Methuen. Pp. 61–107.

Hill, J. N., and R. K. Evans
    1972   A model for classification and typology. In *Models in archaeology,* edited by D. L. Clarke. London: Methuen. Pp. 231–274.

Hole, F., and R. F. Heizer
    1973   *An introduction to prehistoric archeology* (3rd ed.). New York: Holt.

Hough, W.
    1919   Exploration of a pit house village at Luna, New Mexico. *Proceedings of the United States National Museum* **55:**409–431.

Irwin-Williams, C.
    1977   Black boxes and multiple working hypotheses: Reconstructing the economy of early Southwest hunters. *The Kiva* **42:**285–299.

Isaac, G. LL.
    1971   Whither archaeology? *Antiquity* **45:**123–129.

Jeffreys, H.
    1973   *Scientific inference* (3rd ed.). London and New York: Cambridge University Press.

Jelinek, A. J.
    1967   A prehistoric sequence in the Middle Pecos Valley, New Mexico. *University of Michigan, Museum of Anthropology, Anthropological Papers* No. **31.**

    1976   Form, function, and style in lithic analysis. In *Cultural change and continuity: Essays in honor of James Bennett Griffin,* edited by C. E. Cleland. New York: Academic Press. Pp. 19–33.

    1977   The Lower Paleolithic: Current evidence and interpretations. In *Annual Review of Anthropology* **6,** edited by B. J. Siegel. Palo Alto: Annual Reviews Inc. Pp. 11–32.

Johnson, A. E., and R. H. Thompson
    1963   The Ringo Site, southeastern Arizona. *American Antiquity* **28:**465–481.

Jorgensen, J.
    1975   A room use analysis of Table Rock Pueblo, Arizona. *Journal of Anthropological Research* **31:**149–161.

Justeson, J. S.
  1973   Limitations of archaeological inference: An information-theoretic approach with applications in methodology. *American Antiquity* **38**:131–149.
King, D. S.
  1949   Nalakihu: Excavations at a Pueblo III site on Wupatki National Monument, Arizona. *Museum of Northern Arizona, Bulletin* No. 23.
Klejn, L. S.
  1977   A panorama of theoretical archaeology. *Current Anthropology* **18**:1–42.
Kluckhohn, C.
  1939a Discussion. In Preliminary report on the 1937 excavations, Bc 50–51, Chaco Canyon, New Mexico, edited by C. Kluckhohn and P. Reiter. *University of New Mexico Bulletin, Anthropological Series* 3(2):151–162.
  1939b The excavation of Bc 51 rooms and kivas. In Preliminary report on the 1937 excavations, Bc 50–51, Chaco Canyon, New Mexico, edited by C. Kluckhohn and P. Reiter. *University of New Mexico Bulletin, Anthropological Series* 3(2):30–48.
  1939c The place of theory in anthropological studies. *Philosophy of Science* **6**:328–344.
  1940   Conceptual structure in Middle American studies. In *The Maya and their neighbors*, edited by C. L. Hay, R. L. Linton, S. K. Lothrop, A. L. Shapiro, and G. C. Vaillant. New York: Appleton. Pp. 41–51.
Kneale, W.
  1952   *Probability and induction.* London and New York: Oxford University Press.
Krause, R. A.
  1976   Review of *Predicting the past: An introduction to anthropological archaeology* by David H. Thomas, Holt, Rinehart and Winston, New York. *Plains Anthropologist* **21**:159–161.
Krause, R. A., and R. M. Thorne
  1971   Toward a theory of archaeological things. *Plains Anthropologist* **16**:245–257.
Krieger, A. D.
  1944   The typological concept. *American Antiquity* **9**:271–288.
  1949   Analysis and interpretation. In The George C. Davis Site, Cherokee County, Texas. *Memoirs of the Society for American Archaeology* No. 5, 57–237.
  1960   Archeological typology in theory and practice. In *Selected papers of the Fifth International Congress of Anthropological and Ethnological Sciences,* edited by A. F. C. Wallace. Philadelphia: University of Pennsylvania Press. Pp. 141–151.
Leach, E.
  1973   Concluding address. In *The explanation of culture change: Models in prehistory,* edited by C. Renfrew. Pittsburgh: University of Pittsburgh Press. Pp. 761–771.
LeBlanc, S. A.
  1976   Archaeological recording systems. *Journal of Field Archaeology* **3**:159–168.
Levin, M. E.
  1976   On the ascription of functions to objects, with special reference to inference in archaeology. *Philosophy of Social Science* **6**:227–234.
Lipe, W. D.
  1970   Anasazi communities in the Red Rock Plateau, southeastern Utah. In *Reconstructing prehistoric pueblo societies,* edited by W. A. Longacre. Albuquerque: University of New Mexico Press. Pp. 84–139.

Longacre, W. A.
  1968   Archeology: Research methods. In *International encyclopedia of the social sciences*. New York: Crowell-Collier. Pp. 386–392.
Lowther, G. R.
  1962   Epistemology and archaeological theory. *Current Anthropology* **3**:495–509.
MacNeish, R. S.
  1974   Reflections on my search for the beginnings of agriculture in Mexico. In *Archaeological researches in retrospect*, edited by G. R. Willey. Cambridge, Mass.: Winthrop. Pp. 207–234.
McPherron, A.
  1967   The Juntunen Site and the late Woodland prehistory of the upper Great Lakes area. *University of Michigan, Museum of Anthropology, Anthropological Papers* No. 30.
MacWhite, E.
  1956   On the interpretation of archeological evidence in historical and sociological terms. *American Anthropologist* **58**:3–25.
Magers, P. C.
  1975   The cotton industry at Antelope House. *The Kiva* **41**:39–48.
Malik, S. C.
  1962   Comments. *Current Anthropology* **3**:506–507.
Martin, P. S.
  1971   The revolution in archaeology. *American Antiquity* **36**:1–8.
Martin, P. S., and J. B. Rinaldo
  1960   Excavations in the upper Little Colorado drainage, eastern Arizona. *Fieldiana: Anthropology* **51**(1).
Martin, P. S., J. B. Rinaldo, and E. Bluhm
  1954   Caves of the Reserve area. *Fieldiana: Anthropology* **42**.
Moberg, C.-A.
  1971   Archaeological context and mathematical models. In *Mathematics in the archaeological and historical sciences*, edited by F. R. Hodson, D. G. Kendall, and P. Tautu. Edinburgh: Edinburgh University Press. Pp. 551–562.
Moratto, M. J., and R. E. Kelly
  1976   Significance in archaeology. *The Kiva* **42**:193–202.
Morwood, M. J.
  1975   Analogy and the acceptance of theory in archaeology. *American Antiquity* **40**:111–116.
Mueller, J. W.
  1974   The use of sampling in archaeological survey. *Society for American Archaeology, Memoirs* No. 28.
Nelson, N. C.
  1919   The archaeology of the southwest: A preliminary report. *Proceedings of the National Academy of Sciences U.S.A.* **5**:114–120.
Newcomer, M. H.
  1976   Spontaneous retouch. *Staringia* **3**:62–64.
Olson, A. P.
  1963   Some archaeological problems of central and northeastern Arizona. *Plateau* **35**:93–99.
Pastron, A. G.
  1974   Preliminary ethnoarchaeological investigations among the Tarahumara. In *Ethnoarchaeology*, edited by C. B. Donnan and C. W. Clewlow. Los Angeles: University of California, Institute of Archaeology.

Piggott, S.
 1960 Prehistory and evolutionary theory. In *Evolution after Darwin* (Vol. 2): *The evolution of man*, edited by S. Tax. Chicago: University of Chicago Press. Pp. 85–97.

Platt, J. R.
 1964 Strong inference. *Science* **146:**347–353.

Plog, F.
 1973 Laws, systems of law, and the explanation of observed variation. In *The explanation of culture change: Models in prehistory*, edited by C. Renfrew. Pittsburgh: University of Pittsburgh Press. Pp. 649–661.
 1974 *The study of prehistoric change*. New York: Academic Press.

Plog, S.
 1976 The inference of prehistoric social organization from ceramic design variability. *Michigan Discussions in Anthropology* **1:**1–47.
 1977 A Multivariate approach to the explanation of ceramic design variation. Ph.D dissertation, University of Michigan. Ann Arbor: University Microfilms.

Randall-MacIver, D.
 1932 Archaeology as a science. *Antiquity* **7:**5–20.

Redman, C. L.
 1974 Archeological sampling strategies. *Addison-Wesley Modular Publications in Anthropology* No. 55.

Redman, C. L., and P. J. Watson
 1970 Systematic, intensive surface collection. *American Antiquity* **35:**279–291.

Reid, J. J.
 1975 Comments on Environment and behavior at Antelope House. *The Kiva* **41:**127–132.

Reid, J. J., M. B. Schiffer, and J. M. Neff
 1975 Archaeological considerations of intrasite sampling. In *Sampling in archaeology*, edited by J. W. Mueller. Tucson: University of Arizona Press. Pp. 209–224.

Reynolds, W. E.
 1975 The use of roof beams for defining social groups: An application of cluster analysis. *Newsletter of Computer Archaeology* **10:**1–18.

Rick, J. W.
 1976 Downslope movement and archaeological intrasite spatial analysis. *American Antiquity* **41:**133–144.

Riley, T. J.
 1974 Constraints on dimensions of variance. *American Antiquity* **39:**489–490.

Roberts, F. H. H.
 1929 Shabik'eschee Village: A late Basket Maker site in the Chaco Canyon, New Mexico. *Bureau of American Ethnology, Bulletin* No. 92.
 1937 Archaeology in the Southwest. *American Antiquity* **3:**3–33.

Rouse, I.
 1958 The inference of migrations from anthropological evidence. In Migrations in New World culture history, edited by R. H. Thompson. *University of Arizona, Social Science Bulletin* No. 27, 63–68.
 1965 The place of "Peoples" in prehistoric research. *Journal of the Royal Anthropological Institute* **95:**1–15.
 1970 Classification for what? *Norwegian Archaeological Review* **3:**4–12.

Rowe, J. H.
  1962   Worsaae's Law and the use of grave lots for archaeological dating. *American Antiquity* **28**:129–137.
Ruppé, R. J.
  1966   The archaeological survey: a defense. *American Antiquity* **31**:313–333.
Salmon, M. H.
  1976   "Deductive" versus "inductive" archaeology. *American Antiquity* **41**:376–381.
Salmon, W. C.
  1966   *The foundations of scientific inference.* Pittsburgh: University of Pittsburgh Press.
  1967   Carnap's inductive logic. *Journal of Philosophy* **44**:725–739.
  1973   *Logic* (2nd ed.). Englewood Cliffs, N.J.: Prentice-Hall.
Sanders, W. T., and B. J. Price
  1968   *Mesoamerica: The evolution of a civilization.* New York: Random House.
SARG, The Members of
  1974   SARG: A cooperative approach towards understanding the location of human settlement. *World Archaeology* **6**:107–116.
Schiffer, M. B.
  1972   Archaeological context and systemic context. *American Antiquity* **37**:156–165.
  1974   Nomothetic aspects of chipped-stone experiments. *Newsletter of Lithic Technology* **3**:46–50.
  1975a An alternative to Morse's Dalton settlement pattern hypothesis. *Plains Anthropologist* **20**:253–266.
  1975b Behavioral chain analysis: Activities, organization, and the use of space. In Chapters in the prehistory of eastern Arizona, IV. *Fieldiana: Anthropology* **65**:103–119.
  1976   *Behavioral archeology.* New York: Academic Press.
Schiffer, M. B., and W. L. Rathje
  1973   Efficient exploitation of the archeological record. In *Research and theory in current archeology*, edited by C. L. Redman. New York: Wiley. Pp. 169–179.
Schiffer, M. B., and J. J. Reid
  1975   A system for designating behaviorally significant proveniences. In The Cache River Archeological Project: An experiment in contract archeology, assembled by M. B. Schiffer and J. H. House. *Arkansas Archaeological Survey, Research Series* No. 8.
Schiffer, M. B., A. P. Sullivan, and T. C. Klinger
  1978   The design of archaeological surveys. *World Archaeology* **10** (in press).
Scriven, M.
  1962   Explanations, predictions, and laws. In *Scientific explanation, space, time* (Studies in the Philosophy of Science, III), edited by H. Feigl and G. Maxwell. Minneapolis: University of Minnesota Press. Pp. 170–230.
Shepard, A. O.
  1965   Ceramics for the archaeologist. *Carnegie Institution of Washington, Publication* No. 609.
Skyrms, B.
  1966   *Choice and chance: An introduction to inductive logic.* Belmont, Calif.: Dickenson Publishing Co.
Slotkin, J. S.
  1952   Some basic methodological problems in prehistory. *Southwestern Journal of Anthropology* **8**:442–443.

Smith, B. D.
  1977 Archaeological inference and inductive confirmation. *American Anthropologist*
        79:598–617.
Smith, M. A.
  1955 The limitations of inference in archaeology. *Archaeological Newsletter* **6**:3–7.
Solheim, W. G.
  1960 The use of sherd weights and counts in the handling of archaeological data.
        Current Anthropology **1**:325–329.
Spaulding, A. C.
  1953 Statistical techniques for the discovery of artifact types. *American Antiquity*
        18:305–313.
  1960a Statistical description and comparison of artifact assemblages. In The Applica-
        tion of quantitative methods in archaeology, edited by R. F. Heizer and S. F.
        Cook. *Viking Fund Publications in Anthropology* No. 28, 60–83.
  1960b The dimensions of archaeology. In *Essays in the science of culture: In honor of
        Leslie A. White*, edited by G. E. Dole and R. L. Carneiro. New York: Crowell.
        Pp. 437–456.
  1968 Explanation in archaeology. In *New perspectives in archeology*, edited by S. R.
        Binford and L. R. Binford. Chicago: Aldine. Pp. 33–39.
  1971 Some elements of quantitative archaeology. In *Mathematics in the archaeolog-
        ical and historical sciences,* edited by F. R. Hodson, D. G. Kendall, and P.
        Tautu. Edinburgh: University Press. Pp. 3–16.
  1973 The concept of artifact type in archaeology. *Plateau* **45**:149–164.
Speth, J. D., and G. A. Johnson
  1976 Problems in the use of correlation for the investigation of tool kits and activity
        areas. In *Cultural change and continuity: Essays in honor of James Bennett
        Griffin,* edited by C. E. Cleland. New York: Academic Press. Pp. 35–37.
Steward, J. H., and F. M. Seltzer
  1938 Function and configuration in archaeology. *American Antiquity* **4**:4–10.
Stier, F.
  1975 Behavioral chain analysis of yucca remains at Antelope House. *The Kiva*
        41:57–64.
Stjernquist, B.
  1971 Archaeological analysis of prehistoric society. *Scripta Minora Regiae
        Societatis Humaniorum Litterarum Lundensis, 1971–1972* No. 1.
Sullivan, A. P.
  1976 The structure of archaeological inference: A critical examination of logic and
        procedure. Written preliminary examination, Department of Anthropology,
        University of Arizona, Tucson.
Sullivan, A. P. and M. B. Schiffer
  1978 A critical examination of SARG. In *Investigations of the Southwestern An-
        thropological Research Group: An experiment in archaeological cooperation*,
        edited by R. C. Euler and G. J. Gumerman. Flagstaff: Museum of Northern
        Arizona. Pp. 168–176.
Swartz, B. K.
  1967 A logical sequence of archaeological objectives. *American Antiquity* **32**:487–
        497.
Taylor, W. W.
  1948 A study of archeology. *American Anthropological Association, Memoirs* **69**.
  1972 Old wine and new skins: A contemporary parable. In *Contemporary archaeol-*

ogy, edited by M. P. Leone. Carbondale: Southern Illinois University Press. Pp. 28–33.
- 1973 Emic attributes and normative theory in archaeology. *Congresso Internazionale Degli Americanisti, 40th Genoa*. Pp. 67–69.

Thomas, D. H.
- 1971 On distinguishing natural from cultural bone in archaeological sites. *American Antiquity* **36**:366–371.
- 1976 *Figuring anthropology*. New York: Holt.

Thompson, R. H.
- 1956 The subjective element in archaeological inference. *Southwestern Journal of Anthropology* **12**:327–332.
- 1958 Modern Yucatecan Maya pottery making. *Society for American Archaeology, Memoirs* No. 15.

Thompson, R. H., and W. A. Longacre
- 1966 The University of Arizona Field School at Grasshopper, east-central Arizona. *The Kiva* **31**:255–275.

Thorne, R. M.
- 1969 Archaeological theory and method: Some inferences and speculations. *Proceedings, Southeastern Archaeological Conference, 24th* pp. 1–6.

Trigger, B. G.
- 1968 *Beyond history: The methods of prehistory*. New York: Holt.

Tringham, R., G. Cooper, G. Odell, B. Voytek, and A. Whitman
- 1974 Experimentation in the formation of edge damage: A new approach to lithic analysis. *Journal of Field Archaeology* **1**:171–196.

Wasley, W. W.
- 1960 Temporal placement of Alma Neck-Banded. *American Antiquity* **25**:599–603.

Watson, P. J., S. A. LeBlanc, and C. L. Redman
- 1971 *Explanation in archeology*. New York: Columbia University Press.

Watson, R. A.
- 1976 Inference in archaeology. *American Antiquity* **41**:58–66.

Webb, E. J., D. T. Campbell, R. D. Schwartz, and L. Sechrest
- 1966 *Unobtrusive measures: Nonreactive research in the social sciences*. Chicago: Rand McNally.

Wilcox, D. R.
- 1975 A strategy for perceiving social groups in puebloan sites. In Chapters in the prehistory of eastern Arizona, IV. *Fieldiana: Anthropology* **65**:120–159.
- 1976 How the Pueblos came to be as they are: The problem today. Written preliminary examination, Department of Anthropology, University of Arizona, Tucson.
- 1977 The architecture of the Casa Grande and its interpretation. Ph.D dissertation, University of Arizona. Ann Arbor: University Microfilms.
- n.d. Sampling pueblos: The implications of room-set additions at Grasshopper Pueblo. In *Multi-disciplinary research at the Grasshopper ruin*, edited by W. A. Longacre. University of Arizona, Anthropological Papers (in press).

Wilford, L. A.
- 1954 Archaeological method in the eastern United States. In *Method and perspective in anthropology*, edited by R. F. Spencer. Minneapolis: University of Minnesota Press. Pp. 171–191.

Willey, G. R.
- 1953 Inference and analogy in archeology. In *An appraisal of anthropology today*,

edited by S. Tax, L. C. Eiseley, I. Rouse, and C. F. Voegelin. Chicago: University of Chicago Press. Pp. 251–254.

1966   *Introduction to American archaeology* (Vol. 1): *North and Middle America*. Englewood Cliffs, N.J.: Prentice-Hall.

Willey, G. R., and P. Phillips

1958   *Method and theory in American archaeology*. Chicago: University of Chicago Press.

Wilmsen, E. N.

1974   *Lindenmeier: A Pleistocene hunting society*. New York: Harper and Row.

Independent Dating in Archaeological Analysis

JEFFREY S. DEAN

INTRODUCTION

If there is one issue on which nearly all archaeologists can agree, it is the importance of chronology. Control of the temporal variable is crucial to all types of archaeological research, from local culture–historical reconstruction to general processual explanations of human behavior. As we are fond of pointing out, our discipline's major contribution to knowledge of human behavior derives from our control of behavioral data that span long intervals of time (Binford 1962:224, 1972:2; Braidwood 1968:226; Plog 1974:11). Our unequaled ability to deal with long-term, systemic changes in human culture and behavior establishes the credentials of archaeology as a social science. The archaeological study of "process"—processes of technological and sociocultural stability, change, and evolution, processes of adaptation to changing environmental conditions, and so on—is predicated on the accurate measurement of change through time. Similarly, attempts to deal with prehistoric social units and their interactions depend on temporal controls refined enough to establish the absolute contemporaneity (Dean 1969:198) of the inferred social units. In addition, many analytical techniques—nearest-neighbor analysis is one—require that the units of analysis (sites, artifacts, etc.) be shown to be contemporaneous.

The importance of chronological control has stimulated the application

ADVANCES IN ARCHAEOLOGICAL METHOD AND THEORY, VOL. 1

of many dating methods in archaeology. Some of these, such as stratig-raphy and stylistic attribute analysis, are inherently archaeological. Others, such as dendrochronology, radiometry, and archaeomagnetism, are nonarchaeological in that the archaeological origin of the dated mate-rial is irrelevant to the production of dates. The purpose of this paper is to present, within the framework of a provisional model of the archaeologi-cal dating process, an analysis of the general role of independent dating methods and dates in archaeological research. The analysis is intended to isolate some of the *general* problems that arise in connection with the use of such dates and to suggest some ways of resolving these problems. Three rather disparate dating methods—radiocarbon dating, archae-omagnetic dating, and dendrochronology—provide examples to illus-trate the general points raised. None of these techniques is considered in detail; they are used solely for illustrative purposes.

The welter of independent dating methods—each with its own theory, principles, assumptions, and limitations—creates considerable potential for confusion and error in the application of the dates to archaeological phenomena. In addition, the myriad of variables that enters into any archaeological dating exercise can give rise to situations in which the apparent relationship of a date to an archaeological feature is spurious or in which the nature of the relationship is indeterminate. The vast potential for dating uncertainty and error can be mitigated by the development of a coherent theory of the archaeological dating process. Such a theory would, among other things, help isolate sources of dating error and provide formal means of recognizing and dealing with such errors. An integrated archaeological dating theory would include many elements, among them a vocabulary of concepts, a set of assumptions and tenets, a general model of the archaeological dating process, and specific models that relate each independent dating technique to the context of ar-chaeological research. The models would specify sets of conceptual and substantive conditions and relationships that define the structure and operations of the dating process.

Time and space limitations prohibit any attempt to develop a com-prehensive archaeological dating theory here. Rather, I intend to present only a preliminary general model of the archaeological dating process to illuminate the role of independent dates in archaeological analysis. This effort is limited to only two of the many functions performed by models of this type: (*a*) specification of the relationships that link the various dating systems, the dates they produce, past human behavior, and archaeology; and (*b*) the isolation of variables that produce dating problems. Let me emphasize at the outset that what follows is offered not as any sort of final conceptualization, but as a stimulus to the evaluation, criticism, and revision that will lead ultimately to a comprehensive theory of the dating process in archaeology. In line with this orientation, the labels attached to various parts of the model are purely descriptive and provisional.

The preliminary model of the archaeological dating process owes much to Schiffer's (1972, 1973, 1976) analyses of the relationships between human behavior and the material remains of that behavior; to Reid's (1973) elaboration of Schiffer's analyses; to Sullivan's (1976) critical appraisal of these ideas; to Wilcox's (1975, 1976) ideas on the same subjects; and to Clarke's (1973) and Krause and Thorne's (1971) considerations of archaeological systematics. Rather than attempt to apply their ideas directly to the construction of the dating model, I have adapted them to the requirements of my task. Many of the ideas concerning the nature of the dates and dating are grounded in the work of Bannister (1962, 1969), Haury (1935), and Smiley (1955).

DEFINITION OF TERMS

The following discussion of archaeological dating introduces a few new terms and employs some familiar terms in rather special ways. To clarify this presentation, I attempt to adhere strictly to the definitions of the terms given here and to employ them consistently. The term *dating* refers to the placement in time of events relative either to one another or to any established scale of temporal measurement. *Dates* are the "values" that specify the temporal placement of a dated event. These "values" can be either relative—earlier than, later than, etc.—or expressed in the units of a scale of temporal measurement—terrestrial years, radiocarbon years, etc. The nature of such dates varies with the techniques by which they are established and with the units of measurement in which they are expressed. Smiley (1955) provides a typology of dates that makes explicit some of these distinctions and facilitates the application of such dates in archaeological analysis. *Relative placement* involves the positioning of sequential events in the order of their occurrence. Thus, an event can be recognized as being earlier than, contemporaneous with, or later than other events, but the magnitudes of the temporal intervals separating events are unknown. *Time placement* dates are expressed as intervals rather than points on a scale of temporal measurement. Dates of this type represent samples of populations of possible observations that are subject to statistical error, and the dates are expressed in terms of probability models. Thus, there is a finite chance that a time placement date is wrong. Furthermore, the time scales involved in this type of dating are not necessarily constant, nor do they necessarily incorporate standard units of time measurement. A carbon-14 year is not a fixed entity, nor does it correspond exactly to a terrestrial year. An archaeomagnetic year is not a temporal unit at all but a spatial orientation translated into a temporal frame of reference. Smiley's third type of dating is *absolute placement*, which is based on standard time scales with fixed units of magnitude. Absolute dates are expressed as points on standard scales of time measurement.

Independent dates are dates derived by methods that are totally independent of archaeological context and systematics. The theories, principles, and techniques that underlie the production of independent dates are unrelated to archaeological theory and method. The properties that permit certain materials to be dated are imparted to the materials by nonbehavioral and nonarchaeological processes, and the materials would date the same whether they came from an archaeological context or from some other source.

Dating potential refers to the likelihood of an object's yielding a date to some chronometric method. Radiocarbon dating potential varies with the age of the sample; tree-ring dating potential is a function of species and of the character of ring series; archaeomagnetic dating potential varies directly with the quantity of magnetized particles in the sample. *Dating error* applies to situations in which a date is actually wrong owing to human mistakes, equipment malfunction, or unknown or uncontrolled factors. Dating error is distinguished from dating anomaly, which is defined below.

An important set of terms delimits the events to which independent dates are applied. Four types of event are recognized, and they must be carefully distinguished. The *dated event* (E_d) is the event that is actually dated by any chronometric technique in a particular situation (Figure 7.1). The dated event varies with the chronometric method employed. Dendrochronology specifies the year in which a particular layer of xylem cells was produced. Radiocarbon dates on wood are time placement estimates of the growth of groups of rings, while carbon-14 dates derived from other organic materials usually apply to the death of the organism. Archaeomagnetism's E_d is the last time the temperature of a clay object exceeded a critical point. Other chronometric methods provide dates applicable to other events.

Some methods are capable of directly dating more than one event. Dendrochronology has a wide range of potentially datable events: every growth increment in a datable ring series, the germination of the plant, injuries to the plant, the death of the organism, and others. Radiocarbon dates may apply to similar events in the histories of sufficiently long-lived plants, but carbon-14 dates from other organic materials apply only to the

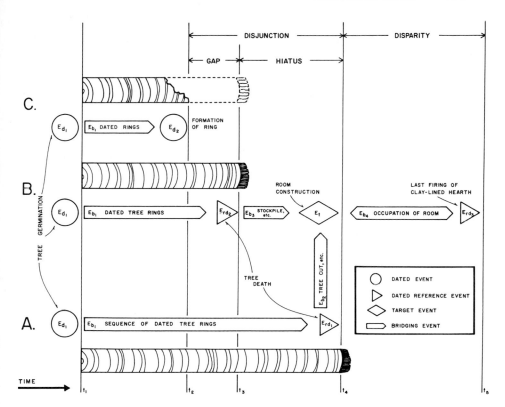

Figure 7.1. Archaeological dating relationships exemplified by tree-ring and archaeomagnetic dates. E_{d1} represent tree germinations at t_1 that are related to the trees' deaths (E_{rd1} and E_{rd2} at t_4 and t_3) and to the formation of a particular ring (E_{d2} at t_2) by the sequence of years recorded in the trees' ring chronologies (E_{b1}). E_{rd3} is the firing of a clay hearth at t_5, and E_t is the construction at t_4 of a room in which the wood and hearth are found. The simplest dating situation is represented by A, in which the relationship between E_{rd1} and E_t is specified by events (E_{b2}) that establish contemporaneity at t_4. B indicates a situation in which a hiatus exists between E_{rd2} at t_3 and E_t at t_4, with the two events joined by other bridging events (E_{b3}). C illustrates a situation in which both a gap between E_{d2} at t_2 and E_r at t_3 and a hiatus between E_r at t_3 and E_t at t_4 exist. A disparity between E_t at t_4 and E_{rd3} at t_5 is spanned by another set of events (E_{b4}) related to the occupation and use of the room.

demise of the organisms. Archaeomagnetic dates apply to only one event—the last time the critical temperature was exceeded. Only a few of the datable events that may be associated with any dating method are related to the events that archaeologists (or other scientists) are interested in dating. For example, the pith date of a roof beam in an archaeological site is totally unrelated to any of the behavioral events associated with that site. The death date of such a tree is far more closely related to the procurement and use of the wood. In contrast, the death date of a tree buried in alluvium is usually difficult to relate to sedimentary events of interest to a geologist. Here the pith date, which indicates when the tree began growing, is the date of interest, because it can be related to the onset of the alluvium that buried it. The potentially datable event that is most closely related to the phenomenon to which the date is to be applied is called the *reference event* (E_r). It is in reference to the date of this event that independent dates are related to nonchronometric occurrences. The reference event often coincides with the dated event, a situation that is symbolized by E_{rd}, but it need not (Figure 7.1). The E_d of tree-ring and carbon-14 dates from the inner portions of long-lived perennial plants can fall centuries earlier than the archaeologically applicable E_r of the plants' deaths. On the other hand, the E_r and E_d are the same for many radio-carbon dates (organisms' deaths) and all archaeomagnetic dates (critical temperature attainment).

The *target event* (E_t) is the event to which the date is to be applied by the chronometrician or other scientist (Figure 7.1). Target events include things such as biological events in the lives of trees and forests, episodes in the alluvial history of drainage systems, behavioral events in the history of a human society, and many others. Usually, but not always, the target events are not directly related to the dated or reference events. For example, the germination date (E_{rd}) of a tree buried in alluvium is only indirectly related to the onset of deposition (E_t). Similarly, the death date of a tree (E_{rd}) may or may not be associated with construction events connected with an archaeological feature (E_t). The radiocarbon date of a deer bone (E_{rd}) is directly related to the killing of the animal by a hunter (E_t), but only indirectly related to the refuse deposit (E_t) in which the bone is found. An archaeomagnetic date from a hearth (E_{rd}) is more closely associated with the last use of the house (E_t) than with its con-struction (E_t).

Bridging events (E_b) are events used to establish a link between a dated event and a target event. The felling of a live tree by humans is a bridging event that relates the death of the tree (E_{rd}) to the construction of a feature (E_t) that contains wood from the tree. Stratigraphic relationships between a dated object and an archaeological feature specify a series of E_b that are used to evaluate the degree of applicability of the date to the E_t represented by the feature.

The term *dating anomaly* refers to a condition in which the chronomet-ric date is not applicable to the target event (Figure 7.1). A dating anomaly exists whenever the dated event is not coterminus with the target event $(E_d \neq E_t)$, the E_d falling either earlier or later than the E_t. Four terms specify the nature of dating anomalies (Figure 7.1), the first three referring to situations in which the E_d falls short of the E_t, the last one to situations in which the E_d is later than the E_t. The *disjunction* is the temporal interval between E_d and E_t. The *gap* is the temporal interval between E_d and E_r. The *hiatus* is the temporal interval between E_r and E_t. The sum of the gap and the hiatus equals the disjunction. The *disparity* is the temporal interval between E_t and E_d when the latter is *later* than the former.

Two terms specify the relationship between E_d and E_t. *Convergence* exists when the two are coeval ($E_d = E_t$). This occurs when both the disjunction (and therefore the gap and the hiatus) and the disparity equal zero. The fact that the dated event is contemporaneous with the target event (convergence exists) does not mean that the former dates the latter. The latter condition prevails only when there is convergence and when the date is relevant to the target event. *Relevance* refers to the degree to which the date is applicable to the E_t. To present an extreme example, a death date (E_{rd}) of A.D. 1250 for a roof beam in Site A is irrelevant to the dating of the construction of a room (E_t) in Site B even though the latter was built in 1250, and the two events converge. Obviously, the date is far more relevant to the construction of the room in which the beam was found. Relevance is a relative rather than an absolute concept, and it must be demonstrated or argued on the basis of archaeological or other evidence. One aspect of relevance specification is the *estimation* of the magnitude of the disjunction or disparity between E_d and E_t, a procedure that is discussed later. Another aspect of establishing relevance is the use of E_b to connect E_d with E_t.

THE DATING PROBLEM IN ARCHAEOLOGY

A simple example of a hypothetical archaeological dating situation illustrates some of the concepts developed in the preceding section and indicates some of the problems that arise in connection with the use of independent dates. Suppose we have a single tree-ring date of A.D. 1180 from a beam in the roof of a masonry room. Before the 1180 date can be applied to any behavioral phenomena associated with the room, a number of problems must be resolved. First, E_t appropriate to the kind of date and the particular dating situation must be specified. Let us take room construction as our E_t for this exercise. Next we must establish the E_r, the potentially datable event in the life of a tree that is most closely associated with the E_t. In this case, the E_r, is the death of the tree. Having established E_t and E_r, we must determine whether the E_d and the E_r are the same. If they are not, if the exterior portion of the log has been destroyed and the outermost dated ring is not the terminal ring, we have a gap between E_d and E_r that must be estimated. Ideally, however, we will be able to show that the date does in fact apply to the tree's terminal ring ($E_d = E_r$) and be spared the necessity of estimating a gap. Let us assume this to be the case for our example and consider the date of 1180 to specify the last year of the tree's life (E_{rd}).

Given a terminal ring date of 1180 for our sample, we must next attempt to assess the relevance of the date to the construction of the room. Having eliminated a gap from our problem, we still must determine whether a disjunction, consisting entirely of a hiatus between E_{rd} and E_t, or a disparity exists, or whether E_{rd} and E_t converge, and if they converge whether E_{rd} is relevant to dating E_t. It should be possible to establish the convergence and relevance of the date of the death of the tree (E_{rd}) to an E_b, the felling of the tree by humans. The issue of relevance then devolves into the problem of evaluating the relationship between E_b, tree felling, and E_t, room construction. This problem is approached through the examination of the archaeological evidence that pertains to other E_b, those involved in room construction. A number of questions would have to be investigated to establish the relevance of the 1180 date to the building of the room. Was the beam cut to fit this particular room, or was it salvaged from an older room or trash deposit? Was the timber part of the original roof, or was it a later repair addition? Is the extant roof the original roof of the room, or a replacement for an earlier roof? A host of such questions, many of them specific to the particular situation, may have to be answered before the relevance of the date for the E_t is established.

As E_t becomes further removed from E_d or E_{rd}, the complexity of the relevance arguments increases as more E_b have to be considered, and the degree of relevance usually declines. Our 1180 date is relevant to the site by virtue of the room's inclusion in the site, but it is far more relevant to the room itself because fewer E_b are involved in relating E_{rd} to E_t. The relevance of the date for other features in the site is argued by analyzing the E_b relationships—architectural, stratigraphic, stylistic, artifactual, etc.—that link the dated room with the other features. Here we are concerned with establishing the relationship of a primary E_t (the construction of the room) to secondary E_t (the building of other features) through the media of E_b, and these arguments of relevance are pyramided on those used to establish the relevance of E_{rd} to the primary E_t.

Despite its manifest complexity, the foregoing example is really fairly simple as dating problems go. It involves only a few of the many problems that can arise in the use of independent dates. The complexity of most dating situations and the number of variables involved in them provide fertile ground for the germination of all kinds of dating anomaly. The model of the archaeological dating process is designed to wring some order from this apparent chaos by isolating general conditions and principles that characterize most dating situations. The model specifies the sources of anomaly-producing variables, provides a priori criteria for detecting potential dating anomalies, and indicates ways in which chronological errors caused by such anomalies can be eliminated or corrected.

THE GENERAL MODEL

The provisional model of the archaeological dating process (Figures 7.2 and 7.3) takes only one of several equally appropriate forms possible. This form is used here because it articulates with other models of archaeological systematics (Reid 1973; Schiffer 1972, 1973, 1976) and because it adequately represents the conditions and relationships that structure the archaeological dating system. Although the model is intended to represent a single system of relationships, it is presented in two aspects to facilitate discussion. The first aspect (Figure 7.2) concerns the interactional relationships among the various components of the model. This aspect serves

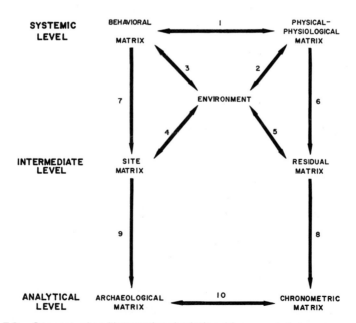

Figure 7.2. Conceptual and interactional relationships among the components of the general archaeological dating model.

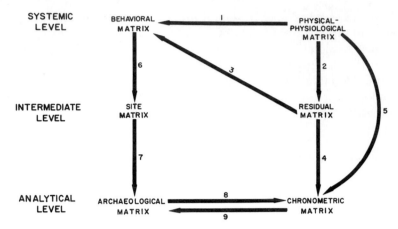

Figure 7.3. Material and information flow among the components of the general archaeological dating model.

as a basis for an analysis of the articulation of chronometry and archaeology in the context of the archaeological dating process. The second aspect (Figure 7.3) indicates the "flow" relationships of the model—that is, the passage of materials and information among the components of the system.

The model is divided vertically into two major *fields* that represent the "content" (concepts, methods, materials, etc.) of the scientific disciplines involved, archaeology on the left, chronometry on the right. Both fields are divided horizontally into three *levels*: systemic, intermediate, and analytical. Levels have temporal as well as structural implications. Events of the systemic level precede those of the intermediate and analytical levels, and intermediate-level events precede analytical-level events. Systemic and intermediate events produce the materials and relationships that are processed on the analytical level.

The levels are composed of units called *matrices*. This term is used to obviate confusion with Schiffer's (1972) concept of "context." Although similar in meaning and placement in the models, "matrix" and "context" are not synonymous. Matrices are networks of conditions, forces, and relationships that encompass the material elements that are the focus of archaeological and chronometric analysis.

The systemic level consists of two matrices, physical-physiological and behavioral. The former includes the physical-chemical and physiological processes that produce the properties that permit the dating of objects by various chronometric methods. The latter is the system of behavioral processes and relationships that impart behavioral information to objects, and it is essentially identical to Schiffer's (1972:157) systemic context.

The intermediate level is really a subunit of the systemic level, because the elements of the former continue to participate in and be affected by environmental interactions (decay, weathering, etc.). Nevertheless, the two levels are distinguished to signify the crucial fact that neither relevant behavioral nor relevant chronological information is imparted to materials on the intermediate level. Any such information added at this level is not relevant to the behavioral and natural events and processes of the systemic level. Processes that modify or destroy behavioral and chronological information operate on the intermediate level. The component labeled "environment" in Figure 7.2 expresses the fact that the elements of the systemic and intermediate levels are connected by networks of environmental interactions.

The intermediate-level site matrix includes the structure and relationships of the material products of human behavior after those products have been removed from participation in human behavioral systems. This unit corresponds in part to Schiffer's (1972:157) archaeological context. The residual matrix is really a component of the physical-physiological matrix and is occupied only by dead organisms whose remains have not been used by human beings or succumbed to weathering or decay. The material remains of an organism pass into the residual matrix upon the death of the organism. The death is usually a result of natural causes; however, the remains of organisms killed but not used by humans also exist in the residual matrix.

The analytical level includes two matrices, archaeological and chronometric, that represent the human activities that process and evaluate information (archaeological data and independent dates) about the material remains of past behavioral and natural events. The archaeological matrix is not the same as Schiffer's (1972:157) archaeological context in that the matrix does not include the materials and relationships in the ground—that is the site matrix. Rather, the archaeological matrix has two major components. The first is the *archaeological record*—that is, those site materials, element attributes, and relationships that are perceived *and* recorded by archaeologists. The second is the behavioral systems within which archaeologists manipulate and interact with the elements of the archaeological record to produce information on the behavioral matrix in which the materials and relationships originated. The chronometric matrix includes the behavioral contexts within which chronometricians derive chronological information from potentially datable materials.

Systemic-level phenomena are important to the analysis of independent dating in archaeology for three reasons. First, it is at this level that material objects are imbued with behavioral and chronological information. Second, the explanation of systemic-level events and processes is a major goal of both archaeology and chronometry. Third, the general and specific theoretical systems that underlie such explanations are structured in no small measure by prevailing conceptions of the conditions and relationships that obtain in the systemic milieu.

The production of behavioral information at the systemic level has been adequately covered by others (Clarke 1973; Krause and Thorne 1971; Schiffer 1972, 1973, 1976; Sullivan 1976), and we can focus here on the chronometric aspect of the problem. The interactions of physical-physiological matrix organic and inorganic elements with each other and with other aspects of their environments (arrow 2) impart to their material remains special properties that allow modern science to date certain events connected with the existence of these entities. The property of tree-ring series that permits them to be dated, crossdatable variation in the widths of the annual rings, is a result of the interaction of the trees' physiological processes with external environmental variables (Fritts 1976). The properties that establish radiocarbon datability are the outcome of four processes (Michels 1973:148–167; Ralph 1971; Sheppard 1975; Willis 1969): (*a*) the production of radioactive carbon-14 atoms in the upper atmosphere; (*b*) the diffusion of carbon-14 atoms throughout the atmosphere to produce a fairly constant ratio of radioactive to nonradioactive carbon throughout the world; (*c*) the absorption by living organisms of carbon atoms in the proportion of radioactive to nonradioactive isotopes that prevails in the atmosphere; and (*d*) the decay of carbon-14 atoms into atoms of nitrogen 14. Archaeomagnetic datability results from the interaction of ferrous inorganic materials with the earth's geomagnetic field, which, because it has changed in orientation over time, provides scales of temporal variation against which suitable materials can be dated (Bucha 1971; Cook 1969; Michels 1973:130–147). This process is triggered when the iron-bearing material is heated to a temperature high enough to free the magnetic particles to respond to the prevailing orientation of the geomagnetic field. When the temperature falls below the critical threshold, the magnetic particles are fixed in the positions they assumed when heated.

Because the systemic level consists of interrelated networks of states and processes, operations that take place in one systemic matrix can affect the other matrices directly (arrow 1) or through the medium of the environment (arrows 2 and 3). Human behavior can affect tree physiology directly, as when logging alters competition relationships among unharvested trees, or indirectly, as when air pollution adversely affects trees' life processes. Human behavior probably has little direct impact on the absorption of carbon by organisms; however, the release into the environment of ancient carbon produced by the burning of fossil fuels and of radioactive products of nuclear explosions has drastically altered the prevailing ratio of radioactive to nonradioactive carbon atoms. Behavioral impact on the earth's geomagnetic field and on the response of magnetic particles to the field has probably been minor.

Intermediate- and analytical-level conditions and relationships are also important variables in the archaeological dating process. Arrows 4 and 5 in Figure 7.2 indicate processes, such as weathering and decay, that link the elements of the site and residual matrices to their environments. Arrows 6 through 9 specify the one-way transfer processes that join the components of successive levels. Events of the physical-physiological and behavioral matrices impinge, respectively, on the elements of the residual and site matrices, and residual and site phenomena affect the elements of the chronometric and archaeological matrices. Arrow 10 represents material, informational, and behavioral exchanges among archaeologists and chronometricians.

The second aspect of the general model (Figure 7.3) illustrates the flow of materials and information through the system. A potentially datable object begins its existence on the systemic level as part of an organism or as an inorganic entity. The material is removed from the physical-physiological matrix (arrow 1) when it is procured for some use by a group of people. Potentially datable materials can also pass directly into the residual matrix (arrow 2) and then be extracted from that matrix for use in the behavioral matrix (arrow 3) or for study in the chronometric matrix (arrow 4). Materials may also pass directly from the physical-physiological matrix into the chronometric matrix (arrow 5), as when a living tree is cored for dendrochronological analysis. Those materials that do pass into the behavioral matrix are usually converted into one or more artifacts, although in some cases, such as the use of the material for food, the residue (bones, corn cobs, etc.) is nonartifactual. As time passes, an artifact may maintain its original function within the behavioral system, or it may undergo a number of transformations. For example, it may be removed from its original context, perhaps modified in some way, and then reused for the same or a different purpose, a process that can be repeated many times. The object may even be consumed, as when wood is used as fuel. If it is not consumed, the object is eventually discarded, either individually or along with many other artifacts and materials when the site is abandoned. At this juncture the materials pass from the behavioral matrix into the site matrix (arrow 6).

The elements that constitute the site matrix undergo further transformations as natural processes and some types of human activity impinge on the site. Decomposition, weathering, erosion, animal activity, and other processes take their toll, altering materials and relationships. Human activities—such as the salvage of building materials, the reutilization of the site locus, and pot hunting—also alter materials and associations in the site matrix. The processes are halted when the site is excavated, and the elements and their relationships are fixed into the archaeological record (arrow 7). At this locus the materials are not only preserved in a field of observed spatial and associational relationships, they also become participants in another behavioral and conceptual system, that of archaeological analysis.

Potentially datable materials are included among the elements recovered from the site. These objects are transferred to the appropriate chronometricians for analysis (arrow 8), where they participate in the behavioral systems that make up the chronometric matrix. Chronometricians provide archaeologists with dates for the samples and with any additional information that can be derived from the specimens (arrow 9). These data are then plugged back into their proper places in the archaeological record for use in extracting information about the behavior of the inhabitants of the site.

Archaeology and chronometry are related by theoretical considerations as well as by the interactions among the elements of the matrices (Figure 7.2) and by the passage of materials and information through the system (Figure 7.3). The most general of these relationships is established by the two disciplines' shared objective of explaining systemic level events and processes. These linkages between the model's two fields are embodied in current understandings of the systemic conditions and interactions that impart behavioral and chronological information to material objects, of the processes of material transfer among matrices and levels, of the intermediate level interactions that destroy or modify behavioral and chronological information, and of the analytical level operations that exploit the informational content of these materials.

Interactions among the elements of the physical-physiological matrix and their environment (Figure 7.2, arrow 2) are explained by ecological theories and by special chronometric models of the interactions that impart datability to various materials. Biological and ecological theories and dendroclimatic models (Fritts 1976:231–238; Fritts *et al.* 1965) specify the environmental variables and relationships that produce datable tree-ring series. The theories of physics, chemistry, and atmospheric science in conjunction with special models—the half-life of carbon 14 and the various schemes for calibrating the radiocarbon and absolute time scales

(Damon *et al*. 1974; Ralph and Michael 1970; Stuiver and Suess 1966)—explain the processes that impart radiocarbon datability to the remains of formerly living organisms. Physical and geological theories coupled with regionally specific models of temporal variability in geomagnetic orientation (Bucha 1971) account for the datable properties of some burned clays. Systemic-level interrelationships between human behavior and the environment (Figure 7.2, arrow 3) are far more complex and subtle than are the environmental relationships of living organisms, isotopes of carbon, and magnetized particles; consequently, the former are less well understood. No general theories explain these behavior–environment relationships, although certain facets of ecological and anthropological theory and some limited models are applicable to these interactions. Systemic interactions between the behavioral and physical-physiological matrices (Figure 7.2, arrow 1) are properly a subject for anthropological theory. However, because of their neglect by anthropologists and their importance to archaeology, explanation of these relationships has by default fallen into the domain of archaeological theory. Intermediate-level environmental interactions of the residual and site matrices (Figure 7.2, arrows 4 and 5) are covered by ecological, geological, and archaeological theories and models.

Archaeologists, like other anthropologists, are concerned with understanding the roles of human culture and behavior in the complex relational networks of the systemic level. Archaeologists pursue this objective through the medium of the archaeological record, which is a record of the current state of the site and not of the material assemblage when it was part of a functioning behavioral system (Binford 1972:333–334; Reid 1973). The task of archaeology, which is performed within the framework of archaeological theory, is to relate the existing assemblage of elements and relationships to the antecedent behavioral system that produced the site. Four aspects of general arch: .ological theory are important to the consideration of independent dating in archaeology. The first deals with the implantation of behavioral information onto material objects and concerns the manufacturing, reuse, and other behavioral matrix processes that alter materials. The second is concerned with the transformations undergone by material elements in their passage from the behavioral into the site matrix (Figure 7.2, arrow 7) and involves conceptions of the recycling, discard, and abandonment behavior of the inhabitants of the site. Another aspect deals with the processes that affect materials during the interval between their entry into the site matrix and excavation of the site. The transformations include environmental interactions (Figure 7.2, arrow 4) and human activities that alter the site elements and their interrelationships. The fourth aspect, which is dependent on the others, involves the analytical-level processes whereby archaeological data are translated into information on the behavior of the people who produced the site.

The structure of chronometric research is similar to that of archaeology. Chronometric materials—plant and animal remains, tree-ring sequences, fired clay, etc.—exist in the present and contain information pertinent to past systemic events. The relationships between these materials and the physical-physiological and residual matrices are specified by the assumptions and principles that structure research in the various chronometric disciplines. These theories are concerned with the implantation of chronological information onto objects on the systemic level, with the modification of this information during transfer to, residence in, and passage out of the residual matrix, and with analytical-level means of extracting chronological information from the materials. Arrow 10 in Figure 7.2 represents a set of relationships that are the special domain of archaeological dating theory, which at present is in a rudimentary state of development.

APPLICATION OF THE MODEL

Establishing the relevance of independent dates for behavioral matrix target events is the major problem involved in the archaeological use of such dates. The detection and elimination of dating anomalies caused either by dating error or by disjunctions or disparities between dated and target events are vital to the resolution of this problem. The dating model's contribution to this endeavor lies in its power to isolate anomaly-producing variables in the dating system. It indicates a priori the points of origin and the nature of possible dating anomalies, alerts archaeologists to the magnitude of this problem, and indicates ways of recognizing and resolving such anomalies. The model's efficacy in this regard is exemplified by applying it to the three chronometric methods chosen to illustrate the dating process. Separate models for each dating system would clarify the roles of these systems in archaeological research and would isolate method-specific anomaly-producing variables that the general model is incapable of revealing. In the absence of specific models, however, the general model will suffice. This analysis considers the effects of anomaly-causing variables for each of the three dating methods at each point in the model, beginning with the physical-physiological matrix and following the flow of materials and information through the system. Only a very few of the many interactions possible at any locus are considered; the analysis is intended to be illustrative, not exhaustive.

Systemic-Level Physical-Physiological Matrix

Physical-physiological variables that create archaeological dating anomalies are, by and large, those processes that endow materials with chronometrically datable properties. Dendrochronological dating potential is affected by the genetic processes that determine species-specific growth responses and by environmental variables that regulate the physiological processes that control tree growth. Factors that suppress climate-sensitive radial growth or that release growth from the control of the variables that produce crossdatable ring variability can destroy, reduce, or modify dendrochronological dating potential. Among the processes that have such consequences are aging, disease, insect infestation, porcupine damage, physical trauma, climatic change, hydrological changes, and many others.

Radiocarbon dating anomalies are produced in this matrix by variation in the four processes that impart carbon-14 datability to organic materials. The amount of time and energy chronometricians devote to calibrating the radiocarbon and absolute time scales attests to the variable nature of these processes, especially those involved in the production of radioactive carbon 14. Physiological variables can cause radiocarbon dating anomalies also, as exemplified by the species-related potential differences between dates derived from animal and annual plant remains and dates from remnants of long-lived perennial plants. All the parts of an animal or annual plant are essentially the same age, and the remains of any part of such an organism yields a radiocarbon date that applies to the organism's death (E_{rd}). Different parts of a tree or shrub can vary in age by centuries, and radiocarbon dates from materials representing the older parts of such plants (E_d) can fall much earlier than the death dates of the organisms (E_r) to produce a gap.

Environmental processes that impinge on the archaeomagnetic dating system include those that relate to the earth's geomagnetic field and to the formation of the materials that are dated. Local disturbances of the geomagnetic field due to the proximity of certain rock types or strong magnetic forces produce dating anomalies. Variations in the geochemical and geophysical processes that control the quantity and sensitivity of magentized particles in the natural deposits that provide the datable material affect archaeomagnetic dating potential.

Natural processes are the most obvious anomaly-producing variables in the physical-physiological matrix. However, human behavior also operates in this domain to cause dating problems. As mentioned previously, human activities that affect the environmental variables that control the physiological processes of organic maintenance and growth significantly alter the tree-ring and radiocarbon dating properties of organisms. Archaeomagnetic dating anomalies are rarely caused by human activity simply because human actions have little impact on the geomagnetic field and on geological processes that produce datable clays.

Intermediate-Level Residual Matrix

The residual matrix is significant for radiocarbon and tree-ring dating because it represents a hiatus between the deaths of organisms (E_r) and the behavioral events with which the remains of the organisms are associated (E_t). The potential magnitude of this problem is illustrated by a surface (residual matrix) fragment of bristlecone pine wood that yielded a radiocarbon date of about 9000 years ago (Ferguson 1969:14). Countless examples of dating anomalies caused by residual matrix disjunctions between E_d and E_t can be extracted from the dendrochronological literature; a couple will suffice. Prehistoric Southwestern pueblos have yielded many instances in which the use of dead wood procured from the residual matrix for construction produced E_d and E_{rd} that are unrelated to the behavioral E_t with which the wood is associated (Dean 1969:144; Robinson 1967:42–45). The common use of driftwood by Alaskan coastal Eskimos (Giddings 1948) produces similar hiatuses between the deaths of trees (E_{rd}) and their incorporation into human behavioral systems (E_t). In addition, natural processes, such as weathering and decay, operate in the residual matrix to create gaps between E_d and E_r that are added to the hiatuses to widen the disjunctions between E_d and E_t.

Systemic-Level Behavioral Matrix

Procurement from either the physical-physiological or the residual matrix marks the entrance of materials into the behavioral matrix where a bewildering variety of things can happen to produce dating anomalies. Many behavioral processes act on the remains of formerly living organisms to widen the disjunctions or disparities between E_d and E_t. Only a few examples of the staggering number of anomaly-producing variables can be given here; in reality the list of possibilities is nearly endless. Procurement activities themselves—tree felling, crop harvesting, hunting, the transportation of materials, and others—can disjoin the sample date (E_d) from that of the behavioral events (E_t) in which the materials participate. Modification of wood (debarking, shaping, carving, etc.) in the manufacture of construction elements or portable artifacts often creates gaps by removing the exterior rings vital for radiocarbon and dendrochronological determinations of the dates of the trees' deaths (E_r). Wear and the intentional or accidental burning of wooden artifacts also produce gaps through the destruction of the youngest growth layers. Even the technology of a people can cause dating anomalies. The use of ground-stone axes, which are unsuitable for working dead wood, fosters the exploitation of living trees, a situation that produces E_r closely related to behavioral E_t. The use of metal tools, which can be applied with equal facility to green or dead wood, leads to the increased exploitation of dead trees and a consequent increase in hiatuses between E_{rd} and E_t. The absence of both ground-stone and metal axes also increases the incidence of hiatuses through the greater utilization of dead wood, which is easier to break than is green wood (O'Bryan 1949; Robinson 1967:37–38).

Differential behavior toward raw materials can affect the relevance of a raciocarbon or tree-ring date for a particular behavioral event. Stockpiling of construction materials widens the hiatuses between the demise of the organisms (E_r) and the use of the materials (E_t). Reuse of material, with or without modification, either for its original purpose or for a different purpose, can drastically alter the relevance of a date for an E_t by widening the hiatus between E_r and E_t. Recycling, the extraction and use of material from the site matrix, also produces dates that are too early for the E_t with which the material is associated. The addition of younger materials to extant features—as exemplified by the insertion of repair elements into existing structures, the reoccupation of previously vacated features, and the discard of refuse into older features—creates disparities characterized by dates that are later than E_t connected with the features involved. One behavioral process, the consumption of material as food or fuel, entirely eliminates the consumed material as a potential source of independent dates.

Behavioral processes have less impact on the relevance of archaeomagnetic dates for two reasons. First, they do not affect the datable properties of the material to the extent that they affect those of radiocarbon and tree-ring materials. The destruction of part of a clay-lined hearth does not alter the archaeomagnetic date that can be derived from the remainder of the hearth. Second, most archaeomagnetically datable material is fairly stationary and not commonly reusable or recyclable. Burned hearths or fired wall or floor plaster are not often reused in any datable form, and most disturbance of such elements is easily detected.

Intermediate-Level Site Matrix

Terminal discard or abandonment of potentially datable materials marks their transition from the behavioral into the site matrix. Materials and relationships contained in this matrix are affected by a wide range of anomaly-producing natural processes. Weathering and decay can destroy the younger portions of perennial plants and thereby produce radiocarbon or tree-ring dates that are too old for the site elements with which the dated materials are associated. Radiocarbon dating disjunctions or disparities result from the site matrix contamination of the samples with older or younger carbon. Various translocative forces—frost heaving, rodent activity, gravity, and others—can destroy the associational relationships among the dated elements and other objects that are crucial to determining the relevance of the dates. Conceivably, natural fires (E_{rd}) could burn abandoned sites and produce archaeomagnetic disparities by fixing the magnetic particles in clay objects into orientations indicative of dates later than any behavioral E_t associated with the site.

Human activities that originate in behavioral systems other than the one(s) that produced a site can disrupt the site matrix enough to create dating anomalies. Reutilization of the site locus not only disturbs the site matrix but often leads to the transferral of site matrix materials into totally different behavioral systems. The site matrix impact of modern pot hunting and construction activity is too well known to require elaboration here.

Analytical-Level Archaeological Matrix (1)

Excavation of a site transfers the materials and relationships of the site matrix into the matrix of archaeological analysis. Chronometric elements, like other components of the archaeological record (sherds, bones, seeds, pollen, etc.), undergo various types of analysis that generate more data that also become part of this matrix. Archaeologists, museologists, and others endeavor to eliminate the effects of natural processes on the materials of the archaeological record, and these processes usually are not significant sources of dating anomalies at this level. Behavioral variables, however, remain extremely important determinants of dating relevance. Crucial in this regard is the archaeologists' perception of the archaeological record. The quality of the dating of a site and its components is directly related to the quality and quantity of data on the chronological samples, their attributes, provenience, and associations. This information enables archaeologists to relate dates to other elements of the archaeological matrix and ultimately to the systemic-level behavioral phenomena that are the focus of their interest.

The treatment accorded potentially datable material is an important variable. Careless collection procedures can produce tree-ring and radiocarbon dating gaps by destroying the younger parts of perennial plants and can create archaeomagnetic dating errors through failure to maintain the proper orientation of fired clay samples. Treating many charcoal fragments from a feature such as a hearth as a single sample lump pieces that have many rings with pieces that have only a few rings and combines fragments that contain inner growth layers with chunks that come from the younger parts of the plants. A radiocarbon date from such a "sample" represents the average date of the *rings* in the sample but has little relevance to the demise of any of the trees involved (E_r) or to any behavioral events associated with the hearth (E_t). In reality, the "dated event" is not an event at all. Collection techniques that are inappropriate for the dating method to be used create dating anomalies. Entrapped moisture often reduces charcoal wrapped in aluminum foil or plastic to an amorphous mush that is useless for tree-ring dating and only marginally useful for radiocarbon dating because the youngest parts of the sample cannot be segregated from the older portions. Inappropriate preservatives can render tree-ring samples unworkable and can contaminate radiocarbon samples.

Analytical-Level Chronometric Matrix

When archaeologists transmit samples to specialists for dating, the material passes into the various behavioral systems of analysis that constitute the chronometric matrix. Here, as is the case in the archaeological matrix, the effects of natural processes are minimal, and behavioral variables are the most common sources of dating anomalies. The chronometricians' perceptions of the material, which are based in large measure on data supplied by archaeologists, is an important variable in this matrix. The specialists' control of dating processes is partly a function of the extent of their knowledge of the samples they are dating, and any information the archaeologists can supply is useful to the chronometricians' assessments of factors that may affect dating potential.

Improper handling of material by chronometricians is just as important a source of dating anomalies as is carelessness on the part of archaeologists. Loss or confusion of samples, sample numbers, or supplementary information, the inadvertent destruction of exterior rings on wood samples, inadequate decontamination procedures, human errors, and equipment malfunction are among the many chronometric matrix behavior-related variables that can produce dating anomalies.

A variable of critical importance that originates in the chronometric matrix is the nature of the date itself (Smiley 1955). The different kinds of date cannot be treated in the same way because they represent different kinds of chronological information. Time placement radiocarbon and archaeomagnetic determinations, which are expressed as means and one sigma dispersal values, cannot be considered to be absolute, nor can they legitimately be analyzed as points in time; the ranges as well as the means must be considered. Absolute tree-ring dates, because they refer to specific terrestrial years and have no associated statistical error, can be analyzed as "points" (of one year's duration) in time. Obviously, these differences are of critical importance in assessing the archaeological and behavioral significance of the dates. Other date-type dependent variables, such as whether or not the date applies to a reference event ($E_d = E_r$) or to some event earlier or later than the reference event ($E_d \neq E_r$), are also important chronometric matrix sources of anomalies.

Analytical-Level Archaeological Matrix (2)

When the dates and other relevant information resulting from chronometric analysis are transmitted to archaeologists, they become integral components of the archaeological record by virtue of their association with the archaeological materials from which they were derived. As archaeological data they are utilized in archaeologists' efforts to understand the behavioral and site matrix conditions and processes that produced the archaeological record. The evaluation of these dates is a purely archaeological process identical in concept to any other archaeological analysis, despite the fact that the dates are derived by methods independent of archaeological systematics.

IMPLICATIONS OF THE MODEL

The model of the archaeological dating process has several implications that are important to an understanding of the role of independent dating in archaeology. First, though we often speak of dating the elements of the archaeological record (pueblos, rooms, pithouses, firepits, and the like), the model clearly indicates that our real goal is the dating of systemic-level events associated with these elements. Of the many such events related to an archaeological feature—its construction, occupation, repair, modification, abandonment, reoccupation, burning, etc.—some may be datable, given the right circumstances, whereas others may not be datable.

Another implication of the model is that the events that are actually dated by various chronometric methods (E_d or E_r or both) occur at different points in the dating system. Thus, not all datable events are necessarily directly associated with the behavioral matrix. Tree-ring and radiocarbon E_r dates mark the passage of materials out of the physiological matrix as a result of organisms' deaths. Death can result solely from natural causes and apply only to a physiological event, or death can be caused by human activities such as the cutting of trees for construction or fuel, the harvesting of crops, or the killing of animals. Material resulting from such activity that passes directly into the behavioral matrix produces a date that is truly relevant to behavioral events, if only those involved in the procurement of the material. If such material exists for a time in the residual matrix before being procured for human use, its date is relevant primarily to the physiological event of its death, and archaeologists are faced with the problem of relating the E_d to behavioral E_t. Dates derived from the remains of organisms that exist within the behavioral matrix, mainly human beings and domesticated plants and animals, are relevant to behavioral events whether or not their deaths were natural or were caused by man. Archaeomagnetic dates usually relate to events of the behavioral matrix, specifically the intentional or accidental firing of clay features. However, as mentioned previously, firing of such materials could occur in the site matrix to produce dating disparities.

A third implication of the model is that independent dates, despite differences in the E_r to which they apply, are in reality integral components of the archaeological data from a site. The materials that provide the dates exist in the archaeological matrix because of their previous participation in a human behavioral system, and the dates attached to them are just as much a part of the archaeological residue of that system as the potsherds and arrow points recovered from the site. The archaeologists' task is to determine how these dates apply to the behavioral events reflected in the site. This process takes place entirely within the archaeological matrix and involves the application of all the principles and techniques of analysis pertinent to the assessment of any other archaeological data. Therefore, if the dates are to be related to the behavioral matrix, the samples must be accorded the same treatment received by the other elements of the archaeological matrix. Many deficiencies in the application of independent dates in archaeology have been due to the treatment of chronometric samples as nonarchaeological temporal indicators rather than as integral components of the archaeological record.

A fourth implication is that there are two basic kinds of dating problem caused by processes operating in any of the matrices. The first is actual dating error, which, given the quality control practices of the various chronometric disciplines, is probably rare. Some processes that do not cause dating errors per se can affect the dating potential of materials to the extent that the relevance of the dates is adversely affected. Second are anomalies that occur because the E_d is not related to the behavioral E_t

with which the dated sample is associated. Anomalies are undoubtedly far more common than actual dating errors. The detection of anomalies is a major problem in the application of independent dates in archaeological analysis. One of the principal contributions of the dating model is that it makes explicit the many ways in which such anomalies can occur.

The model of the archaeological dating process illustrates the complex nature of the role of independent dates in archaeological analysis. An astounding number of variables that can affect either the dating of chronometric samples or the relevance of the dates becomes apparent when the dating system is examined in detail. Anomaly-producing variables arise from natural processes or behavioral activities or both at all loci of the model. Furthermore, the conceptual relationships that structure the behavior of scientists on the analytical level are also important factors in the dating process. To make the best use of independent dates, archaeologists must be cognizant of the complex systems of conditions, events, and interrelationships involved and of the many variables, both general and dating method-specific, that can produce dating anomalies. The application of independent dates in archaeological analysis is not an easy task; however, the development of a general dating theory and of method-specific models would make the procedure more systematic if not any easier.

THE FUTURE OF ARCHAEOLOGICAL DATING THEORY

It is not my intention to go beyond the construction of the provisional model and attempt to develop a comprehensive archaeological dating theory. That is a major undertaking that will require years of thought and debate to accomplish. I am satisfied if I have indicated the complexity of the dating process and the consequent need for more systematic consideration of the place of independent dates in archaeology. Nevertheless, the general model and its ramifications provide a basis for predicting some of the characteristics that archaeological dating theory will assume as it is perfected. A general dating theory will include a body of concepts, assumptions, models, and procedural principles specifying the many variables that produce dating anomalies and the interrelationships of these variables with each other and other components of the matrices in which they operate. Method-specific versions of the general theory will integrate those anomaly-producing variables that are unique to individual dating systems into the conceptual structure of archaeological dating. Such versions will include those aspects of each dating system that affect dating potential and date relevance and will specify the nature of the dates produced by each method. General and method-specific dating theories will provide logical bases for the development of formal principles to guide archaeologists' efforts to relate independent dates to archaeological phenomena and their behavioral antecedents. Finally, archaeological dating theory will be integrated into the anthropological and archaeological theoretical systems that relate behavioral phenomena to other systemic-level phenomena and relate archaeological materials and associations to behavioral conditions, events, and processes.

In addition to these general trends, some rather specific aspects of archaeological dating theory are foreshadowed in the analysis of the model. These include formal procedural guidelines and analytical principles that will enhance archaeologists' control of particular dating problems and their ability to evaluate the relevance of independent dates to archaeological and behavioral phenomena. Better control of dating problems will reduce the incidence of dating anomalies, and formal means of detecting and resolving those anomalies that still exist will enhance dating relevance. Future refinement of archaeological dating theory will undoubtedly produce operational guidelines and analytical principles much more sophisticated than those listed here.

One aspect of dating theory will relate to the definition and control of the specific chronological problem to which independent dates are to be applied. Ideally, the dating problem should be defined on the basis of purely archaeological considerations, and the chronometric technique selected to provide the temporal control most applicable to the problem. Generally, this is a matter of choosing a dating technique with an E_r that is closely related to the behavioral E_t specified by the problem. The degree of relationship between E_r and E_t can be measured by the number of E_b required to connect them; the fewer E_b necessary, the closer is the relationship between E_r and E_t. The intrinsic limitations of various dating methods are important criteria in choosing a chronometric technique. A chronological problem whose solution hinges on temporal resolution of two decades or less cannot be solved by radiocarbon dates, no matter how closely related the carbon-14 E_r and behavioral E_t may be, and more precise techniques such as archaeomagnetism or tree-ring dating must be used. Radiocarbon dating is a poor choice for materials greater than 50,000 years old, just as dendrochronology is inappropriate for materials more than 8000 years old. Other important factors in this decision are the nature of the potentially datable materials available and the geographic limitations of various chronometric methods. If the site produces no wood or charcoal or if it is located in a region where dendrochronology is not applicable, tree-ring dates must be eliminated from consideration. In cases where the range of possible dating methods is severely limited, the nature of the available chronometric techniques may determine the E_t toward which the dating problem is directed.

Once a dating method has been chosen (or dictated by circumstances), collection procedures must be adapted to the sample and data requirements of the appropriate chronometric discipline. Collection techniques that are suitable for tree-ring specimens (Dean, n.d.; Stokes and Smiley 1968:21–36) are inappropriate for samples destined for the radiocarbon laboratory (Sheppard 1975), and dating theory will take these differences into account. Collection of data on chronometric samples and their archaeological matrix associations must be structured by the dating problem—that is, how the dates are to be related to behavioral E_t. Information relevant to E_t, to various E_r, and to the E_b necessary to connect E_r and E_t is especially important in this regard.

Once chronometric dates are reported to the archaeologists, a set of analytical techniques and principles directed toward the detection of anomalous dates, the resolution of these anomalies, and the relating of the dates to behavioral E_t will come into play. The use of these principles within the archaeological matrix constitutes a major point of articulation between archaeological theory and archaeological dating theory. One such principle of archaeological dating will concern the nature of the date involved. The differences among absolute placement, time placement, and relative placement dates are enormously important in assessing the relevance of the dates to archaeological and behavioral phenomena. Relative placement dating is of limited use in measuring rates of change; resolution limitations reduce the applicability of time placement dates to high-frequency events; and absolute dates can measure events of short duration and establish the absolute contemporaneity of behavioral phenomena (Dean 1969:198, 1970:170–173). The different types of date should be employed only in dating situations to which they are suited.

Another principle will involve recognition of the differences between what in dendrochronological parlance are called "cutting dates" and "noncutting dates" (Dean, n.d.). The former (E_{rd}) relate directly to the death of an organism ($E_d = E_r$), whereas the latter (E_d) are relevant to earlier events in the life of the organism ($E_d \neq E_r$). This distinction applies only to materials procured from the physiological or residual matrices and is further restricted to long-lived perennial plants that incorporate elements of widely divergent ages. This distinction is crucial to the evaluation of tree-ring dates and radiocarbon dates from wood, because only "cutting dates" are potentially relevant to behavioral events. Dendrochronologists have established several criteria for distinguishing cutting (E_{rd}) dates from noncutting (E_d) dates (Dean, n.d.), and these criteria should be incorporated into archaeological dating theory.

One very important aspect of archaeological dating theory that has yet to be developed is the estimation of the magnitudes of disjunctions and disparities between E_d and E_t. This complex problem may involve estimating gaps, hiatuses, or disparities, depending on the particular situation and the chronometric method used. Some attempts have been made to estimate gaps between noncutting tree-ring dates and the terminal dates of the trees. In the early days of archaeological tree-ring dating, dendrochronologists often guessed at the terminal dates of samples that yielded noncutting dates, but this inaccurate and misleading practice has long since been abandoned. Some experiments have been made using the sapwood-to-heartwood ratio or the average number of sapwood rings to estimate tree-ring gaps (Douglass 1939), and this promising technique deserves further attention. Kemrer (1974:81–94), Plog (1977:130–138), and others have used size or ring number relationships between samples with noncutting dates and samples with cutting dates to estimate the gaps involved in the former. Gap estimation for radiocarbon dates is even more complex. If wood is used, the time placement nature of the date and the various problems of calibrating the carbon-14 and absolute time scales are added to the gap estimation problems that apply in tree-ring dating. Schiffer (1976:146–149) presents a technique for estimating gaps in radiocarbon dates derived from wood.

Estimating hiatuses between E_{rd} and E_t has received less attention than gap estimation. Generally, hiatus estimation involves the definition of one or more E_b that link E_{rd} and E_t and the calculation of the amount of time represented by the E_b. Schiffer's (1976:140–143) example of the application of a roof construction (E_{rd}) date to the discard of sherds (E_t) found in the fill of the room involves two E_b—the length of occupation of the room and the time required to accumulate the refuse to the depth at which the sherds were found. Estimating disjunctions involves summing estimated gap and hiatus values and can become a very complicated procedure involving many variables.

Disparity estimation can be a fairly simple affair under optimum circumstances. Dating differences between construction and repair timbers can often be used as measures of the disparity between the building and repair events. Similarly, the disparity between a hearth archaeomagnetic date and room construction can be accurately measured if tree-ring dates are available for the construction event. In the absence of evidence of this type, disparity estimates are more difficult, and few attempts to deal with such problems have been made. Estimation of disjunctions and disparities between E_d and E_t is an aspect of dating theory that deserves more attention than it has heretofore received.

Once E_t selection, chronometric method choice, dating, calibration, estimation, and similar problems have been taken care of, the problems of dating anomaly recognition and of dating relevance still exist. Several principles that may be used in resolving these difficulties can be derived from the model. The model clearly indicates the large number of variables that can affect dating potential and the relevance of the dates to behavioral phenomena. Because of the variety of anomaly-producing processes to which any one chronometric sample can be exposed during its passage through the system, the behavioral significance of a single date is uncertain and, in the absence of comparative chronological data provided by other dates, is very difficult to evaluate. Thus, the "strength in numbers" principle stresses the dependence of date evaluation on the availability of as many well-controlled dates as possible.

A second provisional principle is that of clustering (Dean, n.d.). Clustering occurs when a number of dates from an archaeological feature fall within a very few years of one another. The number of years required to define a cluster differs with the various kinds of date and varies directly with the variances associated with the dates. A much shorter time span is necessary to delimit a cluster of tree-ring dates, whose standard deviations are zero, than is required to define a cluster of carbon-14 dates, whose standard deviations may range from 20 to more than 200 radiocarbon years (Long and Rippeteau 1974). Establishing acceptable timespan limits for defining clusters of different kinds of date is another important aspect of archaeological dating theory that remains to be developed. Despite this lack, clustering is still the most powerful tool available for evaluating archaeological dates. As the number of dates per cluster rises, the probability of fortuitous clustering decreases, and the relevance of the dates to behavioral matrix events increases. The best possible dating evidence consists in a tight cluster of cutting dates (E_{rd}) with no evident anomalies. In the absence of cutting dates, clustering often offsets the inherent weaknesses of noncutting dates. The probability of chance clustering of noncutting dates is negligible because there are simply too many variables operating independently at different points in the dating system to produce spurious clusters involving very many noncutting dates. Thus, a cluster of noncutting dates usually approximates quite closely the true date of the materials involved. Clustering is also of great value in isolating dating anomalies in that dates that fall outside a cluster of time placement or absolute dates can be singled out as potentially anomalous and submitted to further examination. The refinement and formalization of the clustering principle and its ramifications will be an important element in the future development of archaeological dating theory.

A third operational guideline could be called the "principle of contextual congruence." This merely means that dating anomalies may be detected on the basis of apparent inconsistencies between the dates and other archaeological data. No matter how distinctive a particular site may be, the archaeologist has a reservoir of accumulated knowledge that enables him to place the site into some sort of temporal, spatial, and relational framework. This frame of reference permits the recognition of dates that are inconsistent with the expected temporal position of the site. More subtle considerations, such as inconsistencies in the associational relationships among the dated samples and other elements of the archaeological record, may reveal potential dating problems. For example, if dates do not correspond with the stratigraphic position of the samples, further examination of the dates is in order.

A final principle, that of "sample attribute consistency," involves congruence between the dates and the physical attributes of the dated samples. Differential surface alteration of construction elements may indicate the use of dead organisms, the recycling of materials, or the addition of repair elements. Certain attributes of tree-ring series show that the trees died of natural causes and thus raise the possibility of signficant hiatuses between the trees' deaths and behavioral E_t. Radiocarbon or tree-ring dates from beams cut to fit a particular room probably apply to the construction of the room, whereas dates from beams cut to standard lengths may apply to stockpiling rather than construction events. The possibilities for the application of this principle are as many and varied as the contexts in which the samples occur and are constrained only by the limitations of the sample attribute data.

CONCLUSIONS

In the foregoing discussion I have attempted to indicate some of the complexities involved in the use of independent dates in archaeology. The general model and its associated concepts specify the temporal, spatial, and relational loci of some of the many vairables that constrain the applicability of such dates to past human behavioral events. Dating accuracy and relevance depend directly on the degree of control that archaeologists have over these variables. The general model and the "principles" that relate independent dates to the archaeological and behavioral matrices are designed to enhance this control. Nevertheless, this effort represents but a halting step toward the development of an adequate theory of the dating process in archaeology. If this exercise has accomplished nothing else, it has clarified the need for such a theory and perhaps indicated at least one direction that the development of archaeological dating theory might take.

Future development of archaeological dating theory will be directed toward improving the concepts and procedures used by archaeologists to relate independent dates to the systemic-level phenomena that are the ultimate concern of archaeological research. The success of this effort will hinge on the elimination of weaknesses in current archaeological dating practice and the resolution of the problems that arise in applying independent dates in archaeological analysis. Some of these problems are pinpointed by the provisional general model. Problem areas that clearly need attention include the relationships between human procurement and use of datable materials on the one hand and the nature of the events recorded by the dates (E_d or E_r or both) on the other; the natural and behavioral processes of the physical-physiological, residual, behavioral, site, archaeological, and chronometric matrices that produce dating anomalies; the practical significance of differences among the various kinds of independent date; techniques for estimating gaps, hiatuses, disjunctions, and disparities; ways of distinguishing "cutting" from "noncutting" dates; the time spans acceptable for defining clusters of various kinds of date; quality control on the assocational and supplementary data crucial to relating the dates to archaeological, site, and behavioral matrix manifestations; the development of "axioms," assumptions, and principles for translating chronometric dates and other archaeological data into information on past human behavior; and many others. Undoubtedly, many unanticipated problems will arise as archaeological dating theory is refined and as new independent dating techniques are developed. As should be evident from this far from exhaustive compilation of presently recognizable problems, archaeological dating theory is in a rudimentary state of development, and the thought and effort of many individuals over a number of years will be required to create a satisfactory framework for the application of independent dates in archaeological analysis. Nevertheless, the need for systemization is manifest, and any time and effort expended in developing archaeological dating theory will be amply rewarded. The greater control of the archaeological dating process that will result from a formal dating theory cannot fail to significantly enhance the quality of archaeology's contribution to the study of human behavior.

ACKNOWLEDGMENTS

I am grateful to Michael B. Schiffer, David R. Wilcox, and three unknown reviewers for critical appraisals of the first draft of this paper. Cory Breternitz, Valerie Clark, and John Hannah aided immensely in the production of the illustrations.

REFERENCES

Bannister, B.
  1962 The interpretation of tree-ring dates. *American Antiquity* **27**:508–514.
  1969 Dendrochronology. In *Science in archaeology: A survey of progress and research,* edited by D. Brothwell and E. Higgs (Rev. ed.). London: Thames & Hudson. Pp. 191–205.
Binford, L. R.
  1962 Archaeology as anthropology. *American Antiquity* **28**:217–225.
  1972 *An archaeological perspective.* New York: Seminar Press.
Braidwood, R. J.
  1968 Archaeology: An introduction. *Encyclopaedia Britannica* **2**:225–227.
Bucha, V.
  1971 Archaeomagnetic dating. In *Dating techniques for the archaeologist,* edited by H. N. Michael and E. K. Ralph. Cambridge, Mass.: MIT Press. Pp. 57–117.
Clarke, D. L.
  1973 Archaeology: The loss of innocence. *Antiquity* **47**:6–18.
Cook, R. M.
  1969 Archaeomagnetism. In *Science in archaeology: A survey of progress and research,* edited by D. Brothwell and E. Higgs (Rev. ed.). London: Thames & Hudson. Pp. 76–87.
Damon, P. E., C. W. Ferguson, A. Long, and E. I. Wallick
  1974 Dendrochronologic calibration of the radiocarbon time scale. *American Antiquity* **39**:350–366.
Dean, J. S.
  1969 Chronological analysis of Tsegi phase sites in northeastern Arizona. *Laboratory of Tree-Ring Research Papers,* No. 3.
  1970 Aspects of Tsegi phase social organization: A trial reconstruction. In *Reconstructing prehistoric pueblo societies,* edited by W. A. Longacre. Albuquerque: University of New Mexico Press. Pp. 140–174.
  n.d. Tree-ring dating in archaeology. *University of Utah, Anthropological Papers* (in press).
Douglass, A. E.
  1939 Notes on beam dating by sap-heart contact. *Tree-Ring Bulletin* **6**:36.
Ferguson, C. W.
  1969 A 7104-year annual tree-ring chronology for bristlecone pine, *Pinus aristata,* from the White Mountains, California. *Tree-Ring Bulletin* **29**:3–29.
Fritts, H. C.
  1976 *Tree rings and climate.* New York: Academic Press.
Fritts, H. C., D. G. Smith, and M. A. Stokes
  1965 The biological model for paleoclimatic interpretation of Mesa Verde tree-ring series. In Contributions of the Wetherill Mesa Archeological Project, assembled by D. Osborne. *Society for American Archaeology, Memoirs* **19**:101–121.
Giddings, J. L., Jr.
  1948 Chronology of the Kobuk-Kotzebue sites. *Tree-Ring Bulletin* **14**:26–32.
Haury, E. W.
  1935 Tree rings—the archaeologists's time-piece. *American Antiquity* **1**:98–108.
Kemrer, M. F.
  1974 The dynamics of western Navajo settlement, A.D. 1750–1900: An archaeologi-

cal and dendrochronological analysis. Ph.D. dissertation, University of Arizona, Tucson. Ann Arbor: University Microfilms.

Krause, R. A., and R. M. Thorne
  1971   Toward a theory of archaeological things. *Plains Anthropologist: Journal of the Plains Conference* **16**:245–257.

Long, A., and B. Rippeteau
  1974   Testing contemporaneity and averaging radiocarbon dates. *American Antiquity* **39**:205–215.

Michels, J. W.
  1973   *Dating methods in archaeology.* New York: Seminar Press.

O'Bryan, D.
  1949   Methods of felling trees and tree-ring dating in the Southwest. *American Antiquity* **15**:155–156.

Plog, F. T.
  1974   *The study of prehistoric change.* New York: Academic Press.

Plog, S.
  1977   A multivariate approach to the explanation of ceramic variation. Ph.D. dissertation, University of Michigan, Ann Arbor. Ann Arbor: University Microfilms.

Ralph, E. K.
  1971   Carbon-14 dating. In *Dating techniques for the archaeologist,* edited by H. N. Michael and E. K. Ralph. Cambridge, Mass.: MIT Press. Pp. 1–48.

Ralph, E. K., and H. N. Michael
  1970   MASCA radiocarbon dates for sequoia and bristlecone-pine samples. In *Nobel Symposium 12: Radiocarbon variations and absolute chronology,* edited by I. U. Olsson. Stockholm: Almqvist & Wiksell. Pp. 619–623.

Reid, J. J.
  1973   Growth and response to stress at Grasshopper Pueblo, Arizona. Ph.D. dissertation, University of Arizona, Tucson. Ann Arbor: University Microfilms.

Robinson, W. J.
  1967   Tree-ring materials as a basis for cultural interpretations. Ph.D. dissertation, University of Arizona, Tucson. Ann Arbor: University Microfilms.

Schiffer, M. B.
  1972   Archaeological context and systemic context. *American Antiquity* **37**:156–165.
  1973   Cultural formation processes of the archaeological record: Applications at the Joint Site, east-central Arizona. Ph.D. dissertation, University of Arizona, Tucson. Ann Arbor: University Microfilms.
  1976   *Behavioral archeology.* New York: Academic Press.

Sheppard, J. C.
  1975   A radiocarbon dating primer. *Washington State University, College of Engineering, Bulletin* No. 338.

Smiley, T. L.
  1955   The geochronological approach. In Geochronology: With special reference to southwestern United States, edited by T. L. Smiley. *University of Arizona, Physical Science Bulletin* No. 2.

Stokes, M. A., and T. L. Smiley
  1968   *An introduction to tree-ring dating.* Chicago: University of Chicago Press.

Stuiver, M., and H. E. Suess
  1966   On the relationship between radiocarbon dates and true sample ages. *Radiocarbon* **8**:534–540.

Sullivan, A.
  1976 The structure of archaeological inference: A critical examination of logic and procedure. Preliminary examination paper, Department of Anthropology, University of Arizona, Tucson. Manuscript on deposit, Arizona State Museum Library, Tucson.
Wilcox, D. R.
  1975 A strategy for perceiving social groups in puebloan sites. In Chapters in the prehistory of eastern Arizona, IV. *Fieldiana: Anthropology* **65:**120–159.
  1976 How the Pueblos came to be as they are: The problem today. Preliminary examination paper, Department of Anthropology, University of Arizona, Tucson. Manuscript on deposit, Arizona State Museum Library, Tucson.
Willis, E. H.
  1969 Radiocarbon dating. In *Science in archaeology: A survey of progress and research,* edited by D. Brothwell and E. Higgs (Rev. ed.). London: Thames & Hudson. Pp. 46–57.

8

Advances in Archaeological Seriation

WILLIAM H. MARQUARDT

Seriation is a deceptively simple technique, the unnecessarily abstruse discussion of which has become an embarrassment to quantitative archaeologists. At the same time, seriation is a mathematically entertaining and eminently useful procedure, the epistemological status of which has been insufficiently explored by archaeologists. If the reader is already confused, let me hasten to add that one purpose of this chapter is to introduce seriation *painlessly* to the serious student. Also, some professional archaeologists may be under the mistaken impression that the seriation activity has been taken over by robots and no longer requires good judgment, careful field work, and plain common sense. Nothing could be further from the truth. An interesting series of mathematically oriented papers on seriation has appeared in the past few years, however, so a second purpose of this chapter is to summarize recent thought on seriation, relating new approaches to the research problems faced today by practicing professionals. I shall not provide a history of seriation, but the interested reader is directed to informative papers on this subject by Johnson (1972:315–318), Kendall (1963), Rouse (1967:154–155), and Rowe (1962). Mathematical terminology will be kept to a minimum in discussion but the reader is asked to make the effort necessary to master the small number of essential concepts introduced. Succeeding sections

ADVANCES IN ARCHAEOLOGICAL METHOD AND THEORY, VOL. 1

will (*a*) explain how seriation works, (*b*) discuss advances in seriation techniques, theory, and epistemology, and (*c*) place seriation within the context of contemporary archaeological research.

Seriation is a descriptive analytic technique, the purpose of which is to arrange comparable units in a single dimension (that is, along a line) such that the position of each unit reflects its similarity to other units. Thus, in Figure 8.1, if units A, B, C, and D are correctly seriated, then A is more like B than it is like C; A is more dissimilar to D than B is dissimilar to D; and so on. As in all seriations, there are two possible "correct" solutions to the problem in Figure 8.1: either A—B—C—D or D—C—B—A. Different methods, including scaling procedures, have been used to effect the ordering. True scaling techniques involve the assignment of numerical values indicating the relative closeness of each unit to all other units. The word seriation does not itself imply a scaling technique, but merely the ranking of units and their subsequent linear ordering on the basis of these ranks. Although seriation is frequently used by archaeologists as a dating technique, it can be presumed to be such only if the ordering criteria are reliable chronological indicators.

In order to seriate, one needs to decide (*a*) the dimension along which units are to be arranged, and (*b*) some unambiguous way to rank units so that they can be ordered along that dimension. If units A, B, C, and D in the above example are persons of ages 5, 20, 30, and 50, respectively, and the dimension of interest is "age," then the four individuals are properly seriated on the basis of chronological age. If the same persons A, B, C, and D are 100 cm, 160 cm, 190 cm, and 170 cm tall, respectively, and the dimension of interest is "tallness," then the four individuals would be seriated differently on the basis of height measurements (Figure 8.2). The examples in Figures 8.1 and 8.2 are trivial, of course, because the ages and heights are already known, and the ordering on these dimensions is clear.

A *matrix* is any rectangular arrangement of numbers; the horizontal lines of numbers are called rows, and the vertical lines of numbers are called columns. All seriation techniques begin with a *data matrix,* with the units to be ordered being listed horizontally as rows, the variables measured on each unit being listed vertically as columns. Each number in a matrix is called an *element.* In the example in Figure 8.2, the matrix has four rows and only one column (Table 8.1). (A matrix with only one row or only one column is called a *vector.*)

Figure 8.1 Seriation is a process of arranging comparable units along a line.

Figure 8.2. The outcome of a seriation depends on the dimension along which units are ordered.

Seriation is most familiar to archaeologists as a relative dating technique, where the dimension of interest is time. Thus, archaeologists must discover some unambiguous way to measure units (for example, graves, excavation units, surface collections) so that they can be inferred to be ordered along the dimension *time*. The kinds of measurements or observations made depend on the nature of the units being seriated; thus, archaeologists have made use of several kinds of data matrices.

One important kind of data matrix is the *incidence* matrix, a matrix in which only the presence or absence of a certain criterion is indicated in the appropriate column for each of the units (rows). Usually a "1" denotes presence of the criterion, "0" its absence. We do this kind of seriation informally when we observe old buildings and attempt to guess their ages on the basis of the presence or absence of certain architectural features. For an illustration of an incidence data matrix, consider the example shown in Table 8.2. Here the seven units are gasoline-powered automobiles, and five possible observations are listed across the top. It will occur to the reader that dozens of unambiguous observations could be made on an object as complicated as an automobile. Some of the observations noted here are more useful indicators of temporal change than others. For example, although radios were installed in automobiles as early as the 1920s, they are commonly considered optional equipment even today. Automatic transmission was perfected a generation ago, but it is still rare in certain classes of automobiles, such as sports cars. When car No. 6 was manufactured in 1965, an automatic transmission was not an option available in the Volkswagen Beetle, nor was an automatic transmission a feature of car No. 7, a 1974 sports car. Finally, we can note that car No. 7 has spoked wheels, but this is for a stylistic reason rather

TABLE 8.1

Data Matrix Consisting of Four Units (Persons) and Only One Variable (Height)[a]

Unit	Height (cm)
A	100
B	160
C	190
D	170

[a] A correct seriation of these data on the dimension "tallness" is shown in Figure 8.2 (this page).

TABLE 8.2

Incidence Data Matrix Representing Five Observations Made on Seven Automobiles[a]

		Observation				
Unit		Running board	Spoked wheels	Electric headlamps	Radio	Automatic transmission
7.	1974 MG B	0	1	1	1	0
6.	1965 Volkswagen Beetle	0	0	1	1	0
5.	1958 Buick station wagon	0	0	1	1	1
4.	1950 Studebaker Commander	0	0	1	1	0
3.	1925 Rolls Royce 40/50 Silver Ghost	1	1	1	1	0
2.	1917 Ford T Coupe	1	1	1	0	0
1.	1892 Peugeot Victoria	0	1	0	0	0

[a] Note that the automobiles are in the correct chronological order, but this is not the best seriation. A "perfect" seriation would place unit 7 between units 3 and 4. This error results from a poor choice of observations.

than a functional reason. Clearly, inferential errors can result from carelessly chosen categories.

A frequent archaeological use of incidence data for seriation is for the relative temporal placement of certain graves. In such cases we assume that the graves represent burials of a single cultural group, having reasonably consistent norms characterizing the cultural practice of human interment, that items found in a grave were in use at the time of the burial, and that each kind of item (artifact type) was in general use in only one discrete time interval. The "best" seriation, based on these assumptions, is one that most closely brings the 1's together in one group in each column.

Another important kind of data matrix is the *abundance* matrix, a matrix in which the elements are numerical indicators of the abundance of some particular characteristic, relative to some absolute minimum. Abundance matrices may be further subdivided into two types. In the first, the elements of the matrix represent percentages or relative proportions of certain characteristics of each unit being seriated. For any single row (unit) the percentages must add to 100% (or, if the elements represent relative proportions, the relative proportions must sum to 1.0). Table 8.3 is an example of an abundance matrix composed of percentages. This is the same kind of matrix that characterized the approach to seriation of ceramic surface collections popularized by Ford and his colleagues (Phillips *et al.* 1951). As Ford describes it, the pottery is first classified into types, and, for each unit to be seriated, percentages of each type are

TABLE 8.3

Hypothetical Abundance of Different Types of Methods of Artificial Illumination in the State of Pennsylvania, 1850–1950[a]

| Year | Types of Artificial Illumination | | | | | Total |
	Candle and oil lamp	Kerosene lamp	Gas lamp	Incandescent electric lamp	Fluorescent electric lamp	
1950	0%	0%	0%	90%	10%	100%
1940	0	0	0	100	0	100
1930	0	0	10	90	0	100
1920	0	5	15	80	0	100
1910	0	5	45	50	0	100
1900	5	10	65	20	0	100
1890	5	15	75	5	0	100
1880	5	30	65	0	0	100
1870	10	40	50	0	0	100
1860	65	5	30	0	0	100
1850	90	0	10	0	0	100

[a] The elements of this abundance data matrix are percentages of types. These data, invented by Mayer–Oakes (1955:176–178) after consulting electrical engineers and published sources (Watkins 1952), provide an example of an abundance matrix with familiar type categories.

calculated. These percentages are then represented as horizontal bars on long narrow strips of graph paper. The strips are "arranged and rear-ranged in relation to one another until the clearest patterning appears" (Ford 1962:42) (see Figure 8.3). The assumptions underlying seriation by percentage matrix are (a) that each artifact type has an incipience, a florescence, and a decline; (b) that each unit constitutes a more or less representative sample of the artifact types in use; and (c) that the units to be seriated represent short ranges of time and come from a limited geographic area. The appropriateness of seriation by percentage matrix and the validity of the presuppositions underlying the practice will be discussed later.

In the second kind of abundance matrix the elements are logically independent ratio-scale variables calculated for each unit. Independent ratio-scale variables are not required to sum to 1 or to 100% for each unit. Unlike percentages (Speth and Johnson 1976:48–49), ratio-scale variables are amenable to analysis by pattern-sensitive similarity coefficients, such as Pearson's r. The variables are chosen in such a way that they either generally increase or generally decrease with the passage of time. Such variables also have the advantage of flexibility, because one can construct them at several levels of analysis: assemblage, type, mode, etc. To use an example similar to the one used above, suppose we wish to seriate chronologically a group of automobiles. Appropriate ratio-scale variables might be a measurement of the area devoted to window glass

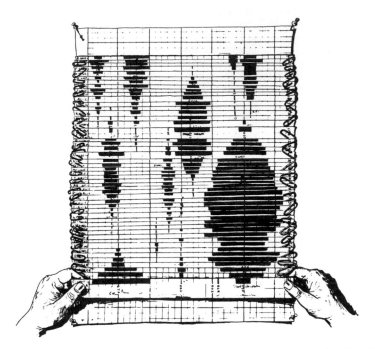

Figure 8.3   Ford's graphical seriation technique. (From Ford 1962, Fig. 8.)

divided by the total surface area, the volume available for the storage of luggage divided by a linear measurement of the wheelbase, or the total weight of various plastic materials used divided by the total weight of the car. All these variables might be expected generally to increase with the passage of time. A detailed example of the use of ratio-scale variables in archaeological seriation is given elsewhere (Marquardt 1974b:64–121, 144–173).

Although there is much room for thoughtful discussion of the cultural assumptions underlying the practice of seriation, and a real need to resolve, in every case, a wide range of practical problems in order to assure comparability between meaningful units, it should be clear by now that seriation is mathematically rather simple. The mathematical problem consists in finding, for a given data matrix, the arrangement of rows (units) that best satisfies the following criterion: In each individual column the elements either (*a*) increase to a maximum and then decrease, or (*b*) increase, or (*c*) decrease. This requirement is interpreted in the "weak" sense; that is, two or more consecutive *identical* elements in a single column do not constitute a violation of the requirement. (A series of numbers that increases, or decreases, in this "weak" sense is said to be increasing, or decreasing, *monotonically*.) An abundance matrix that perfectly satisfies the requirement is sometimes called a Q-matrix (Kendall 1971b:219). Laxton (1976) has proposed a measure of the extent to which an abundance matrix fails to satisfy the properties of a Q-matrix; see also Wilkinson (1971:282).

The mathematical problem is the same, whether the data matrix be composed of percentage, ratio, ratio-scale variable, or the presence/absence of elements. In this regard we may consider the incidence matrix a special case of the abundance matrix. The mathematical problem in the case of incidence data reduces to the task of permuting (rearranging) the rows until the 1's are brought together in one group in each column, to the extent that this is possible. An incidence matrix that perfectly satisfies the requirement is sometimes called a P-matrix (Kendall 1971b:220).

The ordering of units may be carried out by rearranging the n rows (units), as shown in Figure 8.3. Commonly, however, the ordering is done by rearranging the n row–columns of an $n \times n$ matrix of between-unit similarity coefficients until high values cluster about the principal diagonal, a procedure advocated by Robinson (1951). In other words, we do not work directly with the $n \times m$ data matrix, but with an $n \times n$ matrix derived from the data matrix. A simple example will show that these procedures are equivalent for ideal data.

Suppose that we have systematically collected samples of pottery from the surfaces of five archaeological sites and that, for purposes of this example, the pottery sorts neatly into four types, termed Type 1, Type 2, Type 3, and Type 4 (Table 8.4). There are five units (rows), so there are 5! ($5! = 1 \times 2 \times 3 \times 4 \times 5 = 120$) possible arrangements. Instead of rearranging the rows, as in Ford's (1962) procedure, let us generate a matrix of similarity coefficients for all pairs of sites. There are many ways of expressing numerically the similarity between units. Here, we follow

TABLE 8.4

Unseriated Artificial Data Matrix Consisting of Percentages of Four Pottery Types Found on the Surfaces of Five Sites

Unit	Type 1	Type 2	Type 3	Type 4	Total
Site A	0%	20%	10%	70%	100%
Site B	0	40	5	55	100
Site C	50	0	0	50	100
Site D	10	10	10	70	100
Site E	20	0	5	75	100

Robinson's (1951) classic treatment, calculating an index of agreement (*IA*) for each pair of units:

$$IA_{jk} = 200 - \left(\sum_{i=1}^{m} \left| X_{ji} - X_{ki} \right| \right)$$

meaning that the index of agreement between unit *j* and unit *k* is found by subtracting from 200 the sum of the absolute values of the differences between the percentages registered for each type. The figure 200 is used because 200% is the maximum possible disagreement. In this case $m = 4$ in the formula because there are four types represented. Figure 8.4 provides a computational example, and Table 8.5 represents the $n \times n$ similarity matrix obtained in this manner.

Robinson's *IA* coefficient is based on the assumption that similar units will have similar percentages of the various artifact types. It should be clear from the example of Figure 8.4 that the value of *IA* will decrease as the differences between units increase. Table 8.5 is an $n \times n$ symmetric matrix. In any symmetric matrix, the element in the *i*th row and the *j*th column is identical to the element in the *j*th row and the *i*th column. The principal diagonal of a square symmetric matrix S is composed of the elements $s_{11}, s_{22}, \ldots, s_{nn}$, where s_{ij} means the element of S that is located at the intersection of the *i*th row and the *j*th column, and *n* is the number of row–columns. The similarity coefficient of a particular unit with itself will always represent the maximum possible similarity, and in the case of Robinson's *IA*, we observe that the principal diagonal contains the value 200, because the sum of the differences of percentages for one row with

$$IA_{AB} = 200 - \left(\sum_{i=1}^{4} | X_{Ai} - X_{Bi} | \right)$$
$$= 200 - (0 + 20 + 5 + 15)$$

$$= 200 - 40 = \boxed{160}$$

$$IA_{AC} = 200 - \left(\sum_{i=1}^{4} | X_{Ai} - X_{Ci} | \right)$$
$$= 200 - (50 + 20 + 10 + 20)$$

$$= 200 - 100 = \boxed{100}$$

$$IA_{AD} = 200 - \left(\sum_{i=1}^{4} | X_{Ai} - X_{Di} | \right)$$
$$= 200 - (10 + 10 + 0 + 0)$$

$$= 200 - 20 = \boxed{180}$$

etc.

Figure 8.4. Illustration of the calculation of Robinson's *IA*, a similarity coefficient (see Table 8.4 and Table 8.5).

TABLE 8.5

Similarity Matrix (Robinson's Index of Agreement) Obtained from Artificial Data of Table 8.4 by Means of Calculations Illustrated in Figure 8.4

Unit	Site A	Site B	Site C	Site D	Site E
Site A	200	160	100	180	150
Site B	160	200	100	140	120
Site C	100	100	200	120	140
Site D	180	140	120	200	170
Site E	150	120	140	170	200

itself is zero. Because it is a symmetric matrix, the elements on one side of the principal diagonal are a mirror image of those on the other side of the principal diagonal.

We can now rearrange the row–columns so that the higher values will be clustered about the principal diagonal, with decreasing values as "one goes away from the diagonal either vertically or horizontally" (Robinson 1951:295). This results in Table 8.6. Notice that the correct seriated order is C—E—D—A—B (or B—A—D—E—C). Rearranging the rows of the original data matrix (see Table 8.7) confirms that the result is the same: The columns of the permuted data matrix satisfy the "increase-or-decrease-or-increase-and-then-decrease" criterion.

In practice, of course, archaeological data are rarely well-behaved enough to enable such a straightforward rearrangement. In his original article, Robinson (1951:298–301) recommended certain heuristic procedures to help guide the rearrangement process and to evaluate progress in achieving the best ordering. It should also be noted that it is possible, in nonideal cases, for a similarity matrix to be in Robinson form without the corresponding data matrix being a perfect P-matrix (or Q-matrix).

Difficulties inherent in Ford's row rearrangement technique and in Robinson's similarity matrix manipulation technique will be discussed more thoroughly below. It has been the purpose of this section simply to

TABLE 8.6

Square Symmetric Matrix (Robinson Index of Agreement), Rearranged So That the Highest Values Cluster around the Principal Diagonal (Compare with Table 8.5)

Unit	Site C	Site E	Site D	Site A	Site B
Site C	200	140	120	100	100
Site E	140	200	170	150	120
Site D	120	170	200	180	140
Site A	100	150	180	200	160
Site B	100	120	140	160	200

TABLE 8.7

Seriated Artificial Data Matrix Consisting of Percentages of Four Pottery Types Found on the Surfaces of Five Sites (Compare with Table 8.4)

Unit	Type 1	Type 2	Type 3	Type 4	Total
Site C	50%	0%	0%	50%	100%
Site E	20	0	5	75	100
Site D	10	10	10	70	100
Site A	0	20	10	70	100
Site B	0	40	5	55	100

introduce concepts essential to the consideration of advances in the practice of seriation over the past generation.

To summarize, seriation is a unidimensional ordering technique used to arrange items in a series such that the position of an item, relative to other items, reflects its similarity to those other items. Although it need not necessarily be a chronological ordering technique, archaeologists have made frequent use of seriation to arrange units along a temporal dimension. Seriation may be carried out on incidence (presence/absence) data or on abundance data. In the latter case the data are often expressed as relative frequencies or as percentages of certain artifact types found in the units to be seriated. Less frequently, ratio-scale variables have been used in place of percentages or relative frequencies. Seriation can be carried out either by directly rearranging the rows (units) of a data matrix or by manipulating a similarity matrix derived therefrom.

ADVANCES IN SERIATION TECHNIQUES

The works of Ford (1962), discussed above, provide an appropriate place to begin a discussion of advances in thinking about the question of seriation.

Ford's graphical technique has the advantage of simplicity, and, for a relatively small number of units, it is efficient. Over 15 years after its publication, Ford's *A Quantitative Method for Deriving Cultural Chronology* (1962) still contains good advice for the archaeologist beginning to explore unknown or poorly known regions. Ford's technique consists in representing the percentage of each pottery type found in a given unit as a bar of corresponding width on a long strip of graph paper, then arranging and rearranging the strips until the "increase, decrease, or increase and then decrease" pattern emerges in the columns. Naturally, an increase in the percentage of one type must result in the decrease in the percentage of one or more of the other types. To see that this might conceivably be disadvantageous, consider a situation in which a plain pottery consistently employed in association with culinary activities and a decorated ware used only in ceremonies are manufactured. Now suppose that at a later time the production of decorated ceramics is increased, but production of the plain ceramics remains constant. A representative sample of pottery from the later time period would show a higher proportion of decorated pottery. Because the total must sum to 100%, the plain pottery will appear to have decreased in "popularity," when in fact its rate of production remained exactly the same. If we are interested only in a relative chronology, however, this feature of the technique will concern us less than if we are attempting to reconstruct the actual patterns of ceramic change. (This question will be more thoroughly discussed below.) Perhaps a more serious criticism of the technique is that it leaves too much room for subjective judgment about the "best" sequence; it is often difficult for competent workers to agree on such matters. [Régnier (1977) has proposed a computerized algorithm closely following Ford's technique of using the combined information provided by several test excavations.] McNutt (1973) has pointed out that the choice of different typological subdivisions can lead to erroneous sequences even when the data appear to satisfy the assumptions on which the technique is based.

In a paper published in 1959, Meighan proposed a fast graphical seriation technique that involves combining similar types until there are only three major types, then calculating percentages as if there exist only three types in the material. Plotting of the resulting data on triangular graph paper produces a cluster of points along an axis. A straight line is then drawn such that an equal number of points fall on either side of the line, and perpendiculars are drawn from the points to the line to establish the sequence. Because the three types, say A, B, and C, in the Meighan procedure sum to 100% of the assemblage, one of the variables can be expressed in terms of the other two (for example, %C = 100% − %A − %B); thus, the graphing of only two of the three types on ordinary two-dimensional graph paper is sufficient (Ascher 1959).

Like Ford's graphical technique, Meighan's procedure is fast and simple. The latter is useful as a preliminary ordering technique, when time is limited, provided the three types used are reasonably good chronological indicators. Hole and Shaw (1967:76) found that both bad and good data could result in curved plots on triangular graph paper, a situation that always obtains when all three of the types are changing through time (Meighan 1959:204).

As noted above, the Robinson technique proceeds from a square symmetric matrix of similarity coefficients derived from the original data matrix, instead of beginning with the latter and permuting the rows. Robinson's technique was tested on deposits of known chronological order by Brainerd (1951), and used successfully by Belous (1953), Dixon (1956), Flanders (1960), and others. The manipulation of the Robinson agreement matrix is time-consuming and tedious for large numbers of units, however. The procedure is also vulnerable to the same criticism often leveled at Ford's graphical technique: Manual rearrangement of the deposits is unsystematic, and hence prone to unconscious subjectivity.

Dempsey and Baumhoff (1963) became concerned that the Robinson approach of differentially weighting types on the basis of their relative frequencies could introduce error in cases where the incipience, florescence, and extinction of a particular type occurred completely within the time range of concern. They recommended a presence/absence rather than a relative frequency approach, cautioning that built-in similarity between units should be avoided by defining classifications "so that the presence (or absence) of any one type contains no necessary inplication concerning the presence (or absence) of any other type" in the same unit (Dempsey and Baumhoff 1963:499). Their procedure begins with a similarity matrix in which the elements record the number of times a given artifact type is present in both units or absent in both units. Next, the units are split into two groups—presumably "early" and "late"—by comparing, in turn, the similarity coefficient between each unit and the unit having the greatest range of similarity values. One group contains the half of the units with the lowest coefficients of similarity to the chosen unit; the other half contains those with the highest coefficients. Then, the average agreement of each unit with each of the two groups of units is found, and the units are reordered with respect to the signed differences between the average with Group 1 and the average with Group 2. The average–reordering procedure is repeated until no better ordering is possible.

In a comparison of their orderings of real data previously examined by Belous and Heizer, Dempsey and Baumhoff reported a Spearman rank-order correlation of 0.96 with Heizer's results, a 0.77 correlation with those of Belous. The Dempsey–Baumhoff technique, based as it is on presence/absence data, is subject to the same criticism a, other methods based on a binary scale: Incidence of one artifact type is counted as heavily as the occurrence of several hundred such items; hence, potentially interesting information is ignored. Also, as Cowgill (1968b:518), Hole and Shaw (1967:78), Lipe (1964:103–104), and others have pointed out, even the slightest mixing of artifacts from two proveniences may seriously affect the ordering. Cowgill (1968b:518) and Hole and Shaw (1967:78–79) also properly state that Dempsey and Baumhoff are in error when they claim that the Robinson technique is incapable of adequately evaluating types that begin, peak, and end within the time range of interest. (In fact, the Robinson model is based on the assumption that a type will peak in popularity only once, and that no type will end abruptly near its peak of popularity.) Finally, Hole and Shaw (1967:77) indicate that the Dempsey–Baumhoff technique is difficult to carry out and is prone to excessive computational errors.

Renfrew and Sterud (1969) proposed a diagrammatic technique that also begins with a similarity matrix. Proceeding from the assumption that units closest in time will have the highest similarity coefficients, they arrange the units in a linear order, joined by bonds indicating their relative similarity. When loops occur, Renfrew and Sterud provide conventions for restoring the linearity, if such an arrangement is possible for the given data. Further, they introduce a simple "cluster coefficient" that can be calculated before beginning the process. The coefficient varies from 0 (perfect linear ordering is possible) to 100 (a linear ordering is impossible), and they find that their technique is generally reliable for cluster coefficients of less than 60.

The Renfrew–Sterud hand technique is simple and unambiguous. Two different persons should be able to obtain the same ordering if given the same matrix of similarities. Because computation times increase only arithmetically with the number of units being seriated, they recommend the technique as an appropriate means for the preliminary investigation of the structure of a data set or for ordering a matrix of more than 35 units. The technique considers the relationship between closely similar units only, linking according to the magnitude of the similarity coefficients, but cannot take into account weaker links. If there is one main linear relationship within the data structure, the Renfrew–Sterud technique is a fast and systematic means for finding the best sequence.

Statistician Gelfand (1971a,b) offered a generalization of the Renfrew–Sterud double-linkage technique, and has additionally proposed an averaging procedure that has had good results when applied to archaeological data. These techniques are referred to (by Gelfand) as Method I and Method II, respectively.

With Method I, one selects in decreasing order the $n - 1$ largest similarity coefficients such that (*a*) no subscript is included more than twice, and (*b*) all subscripts "communicate"—that is, do not form closed loops (they do not "cluster," in Renfrew and Sterud's sense of the term).

With Gelfand's Method II, one constructs an estimated order for each separate row of the matrix of similarities according to the familiar Robinson pattern of monotonic decrease from the principal diagonal. Then these estimated orders are averaged to give an overall estimated order. It happens that, if there exists a permutation of the matrix that will cast it perfectly into the Robinson form, all n estimated orders of Method II will be identical (Gelfand 1971a:194–195, 1971b:269–271). Gelfand also presents a "continuity index" (Gelfand 1971a:195–196, 1971b:269–271) that enables the comparison of one estimated order with another.

Gelfand's Method II, illustrated here in Figure 8.5, is somewhat more reliable than Method I, although both work well for well-behaved data. Neither technique is complicated, and, for small matrices, both are fast, efficient, and unambiguous. The techniques are easily programmed to be carried out by a digital computer.

Ascher and Ascher (1963) were the first to construct a completely computerized procedure for ordering a similarity matrix of Robinson index of agreement coefficients. The computerized procedure inserts one row (and column) at a time, testing each new row–column in each position. Those row–columns not fully satisfying the monotonic decrease criterion are held aside until all other row–columns are placed. Goodness of fit to the ideal Robinson matrix (similarities monotonically decrease as one moves away from the principal diagonal) is evaluated in terms of the smallest number of negatively signed differences between scores. Then the residual row–columns are inserted, one at a time, in the best possible relationship to the already-ordered row–columns, with the stipulation that the relative position of the latter stay the same.

The Ascher–Ascher program was a step forward at the time of its publication, for it made the sorting of large similarity matrices considerably easier and somewhat more systematic. However, because each placement of a row–column assumes that the previously positioned row–columns are correctly ordered, and because the ordering always begins with the first row–column and proceeds to the nth, the initial input sequence influences the final seriation to a considerable degree. With different initial orders, one may find better (or worse) solutions.

Kuzara, a computer programmer, devised an improved algorithm for the ordering of similarity matrices into the Robinson form (Kuzara *et al.* 1966). Kuzara's program works with the entire similarity matrix at once. The first row–column is moved into the second position, and the new ordering and the previous ordering are compared for goodness of fit, the better of the two orderings being held in storage in the computer. The same row–column is tried in position 3, then 4, and so on, until it has been tried in all positions, with only the single "best" ordering being retained in computer memory. Then the second row–column, the third, etc., are tried in all positions in the same way, until every row–column has been tried in every position. The entire process is then restarted and done again and again, until no improvement is apparent in the orderings. Two criteria are used to determine goodness of fit, criterion A being the sum of the magnitudes of the negatively signed differences, criterion B being the

Step 1: Construct an estimated order for the first row, A. Disregarding the principal diagonal, the largest similarity coefficient in row A is that between A and D, so write down

A—D

Now find the next highest coefficient in row A. It is that between A and B. In order to know whether to link B with the A end of the chain or the D end of the chain, examine the coefficients between B and A and between B and D.

$IA_{BA} = 160$, and $IA_{BD} = 140$. Because 160 is larger than 140, B is assigned to the A end of the chain, rather than to the D end.

The estimated order for row A is, then,

B—A—D

Now find the next highest coefficient in row A. It is that between A and E. In order to know whether to link E with the B end of the chain or the D end of the chain, examine the coefficients between E and B and between E and D.

$IA_{EB} = 120$, and $IA_{ED} = 170$. Because 170 is larger than 120, E is assigned to the D end of the chain, rather than to the B end.

The estimated order for row A is now

B—A—D—E

Finally, the last remaining coefficient in row A is that between A and C. In order to know whether to link C with the B end of the chain or the E end of the chain, examine the coefficients between C and B and between C and E.

$IA_{CB} = 100$, and $IA_{CE} = 140$. Because 140 is larger than 100, C is assigned to the E end of the chain, rather than to the B end.

The final estimated order for row A is thus

B—A—D—E—C

Step 2: Construct an estimated order for the second row, B, in the same manner.
Step 3: Construct an estimated order for the third row, C, in the same manner.
Step 4: Construct an estimated order for the fourth row, D, in the same manner.
Step 5: Construct an estimated order for the last row, E, in the same manner.
In this case, the five resulting estimated orders are identical:

    A: B—A—D—E—C
    B: B—A—D—E—C
    C: B—A—D—E—C
    D: B—A—D—E—C
    E: B—A—D—E—C

Now calculate the average ranks, $T_j, j = 1, 2, ..., n$, where n is the number of rows:

$T_A = 2 + 2 + 2 + 2 + 2 = 10$ because A is ranked second 5 times.
$T_B = 1 + 1 + 1 + 1 + 1 = 5$ because B is ranked first 5 times.
$T_C = 5 + 5 + 5 + 5 + 5 = 25$ because C is ranked fifth 5 times.
$T_D = 3 + 3 + 3 + 3 + 3 = 15$ because D is ranked third 5 times.
$T_E = 4 + 4 + 4 + 4 + 4 = 20$ because E is ranked fourth 5 times.

Now arrange the T_j's in increasing order:

$T_B < T_A < T_D < T_E < T_C$, yielding the seriated order:
B—A—D—E—C

Note: When the matrix can be permuted into a perfect Robinson matrix, as in this case, the estimated orders will be identical for each row; thus the calculation of the average ranks T_j is trivial. See Gelfand (1971b:269) for further discussion and for an example in which the matrix is not capable of being permuted into perfect Robinson form.

Figure 8.5. An illustration of Gelfand's Method II, using the artificial data from Table 8.5, this chapter (see Gelfand 1971a,b for further details).

coefficient first suggested by Robinson (1951:300): the square of the negative differences divided by the sums of squares of all differences, both positive and negative. The higher the value of A or of B, the worse is the fit to the Robinson model. Testing on both ideal and empirical data (Kuzara *et al.* 1966:1453–1454) established the superiority of Kuzara's program over that of Ascher and Ascher in arranging data to fit the Robinson model.

Hole and Shaw (1967) carried out an involved series of experiments, comparing the results of their own computerized seriations of stone tools, bone tools, and ceramics with results of the Meighan graphical technique, the Dempsey–Baumhoff approach, and the Ascher–Ascher matrix-ordering program. The Hole–Shaw algorithm proceeds "by improving a given ordering by examining a selected set of related orderings which presumably contains the ones most likely to be improvements on the original" (Hole and Shaw 1967:15). A subset of the set of all possible orderings is examined, and a matrix coefficient (the sum of the errors— that is, the differences that are negative as one moves away from the diagonal) is calculated and evaluated for each ordering. The best ordering is retained in memory and can be the input ordering for the next cycle. Usually two or three such cycles are sufficient to find an ordering that cannot be further improved (Hole and Shaw 1967:16). The "permutation search" technique of Hole and Shaw does not provide dramatically better results than Meighan's simple graphical technique (Hole and Shaw 1967:69–77), but some of Hole and Shaw's difficulties resulted from badly chosen categories and inadequate sample sizes (Cowgill 1968b:519).

A year after Hole and Shaw's contribution there appeared a new computerized seriation technique by Craytor and Johnson (1968). Craytor created a coefficient H, which is the sum of all the coefficient differences (errors between a perfectly seriated matrix and the one under consideration), and which considers the magnitude as well as the number of differences between similarity scores. Also, the H coefficient takes into account all between-score inequalities, not just those between adjacent scores. The H coefficient, when divided by the product of the number of tested inequalities with the standard deviations of the $\frac{1}{2}(n^2 - n)$ discrete similarity scores, creates matrix coefficient C, a measure that increases as the matrix becomes more perfectly seriated. Craytor's program first generates a random sequencing of the units to be seriated, and calculates a similarity matrix therefrom. In a procedure similar to Kuzara's, every row–column of the similarity matrix is interchanged with every other until high H coefficients indicate high local maxima (relatively good seriations). The permutation search is repeated until the ordering coefficient H does not deviate significantly from the H value of the previous search. Because the calculation of the H coefficient is based on the assumption that all inequalities have the same unit meaning, the Robinson index of agreement is an ideal measure of similarity for Craytor and Johnson (1968:11–12).

The SERIATE program of Craytor was used successfully to order a series of 11 Late Tertiary vertebrate collections into reasonable ecological communities (Johnson 1968:13–14) and to seriate chronologically 26 Upper Paleolithic artifact collections (Johnson 1968:27–43). Low C coefficients in both cases suggested to Johnson the likelihood that there is no overall linear trend in either data set, and analysis with an unweighted pair–group (average-linkage) cluster analysis further partitions the samples. Craytor's algorithm is perhaps the most sophisticated and efficient of the computerized matrix-ordering techniques discussed thus far. However, it is affected by the initial random number supplied by the user. To be reasonably certain that a good seriation has been obtained, it is necessary to run the program a number of times with different initial "random" numbers.

A seriation technique proposed by de la Vega (1977) for the ordering of a similarity matrix makes use of both a clustering algorithm and an ordering algorithm. Within a subset of the units, the program produces a partition of the units into two groups, say α and β, by use of an average-linkage clustering technique. The partial order of elements in α and β is improved according to calculations of F, which is proportional to the number of deviations from the perfect Robinson ordering. An advantage of the procedure is that the final ordering is independent of the starting order. The algorithm has been successful in ordering anthropomorphic statuary (Landau and de la Vega 1971). A detailed example of the algorithm is provided by de la Vega (1977).

The work of Goldmann (1971, 1972) provides an interesting example combining stratigraphic information, typological analysis, and an incidence matrix-reordering technique. Goldmann set for himself the formidable task of refining a regional chronology applicable to about 4000 Bronze Age (about 2000–1400 B.C.) finds from northern, central, and southeastern Europe. Reducing the 4000 finds to about 900 assemblages, he performed a computer-assisted seriation of a 790-unit by 404-type incidence matrix, augmenting his decision-making process by the use of 51 different known stratigraphic sequences (Goldmann 1971:202).

Arguing that formal similarity observed on artifacts by the archaeologist can be the result of "production-similarity" as well as "deposition-similarity," Goldmann believes that a combination of both lines of evidence is necessary to the establishment of a reliable relative chronology. If one can assume that similarity observed by the archaeologist corresponds to a genuine "type" reflecting an idea in the mind of the artifact's manufacturer, and if independent evidence is available to suggest that "the majority of objects grouped into one 'class of similarity' stems from a clearly delimited prehistoric period" (Goldmann 1971:202), then a relative chronology may be established through the seriation of judiciously chosen assemblages. In reality, not all assemblages will provide appropriate qualitative information, so the archaeologist must define among these assemblages "key-finds" (*Leitfunde*) containing representatives of types he considers "relevant to his investigation" (Goldmann 1971:206). The matrix of key-finds is considered to be seriated when, in each column, Goldmann's (1972:20, 27) H coefficient is greater than or equal to 0.5. Goldmann's H is, for any given column (type), the total number of occurrences of the type divided by the inclusive range of the type; for example, if in column i of a seven-row incidence matrix, 1's are recorded for rows 3, 4, 5, and 7, then $H_i = 4/5 = 0.8$.

To my knowledge, Goldmann's is the largest matrix of archaeological data yet seriated by computer. His two FORTRAN programs ARCH and GGG were first tested extensively on 100×50 matrices; the final production run on the complete 790×404 matrix required a little over an hour on an IBM 360-75 computer (Goldmann 1971:202). I have not examined these programs in detail; Wilkinson (1974:31) is of the opinion that Goldmann's programs are inefficient. The entire methodology admits considerable subjectivity, and, as Goldmann himself realizes, it is based on the rather generous assumptions that the assemblages are technologically similar and were comparably collected/excavated/reported. It is to Goldmann's credit that his assumptions and methodology are made explicit (see especially Goldmann 1972:1–28) enough to enable a thorough understanding and critique of his method.

Wilkinson (1974) has also proposed a method for analyzing incidence data matrices directly. All archaeological seriation procedures are based on the assumption that there is a true chronological ordering of the units. If one makes the additional assumption, as Goldmann has, that there is a true chronological ordering of the artifact types, Wilkinson (1974:30–32) proposes a simple but very efficient heuristic algorithm for alternately ordering the rows and columns of an incidence matrix on the basis of the mean positions of the 1's. The algorithm is as follows (Wilkinson 1974:31–32): (1) Calculate the mean positions for 1's in the columns. (2) Order the columns according to these means. (3) Calculate the mean positions for 1's in the rows. (4) Order the rows according to these means. (5) Repeat steps 1–4 until no improvement is possible. In practice, Wilkinson uses the fast AXIS program based on this algorithm to calculate a rough ordering, and then uses another program, POLISH, to refine the seriation. Source listings of both programs are provided by Wilkinson (1974).

Although they differ in specific detail, both Goldmann's ARCH and Wilkinson's AXIS algorithms are procedures for ordering incidence matrices directly. All units and all types are weighted equivalently in determining the best ordering. I shall next describe two other approaches to the ordering of incidence matrices, one by Bordaz and Bordaz, which allows differential weighting of units, and one by Cowgill, which allows differential weighting of types.

The Bordaz–Bordaz procedure begins with the calculation of a Tanimoto distance coefficient (Tanimoto 1961; Rogers and Tanimoto 1960) for each pair of provenience units. Then the units are clustered, and the unit most "typical" of each of the clusters is found. [Clustering procedures for archaeological data are discussed in some detail by Doran and Hodson (1975:173–186).] The most typical member of the cluster is also the most reliable; in information theoretic terms, it is that member which contains the least "noise"; geometrically, the typical member is that unit closest to the centroid of the points constituting the cluster (Bordaz and Bordaz 1970:233–234). An ordering, called by Bordaz and Bordaz a "skeleton" matrix, is established using the typical members alone. The other members of the clusters are then grouped in a systematic way about their respective "most typical" members, producing the final ordering. The Bordaz–Bordaz technique was shown to be successful on model data, satisfactorily ordering 90 excavation units from the Peñitas site in Mexico.

Bordaz and Bordaz use a computer to calculate the distance matrix, form the clusters, and find the typical member for each cluster. An ordering is produced using these typical members, then additional units are added by hand in such a way that (*a*) as few new characteristics are introduced as possible, and (*b*) those units having characteristics most similar to typical members are introduced first. The most innovative facet of the procedure is the initial weighting of certain *units* because they are more "typical."

In Cowgill's (1972) procedure one computes a similarity coefficient between each pair of types (not between pairs of provenience units). Cowgill's similarity coefficient, here denoted as s_C, is calculated as follows (Cowgill 1972:404):

$$s_{C_{ij}} = 0 \text{ if } a_{ij} \text{ is zero}$$
$$s_{C_{ij}} = 1 \text{ if either } b_{ij} \text{ or } c_{ij} \text{ is zero}$$
$$s_{C_{ij}} = (a_{ij} + d_{ij})/n \text{ otherwise}$$

where $s_{C_{ij}}$ is the coefficient of similarity between types i and j, a_{ij} is the number of units in which both i and j occur, b_{ij} is the number of units in which type i is present but type j is absent, c_{ij} is the number of units in which type j is present but type i is absent, d_{ij} is the number of units in which both i and j are absent, and n is the total number of units. As Cowgill notes, s_C is equivalent to s_{SM}, the simple matching coefficient (Sokal and Sneath 1963:133), for cases in which types i and j partially overlap (Cowgill 1972:398–410). A matrix of similarity coefficients thus obtained is analyzed by a standard MDSCAL (Shepard 1962a,b; Kruskal 1964a,b) multidimensional scaling program, and the two-dimensional configuration is inspected in order to gauge the appropriateness of proceeding with a seriation. Working with an ideal matrix, Cowgill (1972:406–409) shows that the order of midpoints of the type ranges (where range means the total number of rows in which the type occurs) is retrieved effectively by MDSCAL. Working from the assumption that a type's probability of occurrence in a given unit is distributed normally with a mean at the predicted midpoint of the type's range and a standard deviation proportional to the number of units in which the type occurs, he derives a formula for predicting the occurrence points for units:

$$L(k)_U = \left(\sum_i x_i / n_i^k \right) \Big/ \left(\sum_i 1/n_i^k \right)$$

where U is some unit (row) in the incidence matrix, L is the predicted "location" of the unit U, x_i is the predicted midpoint for type i (obtained from the MDSCAL configuration), n_i is the number of units in which type i occurs, and the summation is over all types occurring in unit U. The parameter k can be either 1 or 2; in the former condition, less emphasis is given to scarce types in determining the predicted location of units. In either case, it can be seen that, if all the types occurring in unit U occur in the same number of units, the formula reduces to the mean of the predicted midpoints (the x_i's) for all types occurring in unit U (Cowgill 1972:407–422). Interestingly, Cowgill's weighted mean, L, may result in an ordering of the incidence matrix diverging somewhat from the ideal form, even when the data are capable of being cast into the ideal form. There is certainly no reason to make all our results consistent with the idealized model if we know some variables to be more reliable indicators of time trends than others. The inclusion of rare types of an equal standing with common types may introduce an undesirable bias toward the infrequent or idiosyncratic item. Cowgill (1972:420), for example, in working with empirical data, does not consider units having less than three types present. There is, of course, no guarantee that frequently found items are necessarily better indicators of temporal variation. At any rate, Cowgill's weighting technique provides an option that may be useful in many cases. Another advantage of Cowgill's technique is that it can be used to seriate hundreds of units efficiently, provided that the number of types is not very large. Although computer program listings are not provided, Cowgill's (1972) procedure is so clearly described that any competent programmer could easily write his or her own program, provided that some sort of multidimensional scaling program were also available. Both Bordaz and Bordaz' and Cowgill's techniques are intended for the ordering of incidence data.

In Cowgill's procedure, multidimensional scaling is used to estimate the relative positions of the midpoints of the type ranges. If one knows or has a reliable estimate of the date of a type's midpoint, the task of assigning relative dates to the units should be considerably easier. In fact, this is just what South (1977:201–274) has done for historic sites of Colonial America. Although South does not refer to the technique as "seriation," it seems appropriate to describe it here. Working from Nöel Hume's (1970) extensive compendium, South first compiles a table of 78 ceramic types, assigning a median manufacturing date to each type. A simple formula is used to estimate a "mean ceramic date" for a given sample of ceramic fragments.

$$Y = \sum_{i=1}^{m} X_i \cdot f_i \left/ \sum_{i=1}^{m} f_i \right.$$

where X_i is the median manufacturing date for each ceramic type, f_i is the frequency of each type, and the summation is over all m ceramic types represented in the sample. For example, suppose that a ceramic sample contains 30 fragments of a type known to have a median manufacturing date of 1760, 50 fragments of a type with a median date of 1775, and 50 fragments of a type with a median date of 1783. The calculation

$$Y = \frac{(1760)(30) + (1775)(50) + (1783)(50)}{30 + 50 + 50}$$

$$= \frac{52800 + 88750 + 89150}{130} = \frac{230700}{130} = 1774.6$$

yields 1774.6 as an estimate of the "mean ceramic date" for the sample. The investigator of historic sites often has access to documentary evidence concerning dates of manufacture and patterns of commercial distribution of ceramics and other artifacts. These records can be used to confirm functional, social, economic, or other hypotheses about distributions of artifacts in time and space (South 1977:230–235).

A number of individuals have used minimum path approaches to the seriation problem. Wilkinson (1971, 1974) realized that the question of rearranging an incidence matrix with the intention of bunching the 1's together as closely as possible in each column is analogous to the classic graph theoretic question known as the Traveling Salesman problem (Bellmore and Nemhauser 1968). Although the problem has not been "solved"—that is, no nonexhausive algorithm has been discovered that will find *the* shortest tour for a salesman starting from a given city, visiting each of a specified group of cities, then returning to the origin of the tour—heuristic search techniques are known that provide good estimates of the solution. Such a re-entrant path is known as a Hamiltonian circuit (Tutte 1946; Flood 1956). Wilkinson's (1974:105–142) program employs a heuristic search technique in concert with a data-smoothing algorithm that preserves the chronological information contained in incidence matrices. Experiments on ideal and empirical data convinced Wilkinson that the best procedure would be to apply an algorithm that finds the *maximum* Hamiltonian circuit, given a *similarity* matrix (identical to the problem of finding the salesman's *shortest* path, given a *distance* matrix).

The similarity matrix must be "smoothed" to mitigate the effect of "rogue" points (that is, graves that have very few similarities with other graves) (Wilkinson 1974:56–76). Wilkinson suggested that repeated "circle-powering" (see Figure 8.7 below) of a similarity matrix might yield a better-behaved matrix without substantial loss of information. Kadane (1972) also discusses minimum path solutions to the seriation problem. He applies the heuristic method of Little *et al.* (1963) to three data sets, comparing his results with those of Gelfand (1969) and Sternin (1965). Kadane's (1972:12) results are generally satisfactory, but seem to be no improvement over those of Gelfand. The Traveling Salesman problem will be discussed more extensively below.

Several seriation techniques reported in the past few years have utilized one form or another of multidimensional scaling, sometimes called "proximity analysis." Speaking generally, multidimensional scaling techniques fashion a geometric representation of the pattern of a matrix of similarities such that the *rank-order* of geometric distance between points is the inverse of the rank-order of similarities between the units being analyzed. The geometric space (sometimes called a "hyperspace" when more than two dimensions are involved) necessary to represent n units in multidimensional space consists of $n - 1$ dimensions. Often it happens that the rank-order of interpoint distances can be preserved, or nearly preserved, in fewer dimensions than the originally required $n - 1$ dimensions. By means of an iterative procedure, the number of dimensions in which the data are represented is reduced by 1, and a measure of "stress" is calculated that is proportional to the number of violations of the original rank-order. This process is repeated, expressing the data in fewer and fewer dimensions, until the calculated stress becomes too large for adequate representation of the rank-order of interpoint distances.

If a body of archaeological data is capable of being seriated well, it can be represented with little stress in only one dimension. [In practice, it is usually advisable to examine the two-dimensional solution, even when the calculations indicate a good fit is possible in one dimension; see Kendall (1969b:73), Kruskal (1971:129–131), Cowgill (1972:397), and Sibson (1977:84) for comments on this point.] The optimal configuration is influenced by the random number supplied to the computer for the purpose of generating the starting configuration. Hence, multidimensional scaling programs are usually run several times on the same data with different starting configurations; if nearly identical configurations appear several times, it is likely that the best one has been obtained. Examples of multidimensional scaling procedures are the MDSCAL program developed by Shepard (1962a,b) and Kruskal (1964a,b), the TORSCA program of Torgerson and Young (Young 1968), and the versatile Small Space Analysis package developed by Guttman and Lingoes (Lingoes 1973; see Green and Carmone 1970:42–53 for an interesting comparison of these three approaches). A basic introduction to multidimensional scaling is given by Shepard (1972:1–12). Further information concerning the theory and uses of multidimensional scaling can be found in the book edited by Shepard *et al.* (1972; see also Green and Rao 1972; Sibson 1977).

Multidimensional scaling approaches to the seriation problem were advocated by Cowgill (1968a:374, 1968b:519) several years ago. Early uses of multidimensional scaling in archaeology were by Hodson *et al.* (1966), Doran and Hodson (1966), and McPherron (1967). More recent contributions are those of True and Matson (1970), Ammerman (1971), Kruskal (1971), Kendall (1969b, 1970, 1971a), Lingoes (1970), Cowgill (1972), LeBlanc (1975), Drennan (1976), and Graham *et al.* (1976).

A good example of an explicit use of multidimensional scaling for chronological seriation is that reported by Kendall. Kendall's work has contributed significantly to seriation theory as well as to practical seriation techniques. Although his theoretical contributions will be placed in context below, a discussion is necessary here to provide a background for the discussion of a number of techniques. Stimulated by the work of Fulkerson and Gross (1965) on incidence matrices, Kendall proved (1969a) that if an incidence matrix I were capable of being permuted into the ideal "Petrie" (or P-matrix) form (that is, having all the 1's bunched together in each individual column), then that same permutation when applied to the matrix $G = II^T$ would give that square matrix the ideal

"Robinson" form. To transpose a matrix, one simply exchanges its rows and columns (indicated symbolically by a superscript T). Matrix G is the product of I with the transpose of I. Matrix multiplication is not difficult, but there is not room in this chapter to explain the process adequately (for a useful introduction to matrix algebra for the nonmathematician, see Davis 1973:127–169). For purposes of the present discussion, it is convenient to think of the matrix G as composed of elements g_{ij} representing the number of criteria (for example, artifact types) present in both the ith and jth units (for example, graves) (see Figure 8.6.). Cautiously translating this mathematical conclusion to an archaeological context, Kendall (1969b:74) demonstrated that a MDSCAL multidimensional scaling of matrix G produces reliable orderings of the units. For the example shown in Figure 8.6, the indicated MDSCAL order is B—C—E—A—F—D (or D—F—A—E—C—B) (the reader can rearrange the matrices G and I in Figure 8.6 to verify that G becomes an ideal "Robinson" matrix and I becomes an ideal "Petrie" matrix). Kendall (1971b) later generalized this

Example: Units A and B have no criteria in common, so $g_{AB} = 0$; units A and C have criterion 1 and criterion 4 in common, so $g_{AC} = 2$; and so on.

	Criterion					
	1	2	3	4	5	6
Unit						
A	1	0	0	1	1	0
B	0	0	1	0	0	1
C	1	1	1	1	0	1
D	0	0	0	0	1	0
E	1	1	1	1	1	0
F	1	0	0	0	1	0

Incidence matrix I

	Unit					
	A	B	C	D	E	F
Unit						
A	3	0	2	1	3	2
B	0	2	2	0	1	0
C	2	2	5	0	4	1
D	1	1	0	1	1	1
E	3	1	4	1	5	2
F	2	0	1	1	2	2

Similarity matrix $G = II^T$

Figure 8.6. Illustration of the relationship between an incidence matrix and the product of that matrix with its transpose. The element g_{ij} represents the number of criteria present in both unit i and unit j.

result for abundance matrices, proving that, if an abundance matrix **A** were capable of being permuted into the ideal Q-matrix (that is, for each column the numbers increase, or decrease, or increase and then decrease, all in the weak sense), then that same permutation when applied to the matrix $S = A \circ A^T$ would give the ideal "Robinson" form. Matrix **S** is the "circle product" of **A** with the transpose of **A**. That is,

$$S = (A \circ A^T)_{ij} = \sum_{h=1}^{m} \min(a_{ih}, a_{jh})$$

An example, with already familiar data, is given in Figure 8.7. It will be noted that, in this case, $A \circ A^T$ is proportional to Robinson's IA (compare Figure 8.7 with Tables 8.4 and 8.5); this will occur whenever each row (unit) of **A** contains proportions summing to 1.0 (or percentages summing to 100%) (Kendall 1971b:109). Again, Kendall shows (1971a) that a MDSCAL analysis of an $S = (A \circ A^T)$ matrix can yield an appropriate linear arrangement of archaeological units. Experimenting with ideal data, Kendall (1970:128–129, 1971a:225–227) found that the correct order was recovered in a horseshoe-shaped curve. Next, the method was applied to the familiar Münsingen–Rain cemetery data (Hodson 1968), resulting,

	Type			
Unit	1	2	3	4
A	.00	.20	.10	.70
B	.00	.40	.05	.55
C	.50	.00	.00	.50
D	.10	.10	.10	.70
E	.20	.00	.05	.75

Abundance matrix **A**

$$S_{ij} = (A \circ A^T)_{ij} = \sum_{h=1}^{m} \min(a_{ih}, a_{jh})$$

Example

For units A and B, $s_{AB} = \sum_{h=1}^{4} \min(a_{Ah}, a_{Bh})$

$= \min(0., 0.) + \min(.20, .40) + \min(.10, .05)$
$+ \min(.70, .55)$
$= .0 + .20 + .05 + .55 = .80$

	Unit				
Unit	A	B	C	D	E
A	1.00	.80	.50	.90	.75
B	.80	1.00	.50	.70	.60
C	.50	.50	1.00	.60	.70
D	.90	.70	.60	1.00	.85
E	.75	.60	.70	.85	1.00

Similarity matrix $S = A \circ A^T$

Figure 8.7. Illustration of the relationship between an abundance matrix and the circle product of that matrix with its transpose. The element s_{ij} is a similarity coefficient between units i and j.

again, in a roughly horseshoe-shaped curve. Starting at one end of the configuration and reading around the curve to the opposite end, a chronological sequence was obtained that was very close to Hodson's seriation and that was, as well, consonant with the map of the Münsingen–Rain cemetery (Kendall 1971a:227–229). With further experimentation, Kendall was able to "unbend" the horseshoe by inputting to MCSCAL a similarity matrix, $S' = (S \circ S)$, derived from the first similarity matrix (Kendall 1971a:220, 229–236) and opting for a primary, rather than secondary, treatment of ties in the data [see Kruskal (1964a:22) for a discussion of two alternatives for treating tied dissimilarities in a MDSCAL analysis]. Once the horseshoe has been straightened, it is a simple matter to pass a principal component through the two-dimensional array of points, thus arriving at a satisfactory one-dimensional seriation of the units. In another application of the "horseshoe" technique, Boneva (1971) successfully seriated the works of Plato.

In 1975 LeBlanc published a paper in which he calls attention to the limitations of chronological seriation based on "types" alone. He advocates the use of similarity coefficients derived from relative frequencies of certain attributes of a given variable (for example, the variable "paint type" might have the four possible attributes—"matte," "light subglaze," "heavy subglaze," and "glaze"). Although he calls his resulting coefficients Brainerd–Robinson coefficients, they are not. They are actually dissimilarity coefficients computed by first standardizing each attribute so that rare attributes are given as much weight as common ones. An example of the calculation of LeBlanc's standardized dissimilarity coefficient for one pair of units for one given variable is shown in Figure 8.8. After these manipulations, one has an $n \times n$ matrix of dissimilarity coefficients for each variable, where n is the number of units; in LeBlanc's (1975:29–31) example, this would be four 26×26 dissimilarity matrices, based on the variables "slip," "paint," "hue," and "line width." At this point, one has the option of seriating each variable independently. If one wishes to assume that each variable is an equally good indicator of the time trend, all the dissimilarity matrices can be added together. Additionally, of course, it is necessary to standardize the dissimilarity matrices to enable their meaningful combination (LeBlanc 1975:31).

LeBlanc (1975:31–35) displays the results of Guttman–Lingoes (Guttman 1968; Lingoes 1973) multidimensional scaling analysis on each dissimilarity matrix, then on the combined matrix; the results are best with the combined matrix. He also produces an acceptable ordering using only the factor scores obtained from a factor analysis. This procedure will be discussed below. LeBlanc's approach to ordering units based on statis-

Example: To calculate LeBlanc's dissimilarity coefficient between unit 1 (unit 139-303-2) and unit 2 (unit 139-303-4) (see LeBlanc 1975:Table 4) for the "slip" variable, which has three possible attributes: white/red, red, and white.

1. Standardize the attribute "white/red" by setting the maximum value in the column equal to 100, the minimum value equal to 1:

   Max (white/red) = 6.8 is set equal to 100;
   Min (white/red) = 0.0 is set equal to 1.

$$\text{Unit 1 (white/red)} = \frac{(100 - 1)}{(6.8 - 0)} \times (4.6) = \frac{(99)(4.6)}{(6.8)} = 67.0$$

$$\text{Unit 2 (white/red)} = \frac{(100 - 1)}{(6.8 - 0)} \times (5.1) = \frac{(99)(5.1)}{(6.8)} = 74.3$$

2. Standardize the attribute "red" in the same manner:

   Max (red) = 88.7 is set equal to 100;
   Min (red) = 69.4 is set equal to 1.

$$\text{Unit 1 (red)} = \frac{(100 - 1)}{(88.7 - 69.4)} \times (76.3) = \frac{(99)(76.3)}{(19.3)} = 35.4$$

$$\text{Unit 2 (red)} = \frac{(100 - 1)}{(88.7 - 69.4)} \times (83.8) = \frac{(99)(83.8)}{(19.3)} = 73.9$$

3. Standardize the attribute "white" in the same manner:

   Max (white) = 30.6 is set equal to 100;
   Min (white) = 5.6 is set equal to 1.

$$\text{Unit 1 (white)} = \frac{(100 - 1)}{(30.6 - 5.6)} \times (19.1) = \frac{(99)(19.1)}{(25)} = 53.5$$

$$\text{Unit 2 (white)} = \frac{(100 - 1)}{(30.6 - 5.6)} \times (11.1) = \frac{(99)(11.1)}{(25)} = 21.8$$

4. Thus, the resulting values for unit 1 and unit 2 on the "slip" variable, which is composed of the three attributes, are as follows:

	White/red	Red	White
Unit 1	67.0	35.4	53.5
Unit 2	74.3	73.9	21.8

5. Now find the absolute value of the difference for each attribute and sum them to obtain a pooled dissimilarity coefficient:

$$|67.0 - 74.3| + |35.4 - 73.9| + |53.5 - 21.8|$$
$$= 7.3 + 38.5 + 31.7 = 77.5$$

which is LeBlanc's dissimilarity coefficient between unit 1 and unit 2 for the variable "slip."

Figure 8.8. An illustration of the calculation of LeBlanc's pooled dissimilarity coefficient. (See LeBlanc 1975:Table 4.)

tically derived variables is generally a sound one. A Q-mode (across units) factor analysis or any of the forms of multidimensional scaling will probably produce acceptable seriations if the variables being used are primarily sensitive to temporal variation. I advocated the use of factor analysis for ascertaining trend-sensitive variables in an earlier work (Marquardt 1974b:92–121), and I agree with LeBlanc's (1975:22–28) opinion that variables based on attribute frequencies are better indicators of change in artifact morphology than are traditional artifact "types," such as the ceramic types used by Ford (1962). I have reservations about the manner in which LeBlanc combines dissimilarity coefficients, however. Although he is cognizant (LeBlanc 1975:30) of the increased danger of sampling errors when rare attributes are given as much weight as common attributes, it seems to me that such errors may be even more serious than he realizes, especially when masked by the repeated standardizations necessary for the combining of attributes and combining of variables. Also, I do not believe that "micro-seriation," defined by LeBlanc (1975:22) as techniques "which deal with cultural material that falls within periods of 50 or perhaps 100 years," should be distinguished logically from any other kind of seriation; the assumptions are clearly the same. It is not the shortness of the time range or the use of this or that multivariate technique, but the availability of sufficiently complex, well-controlled data that makes fine-grained seriations possible.

Robert Drennan has used multidimensional scaling to order materials from the Middle Formative site of Fábrica San José. Drennan's unit of analysis is the provenience unit, the variables being counts of various attributes observed on ceramics (decoration, details of vessel form, etc.). He generates a dissimilarity coefficient based on the quantity obtained by summing, for each pair of units, the absolute difference in percentages, and dividing the result by 200:

$$\text{Drennan's } D_{ij} = \sum_{a=1}^{m} \frac{P_{ia} - P_{ja}}{200}$$

where D_{ij} represents the dissimilarity between unit i and unit j, m is the number of attributes, P_{ia} is the percentage of occurrence of the ath attribute in unit i, and P_{ja} is the percentage of occurrence of the ath attribute in unit j. The coefficient thus ranges from 0.0 (units i and j have identical percentages) to 1.0 (i and j are maximally dissimilar). Drennan used the multidimensional scaling program MINISSA-I (Lingoes 1973) to obtain a two-dimensional solution for 22 stratigraphic provenience units from four excavations, obtaining a dispersed but interpretable configuration (Drennan 1976:293–296). Further interpretation of the pattern as a "time curve" was aided in this case by a form of localized nonmetric multiple regression in which best fitting lines, or vectors, are passed through the swarms of points symbolizing the units of each of the four excavations. The points were then projected back onto the curve, to form what Drennan (1976:296) calls a "time curve hypothesis." Additional provenience units were then added to the curve one at a time according to D coefficients calculated between the candidate units and each of the 22 units already plotted on the time curve. Drennan (1976:298) found that mixed proveniences and units with small sample sizes could not be scaled reliably. Drennan's statement that the ultimate criterion for determining whether a provenience is mixed is "whether the frequencies of occurrence of the various states [show] strong characteristics of more than one segment of the sequence" seems to beg the question: Why not simply use typological and stratigraphic information to form the sequence? Subjective intervention was necessary at several points in Drennan's analysis. The problem probably lies not in the application of multidimensional scaling, but in Drennan's failure to assure that the variables used were primarily sensitive to temporal changes.

Wilkinson (1974:71–76) has also used multidimensional scaling in seriation, introducing certain modifications of the MDSCAL procedure of Kruskal. Wilkinson's LOCSCAL algorithm involves the calculation of a separate regression for each unit rather than performing a single regression on the interpoint distance matrix. Wilkinson also suggests altering the form of the stress function in order to give less weight to very unusual units (see Sibson 1977 for a detailed discussion of "global" and "local" scaling).

Sibson (1972) proposed that a useful dissimilarity coefficient for analysis by multidimensional scaling is one derived by pairwise rank comparison, a modification of the rank correlation coefficient of M. Kendall (see Figure 8.9). The application of Sibson's transformation has the effect of smoothing data so that multidimensional scaling programs are better able to find local minima. In addition, it has intuitive appeal because it would seem to take into account not only the similarity or dissimilarity of two objects with one another, but the patterns of similarity or dissimilarity values with other objects (Sibson 1971). Further explanation of dissimilarity measurement may be found in Jardine and Sibson (1971:3–34).

An interesting series of experiments in the computer-assisted seriation of incidence data has been reported by Graham *et al.* (1976). They generated a series of four simulated Merovingian cemeteries, the graves varying in number and in diversity of "grave goods" present in each grave. The four data sets were submitted to Wilkinson's (1974) program AXIS and to AXIS used in conjunction with his program POLISH. Also, similarity

			Unit		
Unit	A	B	C	D	E
A	1.00	.80	.50	.90	.75
B	.80	1.00	.50	.70	.60
C	.50	.50	1.00	.60	.70
D	.90	.70	.60	1.00	.85
E	.75	.60	.70	.85	1.00

$\sigma_{ij} = \sum_{i<j} \eta_{ij}$, where η_{ij} is defined to be $+1$ when i and j are ranked in the same order, and 0 when the orders are reversed. The summation is over all possible pairs of coefficients for each pair of units.

For example, for the units A and B, we compute

$$
\begin{array}{lll}
1.00 > .80 \text{ but} & .80 < 1.00 & 0 \\
1.00 > .50 \text{ and} & .80 > .50 & 1 \\
1.00 > .90 \text{ and} & .80 > .70 & 1 \\
1.00 > .75 \text{ and} & .80 > .60 & 1 \\
.80 > .50 \text{ and} & 1.00 > .50 & 1 \\
.80 < .90 \text{ but} & 1.00 > .70 & 0 \\
.80 > .75 \text{ and} & 1.00 > .60 & 1 \\
.50 < .90 \text{ and} & .50 < .70 & 1 \\
.50 < .75 \text{ and} & .50 < .60 & 1 \\
.90 > .75 \text{ and} & .70 > .60 & 1 \\
& \text{Total} = & 8 = \sigma_{AB}
\end{array}
$$

Similarly, $\sigma_{AC} = 1, \sigma_{AD} = 8, \sigma_{AE} = 5, \sigma_{BC} = 0, \sigma_{BD} = 5, \sigma_{BE} = 3, \sigma_{CD} = 3, \sigma_{CE} = 6, \sigma_{DE} = 7$. Thus the Sibson-transformed matrix is as follows:

			Unit		
Unit	A	B	C	D	E
A	10	8	1	8	5
B	8	10	0	5	3
C	1	0	10	3	6
D	8	5	3	10	7
E	5	3	6	7	10

Figure 8.9. Illustration of Sibson's (1972:335) Pairwise Rank Comparison transformation (matrix transformed is the similarity matrix S given in Figure 8.7, this chapter).

matrices derived from the four data sets were analyzed by the multidimensional scaling programs MSDCAL (Shepard 1962a,b; Kruskal 1964a,b) and LOCSCAL (Wilkinson 1974). Coefficients of similarity used were (*a*) a matching coefficient, which simply records the total number of types held in common by a given pair of graves, and (*b*) the Jaccard coefficient (Sokal and Sneath 1963:133), consisting of the number of types held in common by a pair of graves divided by the total number of times in which a type is present in either of the two graves. Finally, the effects of two different transformations of these coefficients were investigated—namely, the circle product transformation of Kendall (1971b; see also Figure 8.7, this chapter) and Sibson's (1972) pairwise rank comparison transformation (Figure 8.9; see also Graham *et al.* 1976:4–13). Appropriateness of the various seriations was gauged by visual examination of representations of the orderings and by calculating Kendall's (Kendall 1975) rank-order correlation coefficient with the "true" order of the simulated graves.

It was found that Wilkinson's programs AXIS and POLISH gave good results, especially when used in concert (annotated source listings of these programs are given in Wilkinson 1974:105–142). Interestingly, the Sibson transformation, so successfully applied to the empirical Münsingen–Rain data (Sibson 1972), caused consistently poorer results when used on the simulated data. Kendall's circle product transformation led to somewhat poorer results than the Sibson transformation, and seemed erratic at best. Contrary to Wilkinson's (1974:60–63) prediction, successive circle powering seems to worsen, rather than better, the seriations. The MDSCAL and LOCSCAL scaling techniques were adjudged equally effective in producing reasonable orderings.

The work of Graham, Galloway, and Scollar, although inconclusive, establishes beyond doubt that the performance of practical seriation techniques is significantly affected by the characteristics of the data sets themselves (for example, number of graves, diversity of grave goods). Their study again underscores the need for corroborative data to aid the interpretation of computer-generated sequences. Multidimensional scaling techniques have been utilized effectively to order archaeological units, but we must continue to evaluate in every case the appropriateness of the result. In the absence of corroboration in the form of stratigraphy, dendrochronology, or other evidence, computer-generated orderings must always be considered hypothetical.

I should like to end this section with brief descriptions of factor analytic approaches to chronological ordering. Factor analysis is actually a set of models and techniques, rather than a discrete mathematical procedure.

Essentially, the goal of factor analysis is to find the minimum number of independent axes necessary to reproduce the variation of the data matrix in a vector space. Originally developed in psychology in an effort to express quantitatively the underlying factors determining individual behavior, factor analytic applications have extended to a wide scale of social and behavioral sciences. Archaeological applications have appeared in print only in the past dozen or so years (e.g., Binford and Binford 1966; Daniels 1967; Glover 1969; Hill 1970; Ahler 1971; Rowlett and Pollnac 1971; Redman 1973; Roper 1974), and productive critical discussion (e.g., Benfer 1972; Doran and Hodson 1975:187–213; Lischka 1975; Read 1974; Roper 1975, 1976; Christenson and Read 1977) has been seen even more recently.

Factor analysis is closely related to principal components analysis, a procedure by which linear relationships are sought within multivariate data sets. Geometrically, one can visualize a swarm of points in m-dimensional space, where m is the number of variables. The first ("principal") axis passes through the ellipsoid of maximum density of the points—that is, the linear relationship of maximum covariance. Each successive axis extracted from the data set is orthogonal to and uncorrelated with all previously extracted axes (geometrically, all the axes are at right angles to one another). Often it happens that the first few axes extracted will account for most of the variance in the data, and the remainder can be ignored. This has the effect of parsimoniously reducing data complexity and considerably simplifying interpretation.

One of the most frequently chosen factor analytic models is that known as "common" factor analysis (Rummel 1970:104–112). This model includes the assumption that the unique parts of the variance attributable to each individual variable are uncorrelated. This contrasts with the principal component model described above, in which all variance—common, specific, and error—is considered at once in defining the patterns of variation. It should be noted, for the benefit of the beginning student of factor analysis, that published terminology is inconsistent regarding the "principal component" model. Some writers refer to a procedure utilizing the component model with the principal axes technique as "principal components factor analysis" (e.g., see Benfer 1975:373–375). Some writers see the distinction between principal components analysis and factor analysis as a difference in emphasis:

> Whereas principal-components analysis is primarily concerned with the definition of linear functions of composite scores having certain optimal statistical properties, factor analysis is concerned with relationships among test variates and relationships of the test variates to derived factors [Overall and Klett 1972:111].

Others favor a sharp distinction between principal components analysis and factor analysis; Doran and Hodson (1975:187–205), for example, express a definite preference for the former. Still others (e.g., Christenson and Read 1977:166) use "factor analysis" as a generic term to refer to all procedures that are used to reduce the dimensionality in a series of correlated measurements, thus including principal components analysis as a subset of factor analysis. I use the term "component factor analysis" below to mean a procedure using the component model (that is, all variance considered at once) (Rummel 1970:112–113, 312–313) with the principal axes factoring technique (Rummel 1970:99, 142, 168, 338–345). [In a previous paper (Marquardt 1974a) I used the term "principal components factor analysis" for this same procedure.]

My own approach to the seriation problem has made use of component factor analysis at two stages of investigation: (1) finding trend-sensitive variables and (2) ordering units on the basis of these trend-sensitive variables. The procedure has produced good results when applied both to artificial data (Marquardt 1977) and to empirical data (Marquardt 1974b; Wynn 1976). I have found that, when independent evidence is available, a component factor analysis can distinguish variables that are primarily sensitive to *temporal* trends from variables primarily sensitive to other linear trends within the data. The process involves several steps, which can be summarized briefly here; further details can be found in Marquardt (1974b, 1977).

The procedure begins with the creation of an $n \times m$ data matrix of n units (rows) and m ratio-scale variables (columns). (By ratio-scale I mean variables that are real number measurements or products, such that a value of zero has meaning for the variable; examples might be the ratio of black polished pottery sherds to the total number of polished pottery sherds in a given provenience unit; the average number of "checks" per square centimeter in a sample of "check-stamped" pottery; the percentage of all red-slipped bowl sherds in a provenience unit which have black painted designs.) The variables are chosen in such a way that they are as independent from one another as possible (for example, if one of the proposed variables is the percentage of slipped pottery in a given unit that is *white*, we shall not also include a variable that records the percentage of slipped pottery that is *red*). The data matrix that eventually results will include variables that independent evidence suggests are time-sensitive, variables suspected to be time-sensitive, and variables known not to be time-sensitive. A Pearson's r correlation matrix is calculated, and this $m \times m$ similarity matrix is factor-analyzed, using the principal axes technique. If there is a strong linear trend in the data set, the principal axes technique will assure that the first factor extracted will account for the variance of the maximum linear relationship. If the known time-sensitive variables have been judiciously chosen, they will load highly on (that is, will be highly correlated with) a single factor. The sign of each loading will indicate the direction of the trend relative to other high-loading variables. Variables that load highly *on the same factor* as the known time-sensitive variables may be inferred to be good candidates for additional time-sensitive variables. As a rule of thumb, I expect the first two factors to account for at least 50% of the variance; any less than this amount should call for a re-evaluation of the variables. It is good practice to include one or two "nonsense" variables as a check; I have used a vector of random numbers for this purpose. Variables that load with nonsense variables are viewed with suspicion.

To summarize, when independent evidence is available, a factor analysis can be used to define useful time-sensitive variables. The candidate variables are ratio-scale measurements, averages, percentages, or proportions that are composed in such a way that they are logically independent. Additionally included among the variables are some expected, on the basis of supplementary evidence, to be time-sensitive, and others not expected to be time-sensitive. An R-mode (across variables) factor analysis of an $m \times m$ correlation matrix, using the principal axes technique, will disclose a main factor attributable to "time," and the "known" time-sensitive variables will load highly on this factor. Additional variables loading highly on the factor are inferred also to be time-sensitive. The most reliable trend-sensitive variables (TSV's) are (*a*) those based on logically independent measures, (*b*) those generally increasing or generally decreasing through time, and (*c*) those possessing few "zero" readings.

Once the first part of the two-step operation (creating a number of reliable trend-sensitive variables) is solved, the second part (determining the proper order of the units, based on the trend-sensitive variables) is a good deal easier. Using *only* the TSV's determined in step 1, one generates an $n \times n$ matrix of similarity coefficients and analyzes this matrix with a Q-mode (across units) factor analytic technique or one of the various multidimensional scaling programs. I have obtained good orderings on both ideal and empirical data by using a component factor analysis for which the input is an $n \times n$ matrix of similarity coefficients ranging in value from 0.0 (maximum dissimilarity) to 1.0 (maximum similarity). One similarity coefficient satisfying this criterion is the scaled taxonomic distance coefficient Δ^*, where

$$\Delta_{jk}^* = 1.0 - (\Delta_{jk}/\Delta_{max})$$

$$\Delta_{jk} = \left(\sum_{i=1}^{m} X_{ji}^2 + \sum_{i=1}^{m} X_{ki}^2 - 2 \sum_{i=1}^{m} X_{ji} \cdot X_{ki} \right)^{1/2}$$

where Δ_{max} is the largest of the Δ_{jk}'s;

X_{ji} is the element of the $n \times m$ data matrix at the intersection of row (unit) j and column (variable) i;

X_{ki} is the element of the $n \times m$ data matrix at the intersection of row (unit) k and column (variable) i;

n is the number of rows (units);

m is the number of columns (variables);

Δ_{jk} is the taxonomic distance between units j and k.

It should be clear that the Δ_{jk}^{*} (scaled taxonomic distance) coefficient is actually a similarity coefficient ranging in value from zero (minimum similarity) to unity (maximum similarity).

The $n \times n$ matrix of scaled distance coefficients is factor-analyzed, the two most significant factors (that is, the first two to be extracted) being retained for consideration. The loadings of all n units on each of the two factors are plotted on a two-dimensional graph. The variables are primarily sensitive to a particular linear trend; hence the order of the units on the graph will indicate their relative score on this linear trend. In the case of chronological seriation, one factor-analyses an $n \times n$ similarity matrix calculated from variables known to be primarily sensitive to temporal variation (see Marquardt 1974b:64–184, 1977).

I have found that the plot of the loadings on factors 1 and 2 usually takes the form of a crescent-shaped scatter of points (Marquardt 1977: Figs. 1 and 2). Elsewhere I provide three techniques for the generation of a one-dimensional ordering of the units, each of which provides a good estimate of the minimum Hamiltonian circuit through the points (Marquardt 1974b:152–163). I also suggest rules of thumb for estimating taxonomic contemporaneity (1974b:163–169).

Another approach to step 2 (the ordering of units on the basis of trend-sensitive variables) is LeBlanc's (1975:30–31) procedure of plotting the factor scores for the principal factor, reading the order directly from the plot. A *factor score* (Rummel 1970:108) is a measure of a unit's contribution to the variance accounted for by a certain factor. If we feel comfortable with the interpretation of the principal factor as "time," then LeBlanc's technique has intuitive appeal. Use of the principal axes factoring technique will assure that a large part of the variance will be accounted for by the first factor extracted. If one takes pains to "stack the deck" so that most of the variance in the unit × variable data matrix is temporal variance, then it is probably safe to think that the principal factor will be attributable to time.

It should be evident that most advances in seriation technique have been concerned with improving *ordering* procedures, which I have called step 2. Very little attention has been given to step 1: the process of generating data matrices that contain information explicitly appropriate to the archaeological seriation problem.

The simulation experiments of Graham *et al.* (1976) show that the performance of certain ordering techniques and matrix transformations varies from data set to data set. Mathematicians, statisticians, and computer programmers have contributed an invaluable perspective to our work, but we archaeologists cannot expect them to solve our chronological problems for us. We must continue to re-evaluate the cultural assumptions tacitly underlying our ordering procedures, and we must devote some time to ascertaining the kinds of data appropriate for the archaeological questions we ask. It does no good to have efficient matrix ordering techniques if we are uncertain of the data contained in the matrices. Surely, at the least, temporal, functional, spatial, stylistic, and idiosyncratic variance characterizes our raw data. This does not even take into account postdepositional processes. If archaeologists want chronological orderings, they must develop methods of distinguishing, in each instance, variables primarily sensitive to temporal change from those primarily sensitive to other factors.

ADVANCES IN SERIATION THEORY

It is important to differentiate the mathematical aspects of seriation from its application in archaeology and other fields. The essence of the mathematical seriation problem is this: Given a matrix of n rows and m columns of which the elements are nonnegative real numbers, find the permutation of rows that best satisfies this criterion: In each column the elements increase to a maximum and then decrease, or increase, or decrease, in the "weak" sense (two or more consecutive identical elements do not violate the criterion). The principles of the technique were used by Petrie (1899) to "sequence-date" 900 graves excavated in Egypt during the years 1894–1899. The task was accomplished in part by a thorough analysis of 804 varieties of pottery classified into nine larger groups and the arrangement of the graves in serial order based on the presence of certain varieties. In Petrie's work one finds the first articulation of what Kendall (1963:659) has called the Concentration Principle: Other things being equal, arrangements that reduce the ranges of varieties are to be preferred to those that do not. A detailed study of Petrie's work led Kendall (1963) to propose an analytical formulation of the Concentration Principle applicable to abundance matrices. Assuming the number of items of a given type in a given unit to be distributed as a Poisson variable, Kendall (1963:664) derived a scoring function, the minimization of which results in a seriation. Later, Wilkinson (1974:77–80) proposed two probabilistic models for incidence matrices, the first based on the assumption that there is a fixed probability that a unit contains a given artifact type, the second based on the assumption that there is a fixed probability that a representative of a type in general use is contained in the unit. Both Kendall's and Wilkinson's probabilistic models, while intrinsically interesting, incorporate assumptions probably unsuited to actual archaeological application.

In 1965, Fulkerson and Gross proposed a graph theoretic method for casting an incidence matrix into the ideal Petrie form. They were concerned with incidence matrices in which the rows represented mutant micro-organisms, the columns the intersections of mutant genes, but the mathematical objective is the same: reordering the rows to produce a matrix with column-consecutive 1's. Kendall's (1969a,b) important extension of Fulkerson and Gross's work and his later generalization of it to abundance matrices (Kendall 1971a,b) have been discussed above.

Wilkinson (1971, 1974) realized the similarity between the archaeological seriation problem and the Traveling Salesman problem, a question that has received considerable interest in operations research (Ackoff 1956:278). A historical review of the Traveling Salesman problem is found in Bellmore and Nemhauser (1968). Various heuristic solutions are discussed by Dantzig et al. (1954), Croes (1958), Little et al. (1963), Netter (1971), Christofides and Eilon (1972), and Lin and Kernighan (1973). The Traveling Salesman problem is equivalent to the task of minimizing the sum of dissimilarity coefficients between adjacent units. Laporte (1976) suggests that this procedure is more appropriate for small matrices, while the procedure of minimizing the "score," suggested by Doran and Powell (1972), is more appropriate for large matrices. The score (Laporte 1976:251) is simply the sum, over all columns, of the range of the nonzero elements in each column (see also Doran and Hodson 1975:277).

Robinson (Brainerd 1951; Robinson 1951; Matthews 1963; Kendall 1963) seems to have been the first to realize that an $n \times n$ matrix of between-unit similarity coefficients would have higher values near the principal diagonal if the units were arranged in a perfect seriation. In general, the grouping of high values of any similarity matrix together is of practical value. Sokal and Sneath (1963:175–179) discuss the shading of a similarity matrix according to the strength of the similarity, darker squares indicating higher values, and mention (1963:178) that "one can visualize the search for group structure as a rearranging of rows and columns . . . in such a way as to obtain the optimum structure in the system."

The systematic grouping of comparable units together at certain levels of computed similarity is called *cluster analysis,* a term that, like factor analysis, includes a wide range of models and techniques. [Cluster analytic applications in archaeology are described by Cowgill (1968a), Doran and Hodson (1975:173–185), and Hodson (1970); see also Hodson *et al.* (1971).] Johnson (1968, 1972) advocates the use of seriation as a first step in the search for meaningful clusters, adopting the shading procedure described by Sokal and Sneath (see, e.g., Johnson 1972:349, Figure 8.14). A similar application of matrix ordering as a preliminary analytical procedure is described by McCormick *et al.* (1972). Their sorting algorithm proceeds by a permutation search technique, placing each column in such a way that the "measure of effectiveness" (a value proportional to the sums of products of neighboring elements, taken over both rows and columns) obtains its maximum value.

McCormick *et al.*'s technique is applicable to any matrix with nonnegative elements, including nonsymmetric abundance matrices (called by them "object-attribute" matrices). They illustrate this procedure by successfully clustering ordinal data from 53 aircraft types and 37 aircraft functions, each element of the matrix being a score of 0, 1, or 2, indicating the aircraft's ability to perform the given function. Although the authors (McCormick *et al.* 1972:1008) see wider applications for their "bond-energy" algorithm, I believe that "clustering" techniques such as theirs and Johnson's are methodologically suspect except in very special cases in which a single linear dimension can be demonstrated to account for most of the variance (see Doran and Hodson 1975:169–177 for a more detailed consideration of this point).

Interestingly, McCormick *et al.* perceive their problem as part of a general class of allocation problems called in operations research Quadratic Assignment problems. Similarities between seriation and the Quadratic Assignment problem have been pointed out in an important series of papers by Hubert and Schultz (Hubert 1976; Hubert and Schultz 1976a,b). Lenstra (1974) has noted that any clustering problem of the type considered by McCormick *et al.* can be stated as *p* Traveling Salesman problems, where *p* is the number of dimensions. Generalizing from the work of Wilkinson (1971) and Lenstra (1974), López *et al.* (1976) note that, with a modified measure of performance, the bond-energy algorithm of McCormick *et al.* is also equivalent to doing two independent seriations: one for the rows and one for the columns.

It should be stressed that matrix ordering techniques that simply bring higher values together are not necessarily relevant to the seriation problem. For example, Deutsch and Martin (1971) describe an efficient algorithm that accomplishes this task by alternatively rearranging rows and columns on the basis of calculated row and column moments. [An identical procedure is reported by de la Vega (1977), who attributes the algorithm to Tonnelier.] Their method is successful in "clustering" high values about the diagonal, and, in fact, they show (Deutsch and Martin 1971:1361–1362) in an archaeological example that an $n \times n$ matrix of Robinson's *IA* coefficients can be successfully rearranged by their approach. But, although for seriation this will be useful for ordering an $n \times n$ *similarity matrix*, the clustering of high values about the diagonal of an $n \times m$ *data matrix* will not necessarily produce an acceptable seriation.

In sum, the graph theoretic concept of the Hamiltonian circuit has provided a valuable perspective on seriation theory, and the work of Wilkinson and Kendall is especially important in this development. Obviously, seriation, the Traveling Salesman problem, and the Quadratic Assignment problem are closely related (see Hubert 1974 for a formal consideration of these problems in graph theoretic terms; Hill 1974 provides an instructive comparison of seriation with principal components analysis, "correspondence analysis," and canonical correlations). Although developments in operations research can result in progress in seriation theory, archaeologists must continue to evaluate the appropriateness of various methods to *archaeological* problems. There is always a tendency to apply techniques from other fields immediately because they have been shown to be effective for homologous problems. However, formal similarities may mask important differences in assumptions and objectives. We must avoid the uncritical adoption of theory as steadfastly as we resist the uncritical application of techniques.

SERIATION IN CONTEXT

Between the ideal models of seriation theory and the various practical seriation techniques employed by archaeologists lies the less frequently discussed realm of seriation epistemology. Among the many relevant questions that might be asked are: Are the assumptions of seriation theory appropriate? What kinds of artifacts or attributes of artifacts are likely to be reliable temporal indicators? What kinds of situations are likely to promote rapid technological change? rapid stylistic change? What happens to the rate of technological or stylistic innovation in times of stress? in times of cultural contact? How can we be reasonably certain for a given assemblage that we have isolated temporal variance, from, say, functional, stylistic, idiosyncratic, or error variance?

Whallon (1972:32) noted several years ago that the mathematical development of seriation had reached a greater level of sophistication than had archaeologists' knowledge of the nature of archaeological data. His assessment is still true today, but some progress has been made in the latter direction. Advances in the epistemology of seriation have included critical examinations of seriation's underlying assumptions; its relationship to chronological inference in both real and simulated material cultural contexts; and the exploration of alternative strategies for chronological investigation.

In one of the most thorough discussions of the appropriateness of chronological seriation in various archaeological contexts, Rouse delineates five major areas of concern: (a) the units to be seriated, (b) the traits characterizing these units, (c) the cultural tradition, (d) the local area, (e) the historical pattern. He suggests that "events" are what are ideally seriated (1967:158), but he also recognizes that "some length of time is required to produce any unit of seriation" (1967:162). Fabrication units, deposition units, and occupation units are all proper items for seriation, but in all cases Rouse considers it advisable that units be unambiguously identifiable, and complex enough to provide recognizable, chronologically significant trait associations. Criteria for characterization of the units should be established on the basis of the kind of unit and the purpose of the seriation. Thus, Rouse suggests that fabrication units be seriated with respect to "the pattern of occurrence of their modes" (where a mode consists of a series of attributes recurring on corresponding features of a number of artifacts), that large deposition units be seriated on the basis of relative type frequencies (as Ford has done), and that components and other habitation units be seriated in phases, according to the developmental pattern within their local cultural tradition. To be reliable, seriation needs to be limited to a single cultural tradition and restricted to a certain local area. Occurrence, frequency, and development patterns can be obtained, depending on the nature of the units to be seriated and the interests of the investigator.

One can only agree with Rouse that careful attention to all five aspects—units, traits, tradition, area, and pattern—is requisite to reliable chronological seriation. Although seriation by attention to the relative frequency of types is an effective way to establish a long-term developmental chronology for a specific area, I do not agree completely with Rouse's statement that "types are the best kind of criterion to use in seriating surface collections or other deposition units" (1967:171). With such units, Rouse says that "one is dealing with completed artifacts, after they have been used and deposited in the ground, rather than with the procedure of manufacture'' (1967:171). With reasonably complex artifacts—for example, painted ceramics—it seems to me it is precisely the procedures of manufacturing with which we are concerned, if ''manufacture'' is understood to include the decoration as well as the shaping and firing of the pottery. If we have available sufficiently complex data and are concerned to differentiate precisely between certain units, then the attention to particular modes, to use Rouse's term, is by far preferable to the use of types (Rowe 1959). I agree with Rouse (1967:179–180) that in seriation one studies changes in the criteria of archaeological units, but his conceptual scheme admits only modes, types, and phases as suitable criteria for judging chronological change. I would add trend-sensitive variables as a fourth kind of permissible temporal criterion, while agreeing fully with Rouse (1967:189) that supplemental chronological techniques—for example, stratigraphy and dendrochronology—are essential to avoidance of circularity in reasoning.

In 1970 Dunnell proposed that a seriation cannot be presumed to be a chronology unless three conditions are met: (*a*) All units included in a seriation must be of comparable duration; (*b*) all units must belong to the same cultural tradition; (*c*) all units must come from the same local area. These three conditions will be discussed in turn.

It seems obvious that in all but the most trivial of circumstances it will be impossible to determine whether or not a given collection of artifacts was deposited in the same length of time as another given collection of artifacts. The question is more practically stated by Dunnell (1970:312) when he asserts that, for purposes of a given seriation, variation in the duration of the units ''cannot be so great as to affect the distribution of the denotata of the classes used to create the ordering.'' Dunnell's (1970:313) solution is to remove the units that do not fit the ideal seriation model. This has two implications: (*a*) that acceptable chronological seriations may be carried out only on ideal data—that is, data for which, for a single ''best'' ordering, the denotata of the various criteria are continuous, in the case of incidence data, or are distributed unimodally, in the case of frequency or other abundance data; (*b*) that truly contemporaneous units cannot be tolerated in a seriation because their temporal positions would be ambiguous. Cowgill's (1972:385) requirement for the duration of archaeological units being seriated seems more practical: ''For any two units whose chronological positions are claimed to be reliably or usefully distinguished, both [should] have durations that are at least not much greater than their time differences, and preferably durations that are considerably smaller than their time difference.''

It may be unrealistic to expect a precisely unimodal curve of any class of artifacts or attributes. What we wish to establish in a chronological seriation is the "best" general ordering of a set of units on the basis of time; if our criteria for ordering the units are primarily sensitive to time, we may expect some ambiguities in the ordering of the units for the reason that some of the units may be very close in time. A good seriation technique should be capable of indicating contemporaneity as well as differences in time between given units. For other discussions of criteria for a "good" seriation, see Cowgill (1972:383–387), Graham *et al.* (1976:1), and Kendall (1971a:237).

Dunnell's second criterion for inferring that a seriation is a chronology is that seriated units belong to the same cultural tradition. For a given seriation, Dunnell (1970:313) proposes that the "set of classes employed to do the ordering be relevant to all the units." According to Dunnell, if more than a single tradition is represented in the data, more than one independent solution will obtain. The only remedy, according to Dunnell, is to remove the offending units and seriate them separately; the assumption is that "the application of the seriation model will produce as many independent orders as there are traditions represented" (1970:313). In principle, I agree with Dunnell on this point, but it should be stressed that the recalcitrant units may well represent error variance (a mixed provenience, perhaps) or spatiofunctional variance rather than a separate tradition.

Dunnell's third requirement for a chronological seriation is that the units to be seriated come from the same local area. He points out that the notion of "local area" is, at best, an ambiguous concept. Because variation in form can occur across space as well as through time, he asserts that, if the criteria used "are defined on the basis of attributes which show little variation in space and much variation in time, [then] the classes so created will have distributions that are *primarily* the result of change through time and not change through space" (Dunnell 1970:315; emphasis in original). He goes on to say that the effects of spatial variation can be minimized by carrying out several seriations of the same units using different classes of artifacts—for example, projectile point types, pottery types, scraper types, burial types, and house types (Dunnell 1970:316). As Rouse (1967:158–166, 194) observes, however, different kinds of criteria are appropriate to the seriation of different kinds of units. The likelihood of the availability of several classes of such units, each complex enough and abundant enough for adequate seriation, is very slight. Hole and Shaw (1967) experienced this difficulty in seriating their Near Eastern materials: Their pottery seriated well, but the chipped stone and other artifacts did not, primarily because of inadequate sample sizes for the nonceramic artifact classes (Cowgill 1968b:519). Carrying out multiple seriations is one solution, but, in most cases, an impractical one. It would probably be an inefficient usage of time and financial resources for most archaeologists.

In sum, Dunnell's reasoning is logically indisputable, but his suggestions are applicable to ideal, not empirical, data. Confusion can result from failing to distinguish the mathematical seriation problem from the practical seriation problem in archaeology. Dunnell seems to be addressing the latter from the rigorous framework of the former.

Archaeological seriation has two aspects: the mathematical problem and the archaeological interpretive problem. The archaeological interpretive problem can easily be obfuscated by the mistaken notion that ideal models are directly applicable to real situations. A more profitable approach is the search for efficient techniques that will yield reliable results when applied to empirical data.

Perhaps the most difficult part of our task is relating the ideal models and practical techniques to the systematic investigation of human behavior. Some progress has been made in this direction, using both empirical and simulated data. For example, Dethlefsen and Deetz found that gravestone designs in eighteenth century New England did change according to the patterns expected of type frequency data. Their research (Dethlefsen and Deetz 1966) revealed a gradual replacement of the "death's head" by the "cherub" motif, then a replacement of the latter by the "urn and willow" design. Although this pattern of replacement was widespread, they discovered differences in the time and rate of replacement, as well as in patterns of motif overlap. In Boston and Cambridge, for example, death's head and cherub motifs had long periods of contemporary use. The cherub appears to have diffused outward from the Boston area roughly at the rate of 1 mile per year (Deetz and Dethlefsen 1965, 1971). They suggest that the Great Awakening of 1740–1760 may have had an effect on the replacement of the stern death's head with the angelic cherub figure.

The durability of gravestones and the ease with which they can be dated make them valuable sources of information. Such well-controlled and documented studies bearing on the seriation problem are rare in archaeology and should be encouraged whenever possible. Recently intensified interest on the part of archaeologists (e.g., Binford 1973:241–244; Longacre 1974; Rathje 1974) in ethnographic studies promises to shed additional light on the behavioral correlates of material culture.

The work of David (1972) provides a valuable perspective on the use of frequencies of pottery types in archaeological inference. After a detailed study of pots from 15 women's quarters in the Fulani village of Bé, David (1972:141) is convinced that ceramic representation in the archaeological record is generally a function of (*a*) the relative frequency of pot types at any given time, (*b*) the life span of pots, and (*c*) the duration of the level in which the assemblage is found. David's census of the ages of various pots in Fulani households reveals significant contrasts in their longevity. For example (David 1972:141, Table 1), the median age for bowls and small and medium cooking pots is between 2 and 3 years, while the median age for large cooking and storage vessels is three to four times this age. In similar observations of pottery function and longevity among the Conibo of Peru, DeBoer (1974) reports considerably shorter ceramic life spans. He provides an interesting discussion of the possible uses, and limitations, of ceramic longevity data for the estimation of population and village duration. The studies of David (1972) and DeBoer (1974) may be compared with Foster's (1960) estimates of pottery life span in four households in Tzintzuntzan, Mexico. Foster (1960:608) hypothesizes that life spans of pottery depend on (*a*) basic strength of the pottery, (*b*) functions of the pottery, (*c*) the mode of use, particularly whether cooking is done on a stove or on the ground, (*d*) causes of breakage (carelessness, presence of children or domestic animals), and (*e*) pottery costs.

Stimulated by the work of David and Hennig (1972), Hatch (1976) and his colleagues have simulated by computer the manufacture, breakage, and accumulation of potsherds. Studies of this nature, based on actual ethnographic observations, can provide insight into the formation of the archaeological record. Efforts (e.g., Schiffer 1976) to formulate explicit models for the description and explanation of archaeologically observable behavioral processes also are to be welcomed. Such models provide a framework for profitable communication among archaeologists who recognize the importance of investigating the relationships between the archaeological record and the cultural and natural processes that produce it.

In sum, study of well-documented archaeological cases, ethnographic observations of the formation of the archaeological record, and experimentation with simulated archaeological data are all important to the evaluation of archaeological seriation and its improvement or replacement, should it be found wanting.

Some alternatives, in fact, have been suggested. As a supplement to type frequency seriation, "arrangement" has been proposed by Schiffer (1975:257) for the chronological ordering of sites having "intermittent and varying durations of occupation"—that is, sites that might violate Dunnell's first criterion, discussed above. Archaeologists have generally solved the "comparable duration of units" problem by augmenting with supplementary evidence (stratigraphic, usually) seriations obtained by ordering units of presumed short temporal duration. Schiffer (1975:258) assumes that, within the same cultural tradition in the same local area, there is a true chronological ordering of artifact types. In one version of "arrangement," the relative dates of initial occupation and final abandonment of sites are inferred directly from the appearance and disappearance of certain artifact types; the true sequence of types is assumed to be already known through the application of conventional type frequency seriation. As Schiffer notes, the technique would not properly arrange intermittently occupied sites. The second version of "arrangement" also begins at the point when an agreeable seriation has been produced. Type frequencies are plotted against a scale of "relative time," and an algebraic equation for each type is fitted to each frequency curve as if the units of relative time were equivalent in duration (Schiffer 1975:259). The total amounts of all types that would be deposited over continuous or discontinuous intervals are estimated by substituting type frequency data into algebraic functions obtained by Riemann integration of the linear functions derived earlier. Finally, the predicted artifact counts are compared with actual artifact counts from multicomponent sites by means of the Pearson correlation, high positive values of Pearson's r indicating, Schiffer hypothesizes, probable times of site occupation. Schiffer's use of integral calculus on relative frequency data for which the equivalence of time units cannot be demonstrated would probably be considered preposterous by a serious mathematician, but his technique is nonetheless intuitively appealing. I am skeptical that "arrangement," as articulated by Schiffer, would be any more systematic or provide more reliable results than the traditional process of seriating multiple provenience units and using stratigraphic or other supplementary information to confirm sequences. His proposed experiments on both simulated and empirical data (1975:260–262) will provide further basis on which to judge the technique's efficacy.

Another approach to seriation epistemology has been taken by Kintigh (1973, 1974) in the context of the application to archaeological inference of techniques developed in artificial intelligence research. Inspired by the successes of the DENDRAL program (Buchanan *et al.* 1971) in the generation of hypotheses about complex organic molecules, given mass spectrometer data, Kintigh has begun work on a LISP program that will select likely archaeological hypotheses based on its own archaeological "knowledge," test these propositions, and use the result to generate and test additional hypotheses. Doran (1972:434–449) has also argued, following Amarel (1971), that automatic hypothesis generation can be valuable in archaeology because its hallmarks—(*a*) appropriate representation, (*b*) evaluation procedures, and (*c*) search strategies—are all important to the generation of archaeological knowledge.

In sum, contributions to seriation epistemology have taken the form of (*a*) studying the relationship of the ideal seriation model to real situations; (*b*) exploring the relationship of seriation to the formation of the archaeological record (in well-controlled archaeological contexts, in living societies, and in simulated situations), and (c) studying the process of archaeological inference itself.

It should be stressed again that seriation is a descriptive analytic technique for arranging units along a single dimension. In archaeology it has been used to suggest *chronological* orderings of archaeological units, and it has generally been successful at this task. Although I have quibbled (Marquardt 1974b:188–198) with some of his statements, I am in agreement with Plog (1973:189) that "chronologies cause us to think of time as a series of successive units rather than as a continuous flow." If we do think in this way, then it is not surprising that seriation plays virtually an axiomatic role in archaeological inference.

Plog suggests we might realize seriation's potential as a diachronic tool by generating "a data base from which we would work in attempting to explain variability in the way that human populations adopt innovations" (1973:191–192). Some earlier anthropological works, notably those of Barnett (1953), approached the explanation of culture change with concepts centering on the individual's acceptance of innovations, and archaeologists have offered explanations for the distribution of various pottery types, manufacturing techniques, and design details in which both temporal and spatial considerations were important. As one example of the latter sort of study, Menzel *et al.* (1964) hypothesized phases of diversity and unity in stylistic features within the Ica Valley, suggesting that stylistic changes were often influenced by neighboring developments.

Ethnographic observations, such as those of DeBoer, discussed above, have shown that type frequencies in the archaeological record may bear little resemblance to frequencies of certain items in use by a human group at one given time. This sort of information may help us to choose our variables or types more effectively, but it does not invalidate the seriation technique itself (Springer 1977 has recently made a similar argument). I agree with Cowgill (1972:386) that obtaining a chronological ordering will often require only a small fraction of the available data. Used in isolation, seriation is surely an inadequate technique for investigating cultural process or, for that matter, for reconstructing culture history. Used in concert with other techniques in a well-advised research strategy, it will continue to be an important archaeological tool.

THE PRACTICE OF SERIATION

As with any analytical technique, seriation must be employed judiciously. *Strategies and techniques used in the field must be coordinated with the research questions being asked and must be appropriate to the nature of the archaeological record in the region being investigated.* Steps must be taken to be sure that surface collections are representative samples, that excavations are carefully carried out, that proveniences are unmixed: These are, of course, advisable whether or not seriation is to be employed.

Although many computer-assisted techniques are available, archaeologists should not hesitate to sort by hand if the number of units is relatively small. The methods of Gelfand (1971a,b), for example, are unambiguous and efficient for problems on the order of 10 units. Even if the number of units is large, samples drawn from these units can be seriated individually; at the least, this procedure can suggest hypotheses for further testing, and may help guide the choice of additional sites or areas for investigation when time in the field is limited. It goes without saying that a computer can be of invaluable assistance in the efficient processing of large data sets. Programs are easily obtained for many of the computer-assisted techniques mentioned in this paper—for example, SE-RIATE (Craytor and Johnson 1968), AXIS and POLISH (Wilkinson 1974), Small Space Analysis (Lingoes 1973), TORSCA (Young 1968), and Statistical Package for the Social Sciences (SPSS) (Nie *et al.* 1975). Factor analytic programs and multidimensional scaling programs, such as MDSCAL (Shepard 1962a,b; Kruskal 1964a,b), are available at many computing facilities. If archaeologists want to use techniques for which programs are not readily available, the assistance of a computer programmer will be needed. A competent programmer can produce a working program in a matter of a few hours or a few days, depending on the complexity of the algorithm. The budgeting of wages for a computer programmer may be a wise investment, particularly for large-scale or long-term projects in which substantial amounts of data are processed, or in which the time available for report preparation is limited.

Although they have their limitations, incidence data can be useful in seriation. This kind of information is most reliable when the units represent "closed finds," such as graves. Because it is the *incidence* of certain criteria that we are recording for each unit, rather than an absolute number or relative proportion, it is especially important that mixing of materials between units be minimized.

Various forms of abundance data have been used. Again, although seriation according to the frequency of types has inherent limitations, it has produced and can continue to produce reasonable results. Types must be chosen carefully, however. Descriptive statistical analyses can help suggest or confirm reliable types (Spaulding 1953). If the results of type frequency seriations are ambiguous, one should re-evaluate the criteria used for classification and the methods used to collect the samples being seriated. Steps must be taken to maximize spatiotemporal variance and minimize spatiofunctional variance if the objective is a chronological seriation. Supplementary information should be sought in order to provide independent confirmation or disconfirmation of sequences.

If sufficiently complex data are available, logically independent trend-sensitive variables are preferable to type frequencies for chronological investigation. Use of independent ratio-scale variables avoids the closed array effect caused by the use of percentages or relative proportions.

The productive debates of the past 10 years stimulated a re-evaluation of some of archaeology's oldest and most reliable tools, including seriation. As Watson has stated:

> There is undeniable potential for immensely increased information from our data if we explore these new theoretical and methodological questions, while applying new and better methods to old questions like the explanation of culture change. The prehistorian as philosopher of science emerged in the 1960's; the 1970's should be devoted to the operationalizing of theory by the nomothetically-oriented prehistorian as excavator of the past [1973:51].

Further advances in seriation theory, epistemology, and techniques may be anticipated in the future. Whether individuals perceive their efforts to be idiographic or nomothetic, primarily humanistic or primarily scientific, the establishment of reliable chronologies will always be important in archaeology.

ACKNOWLEDGMENTS

Although I am alone responsible for errors of omission or interpretation, I am grateful to the following people who offered valuable constructive criticism: Robert Benfer, Linda Gorski, David Ives, Keith Kintigh, Michael Schiffer, and Vin Steponaitis. Additionally, four reviewers—Charles McNutt, Robert Whallon, and two anonymous persons—are thanked for their detailed criticisms and bibliographic suggestions. Finally, I thank Michelle Millot for typing with great care both the first and the revised versions of the chapter.

REFERENCES

Ackoff, R. L.
1956   The development of operations research as a science. *Operations Research* **4:** 265–295.
Ahler, S. A.
1971   Projectile point form and function at Rodgers Shelter. *Missouri Archaeological Society, Research Series* No. 8.

Amarel, S.
  1971   Representation and modeling in problems of program formation. *Machine Intelligence* **6**: 411–466.
Ammerman, A. J.
  1971   A computer analysis of epipalaeolithic assemblages in Italy. In *Mathematics in the archaeological and historical sciences,* edited by F. R. Hodson, D. G. Kendall, and P. Tăutu. Edinburgh: Edinburgh University Press. Pp. 133–137.
Ascher, M.
  1959   A mathematical rationale for graphical seriation. *American Antiquity* **25**:212–214.
Ascher, M., and R. Ascher
  1963   Chronological ordering by computer. *American Anthropologist* **65**:1045–1052.
Barnett, H. G.
  1953   *Innovation: The basis of cultural change.* New York: McGraw-Hill.
Bellmore, M., and G. L. Nemhauser
  1968   The traveling salesman problem: A survey. *Operations Research* **16**:538–558.
Belous, R. E.
  1953   The central California chronological sequence re-examined. *American Antiquity* **18**:341–353.
Benfer, R. A.
  1972   Factor analysis as numerical induction: How to judge a book by its cover. *American Anthropologist* **74**:530–554.
  1975   Morphometric analysis of Cartesian coordinates of the human skull. *American Journal of Physical Anthropology* **42**:371–382.
Binford, L. R.
  1973   Interassemblage variability—the Mousterian and the "functional" argument. In *The explanation of culture change,* edited by C. Renfrew. London: Duckworth. Pp. 227–254.
Binford, L. R., and S. R. Binford
  1966   A preliminary analysis of functional variability in the Mousterian of Levallois facies. *American Anthropologist* **68**:238–295.
Boneva, L. I.
  1971   A new approach to a problem of chronological seriation associated with the works of Plato. In *Mathematics in the archaeological and historical sciences,* edited by F. R. Hodson, D. G. Kendall, and P. Tăutu. Edinburgh: Edinburgh University Press. Pp. 173–185.
Bordaz, V. von H., and J. Bordaz
  1970   A computer pattern recognition method of classification and seriation applied to archaeological material. In *Archéologie et calculateurs: Problèmes sémiologiques et mathématiques.* Paris: Centre National de la Recherche Scientifique. Pp. 229–274.
Brainerd, G. W.
  1951   The place of chronological ordering in archaeological analysis. *American Antiquity* **16**:301–313.
Buchanan, B., E. Feigenbaum, and J. Lederberg
  1971   A heuristic programming study of theory formation. *Stanford University, Computer Science Department, A.I. Memo* No. 145.
Christenson, A. L., and D. W. Read
  1977   Numerical taxonomy, R-mode factor analysis, and archaeological classification. *American Antiquity* **42**:163–179.

Christofides, N., and S. Eilon
1972 Algorithms for large-scale traveling salesman problems. *Operational Research Quarterly* **23**:511–518.

Cowgill, G. L.
1968a Archaeological applications of factor, cluster, and proximity analysis. *American Antiquity* **33**:367–375.
1968b Review of *Computer analysis of chronological seriation*, by F. Hole and M. Shaw. *American Antiquity* **33**:517–519.
1972 Models, methods, and techniques for seriation. In *Models in archaeology*, edited by D. L. Clarke. London: Methuen. Pp. 381–424.

Craytor, W. B., and L. Johnson, Jr.
1968 Refinements in computerized item seriation. *University of Oregon, Museum of Natural History, Bulletin* No. 10.

Croes, G. A.
1958 A method for solving traveling salesman problems. *Operations Research* **6**:791–814.

Daniels, S.
1967 Statistics, typology, and cultural dynamics in the Transvaal Middle Stone Age. *South African Archaeological Bulletin* **22**:114–125.

Dantzig, G., R. Fulkerson, and S. Johnson
1954 Solution of a large-scale traveling salesman problem. *Operations Research* **2**:393–410.

David, N.
1972 On the life span of pottery, type frequencies, and archaeological inference. *American Antiquity* **37**:141–142.

David, N., and H. Hennig
1972 The ethnography of pottery: A Fulani case seen in archaeological perspective. *Addison-Wesley Modular Publications, McCaleb Module* No. 21.

Davis, J. C.
1973 *Statistics and data analysis in geology.* New York: Wiley.

DeBoer, W. R.
1974 Ceramic longevity and archaeological interpretation: An example from the Upper Ucayali, Peru. *American Antiquity* **39**:335–343.

Deetz, J., and E. Dethlefsen
1965 The Doppler effect and archaeology: A consideration of the spatial aspects of seriation. *Southwestern Journal of Anthropology* **21**:196–206.
1971 Some social aspects of New England colonial mortuary art. In Approaches to the social dimensions of mortuary practices, edited by J. A. Brown. *Society for American Archaeology, Memoirs* **25**:30–38.

de la Vega, W. F.
1977 Deux algorithmes de sériation. In Raisonnement et méthodes mathématiques en archéologie, edited by M. Borillo, W. F. de la Vega, and A. Guenoche. *Centre National de la Recherche Scientifique, Séminaire du Laboratoire d'Informatique pour les Sciences de l'Homme* No. 1, 146–155.

Dempsey, P., and M. Baumhoff
1963 The statistical use of artifact distributions to establish chronological sequence. *American Antiquity* **28**:496–509.

Dethlefsen, E., and J. Deetz
1966 Death's heads, cherubs, and willow trees: Experimental archaeology in colonial cemeteries. *American Antiquity* **31**:502–510.

Deutsch, S. B., and J. J. Martin
  1971   An ordering algorithm for analysis of data arrays. *Operations Research* **19:**1350–1362.
Dixon, K. A.
  1956   Archaeological objectives and artifact sorting techniques: A re-examination of the Snaketown sequence. *Western Anthropology* **3.**
Doran, J. E.
  1972   Computer models as tools for archaeological hypothesis formation. In *Models in archaeology*, edited by D. L. Clarke. London: Methuen. Pp. 425–452.
Doran, J. E., and F. R. Hodson
  1966   A digital computer analysis of Palaeolithic flint assemblages. *Nature* **210:**688–689.
  1975   *Mathematics and computers in archaeology*. Cambridge, Mass.: Harvard University Press.
Doran, J. E., and S. Powell
  1972   Solving a combinatorial problem encountered in archaeology. In *Some research applications of the computer*. Radnor, Pa.: Atlas Computer Laboratory, Chilton. Pp. 47–52.
Drennan, R. D.
  1976   A refinement of chronological seriation using nonmetric multidimensional scaling. *American Antiquity* **41:**290–302.
Dunnell, R. C.
  1970   Seriation method and its evaluation. *American Antiquity* **35:**305–319.
Flanders, R. E.
  1960   A re-examination of Mill Creek ceramics: The Robinson technique. *Iowa Archaeological Society, Journal* **10:**1–35.
Flood, M. M.
  1956   The traveling-salesman problem. *Operations Research* **4:**61–75.
Ford, J. A.
  1962   A quantitative method for deriving cultural chronology. *Pan American Union, Technical Manual* No. 1. (Reprinted as *University of Missouri, Museum of Anthropology, Museum Brief* No. 9.)
Foster, G. M.
  1960   Life-expectancy of utilitarian pottery in Tzintzuntzan, Michoacán, Mexico. *American Antiquity* **25:**606–609.
Fulkerson, D. R., and O. A. Gross
  1965   Incidence matrices and interval graphs. *Pacific Journal of Mathematics* **15:**835–855.
Gelfand, A. E.
  1969   Seriation of multivariate observations through similarities. *Stanford University, Department of Statistics, Technical Report* No. 146.
  1971a Rapid seriation methods with archaeological applications. In *Mathematics in the archaeological and historical sciences*, edited by F. R. Hodson, D. G. Kendall, and P. Tǎutu. Edinburgh: Edinburgh University Press. Pp. 186–201.
  1971b Seriation methods for archaeological materials. *American Antiquity* **36:**263–274.
Glover, I. C.
  1969   The use of factor analysis for the discovery of artifact types. *Mankind* **7:**36–51.
Goldmann, K.
  1971   Some archaeological criteria for chronological seriation. In *Mathematics in the*

archaeological and historical sciences, edited by F. R. Hodson, D. G. Kendall, and P. Tăutu. Edinburgh: Edinburgh University Press. Pp. 202–208.

1972   Zwei Methoden chronologischer Gruppierung. *Acta Praehistorica et Archaeologica* **3**:1–34.

Graham, I., P. Galloway, and I. Scollar
1976   Model studies in computer seriation. *Journal of Archaeological Science* **3**:1–30.

Green, P. E., and F. J. Carmone
1970   *Multidimensional scaling and related techniques in marketing analysis.* Boston: Allyn & Bacon.

Green, P. E., and V. R. Rao
1972   *Applied multidimensional scaling: A comparison of approaches and algorithms.* New York: Holt.

Guttman, L.
1968   A general nonmetric technique for finding the smallest coordinate space for a configuration of points. *Psychometrika* **33**:469–506.

Hatch, J. W.
1976   "Change" versus "noise" in ceramic frequency seriation. Paper presented at the 1976 Meeting of the Society for American Archaeology, St. Louis.

Hill, J. N.
1970   Broken K Pueblo: Prehistoric social organization in the Southwest. *University of Arizona, Anthropological Papers* No. 18.

Hill, M. O.
1974   Correspondence analysis: A neglected multivariate method. *Applied Statistics* **23**:340–354.

Hodson, F. R.
1968   *The La Tène cemetery at Münsingen-Rain.* Bern: Stämpfli.
1970   Cluster analysis and archaeology: Some new developments and applications. *World Archaeology* **1**:299–320.

Hodson, F. R., D. G. Kendall, and P. Tăutu (editors)
1971   *Mathematics in the archaeological and historical sciences.* Edinburgh: Edinburgh University Press.

Hodson, F. R., P. H. A. Sneath, and J. Doran
1966   Some experiments in the numerical analysis of archaeological data. *Biometrika* **53**:311–324.

Hole, F., and M. Shaw
1967   Computer analysis of chronological seriation. *Rice University, Studies* **53**(3).

Hubert, L.
1974   Some applications of graph theory and related non-metric techniques to problems of approximate seriation: The case of symmetric proximity measures. *The British Journal of Mathematical & Statistical Psychology* **27**(2):133–153.
1976   Seriation using asymmetric proximity measures. *The British Journal of Mathematical & Statistical Psychology* **29**(1):32–52.

Hubert, L., and J. Schultz
1976a   A note on seriation and quadratic assignment. *Classification Society Bulletin* **3**(4):16–24.
1976b   Quadratic assignment as a general data analysis strategy. *The British Journal of Mathematical & Statistical Psychology* **29**(2):190–241.

Jardine, N., and R. Sibson
1971   *Mathematical taxonomy.* New York: Wiley.

Johnson, L., Jr.
  1968   Item seriation as an aid for elementary scale and cluster analysis. *University of Oregon, Museum of Natural History, Bulletin* No. 15.
  1972   Introduction to imaginary models for archaeological scaling and clustering. In *Models in archaeology*, edited by D. L. Clarke, London: Methuen. Pp. 309–379.
Kadane, J. B.
  1972   Chronological ordering of archaeological deposits by the minimum path length method. *Carnegie-Mellon University, Department of Statistics, Technical Report* No. 58.
Kendall, D. G.
  1963   A statistical approach to Flinders Petrie's sequence dating. *International Statistical Institute, Bulletin* No. 40, 657–680.
  1969a Incidence matrices, interval graphs, and seriation in archaeology. *Pacific Journal of Mathematics* **28**:565–570.
  1969b Some problems and methods in statistical archaeology. *World Archaeology* **1**:68–76.
  1970   A mathematical approach to seriation. *Philosophical Transactions of the Royal Society of London, Series A* **269**:125–135.
  1971a Abundance matrices and seriation in archaeology. *Zeitschrift für Wahrscheinlichkeitstheorie* **17**:104–112.
  1971b Seriation from abundance matrices. In *Mathematics in the archaeological and historical sciences,* edited by F. R. Hodson, D. G. Kendall, and P. Tăutu. Edinburgh: Edinburgh University Press. Pp. 215–252.
Kendall, M. G.
  1975   *Rank correlation methods.* London: Griffin.
Kintigh, K. W.
  1973   A seriation rule synthesizer. Manuscript on deposit, Museum of Anthropology, University of Michigan, Ann Arbor (xerox).
  1974   An artificial intelligence approach to the discovery of structure in archaeological data. Manuscript on deposit, Museum of Anthropology, University of Michigan, Ann Arbor (Xerox).
Kruskal, J. B.
  1964a Multidimensional scaling by optimizing goodness of fit to a nonmetric hypothesis. *Psychometrika* **29**(1):1–27.
  1964b Nonmetric multidimensional scaling: A numerical method. *Psychometrika* **29**(2):115–129.
  1971   Multidimensional scaling in archaeology: Time is not the only dimension. In *Mathematics in the archaeological and historical sciences,* edited by F. R. Hodson, D. G. Kendall, and P. Tăutu. Edinburgh: Edinburgh University Press. Pp. 119–132.
Kuzara, R. S., G. R. Mead, and K. A. Dixon
  1966   Seriation of anthropological data: A computer program for matrix ordering. *American Anthropologist* **68**:1442–1455.
Landau, J., and W. F. de la Vega
  1971   A new seriation algorithm applied to European protohistoric anthropomorphic statuary. In *Mathematics in the archaeological and historical sciences,* edited by F. R. Hodson, D. G. Kendall, and P. Tăutu. Edinburgh: Edinburgh University Press. Pp. 255–262.
Laporte, G.
  1976   A comparison of two norms in archaeological seriation. *Journal of Archaeological Science* **3**:249–255.

Laxton, R. R.
   1976   A measure of pre-Q-ness with applications to archaeology. *Journal of Archaeological Science* **3**:43–54.
LeBlanc, S. A.
   1975   Micro–seriation: A method for fine chronologic differentiation. *American Antiquity* **40**:22–38.
Lenstra, J. K.
   1974   Clustering a data array and the traveling-salesman problem. *Operations Research* **22**:413–414.
Lin, S., and B. W. Kernighan
   1973   An effective heuristic algorithm for the traveling-salesman problem. *Operations Research* **21**:498–516.
Lingoes, J. C.
   1970   A general nonmetric model for representing objects and attributes in a joint metric space. In *Archéologie et calculateurs: Problèmes sémiologiques et mathématiques*. Paris: Centre National de la Recherche Scientifique, Pp. 277–297.
   1973   *The Guttman-Lingoes nonmetric program series*. Ann Arbor, Mich.: Mathesis Press.
Lipe, W. D.
   1964   Comment on *The statistical use of artifact distributions to establish chronological sequence*, by P. Dempsey and M. Baumhoff. *American Antiquity* **30**:103–104.
Lischka, J. J.
   1975   Broken K revisited: A short discussion of factor analysis. *American Antiquity* **40**:220–227.
Little, J. D. C., K. G. Murty, D. W. Sweeney, and C. Karel
   1963   An algorithm for the traveling salesman problem. *Operations Research* **11**:972–989.
Longacre, W. A.
   1974   Kalinga pottery making: The evolution of a research design. In *Frontiers in anthropology*, edited by M. Leaf. New York: Van Nostrand. Pp. 51–67.
López, A., G. Espinosa, and R. Carvajal
   1976   A relationship between seriation and cluster analysis. *Universidad Nacional Autonoma de Mexico, Instituto de Investigaciones en Matematicas Aplicadas y en Sistemas, Comunicaciones Téchnicas, Serie Naranja: Investigaciones* **7**(128).
McCormick, W. T., P. J. Schweitzer, and T. W. White
   1972   Problem decomposition and data reorganization by a clustering technique. *Operations Research* **20**:993–1009.
McNutt, C. H.
   1973   On the methodological validity of frequency seriation. *American Antiquity* **38**:45–60.
McPherron, A.
   1967   The Juntunen site and the Late Woodland prehistory of the Upper Great Lakes area. *University of Michigan, Museum of Anthropology, Anthropological Papers* No. 30.
Marquardt, W. H.
   1974a A statistical analysis of constituents in human paleofecal specimens from Mammoth Cave. In *Archeology of the Mammoth Cave area*, edited by P. J. Watson. New York. Academic Press. Pp. 193–202.

Marquardt, W. H.
  1974b A temporal perspective on late prehistoric societies in the eastern Cibola area: Factor analytic approaches to short-term chronological investigation. Ph.D. dissertation, Washington University, St. Louis. Ann Arbor: University Microfilms.
  1977 A factor analytic approach to seriation. Manuscript on deposit, Dept. of Anthropology, University of Missouri-Columbia (Xerox).
Matthews, J.
  1963 Application of matrix analysis to archaeological problems. *Nature (London)* **198**:930–934.
Mayer-Oakes, W. J.
  1955 Prehistory of the upper Ohio valley: An introductory archaeological study. *Pittsburgh, Carnegie Museum, Annals* No. 34.
Meighan, C. W.
  1959 A new method for the seriation of archaeological collections. *American Antiquity* **25**:203–211.
Menzel, D., J. H. Rowe, and L. E. Dawson
  1964 The Paracas pottery of Ica: A study of style and time. *University of California, Publications in American Archaeology and Ethnology* No. 50.
Netter, J. P.
  1971 An algorithm to find elementary negative-cost circuits with a given number of arcs—the traveling salesman problem. *Operations Research* **19**:234–236.
Nie, N. H., C. H. Hull, J. G. Jenkins, K. Steinbrenner, and D. H. Bent
  1975 *Statistical package for the social sciences.* Second edition. New York: McGraw-Hill.
Nöel Hume, I.
  1970 *A guide to artifacts of Colonial America.* New York: Knopf.
Overall, J. E., and C. J. Klett
  1972 *Applied multivariate analysis.* New York: McGraw-Hill.
Petrie, W. M. F.
  1899 Sequences in prehistoric remains. *Journal of the Anthropological Institute* **29**:295–301.
Phillips, P., J. A. Ford, and J. B. Griffin
  1951 Archaeological survey in the lower Mississippi alluvial valley, 1940–1947. *Harvard University, Peabody Museum of American Archaeology and Ethnology, Paper* No. 25.
Plog, F. T.
  1973 Diachronic anthropology. In *Research and theory in current archeology,* edited by C. L. Redman. New York: Wiley (Interscience). Pp. 181–198.
Rathje, W. L.
  1974 The garbage project: A new way of looking at the problems of archaeology. *Archaeology* **27**:236–241.
Read, D. W.
  1974 Some comments on typologies in archaeology and an outline of a methodology. *American Antiquity* **39**:216–242.
Redman, C. L.
  1973 Multistage fieldwork and analytical techniques. *American Antiquity* **28**: 61–79.
Régnier, S.
  1977 Sériation des niveaux de plusieurs tranches de fouille dans une zone archéologique homogène. In Raisonnement et méthodes mathématiques en ar-

chéologie, edited by M. Borillo, W. F. de la Vega, and A. Guenoche. *Centre National de la Recherche Scientifique, Séminaire du Laboratoire d'Informatique pour les Sciences de l'Homme* No. 1, 146–155.

Renfrew, C., and G. Sterud
    1969   Close-proximity analysis: A rapid method for the ordering of archaeological materials. *American Antiquity* **34**:265–277.

Robinson, W. S.
    1951   A method for chronologically ordering archaeological deposits. *American Antiquity* **16**:293–301.

Rogers, D. J., and T. T. Tanimoto
    1960   A computer program for classifying plants. *Science* **132**:1115–1118.

Roper, D. C.
    1974   The distribution of Middle Woodland sites within the environment of the lower Sangoman River, Illinois. *Illinois State Museum, Reports of Investigations* No. 30.
    1975   Reporting the results of a factor analysis: Some suggested guidelines. *Newsletter of Computer Archaeology* **10**(3):1–5.
    1976   Nominal data and factor analysis: A comment on Geier. *Plains Anthropologist* **21**:231–236.

Rouse, I.
    1967   Seriation in archaeology. In *American historical anthropology: Essays in honor of Leslie Spier*, edited by C. L. Riley and W. W. Taylor. Carbondale: Southern Illinois University Press. Pp. 153–195.

Rowe, J. H.
    1959   Archaeological dating and cultural process. *Southwestern Journal of Anthropology* **15**:317–324.
    1962   Worsaae's Law and the use of grave lots for archaeological dating. *American Antiquity* **28**:129–137.

Rowlett, R. M., and R. B. Pollnac
    1971   Multivariate analysis of Marnian La Tène cultural groups. In *Mathematics in the archaeological and historical sciences*, edited by F. R. Hodson, D. G. Kendall, and P. Tăutu. Edinburgh: Edinburgh University Press. Pp. 46–58.

Rummel, R. J.
    1970   *Applied factor analysis*. Evanston: Northwestern University Press.

Schiffer, M. B.
    1975   Arrangement vs. seriation of sites: A new approach to relative temporal relationships. In The Cache River Archeological Project: An experiment in contract archeology, assembled by M. B. Schiffer and J. M. House. *Arkansas Archeological Survey, Research Series* No. 8, 257–263.
    1976   *Behavioral archeology*. New York: Academic Press.

Shepard, R. N.
    1962a   The analysis of proximities: Multidimensional scaling with an unknown distance function I. *Psychometrika* **27**(2):125–140.
    1962b   The analysis of proximities: Multidimensional scaling with an unknown distance function II. *Psychometrika* **27**(3):219–246.
    1972   Introduction. In *Multidimensional scaling: Theory and applications in the behavioral sciences* (Vol.1): *Theory*, edited by R. N. Shepard, A. K. Romney, and S. B. Nerlove. New York: Seminar Press. Pp.1–20.

Shepard, R. N., A. K. Romney, and S. B. Nerlove (editors)
    1972   *Multidimensional scaling: Theory and applications in the behavioral sciences* (Vol. 1): *Theory*. (Vol. 2): *Applications*. New York: Seminar Press.

Sibson, R.
   1971   Some thoughts on sequencing methods. In *Mathematics in the archaeological and historical sciences,* edited by F. R. Hodson, D. G. Kendall, and P. Tăutu. Edinburgh: Edinburgh University Press. Pp. 263–266.
   1972   Order invariant methods for data analysis. *Journal of the Royal Statistical Society, Series B* **34**:311–349.
   1977   Multidimensional scaling in theory and practice. In Raisonnement et méthodes mathématiques en archéologie, edited by M. Borillo, W. F. de la Vega, and A. Guenoche. *Centre National de la Recherche Scientifique, Séminaire du Laboratoire d'Informatique pour les Sciences de l'Homme* No. 1, 73–97.

Sokal, R. R., and P. H. A. Sneath
   1963   *Principles of numerical taxonomy.* San Francisco: Freeman.

South, S.
   1977   *Method and theory in historical archeology.* New York: Academic Press.

Spaulding, A. C.
   1953   Statistical techniques for the discovery of artifact types. *American Antiquity* **18**:305–313, 391–393.

Speth, J. D., and G. A. Johnson
   1976   Problems in the use of correlation for the investigation of tool kits and activity areas. In *Cultural change and continuity,* edited by C. Cleland, New York: Academic Press. Pp. 35–57.

Springer, J. W.
   1977   A ceramic sequence from southern Louisiana and its implications for type frequency seriation. Manuscript on deposit, Department of Anthropology, Northern Illinois University, DeKalb (Xerox).

Sternin, H.
   1965   Statistical methods of time sequencing. *Stanford University, Department of Statistics, Technical Report* No. 112.

Tanimoto, T. T.
   1961   A nonlinear model for a computer-assisted medical diagnostic procedure. *Transactions of the New York Academy of Sciences, Series 2* **23**:576–578.

True, D. L., and R. G. Matson
   1970   Cluster analysis and multidimensional scaling of archaeological sites in northern Chile. *Science* **169**:1201–1203.

Tutte, W. T.
   1946   On Hamiltonian circuits. *Journal of the London Mathematical Society* **21**(No. 82, Part 2):98–101.

Watkins, C. M.
   1952   Artificial lighting in America: 1830–1860. *Smithsonian Institution, Annual Report, 1951.* Pp. 385–407.

Watson, P. J.
   1973   Explanation and models: The prehistorian as philosopher of science and the prehistorian as excavator of the past. In *The explanation of culture change,* edited by C. Renfrew. London: Duckworth. Pp. 47–52.

Whallon, R., Jr.
   1972   The computer in archaeology: A critical survey. *Computers and the Humanities* **7**:29–45.

Wilkinson, E. M.
   1971   Archaeological seriation and the traveling salesman problem. In *Mathematics in the archaeological and historical sciences,* edited by F. R. Hodson, D. G.

Kendall, and P. Tăutu. Edinburgh: Edinburgh University Press. Pp. 276–283.

1974 Techniques of data analysis—seriation theory. *Archaeo-Physika* **5:**1–142.

Wynn, J. T.

1976 The Marquardt seriation method applied in the Tairona area, Colombia. Paper presented at the 1976 Meeting of the Society for American Archaeology, St. Louis.

Young, F. W.

1968 A FORTRAN IV program for nonmetric multidimensional scaling. *University of North Carolina, L. I. Thurstone Psychometric Laboratory, Report* No. 56.

9

A Survey of Disturbance Processes in Archaeological Site Formation

W. RAYMOND WOOD and DONALD LEE JOHNSON

INTRODUCTION

The context of archaeological remains has always been a matter of keen interest to prehistorians, for the relationships of cultural features to one another—and to the natural features of a site—are the foundations of our discipline. If we fail to record the context, or if we misread or misinterpret that context, proper archaeological interpretation is impossible.

It is therefore obvious that a study of archaeological context must go hand in hand with an understanding of the matrix in which remains are embedded. In many cases, it is no more possible for us to understand the nature of the past without an understanding of soil dynamics than it is for a marine biologist to comprehend his discipline without an understanding of the nature of ocean water and its movements. This is true for any practicing archaeologist, in the field as well as in the task of interpretation.

Archaeologists have long operated under the assumption that past human activities are reflected in the patterned distribution of artifacts. Childe (1956:1), among many others, spoke of human behavior's being "fossilized" in the archaeological record, and stated that it was "the archaeologist's business to reconstitute that behaviour as far as he can. . . ."

ADVANCES IN ARCHAEOLOGICAL METHOD AND THEORY, VOL. 1

The major bone of contention here is the *degree* to which the distribution of artifacts can be attributed to past behavior. Binford (1964:424) took what appears to be an extreme and untenable position when he said that the archaeological record is a " 'fossil' record of the *actual operation* of an extinct society" (our emphasis). Thompson and Longacre have gone further and asserted that

> *all* of the material remains in an archaeological site are highly patterned or structured *directly* as a result of the ways in which the extinct society was organized and the patterned ways in which the people behaved [1966:270; our emphasis].

Krause and Thorne, however, have taken exception to this generalization:

> We might agree that all the materials in an archaeological site *may be* structured or highly patterned. But we think it is stretching the point to assume that *all* archaeologically derivable patterning can be directly attributed to the behavior of the site's prehistoric inhabitants [1971:246].

That is, since debris distribution is the result of purposeful human activity, it *may* be patterned; but it does *not* follow that the patterning of the debris and the patterning of the human behavior that produced it are identical. And before any such demonstration of artifact/behavior isomorphism is complete, the processes must be known that may have acted on the matrix in which the debris was incorporated, and their effects assessed. This matrix is usually soil, the upper few decimeters of the earth's mantle, which is subject to modification and transport by numerous chemical, biological, and mechanical processes.

This line of reasoning was anticipated and developed in some detail first by Ascher (1968) and, more recently, by Schiffer (1972, 1976). Both authors are concerned with the processes of site formation, and with its subsequent history. Ascher pointed out that entropy and decreasing entropy take place at different rates in a living community. After a site is abandoned, natural processes begin

> disorganizing matter that was once arranged in patterns by human effort . . . The recognition of man's purposeful arrangements depends on *distinguishing between* the action of natural agents and the action of human agents. . . . Indeed, the heavy use in archaeological literature of the ambiguous term "feature" to describe any apparent patterning of objects is a tacit admission that the contributions of natural and human factors to an archaeological matrix are often indistinguishable. . . . Since the connection between the archaeological present and the ethnographic past lies along the route of increasing disorder, the advancement of interpretation depends on knowing what happens along that route [Ascher 1968:46–47, 52].

Schiffer (1976:15–16) has also noted some of the natural processes ("n-transforms") that act to modify the archaeological record—that is, that translate systemic context into archaeological context.

Soil is not a static body; it is a dynamic, open system, in which a variety of processes may act to move not only soil matter, but objects (including artifacts), from one position to another. It must therefore be included as one of the major natural features we must contend with in interpreting the archaeological record.

Although soil scientists have long been aware of the dynamic nature of soil, only recently have prehistorians begun to apply this concept systematically to field situations, at least in the New World. The purpose of this chapter is to explore various processes of soil mixing, and to suggest how mixing may affect archaeological context. We feel that it is just as important for us to be aware of the factors and processes that *disturb* soil horizons and their contents as it is to know the factors and processes leading to artifact *deposition* in natural or cultural deposits. As we shall see, the term *in situ*, used to denote undisturbed artifacts, is probably more optimistic than realistic—especially in certain kinds of soils.

TWO GENERAL SOIL-FORMING PROCESSES

Two contrasting sets of processes operate in soil development: *horizonation*, where soil materials are differentiated into profiles having horizons, and *homogenization* (or haploidization), where horizon formation is impeded, or where horizons and their contents may be mixed or otherwise disturbed. Homogenization is as important a general process as horizonation, both to soil scientists (Buol *et al.* 1973:91) and to archaeologists. These two sets of processes, however, are not mutually exclusive; for example faunal mixing of organic matter in the A horizon of forest and prairie soils appears essential for A horizonation in such soils (Hole and Nielsen 1970:29; Buntley and Papendick 1960:128; Soil Survey Staff 1975:293, 298, 309).

The various processes of homogenization are collectively termed *pedoturbation*—a synonym for "soil mixing." Pedoturbation is the biological, chemical, or physical churning, mixing, and cycling of soil materials (Buol *et al.* 1973:89, 94).

Hole (1961) listed and defined nine processes of pedoturbation that cause soil mixing (Table 9.1). A scan of the list shows that certain processes are obviously more common in some regions than in others, whereas some may be only local in their occurrence. Archaeologists should be thoroughly familiar with those processes in Table 9.1 that operate in their activity region and gain some facility for perceiving their effects. Parenthetically, it should be noted that the nine processes of pedoturbation may not be mutually exclusive. For example, genesis of

TABLE 9.1

Pedoturbation Processes[a]

Process[b]	Soil-mixing vectors
Faunalturbation	Animals (burrowing forms especially)
Floralturbation	Plants (root growth, treefall)
Cryoturbation	Freezing and thawing
Graviturbation	Mass wasting (solifluction, creep)
Argilliturbation	Swelling and shrinking of clays
Aeroturbation	Gas, air, wind
Aquaturbation	Water
Crystalturbation	Growth and wasting of salts
Seismiturbation	Earthquakes

[a] Modified from Hole (1961).
[b] Shortened terminology.

solifluction lobes on slopes of cold regions reflects the combined action of cryoturbation, graviturbation, and aquaturbation, but it is treated in this paper under graviturbation. We now wish to examine these nine processes in detail.

FAUNALTURBATION: DISTURBANCE BY ANIMALS

Faunalturbation refers to the mixing of the soil by animals. Surely every archaeologist has seen the effects of burrowing animals time and again. At death, plants and animals contribute material to the soil—but in life, they distort it, sometimes minutely, sometimes profoundly.

On disuse, animal burrows in one soil horizon are commonly filled with material of a different color and texture from a different horizon, so they often appear in excavation profiles as the conspicuous tubular features known as krotovina, which are so familiar to archaeologists. Animals most responsible for them are rodents and other burrowing mammals, crayfish, various insects, and earthworms.

Burrowing Mammals

Many species of mice, voles, moles, gophers, squirrels, and shrews have elaborate complexes of tunnels, principally in the surface soil. They are sometimes as efficient as humans in churning the top soil, although their work may be more discontinuous, spatially and temporally, than that of people (Figure 9.1). In the Southwestern United States, burrowing mammals and insects may collectively mix and obliterate soil horizons over relatively short periods, sometimes measured in a few decades (Gile

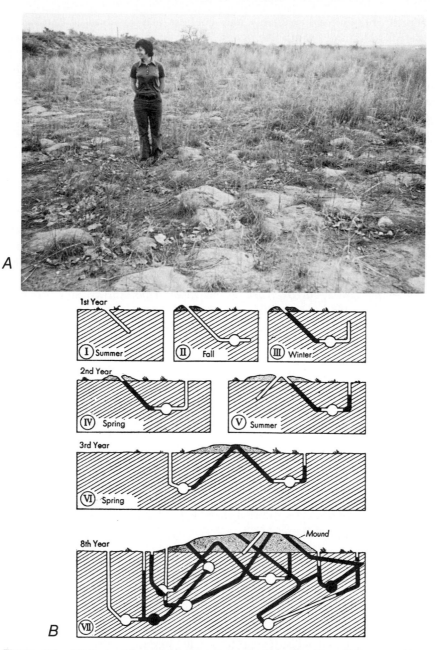

Figure 9.1.   (*A*) Rodent (gopher) burrow mounds, Canadian River Valley, west Texas. (*B*) Evolution of a *Citellus* burrow and mound (after Ogner). [From Grassé (1955) and Bourlière (1964).]

1966, 1975b). Ground squirrels and gophers are so abundant in some places (for example, south Texas) as to turn over 15–20% of the surface soil in a single season, thus completely mixing it in five or six years (Thorp 1949:190). Some rodents burrow more deeply, and annually bring to the surface an estimated 7200–14,000 kg/ha (20–40 tons/acre) of subsoil material (Thorp 1949: Matelski 1959). During winters in Wyoming and elsewhere, gophers burrow in snow and then may fill the tunnels with soil, which remains on the soil surface as "rodent eskers" when the snow melts (Laycock 1958; Thorp 1949:188; Daubenmire 1959:35). Gophers in California are estimated to bring about 2.5 metric tons/km² (7 tons/mi²) of subsoil to the surface annually (Grinnell 1923). In the Arctic, ground squirrels (*Citellus undulatus*) burrow selectively into southeast facing slopes where solifluction lobes are well-developed, excavating annually 18,000 kg/ha (8 tons/acre) (Price 1971:100). Extensive mound systems were formed by burrowing kangaroo rats (*Dipodomys spectabilis baileyi*) in 23–30 months in the Blackwater Draw area of eastern New Mexico (Best 1972:201). In the Rajasthan Desert of Pakistan, the total number of openings of gerbil burrows are about 2,000,000/km²/day in cultivated areas, and 60,000/km²/day in uncultivated areas (Sharma and Joshi 1975:268).

Larger mammals, like foxes, prairie dogs, badgers, skunks, armadillos, oppossum, rabbits, and woodchucks, also burrow deeply, commonly through the subsoil, with some burrowing to depths of several meters (Bourlière 1964:72–88). As a manifestation of the pedoturbation activities of large mammals, human bones, casket handles, and other burial items frequently occur on the surface near entrances of woodchuck burrows in some cemeteries of the Midwest (C.S. Alexander, 1975 personal communication). The bones are brought up from depths of 2.5 m (7 ft), apparently during the course of burrowing activities of these mammals.

Some of the largest mammals may have a profound effect on soils. It is well known that, in addition to deflation and solution, many of the depressions on the High and Central Plains of North America owe their origin to the wallowing activities of bison.

Crayfish

Crayfish are nearly as effective as burrowing mammals in mixing soils on landscapes with shallow or fluctuating water tables. Their burrows leading to the surface may be 5–8 m (15–25 ft) deep, reflecting their need to have contact with the water table. Small chambers occur at the base of the passageways, about 15 × 25 cm (6 × 10 in.). Crayfish deposit small, pea- to marble-sized balls of earth at the surface around the entrances to their tunnels, forming earthen "chimneys" of up to 1.5 kg (3 lb) or so of earth (Figure 9.2). When crayfish are abundant, and when they rebuild their chimneys several times a season, upward of several 1000 kg/ha (several tons per acre) of earth will be moved to the surface. Crayfish are common in poorly and imperfectly drained soils in eastern United States from the Canadian border to the Gulf Coast, favoring within that area Alfisols, Mollisols, and Ultisols (Thorp 1949:186–188; and many personal observations of the writers).

Ants, Termites, and Other Insects

The effect and importance of ants and termites as agents of soil mixing has rarely been appreciated, even by many soil scientists. There are many species adapted to a wide variety of habitats, from forest to plains, at many latitudes, and from low to high altitudes (Figure 9.3). Indeed, archaeologists frequently consult anthills in the course of surface reconnaissance for clues to subsurface remains. Glass trade beads are brought to the surface from graves; and small crumbs of pottery and burned earth may also be carried from buried features to the surface through a culturally sterile horizon.

In North America the effects of ants and termites on soil horizons and particles in them is probably most pronounced in the west, where their earthworks and subterranean burrows appear to be larger and more extensive, if not more numerous, than in the east. These insects affect the soil most directly in carrying material from as deep as 2 m (6 ft) to the surface, thereby mixing and homogenizing it, as well as providing channels for surface water and, especially, air to move downward (Baxter and Hole 1967; Czerrvinski *et al.* 1971; Gile 1975a,b; Green and Askew 1965; Heath 1965; Hesse 1955; Lee and Wood 1971a,b; Salem and Hole 1968; Wiken *et al.* 1976). "A species of ant . . . builds large mounds 1 to 1½ ft high by 2 to 3 feet in diameter. The number of mounds may reach 40 or 50 or more per acre. Since they are active only for a limited number of years and are replaced by new mounds, a very considerable percentage of the total area may be worked over in a relatively short time" (Curtis 1959:279–280; see also Salem and Hole 1968; Thorp 1949). Wiken *et al.* (1976:424) estimated 1150 ant (*Formica*) mounds per hectare (2875 per acre) in British Columbia, with an estimated mound volume of 54 m³/ha. Ant-affected soils in the region have marked changes in particle size distribution, chemical properties, and structure. Mound microrelief (earth hummocks) landscapes on high pastures of the Swiss Jura are built by the yellow field ant *Lasius flarus* F., and may evolve in a period as short as 10–15 years (Schreiber 1969). The general pedogenetic processes of leach-

Figure 9.2. (*A*) Crawfish chimney, southern Indiana (pen is 15 cm long). (*B*) Field of crawfish chimneys.

Figure 9.3. (*A*) Ant mound on the high plains, western Nebraska. (*B*) Termite mound with an ant bear hole (where man is standing), Rhodesia. (Photograph courtesy P. Watson.)

ing and horizonation are reversed in such ant-affected soils (Wiken *et al.* 1976:422).

Termites are equally (if not more) effective as pedoturbators, their principal activity being that they, too, bring fine earth subsoil fractions to the surface (Gile 1975b; Watson 1967; Lee and Wood 1971b). Lee and Wood (1971b:53) conclude that "termites have developed the capacity to burrow and mold structures from soil and organic matter to a level unknown in any other group of soil animals."

Termite pedoturbation in the tropics is keenly appreciated by tropical pedologists and ecologists (Watson 1967; Thorp 1949; Lee and Wood 1971a,b). Even casual visitors are impressed with the number and size of termitaria that dot many tropical landscapes. A growing number of pedologists now believe that many of the stone lines in or under oxic horizons on old stable landscapes in the tropics and subtropics are of biologic origin (Heath 1965; Ollier 1959; Thorp 1949, and 1976 personal communication). The process of upward movement of subsoil fines brought to the surface by termites will eventually produce a "biomantle" many meters thick without horizons and result in a "lag" concentration of resistant stones at depth (Figure 9.4). According to the Soil Survey Staff (1975:36), "Stone lines are so common that one must consider it probable

Figure 9.4. Stone line in a tropical soil due to activity of termites in Africa (photograph courtesy of James Thorp).

that oxic horizons are mainly in very old biomantles or transported sediments.'' Such stone lines and biomantles appear as pedolithologic discontinuities (Heath 1965; Ollier 1959).

A common misconception is that the pedoturbation activities of termites are limited to the tropics. Nothing could be further from the truth. In North America, termites are known to mix horizons and objects in the soil, change the character of soil within horizons, cause horizons to be inverted, create new horizons (cambic B's), obliterate pre-existing (argillic) horizons, and affect the spatial boundaries of different soils (Gile 1975b; Soil Survey Staff 1975:21). One of us (D.L.J.) studied, photographed, and sampled termitaria (termite structures) during the summer of 1971 in a transect that extended from Missouri to California. These termitaria are often inconspicuous initially to untrained eyes, but with experience are seen in incredible numbers across the plains and western states.

Cicada nymphs and other burrowing insects have considerably modified the profiles of Aridisols and related soils in Idaho, Utah, Nevada, and California (Hugie and Passey 1963; and observations of the authors). Much of the ''cylindrical blocky'' structural peds that dominate the profiles of such soils are in reality insect krotovina fillings, principally of cicada nymph burrows.

Earthworms

Perhaps the most widely recognized faunal agent for soil mixing is the earthworm, which has this distinction in part because of the classic study by Darwin, *The Formation of Vegetable Mould through the Action of Worms,* first published in 1881.

Earthworms not only modify soil, and move objects within it, they actually *create* distinctive soil types. Worms are common at many latitudes and altitudes in all except very dry or very acid soils. Although they carry out their activities near the surface when the soil is moist, their burrows may extend to depths of 3 m (9 ft) or more during drought, or when the ground is cold or frozen.

They burrow by pushing the soil aside or by ingesting it before them, either leaving their castings behind, or extruding them at the surface (Figure 9.5). In worm-rich areas, soil material is passed time and again through their systems every few years, thereby gently but effectively churning the soil. Darwin (1896:305) noted that, in parts of England, more than 3600 kg/ha (10 tons/acre) of earth annually passed through their bodies and was brought to the surface. Other authors have reported a range of 360–9000 kg dry weight per hectare (1–25 tons/acre) of earth-

Figure 9.5. (*A*) Earthworm middens built during January thaw, 1973, in east-central Illinois. (*B*) Close-up of earthworm midden composed of leaf-covered soil mounds.

worm casts deposited annually on the soil surface (Evans and Guild 1947; Evans 1948).

One of the most familiar consequences of earthworm action is the blurring of natural or cultural boundaries in the soil. Most of us are familiar with the fact that pit outlines are frequently blurred near the surface, and become increasingly sharply defined with increasing depth. Responsibility for the phenomenon of blurring is assignable largely to earthworms, although other processes and microfauna contribute to it as well.

The number of earthworms in an area depends on several factors: temperature, moisture, soil reaction (pH), and vegetation. Studies have shown that in the mid-latitudes earthworms concentrate in areas where ash, hickory, tulip tree, dogwood, and certain other species of trees are common; they are especially fond of the fallen leaves of these trees. The leaves of red oak, on the other hand, are generally avoided (Thorp 1949:180–182).

The importance of earthworms and other soil animals to soil formation has long been recognized—for example, sombric mineral horizons, and mor, mull, and moder organic horizons (Canada Soil Survey Committee 1970). The Soil Survey Staff of the U.S. Department of Agriculture has defined three great groups of Mollisols that have derived largely from the actions of worms and their predators: Vermiborolls, Vermudolls, and Vermustolls. Although not widespread in North America, Vermiborolls and Vermudolls are extensive locally and are thus important to American archaeologists, and all three occur extensively on other continents (Soil Survey Staff 1975:293, 298, 309). There are large areas in the Midwest, such as in eastern South Dakota, where horizonation has been almost completely obliterated to a depth of 1 m (3 ft) by the action of earthworms (Buntley and Papendick 1960:128)—a graphic illustration of the fact that biologic activity is greater in grassland soils than in forest soils (Buol *et al.* 1973:245). In fact, earthworms play a principal role in the development of A horizons of many if not most grassland and forest soils in the mid-latitudes (Nielsen and Hole 1964; Hole and Nielsen 1970; Jacks 1963; Bocock and Gilbert 1957; Gilbert and Bocock 1960; Scully 1942; Wilde 1958).

In addition to simply churning the soil material itself, however, earthworms have another and more profound effect on archaeological remains. Darwin, nearly a century ago, wrote:

> Archaeologists are probably not aware how much they owe to worms for the preservation of many ancient objects. Coins, gold ornaments, stone implements, etc., if dropped to the surface of the ground, will be buried by the castings of worms in a few years, and thus be safely preserved [Darwin 1896:176].

It is worth noting that Darwin did not overlook the fact that loess and slopewash or colluvium (he, of course, used other terms) aided the earthworms in their "work of concealment" (1896:228, 309). Cornwall has described this process rather succinctly:

> One effect of the bringing by worms of their castings to the surface is to sink into the soil, and eventually bury, any body lying on it which is too large to be swallowed by them. This sinking is assisted by the collapse, below, of old worm-tunnels and the falling in of the subsoil which has been penetrated by them. The resultant rate of sinking of stones and other bodies is commensurate with the surface accumulation and may amount to as much as [5 mm] annually [Cornwall 1958:52].

Such action is capable of burying surface features very rapidly. Indeed, one of us (D.L.J.), while spading a yard in Champaign, Illinois, in 1970 discovered a buried brick patio under 7 cm (3 in.) of worm-worked top soil. The mortarless bricks, which had been laid during or after 1949 (when the adjacent house was built), apparently had been gradually covered over and "lowered" by earthworms depositing their castings at the surface between and over the bricks. Several months after clearing, the process was renewed when worm castings were observed again accumulating above the bricks. Like ants and termites, then, earthworms can also produce stone lines (and artifact lines?) at depth while concomitantly producing overlying biomantles.

Since earthworm activity decreases with depth, objects nearer the surface will sink more rapidly than those at a greater depth. Materials left on the surface may, over a long period of time, be concentrated into an "artificial" subsurface layer in which vertical stratification is all but erased and objects from different time periods are placed in spurious association. Other complications can be readily envisioned by the active field archaeologist. We heartily endorse Cornwall's (1958:51) recommendation to consult Darwin's original work, which is based in part on studies made by him and his sons on Roman ruins in England.

FLORALTURBATION: DISTURBANCE BY PLANTS

Floralturbation is the mechanical mixing of soil by plants, as occurs during root growth and decay, where krotovina-like structures termed *root casts* are produced (Figure 9.6), and during tree fall, when uprooted trees bring masses of earth to the surface. Of the two processes, treefall is by far the more important. The natural falling of dead trees may leave shallow depressions where roots and adhering rock and soil are torn up; even larger depressions may be left by live, windthrown trees. As the trees decompose, adhering soil and regolith settles to form mounds of low

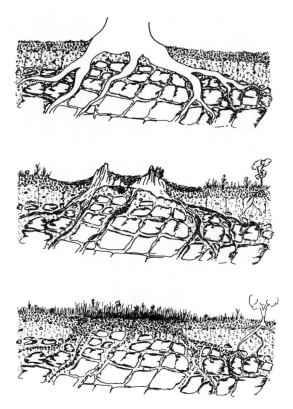

Figure 9.6. A three-stage diagram showing the formation of root casts. (From Limbrey 1975:Fig. 31.)

relief, variously called *blowdown mounds* and *tree-tip mounds* (Figure 9.7). The mounds, together with the depressions, produce a form of microrelief, called *cradle–knoll* topography, common in many forested lands of the world (Denny and Goodlett 1956; Lutz 1960; Shcherbakov and Bakanin 1969; Booij 1975; Blancaneaux 1973; Baxter 1967:99; also Milfred *et al.* 1967:57–58, 192; Hole and Schmude 1959; Gaikawad and Hole 1961; Mueller and Cline 1959). Treefall causes inversion and mixing of horizons and, of course, mixes any artifacts contained within them.

It is estimated that cradle–knoll topography occupies about 20% of forest lands in parts of the Great Lakes region of North America (Buol *et al.* 1973:253; Milfred *et al.* 1967:58). The interrupted character of the A_2 (albic) and Bhir (spodic) horizons of many of the Spodosols of North America and Eurasia may well be due principally to treefall. In 1975, one of us (D.L.J.) went on a 1600 km soil inspection trip through Wisconsin

Figure 9.7.   Treefall in Brownfield Woods, Champaign County, Illinois. This is the first step toward the formation of cradle–knoll topography.

led by F. D. Hole, during which cradle–knoll topography was observed over vast areas of that state. Indeed, most forested areas of the Midwest visited by the authors, especially Wisconsin, Illinois, and Indiana, show evidence of treefall.

Most treefall is caused by high winds during storms (termed "windthrow"). Hurricanes, tropical depressions, frontal systems and associated high winds, and tornadoes are responsible for most cradle–knoll topography in the world. To lend perspective, on the basis of observed tornado frequency and average path area, the probability is such that every part of the surface of Illinois will experience a tornado (and thus trees in woodlands suffer windthrow) once every 1000 years (unpublished study by meteorologist Jack Linde, 1971 personal communication).

Although wind is the active factor ultimately responsible for most treefall, tree type, tree size (diameter), soil substrate, and moisture conditions appear to be important passive factors. In Menominee County, Wisconsin, Nielsen (1963) counted 141 cradle–knolls per acre under mature hemlock forest on silty soils, but only 4 per acre under jack pine on sandy soils (tree size was not considered in the study and may have been an additional factor). Of 250 cradle–knolls in silty soils examined by Nielsen, the average vertical distance (relief) between the bottom of the cradle and the top of the knoll was 0.4 m (1.3 ft); the horizontal distance, or length, was 1.2 m (4.0 ft); and the average slope for a line drawn between the two points was 31%. On sandy soils corresponding figures were 0.2 m (0.6 ft), 0.8 m (2.6 ft), and 27%. [According to Buol *et al.* (1973:253), the relief of cradle–knolls may be as much as 1 m, and the length 3 m.] The maximum slope of the steepest knolls measured by Nielsen was 45°, or 100%. Incipient soils a few centimeters thick have formed on the cradle–knolls. Orientation of the cradle–knolls show that westerly winds caused the treefall, and on slopes greater than 8% treefall was preferentially downslope.

Where root development is shallow because of closeness to bedrock or the presence of a fragipan, or because of the water table, trees will have a high susceptibility to windthrow, other things being equal (Mueller and Cline 1959). Data obtained by Mueller and Cline, and by Olson and Hole (1967), indicate that, in soils with fragipans, soil mixing is limited to the layer of soil above the fragipan. These authors, together with Denny and Goodlett (1956:65), estimate that most of the A and B soil horizons in the northern hardwood regions of North America will be floralturbated over 500 years.

> The amount of material moved by treefall on slopes is impressive. Based on measurement of mound volumes and on frequency estimates derived from counts of tree rings, Denny and Goodlett calculate that since the retreat of ice from northern Pennsylvania some 10,000 years ago, treefall alone has moved a soil mantle 20 cm thick 45 m downslope [Malde 1964:11].

Table 9.2 shows the relationship between tree diameter, soil moisture, and substrate conditions, and the volume and areal extent of disturbed soil by treefall in central New York; Table 9.3 relates tree diameter alone to volume and areal extent of disturbed soil.

A graphic example of archaeological floralturbation operating together with faunalturbation is given at a multicomponent site (21 CA 58) that occurs on two terraces of Gull River and Gull Lake in Cass County, Minnesota (Neumann 1978). The terrace surfaces are ''marked by numerous hummocks,'' the product of treefall in a now lightly wooded area (about 760 trees/ha). Neumann (1978:90) reports that beginning a few cm below the surface and continuing past 65 cm, there were at least six different "temporal groups" of artifacts scattered over the upper terrace. Concentrated between 5 and 30 cm there were five recognizable ceramic types: Sandy Lake Cord-Impressed and Sandy Lake Smooth (A.D. 1300–Historic: . . . Kathio (A.D. 800–1300) . . . ; St. Croix Stamped (Dentate) (A.D. 500–700) . . . ; Brainerd Net Impressed (A.D. 600–800) . . . ; and Malmo–Kern (800 B.C.–A.D. 800–200) . . . . These materials were contained within a matrix with no apparent cultural stratigraphy and no perceptible natural stratigraphy. The frustrating nature of the site can be appreciated for, given the above, this suggests an extreme of 2500 years packed into 25 cm.

While treefall was the most obvious pedoturbatory process operating, Neumann believed activities of ants and earthworms were also important.

In the foregoing discussion we have focused on the soil- and artifact-mixing capabilities of floralturbation. We wish to conclude this section by stressing the importance of treefall to archaeologists in paleoecological reconstructions, drawing in part on observations by Malde (1964:11–12) and by Denny and Goodlett (1956). With time, the microrelief generated by treefall is obliterated, but the disturbed soil mantle remains. Fines eroded from the soil surface during repeated mantle turnover by treefall may serve to concentrate a veneer of stones at the surface. Such stone pavements resemble landscapes produced by frost action in cold regions. Thus, it is ecologically important to separate mixing by frost action from

TABLE 9.2

Relationship between Tree Size (Diameter), Soil Drainage, Horizon Restrictions (Fragipan versus Calcareous Till), and Total Volume and Areal Extent of Soil Mixed by Windthrow of 100 Trees[a]

Approximate tree diameter (cm)	Drainage class	Surface area disturbed (m²)		Soil volume disturbed (m²)	
		Fragipan restriction	Calcareous till restriction	Fragipan restriction	Calcareous till restriction
10	Good[b]	232[c]	116	162	69
	Poor[b]		260	34	127
20	Good	316[c]	223	223	164
	Poor		446	91	223
30	Good	493[c]	353	281	259
	Poor		628	150	318
40	Good	660[c]	525	337	354
	Poor		837	207	413

[a] Modified from Mueller and Cline (1959: 110, Table 5).

[b] The Good category here is the combined Good and Moderately Good Drainage classes of Mueller and Cline; the Poor category is the combined Poor and Very Poor classes.

[c] Because wetness did not appreciably affect surface area disturbed on fragipan soils, no distinction was made between the Good and Poor drainage classes.

mixing by treefall. Ground disturbed by frost action is often sorted into rings, stripes, and polygons of stones, often with slabs standing on end or tilted, often jigsawed together. Soil disturbed by frost action may be crudely sorted in a wide range of geometric forms and features (see next section). On the other hand, mixing by treefall results in nonsorted mantle, except for the accumulation of stones on the surface.

> The ecologic significance of soil disturbed by treefall is clear. If treefall can be recognized and differentiated from disturbance caused by freezing, the former presence of forests is established, even where trees are absent. Furthermore, treefall replenishes the alluvial soil of bottomlands by slowly moving large volumes of soil to the floors of valleys. In forested areas, treefall may be the principal mechanism of soil movement [Malde 1964:12].

CRYOTURBATION: DISTURBANCE BY FREEZE–THAW ACTION

Archaeologists in cold regions face a legion of problems that are rare in warm, temperate regions and absent in warm, tropical settings. Freeze–thaw and related phenomena in Arctic, mountain, and many mid-latitude lands of the world pose perennial and profound problems to anyone concerned with soil disturbance. In such areas, the soil and regolith often are continuously disturbed by a variety of freeze–thaw processes, which may not only prevent the development of a normal soil profile, as in tundra, but which may also destroy any horizonation that develops.

Since the term *cryoturbation* is ill-defined and has been used to refer to a variety of different freeze–thaw processes (Edelman *et al.* 1936; Davies 1969:30; French 1976:34; Washburn 1973:316; Embleton and King 1968:590–591) our usage in this chapter is of necessity very broad, including all freeze–thaw and periglacial processes, except for mass wasting, that mix soil. Periglacial and other nonfrost action forms of mass wasting are covered in the next section, Graviturbation.

TABLE 9.3

Relationship between Tree Size (Diameter) and the Total Areal Extent and Volume of Disturbed Soil by Windthrow of 100 Trees[a]

Approximate tree diameter (cm)	Soil surface area disturbed (m^2)	Soil volume disturbed (m^3)
10	422	99
20	647	177
30	984	255
40	1339	332

[a]Modified from Mueller and Cline (1959: 110, Table 5).

The genesis, classification, and characteristics of the many cold climate soil and geomorphic features are the subject of a voluminous literature, a general overview of which may be obtained by consulting Washburn (1973), French (1976), and Embleton and King (1968). Because space limitations preclude little more than a superficial coverage of cryoturbatory processes and features, we shall focus on, and emphasize, those aspects most relevant to archaeologists. To do this most conveniently we follow a modified format of Washburn (1973), introducing first the subject of frozen ground, then a discussion of the physics of soil freezing, followed by a coverage of cryoturbatory processes and features.

Frozen Ground

Frozen ground includes *permafrost* and *seasonally frozen ground,* and it is important to distinguish between them. Permafrost is perennially frozen soil or other substrate of variable depth. Seasonally frozen ground is ground frozen by low seasonal temperatures which remains frozen only during the winter. Thus, seasonally frozen ground occurs wherever the soil freezes to any depth, whether it is in Georgia, Colorado, or Alaska. By this definition, the active layer above permafrost is seasonally frozen ground.

Permafrost is widespread in high latitudes covering over a quarter (including glaciers) of the land area of the earth, which includes 80% of Alaska and 50% of Canada (Washburn 1973:21). Seasonally frozen ground covers *nearly 50% of the land area of the planet* (all of the high latitudes and most of the middle latitudes). Figure 9.8 shows the permafrost areas of the Northern Hemisphere. Figure 9.9 shows the maximum depth of frost penetration in the United States. The depth of winter freezing in both permafrost and nonpermafrost regions, wherever the soil freezes, can be estimated by the following equation (Terzaghi 1952:41):

$$Z = \left(\frac{2tTk_h}{72n \text{ cal/cm}^3 + T/2(0.53 + 0.4n) \text{ cal/cm}^3} \right)^{1/2}$$

where Z = depth of winter freezing (cm)
      t = freezing period (sec)
      T = mean temperature of freezing period
      k_h = thermal conductivity (cal/cm sec °C)
      n = porosity of soil.

The Freezing Process

The thermodynamics of freezing soil are very complex, and the processes involved have been summarized at progressive temporal stages of

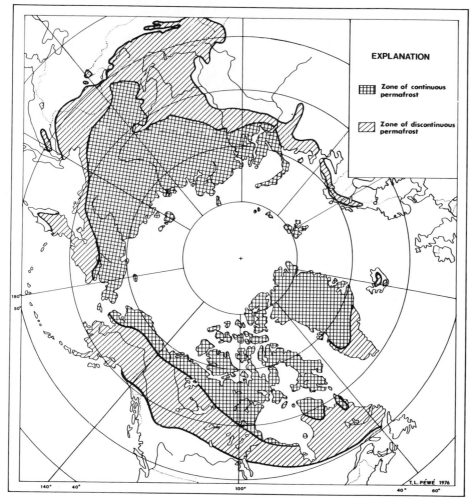

Figure 9.8. Permafrost map of the Northern Hemisphere compiled from all available sources (by T. L. Péwé, Arizona State University, 1976).

understanding by Bouyoucos and McCool (1928), Taber (1929, 1930), Beskow (1935), Troll (1944), Johnson (1952), Penner (1959), Leary *et al.* (1968), Anderson (1970, 1971), Washburn (1973), Johnson and Hansen (1974), and French (1976). Over the past two decades a tremendous amount of additional foreign and domestic research on the theory, physics, and effects of frost action has been published. *The Bibliography of Cold Regions Science and Technology,* published annually by the U.S. Army Cold Regions Research and Engineering Laboratories (CRREL),

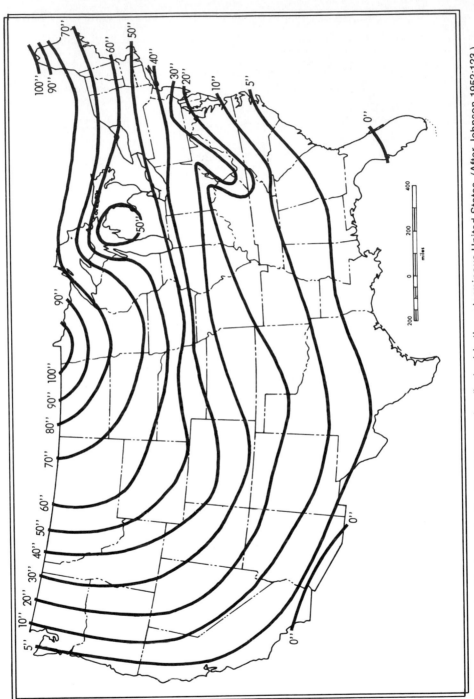

Figure 9.9. Maximum depth of frost penetration (inches) in the coterminous United States. (After Johnson 1952:123.)

contains most references to the subject (see also USA CRREL *Technical Publications,* Special Report 175, June 1972, and Supplement of April 1, 1973). Much of the above-cited research was done with airfield design improvements in mind.

Normally, soil freezes from the surface downward. There are two exceptions: One is where permafrost is present, in which case the soil may freeze both from above and from below. The other is where freezing occurs from the side, as along a bank or cliff. The following discussion [adapted from Johnson and Hansen (1974:89) and Johnson *et al.* (1977)] assumes that the soil freezes from the top down.

When water freezes, it expands approximately 9%. However, early researchers noted that when soil freezes the actual expansion is usually far more than that due to expansion by growth of ice crystals alone. This fact was long a puzzle until Taber (1916) showed experimentally that, when soils freeze, the force of crystallization causes additional water to be drawn to the freezing front from below (soil freezing has the same effect on capillarity as does surface evaporation of soil water). The additional water augments ice formation at the freezing plane; ice segregates as ice lenses that begin forming parallel to the ground surface and perpendicular to the direction of heat flow (upward). The soil thus begins expanding in the direction of least resistance—upward. As the freezing plane moves downward, more ice segregates, ice lensing continues, and expansion proceeds as long as capillary water movement from below continues. Thus, there are two essential keys to a general understanding of frost action in soils: (*a*) capillary movement of water from below, and (*b*) ice lensing and concomitant heaving upward. Also contributing to heaving, but to a lesser extent, is the expansion of water on freezing. The result of these forces is a heaved soil.

Frost action is most pronounced in moist or wet soils, especially those with a high water table. When the rate of frost penetration into a moist or wet soil is initially slow (for example, 1–2 cm/day), decreasing to almost a standstill, and a capillary flow of moisture feeds the freezing front, ice will segregate at the liquid–solid interface. Under such steady-state conditions, maximum frost heave is governed by the maximum rate and amount of ice lens growth, which in turn is dependent on the rate of capillary water flow to the freezing boundary (this process must be accompanied by a heat flow to remove the latent heat of fusion that is released in the freezing process). In this way some soils may heave up to 70% of their original volume (CRREL motion picture, "Frost Action in Soils"), and soil moisture content may rise from an initial 19% before freezing to 55% afterward. The rate of capillary flow in any soil is governed principally by texture and the amount of water available, although other factors may be contributory (Johnson and Hansen 1974).

On the other hand, if the rate of frost penetration is relatively fast, little or no ice segregates, and the soil simply "solid" freezes. The 9% expansion of water on freezing, augmented by some capillary flow, accounts for frost heave in solid freezing (often called concrete freezing). The amount of frost heave associated with solid freezing may be appreciably less than that associated with ice lens formation.

Cryoturbatory Processes and Features

The freeze–thaw processes and features that mix soil include frost heaving, mass displacement, frost cracking, frost sorting, patterned ground, involutions, stone pavements, string bogs, palsas, and pingos (Washburn 1973). The regional place of occurrence in seasonally frozen ground of these processes and features, whether in permafrost areas or nonpermafrost areas, and their archaeological significance are given in Table 9.4.

Frost Heaving (Upfreezing) of Artifacts

When frost penetrates soil and reaches a buried artifact with less thermal conductivity than the surrounding soil (for example, bone or wood), the artifact may be moved up providing that (a) the frozen soil firmly adheres to it, (b) the skin friction of the buried, unfrozen portion of the artifact is overcome by the upward thrust of the heaving soil, and (c)

TABLE 9.4

Freeze–Thaw Processes: Regional Occurrence, and Archaeological Importance[a]

Freeze–thaw processes and features	General occurrence in seasonally frozen ground	
	Permafrost areas	Non-permafrost areas
Frost wedging	X	X
Frost heaving (upfreezing)	X[b]	X[b]
Mass displacement and involutions	X[b]	X[b]r[c]
Ice wedges	X[b]	X[b]r[c]
Frost cracking	X[b]	X[b]r[c]
Frost sorting	X[b]	X[b]
Patterned ground	X[b]	X[b]r[c,d]
Stone pavements	X[b]	X[b]

[a]Compiled in part from Washburn (1973) and French (1976).
[b]Archaeologically important.
[c]Relic features formed under more extensive periglacial conditions in the Pleistocene.
[d]According to one of the referees of this chapter, nonrelic patterned ground is as widespread outside the permafrost belt as inside it.

the overburden pressure (surcharge) on the artifact is sufficiently low so that heave forces can overcome it. This process is called *frost pull*. However, if any artifact, such as stone, obsidian, or metal, conducts heat better than the surrounding soil, ice may form under it and push it upward. This process is called *frost push*. The distinction between the two processes is important.

The amount of frost heaving an object experiences, then, is due in part to various interrelated *soil–environmental factors,* such as soil texture, frequency and rate of frost penetration, amount of soil moisture, and overburden pressure, plus other factors as noted above [see Johnson and Hansen (1974) and Johnson *et al.* (1977), and references therein]. Also important are the *physical factors* of the objects themselves—namely, their geometry and their density–thermal conductivity attributes. Geometry includes the geometric form of an object (cylinder, parallelepiped, etc.), its surface area, and its effective height (which compensates for and includes the object's orientation, and its length–width parameters).

Other things being equal, an artifact's *effective height* will determine the relative amount of frost heaving it will experience (Figure 9.10). Accordingly, artifacts oriented in soil with their long axes at a greater angle from the horizontal would have greater effective heights and experience greater frost heave than would artifacts with equivalent lengths that are flat-lying. Likewise, vertically oriented long objects would have greater effective heights and experience more frost heave than would

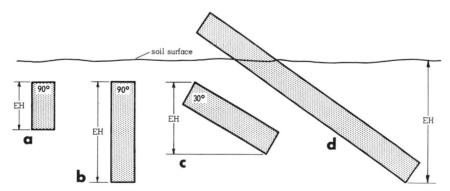

Figure 9.10. Diagram showing the relationship between the effective height (EH), length, and orientation of a buried object. Object *a*, whose long axis is oriented 90° from the horizontal, has an effective height equal to its length. In object *b*, the effective height is also equal to its length, and both are twice that of *a*. Object *c*, with its long axis 30° from the horizontal, is the same length as *b* but has a smaller effective height. Object *d* is longer and oriented differently than *c*, and partly protrudes above the soil surface; the vertical dimension of the *buried* portion is the effective height.

vertically oriented short ones. In addition to being frost-heaved upward, artifacts oriented at differing angles tend to rotate toward the vertical with each freeze–thaw cycle. Also, artifacts buried near the surface will experience more freeze–thaw cycles and thus move upward faster than will objects buried deeper. Since upward movement is cumulative, the longer an object is buried, the greater will be its upward displacement.

These generalizations were validated by a series of laboratory experiments performed by one of us (D.L.J.) and several collaborators (Figures 9.11 and 9.12). Other laboratory experimental data are either supportive or partially supportive (Corte 1962a,b; Bowley and Burghardt 1971). Results from outdoor experimental plots also either support or partially support these frost-heave models (Washburn 1969, 1973:71–80; Johnson and Hansen 1974; Decker and Ronningen 1957; Holmes and Robertson 1960; Chambers 1967; Jahn 1961; Fahey 1974; see also summary by French 1976:30–33). They are also shown to be archaeologically valid through analyses of lithic material (Figure 9.13) from the extensively cryoturbated Hungry Whistler Site in the Rocky Mountains (Benedict and Olson 1978).

Frost heaving can thus potentially have the effect of reorienting and vertically translocating artifacts within a soil profile or sediment, and the principle of stratigraphic superposition, which is used in relative dating in archaeology, may not always be valid. Soils or sediments containing artifacts can thus have a "disturbed" stratigraphy, possibly leading to

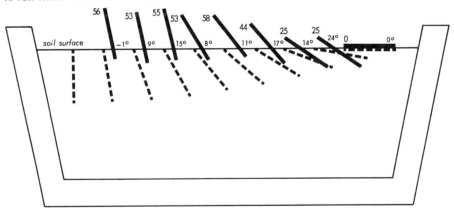

Figure 9.11. Total length movement and angular rotation of dowels. The dashed line indicates position of original dowel emplacement; the solid line shows relative positions of dowels after three freeze–thaw cycles. The total length movement (millimeters) is given by the number at the top of the dowel; the degrees of angular rotation is given by the lower number. (The 90° dowel was accidentally disturbed during the experiments, so the results are not given.)

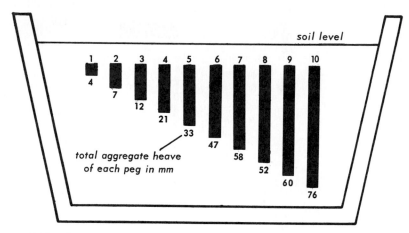

Figure 9.12. Cross section of wooden pegs in a soil-filled styrofoam freezing chamber; the number at the top of each peg indicates its length in centimeters; after seven freeze–thaw cycles, the pegs moved up an amount shown by the number at their base.

misinterpretations of relative artifact ages if such interpretations are based on position within a soil profile. If translocated materials (wood, charcoal, bone) are used for radiometric dating, the dates will be at variance with their stratigraphic position. The upfreezing of artifacts occurs in permafrost regions as well as in nonpermafrost regions (Table 9.4), potentially including most of the mid-latitude areas of North America, Eurasia, and South America.

Mass Displacement and Involutions

Mass displacement is a cryoturbatory process of "*en-masse* local transfer of mobile mineral soil from one place to another within the soil as a result of frost action" (Washburn 1969:90). It includes upward as well as lateral movements. The possible causes are artesian pressure, cryostatic pressure, and changes in density and intergranular pressure (Washburn 1973:86–90). Involutions are defined as "aimless deformation, distribution, and interpretation of beds produced by frost action" (Sharp 1942:115). Freezing-induced pressures (cryostatic pressures) in seasonally frozen ground can result in the contortion, deformation, and displacement of soil and sediments. Apparently, as the freezing front advances downward in autumn, the unfrozen saturated soil below is subjected to increasing cryostatic pressure. The cryoturbated sediments and

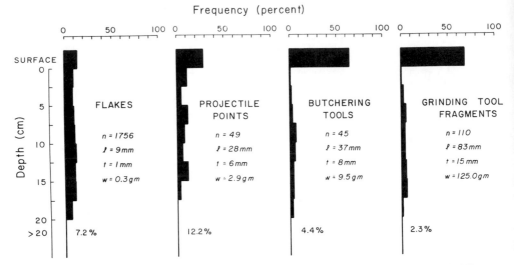

Figure 9.13. Vertical distribution of artifacts at the Hungry Whistler site (5 BL 67), Colorado Front Range. The site is above the present timberline (3500 m above sea level) in a severe periglacial environment. Its mean air temperature is −2°C, its annual precipitation approximately 900 mm. The site was occupied between 5800 ± 125 B.P. (I-3267) and 5300 ± 130 B.P. (I-4418) and has experienced at least three intervals of Neoglacial frost disturbance. Patterned ground is active today in wet microenvironments adjacent to the excavation area.

Four artifact classes are plotted, with data on number of specimens (*n*), median length (*l*), median thickness (*t*), and mean length (*w*). Consistent with frost-heaving theory, the data suggest that artifacts with large vertical dimensions are ejected at the ground surface more rapidly than smaller artifacts, at least within the range of dimensions represented here. Upfreezing is most rapid in the upper 5 cm of soil, the duplicated layer affected most strongly by diurnal freezing and thawing; within this zone there are relatively few artifacts. (Illustration from Benedict and Olson 1978.)

soils at the Dry Creek Site in interior Alaska show involutions, mass displacement features, and other evidence of past cryostatic pressures (Thorson and Hamilton 1977:162). Because it is liquid water under cryostatic pressure that actually deforms the soil, the direct pedoturbatory process is aquaturbation, covered later in this chapter.

Frost Cracking, Ice Wedges, and Sand Wedges

"Frost cracking is fracturing by thermal contraction at subfreezing temperatures" (Washburn 1973:90). When cracks form in seasonally frozen ground, they may be filled by water that refreezes, forming *ice wedges,* or by sand, which forms *sand wedges.* Both types form by repeated frost cracking and infilling. Some ice wedges, on thawing, may be infilled with sand or soil and become *ice wedge casts*. According to Washburn (1973:92), ice wedges start as ice veins that become the focus of subsequent cracking. Ice wedges may grow to enormous size, over 50 m deep and up to 10 m wide, and develop laterally to the extent that the volume of ice exceeds that of the soil (Dostovalov and Popov 1966; Shumskii 1964:199). The intervening soil is squeezed and deformed into columns. Laterally coalescing ice wedges may, it is hypothesized, eventually form enormous stratiform sheets of ground ice that measure up to 80 m thick (Gerasimov and Markov 1968:14; Grave 1968a:53, 1968b:9; Popov 1962; Shumskii and Vtyurin 1966). If such ground ice masses ever thawed, any archaeological sites on the superposed tundra sod (and probably there are many) would settle downward an equivalent distance with obvious attendant mixing.

The Wasden Site, a stratified megafaunal butchering site with extinct animals in Birch Creek Valley, Idaho, reportedly has several levels of presumed ice wedge casts[1] (Dort 1976 personal communication). Involutions and flame structures are also reported to be present in this and other collapsed lava tubes in the valley.

Sorting by Frost Action

As a result of a number of experiments Corte (1962a,b,c, 1963, 1966a,b) concluded that, as a freezing front moves through soil, finer materials tend to migrate ahead of the freezing front, while coarser materials are left above. The result is a sorted soil or sediment, coarse above, fine below (assuming that freezing is from the surface down—obviously not a safe assumption in permafrost areas). Corte's conclusions have been supported by some investigators (Jackson and Uhlmann 1966; Pissart 1966) and challenged by others (Inglis 1965; Kaplar 1970).

In experiments carried out by one of us (D.L.J.), three 1000-ml beakers were filled with 17, 25, and 30 mm of homogeneous mixed-fraction sand, saturated and overtopped with 50 mm of water, and subjected to eight freeze–thaw cycles. Two things happened: (*a*) Particle sorting occurred, with fines concentrating below and coarse particles above; and (*b*) the sediment surface developed a convex-upward form (cf. the "edge effect" of Johnson *et al.* 1977). Although much research needs to be done on this problem, it is probable that freeze–thaw activity will sort and stratify disaggregated mixed-sized sediment that is water-saturated. Various implications for archaeologists may be envisioned.

---

[1] One of the referees (unidentified) of this chapter believes that such ice wedge casts are very difficult to document fully and that their identification should be contingent upon such documentation.

Patterned Ground

The literature of this subject is vast indeed, and a detailed review of patterned ground form and process is beyond the scope of this discussion. The following brief treatment focuses on the archaeological implications of the subject. It is based mainly on Washburn's classic paper (Washburn 1956).

"Patterned ground is a group term for the more or less symmetrical forms, such as circles, polygons, nets, steps, and stripes, that are characteristic of, but not necessarily confined to, mantle subject to intensive frost action" (Washburn 1956:824). Five basic geometric forms are recognized: *circles, polygons, nets, steps,* and *stripes.* Each form may be sorted or unsorted, thus giving ten principal categories of patterned ground. The character of circles and polygons is self-evident. Nets are intermediate between polygons and circles in plan. Steps are benchlike features with downslope borders of stones and vegetation that embank bare ground upslope.

> Circles, polygons and nets usually occur on flat or nearly flat surfaces. As slope angle increases to 2–3°, however, these forms become elongated due to mass wasting and, depending upon local conditions, may change to stripes further down the slope. Steps are the transitional form in this sequence [French 1976:185].

Figure 9.14 shows the relationship between angle of slope and the various patterned ground forms. Figure 9.15 shows sequential cross sections of sorted polygons. Figure 9.16 shows sorted stone circles.

The nuances of frost action that are responsible for patterned ground are by no means universally agreed upon. Washburn (1956, 1969, 1970, 1973), after reviewing nineteen hypotheses for patterned ground formation, concluded:

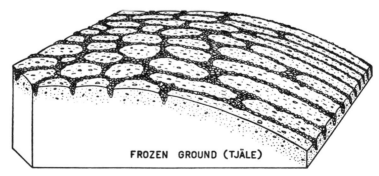

FROZEN GROUND (TJÄLE)

Figure 9.14. Diagram showing relationship between angle of slope and presence of stone rings and stone stripes. (After Sharpe 1938/1960:Fig. 5.)

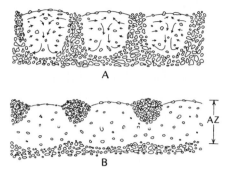

Figure 9.15. Sequential cross sections of sorted stone polygons (*A*) showing flow and material transfer directions caused by ice wedging in which stones within the active zone of the permafrost (AZ) have not yet been brought to the surface, and (*B*) illustrating "floating" stone borders where most rocks within the active zone have surfaced. (From *The Origin of Landscapes: A Synthesis of Geomorphology* by H. F. Garner. Copyright © 1974 by Oxford University Press, Inc. Reprinted by permission.)

Figure 9.16. Sorted stone circles in the bottom of a small drained pond along Denali Highway, on the south side of the Alaska Range at Alpine Creek (U.S. Geological Survey photograph number 1764, by T. L. Péwé, 14 June 1958).

(1) Patterned ground is of polygenetic origin; (2) similar forms of patterned ground can be due to different genetic processes; (3) some genetic processes may produce dissimilar forms; (4) there are more genetic processes than there are presently recognized terms for associated forms [1973:137].

The archaeological implications of patterned ground are obviously enormous.

Stone Pavements

Stone pavements in cold, periglacial regions are very similar to the desert pavement of dry lands. They consist of rock fragments of pebbles, cobbles, and boulders fitted together as a mosaic, with a flat side up (Washburn 1973:149). The processes that form them are thought to be mainly vertical sorting and upfreezing of coarse particles by frost heave, and the removal of fines by wind and meltwater.

Since the frost action processes and features described in this section depend so heavily on the presence of water, an important consideration is whether one is working in low, wet tundra, or in high, dry tundra. Most of the processes and features described above would be found in the low, wet areas.

GRAVITURBATION: MASS WASTING

Graviturbation as used in this discussion is essentially mixing during mass wasting. Graviturbation is the mixing and movement of soil and rock debris downslope, including subsidence, principally under the influence of gravity, without the aid of the flowing medium of transport such as air, water, or glacier ice. It includes a host of different processes, all of which are of significance to archaeologists and others concerned with pedoturbation. Table 9.5 lists the individual graviturbation processes. Those processes listed under Rapid movements are self-evident, and where they occur they have great archaeological implications. Those listed under Slow movements are more subtle processes and, over the long run, are of equal if not greater archaeological importance. It is the slow graviturbative processes that we wish to focus our attention on—in particular, solifluction, creep, and subsidence.

Solifluction, Gelifluction, and Frost Creep

"Solifluction is regarded as one of the most widespread processes of soil movement in periglacial regions" (French 1976:135). It refers to the slow downslope flowing of water-saturated soil and regolith. As originally

TABLE 9.5

Graviturbation Processes[a]

Slow movement	Rapid movements
Creep	Earthflows
Talus creep	
Soil creep	Mudflows
Frost creep	
Solifluction	Slushflows
Gelifluction	Debris avalanche
Soil flow	Snow avalanche
Subsidence	Landslide
	Slump
	Rockfalls
	Rockslides
	Debris slides

[a] Modified from Sharpe (1938).

defined, it is a process that occurs in all environments, not just in cold regions. To clarify the problem, the term *gelifluction* was coined to describe the solifluction of permafrost areas (see Benedict 1976:57 for a review).

Frost creep is the "ratchetlike downslope movement of particles as the result of frost heaving of the ground and subsequent settling upon thawing, the heaving being predominantly normal to the slope and the settling more nearly vertical" (Washburn 1967:14). Frost creep and gelifluction are intimately associated processes because both are accomplished by ice segregation (Figure 9.17). Of the two processes, gelifluction is assumed to be the more dominant. The term gelifluction as used here will thus imply the operation of both processes. Gelifluction occurs in both permafrost and nonpermafrost areas (Benedict 1976:65–66).

In continuous permafrost, with summer thawing limited to shallow depth, thaw water cannot infiltrate the underlying permafrost, and so it remains in the thawed (active) layer, saturating it, and permitting the slow flowage of that layer downslope. Gelifluction can occur on slopes as gentle as 1° (St-Onge 1965:40). The deposits and landforms associated with gelifluction include *gelifluction sheets, lobes, benches* and *terraces,* and *streams* (Figure 9.18; see also Washburn 1973:189; Benedict 1976:60). Maximum velocities of up to 25 cm/yr have been recorded for some gelifluction lobes and terraces, but the median maximum velocity from a number of studies is 3 cm/yr (Benedict 1976:57).

A clear example of how gelifluction processes and deposits can complicate the lives of archaeologists is shown at the Iatayet excavations, Cape

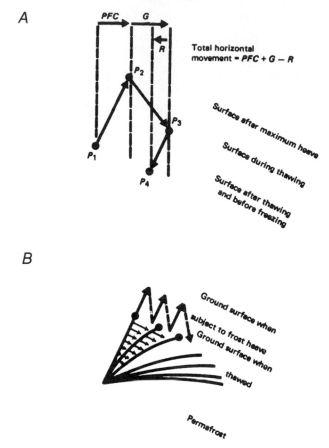

Figure 9.17. Diagram illustrating the components of solifluction. (A) The movement of a surface particle due to frost creep, gelifluction, and retrograde movement. (B) The frost-creep mechanism. [After French (1976), Washburn (1967), and Dylik (1969).]

Denbigh, on the west coast of Alaska (Hopkins and Giddings 1953:17–18). There are numerous and complex folds in the Denbigh flint layer in several parts of the site, although they do not find expression on the surface. The folds formed as the result of the formation of gelifluction lobes in the sandy silt overlying the Denbigh occupational layer. This movement took place during a cold period long after the Denbigh occupation ended, and before the sediments were deeply buried and immobilized by permafrost. Not only is the Denbigh flint layer folded upon itself, but there are gaps in the layer where they have been entirely moved downslope. At the Engigstciak site, in northwestern Yukon Territory, Mackay *et al.* (1961:25) found that the original stratigraphic relationships in some parts of the site had been virtually destroyed by pedoturbation. Gelifluction had, in places, reversed the stratigraphic sequence, leading the authors to comment that "it is surprising indeed that any general succession of beds is recognizable" (Mackay *et al.* 1961:36).

Frost creep is a very important graviturbation process in regions of seasonal freeze and thaw beyond areas of gelifluction activity. This would include most of the middle latitudes of both hemispheres. Although the actual role of frost heaving in nonperiglacial areas is difficult to separate from other forms of creep, it is generally agreed among geomorphologists that frost creep is probably most significant. In just one 24-hour period on a 10° slope at Turkey Run, Indiana, one of the authors measured 12-cm-high frost-heave pillars of segregated ice and soil that covered the whole valley side slopes (Figure 9.19).

Soil Creep

Creep unrelated to frost action may be seasonal or continuous (Schumm 1964), and it occurs ubiquitously. Textbook photographs and our own observations of fenceposts, telephone poles, and cemetery headstones tilted downslope, and the upslope curvature of many tree trunks, prove that the soil in which they are embedded creeps downslope. Such observations have been made at all latitudes and in many different global environments, although quantitative data are scarce.

Creep not resulting from frost action may be caused by various processes that can markedly affect archaeological materials. Most important are wetting and drying, biotic activity, and erosion of fine particles by sheetwash and rills. According to Young (1960), colloidal components swell on wetting, and expansion is perpendicular to the slope. On drying, the colloids shrink downslope (similar to frost action), causing net downslope movement. Small animals burrowing on slopes, and large animals treading on slopes, will cause net downslope movement. The wedging and prying of plant roots and the swaying of trees and bushes in wind, plus the decay of plant roots and organic matter, also result in downslope soil movement.

Detailed observations of creep processes not associated with freeze–thaw conditions were made by Schumm (1956b) on badland topography in South Dakota. Rain falling on the permeable Chadron formation is absorbed by clays, which first swell and aggregate, then slump downslope. On similar terrain in drier areas where rainfall is concentrated into shorter periods of time, swelling clays may aggregate even more, producing sheets of aggregates, which move gradually downslope. Erosion increases from the base of slopes to the crests. Rates of creep from various regions

A

B

Figure 9.18. (A) Turf-banked lobe, and (B) lobate stone-banked terrace, both on Niwot Ridge, Colorado Front Range; (C) turf-banked terraces on a 20–25° northeast-facing snow accumulation slope, Old Man Range, central Otago, New Zealand. (After Benedict 1976.)

Figure 9.18C. See legend facing page.

are shown in Table 9.6. The rate of creep on slopes in general is proportional to the gradient (Culling 1963).

The graviturbatory role of creep is to translocate surface and shallowly buried archaeological materials downslope, or to bury such materials if they originally occurred at the slope bottom. Hence, Cumulic Haplaquolls (Peotone Series) in the Midwest are preferred sites of burial by soil creep (personal observations of the writers). Near Junín, Peru, preceramic occupational debris in shelters has crept downslope a distance ranging from 20 to 300 m on slopes varying from 10° to 44° (Rick 1976:134). An interesting and important observation is that heavier and denser objects were moved farther downslope than lighter and less dense ones. As Rick points out, this is exactly the opposite of the effects of fluvial action (Rick 1976:144).

Similarly, the widespread occurrence of pottery fragments at depth in Oxisol profiles on the Palau Islands in the Pacific (Vessel and Simonson 1958) suggests graviturbation, probably soil creep. Vessel and Simonson point out that laboratory data suggest that the present B_{23} horizon was at one time an A horizon, covered over by gravitative transfer of materials

Figure 9.19.   Frost-heave pillars of segregated ice formed overnight on a 10° slope in December 1975, Turkey Run, Indiana.

downslope from above. It also appears that graviturbation processes were responsible for the late nineteenth-century confusion about the antiquity of artifacts found in the Trenton Gravels of the Delaware River Valley (Holmes 1893).

Subsidence

Subsidence is the downward displacement of surface earth materials without a free surface and without appreciable horizontal displacement. Subsidence occurs most commonly by settling, compaction, or densification of earth materials. It may also occur by solutional sapping of soluble substrate, followed by settling and compaction. Normal faulting may sometimes accompany subsidence, as in the case of Lake Texcoco sediments encasing the artifacts at the Tlapacoya Early Man Site near Mexico City (personal observations of authors). The faulting at the Dry Creek Site in Alaska (Thorson and Hamilton 1977) may in part be subsidence-related. Both sites, however, are in tectonically unstable areas, so that seismiturbation (shock-related) processes are also likely involved.

ARGILLITURBATION: DISTURBANCE BY EXPANDING AND CONTRACTING CLAYS

Argilliturbation is soil mixing caused by seasonal swelling and shrinking of expansible clays in soils. Such soils are called Vertisols (Grumusols;

TABLE 9.6

Rates of Slow Mass Wasting Processes and Comparison with Soil Erosion Rates[a]

Surficial creep[b]	Cm² yr⁻¹	Surface velocities of mass-wasting processes[c]	Mm yr⁻¹	Soil wash[d]	Mm yr⁻¹
Malaya (Eyles and Ho 1970)	12.4	Depth creep (Ter-Stepanian 1965)	110	S. Dakota (Schumm 1956a)	13.4
N. T., Australia: granite (Williams 1973)	7.3	Gelifluction (Jahn 1960)	65	New Mexico (Leopold et al. 1966)	4.7
Alaska: till (Barr and Swanston 1970)	7.0	Talus creep (Caine 1964)	50	France: bare soil (Gabert 1964)	4.6
Ohio (Everett 1963)	6.0	Gelifluction (Williams 1966)	45	Java (Coster 1933)	0.7
N. T., Australia: sandstone (Williams 1973)	4.4	Gelifluction (Harris 1972)	35	Madagascar: crops (Roche 1954)	0.5
N. S. W., Australia: sandstone (Williams 1973)	3.2	Depth creep (Kojan 1967)	30	N. S. W., Australia (Williams 1973)	0.1–0.05
S. Alps, N. Z. (Owens 1969)	3.2	Gelifluction (Washburn 1973)	25	N. T., Australia (Williams 1973)	0.05
Scotland (Kirkby 1967)	2.1	Gelifluction (Rudberg 1962)	24		
N. S. W., Australia: granite (Williams 1973)	1.5	Soil creep (Barr and Swanston 1970)	6		
England (Young 1960)	0.9	Depth creep (Mitchell and Eden 1972)	2		
		Soil creep (Kirkby 1967)	2		
		Soil creep (Everett 1963)	1		

[a] After Carson (1976).
[b] Cm² yr⁻¹ denotes area enclosed by annual velocity profile (also expressed as cm³/cm/year).
[c] Mm yr⁻¹ denotes downslope travel vector.
[d] Mm yr⁻¹ denotes vertical lowering of ground surface.

also some Rendzinas) and are referred to as "self-swallowing soils" (Oakes and Thorp 1951). They are extensive in the seasonally wet and dry tropics and subtropics, where they are variously called Black Cotton Soils, Regur, Tirs, and Dark Clay Soils of warm regions (Dudal 1963, 1965; Oakes and Thorp 1951). They also occur in the middle latitudes where conditions permit. In North America, Vertisols occur in Texas, Alabama, Arizona, California, and Oregon, and locally in certain other states (Buol *et al.* 1973:218; Parsons *et al.* 1973).

Abundant expansible soil clays (montmorillonite), plus an alternately wet and dry climate, seem to be fundamental prerequisites to Vertisol development. During dry periods such soils shrink and crack. The drier the weather, the wider the cracks develop, up to a point. Surface soil gradually fills the cracks through wind action, animal traffic, and soil in-washing at the onset of rainfall (Figure 9.20). The soil thus wets from the top down and, mainly, inward (sideward) from the cracks. Being wetted first, the cracks close first, while sideward wetting continues. This process generates great lateral and upward pressures, which create soil slickensides and a peculiar wedge-shaped soil structure. The intercrack portion of the soil may be forced upward by these pressures, creating a mound microrelief on the surface called *gilgai*. If the gilgai forms on sloped lands, the mounds and depressions tend to run together, forming

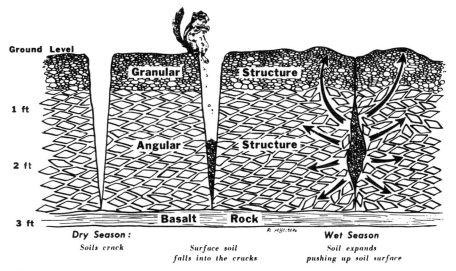

Figure 9.20. Sketch illustrating wetting (swelling) and drying (shrinking) cycles of Vertisols. (Reprinted by permission from *Soil Genesis and Classification*, by S. W. Buol, F. D. Hole, and R. J. McCracken, © 1972 by Iowa State University Press, Ames, Iowa, 50010.)

linear gilgai, somewhat analogous to stone stripes forming from stone rings in permafrost regions (cf. Figure 9.11). Normal and linear gilgai are especially widespread in Australia (Thorp 1957; Beckmann *et al.* 1973; Russell and Moore 1972; Halsworth and Beckmann 1969; Halsworth *et al.* 1955; Mabbutt 1965; Jessup 1960; Ollier 1966), where they may merge with other Vertisol-generated patterned ground resembling permafrost phenomena (Paton 1974; Harris 1968).

Linear gilgai has been called "fingerprint topography" in the United States (Tanner 1958; Crooks 1958) because of its fingerprint-like appearance on aerial photography (Figure 9.21). In Love County, Oklahoma, large, loose slabs of limestone, whose long axes are oriented orthogonally to the slope, project out of the fingerprint pattern and resemble tipped tombstones. These megaliths are organized in annular rosette-like patterns around certain hillocks in the area. They appear intriguingly anthropogenic, but they merely reflect the pedoturbatory nature of Vertisols.

Stone pavements of wave-rounded boulders and cobbles occur on the surface of Vertisols developed on tectonically raised marine terraces along the California coast and on the offshore islands. The origin of these stone pavements is due to the long-term vertical churning action of the Vertisols (Johnson and Hester 1972:52). The stones were originally

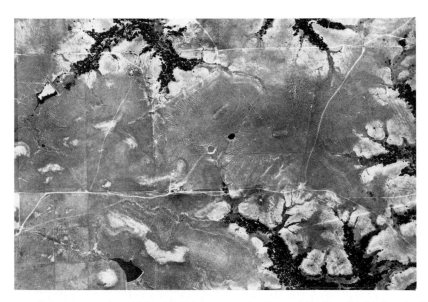

Figure 9.21. Aerial view of fingerprint topography (linear gilgai—a Vertisol variant), Love County, Oklahoma.

marine-eroded and rounded in the wave zone before the terraces were uplifted. After uplift, soil developed over the marine terraces, leaving the stones buried. As the soils evolved to Vertisols, the stones were gradually transported vertically to the surface, as shown in Figure 9.22. Once the larger stones reach the surface, they cannot move down again unless they are smaller than the cracks that develop during the dry season. Interestingly, when pits were dug into these Vertisols, late Canaliño artifacts were found at the *bottom* of the profiles, showing that archaeological materials are being intrusively mixed (Figure 9.23).

In many deserts of the world, similar stone pavements exist that are

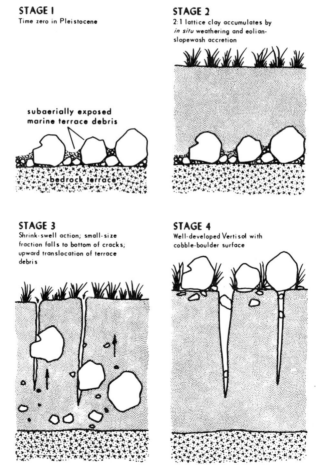

STAGE 1
Time zero in Pleistocene

STAGE 2
2:1 lattice clay accumulates by *in situ* weathering and eolian-slopewash accretion

subaerially exposed marine terrace debris

bedrock terrace

STAGE 3
Shrink-swell action; small-size fraction falls to bottom of cracks; upward translocation of terrace debris

STAGE 4
Well-developed Vertisol with cobble-boulder surface

Figure 9.22. Hypothetical model of seasonal shrink–swell process and evolution of Vertisols and stone pavements. (After Johnson and Hester 1972.)

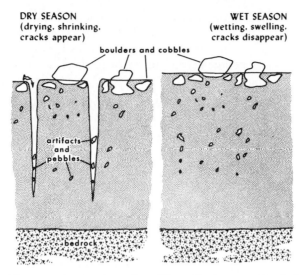

DRY SEASON
(drying. shrinking,
cracks appear)

WET SEASON
(wetting. swelling.
cracks disappear)

Figure 9.23. Diagram showing how Canaliño artifacts were mixed at depth in Vertisols on San Miguel Island, California.

termed "desert pavement," "gibber plains," and so on (Mabbutt 1965; Cooke and Warren 1973). They are interpreted by many as being solely due to the removal of finer material by wind or water. In many cases, and in most cases observed by the authors, a stone-free zone exists below the pavement, although stones reappear deeper in the profile. This stone-free layer is often vesicular, especially in deserts and intermontane basins of western North America. In Australia the soil surface is gilgaied, and the stone-free layer coincides with the B_2 horizon of massive clay (Jessup 1960; Mabbutt 1965:139). The fine fraction of the stone-free layer is usually a sandy clay, clay loam, or clay that cracks on drying (Mabbutt 1965; Springer 1958). Desert pavement and gibber plains that occur on soils with underlying stone-free vesicular layers that crack when dry strongly suggest that the stones have migrated to the surface from below (as on the marine terraces in California) and are not due solely to removal of fines by wind or water.

However, still another process, aeroturbation, is involved in creating desert pavement (see next section). The archaeological implications of Vertisols and desert soils that shrink and swell, and of argilliturbation in general, are profound indeed. Archaeological materials on the surface of such widely occurring soils may have come from below, and those found at depth may have come from above. Duffield (1970) has summarized the headaches that Vertisols give to archaeologists; they churn "archaeological features into a homogeneous mass and totally destroy the original context of a site.'' He also points out that Vertisols are difficult to farm under primitive conditions, and may have acted as barriers to the expansion of horticultural peoples (Duffield 1970:1055).

AEROTURBATION: DISTURBANCE BY SOIL GAS AND BY WIND

Aeroturbation occurs when soil gas disturbs the fabric of the soil, or when the wind winnows fines from the soil, leaving coarse particles behind as a mixed lag deposit. Both forms of aeroturbation occur most commonly in, but are not limited to, deserts.

Aside from the marginally relevant studies cited by Hole (1961:376), the only situation known to the authors where aeroturbation by soil gas may be an important archaeological mixing process is in the formation of desert pavement and the underlying vesicular layer described earlier. The original statement describes a laboratory experiment that was designed to shed light on the origin of the pavement and of the subjacent vesicular layer:

> The behavior of sieved soil from the vesicular layer of profile No. 1 as water was added in the laboratory sheds some light. Immediately upon becoming wet, the particles of the upper 3 or 4 mm. seemed to become so oriented as to hold water on top for the several minutes required for infiltration. Upon becoming moist, the particles below the surface appeared to become rearranged and closely packed with air moving from the disappearing medium sized pores into the larger spaces now created. As infiltration of water continued, some of the air bubbles moved toward the top of the soil and eventually escaped. Of these, a few left tubules behind which in certain instances remained open after the bubble escaped. In most cases, however, the end was closed by wet soil particles. Other bubbles were displaced by soil particles which immediately occupied the space vacated as the bubble moved upward. Repeated wetting and drying caused a continual rearrangement of soil particles and voids. Sometimes, when a crust of finer particles surrounding relatively large voids near the pebbles became wet, it collapsed and filled the space. *Repetition of this process brought some of the pebbles to the top* [our emphasis]. Only a few small cracks appeared when the soil was dried. These cracks, along with open vesicles and collapsible spheroidal voids near the surface were the places where wetting took place most rapidly. When the surface of the soil was again dry, its surface was marked by a few pores and numerous depressions left by the escape of bubbles from the wet soil. The interior consisted of vesicular and spheroidal voids encased by the otherwise closely packed soil particles [Figure 9.24]. Its appearance closely resembles the natural soil before its mutilation. Possibly formation is similar in both cases [Springer 1958:65–66].

Wind winnowing of fines (deflation) is the more common aeroturbative process. Desert deflation has telescoped (lowered) and rearranged countless archaeological materials as an active process in the formation of

Figure 9.24. Vesicular structure, artificially reconstituted (left) and natural (right). Each space on the scale is 1 mm. (Reproduced from *Soil Science Society of America Proceedings,* Volume 22, 1958, page 65, by permission of the Soil Science Society of America, Inc.)

desert pavement, especially on desert playas. The process is so self-explanatory that elaboration is probably unnecessary. However, an example of deflation mixing of archaeological materials is illuminating.

In late October, 1976, one of us (D.L.J.) participated in a Friends of the Pleistocene field trip at China Lake, California, to assess the geologic and chronological context of Paleo-Indian lithic materials (fluted points) and extinct fauna. China Lake is a playa lake in the northwestern Mojave Desert. During the Wisconsin glacial epoch the lake was one of many in the area that held water, which attracted birds such as ducks, geese, and eagles, and rodents, plus large now-extinct Rancholabrean mammals (canids, felids, horse, bison, camel, deer, and proboscideans; Fortsch 1976). Fluted points and other lithic materials occur in abundance, mixed together with the extinct fauna as a surface lag deposit of sandblasted desert pavement (Davis and Fortsch 1970; Davis 1975a,b; Davis and Shutler 1969). The three-dimensional integrity and chronological context of the archaeological sites has been almost completely destroyed by post-Pleistocene deflationary removal of fines. One of the field trip leaders (G.I. Smith) noted that nature had done the excavating and, unfortunately, had left a two-dimensional chronologically blurred site context for archaeologists.

AQUATURBATION: DISTURBANCE BY ARTESIAN ACTION

Aquaturbation occurs when water under pressure disturbs the soil. The pressure may be artesian or cryostatic, as mentioned earlier. French (1976:40) points out that cryostatic pressures are essentially hydrostatic in nature, since they develop in pockets of unfrozen soil. Johnsgard (1971) puts forth persuasive evidence that all involutions in soils and sediments that are seasonally frozen are produced by artesian action. In laboratory simulation of freezing-induced pressures, Pissart (1970:37–43, 1973) measured pressures in excess of 4 kg/cm² (Figure 9.25). The pressures are generated "not only during the freezing process when a closed system exists (cryostatic pressure *senso stricto*), but also when temperatures have dropped well below zero" (French 1976:41). These latter pressures may occur within any freezing body, and they are not restricted, as are the cryostatic pressures, to the seasonally thawed layer of permafrost.

On the basis of extensive studies of mixed and involuted soils in North Dakota and Minnesota, Johnsgard (1971:613–614) observed that the process occurs in low-lying, poorly or imperfectly drained landscape situations with high water tables, where underlying sediments tend to have low permeability. Soils typically are Solonchaks (Calciaquolls) and Humic Gleys (Hapaquolls). As the soil freezes downward during the winter, often to a depth of 1 m or more, pressures build below the frozen zone. When the soil begins thawing, localized points of weakness develop to where eventually the soil below, being saturated and under pressure, erupts through the frozen layer and is injected into the thawed and supersaturated portion of the overlying soil. This seasonal "toothpaste" squirting action contorts, mixes, and involutes the soil through time to produce the eye-striking "flame structures" common in depressions in the High Plains of North America. This type of soil mixing takes place near the soil surface, within the depth to which freezing normally occurs.

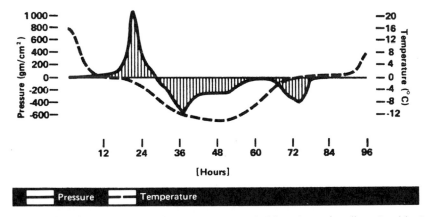

Figure 9.25. Freezing-induced pressures recorded in a tray of sediment subject to freezing and thawing. [After Pissart (1973) and French (1976:Fig. 3.11).]

Since involutions occur in a variety of different regions in the middle and high latitudes, aquaturbation has special significance for archaeologists who claim these regions as their domain. A number of archaeological sites display what appear to be involutions, examples being the Dry Creek Early Man Site in Alaska (Thorson and Hamilton 1977), the Wasden Paleo-Indian Site in Idaho (Dort, 1977 personal communication), and the Dutton Paleo-Indian Site on the high plains of eastern Colorado (Figure 9.26).

Artesian aquaturbation not associated with seasonally frozen soil has created temporary confusion for Quaternists at several important spring and bog sites in North America. At one, the Tule Springs Site near Las Vegas, Nevada, claims were originally made that humans were present in the area in company with extinct megafauna some 23,000 radiocarbon years ago (Harrington and Simpson 1961). The evidence consisted of associations of artifacts and organic materials, which were carbon-14 dated. Subsequent work revealed that a mixing of soil material, organic debris, artifacts, and megafaunal bones of widely varying ages had occurred as a result of artesian aquaturbation in the feeder conduits of the

Figure 9.26. Involutions (flame-structures) caused by aquaturbations, Dutton Site, eastern Colorado. The site is low-lying and is poorly drained, and surface freezing pressures ultimately caused deformation of the saturated soil. (Photograph courtesy of J. Albanese.)

springs (Haynes 1967:45–48). The antiquity of humans at the site was placed at no earlier than 12,000 years ago.

Aquaturbation in certain springs along the lower Pomme de Terre River in the western Ozark Highland has also caused temporary confusion for archaeologists and related workers. The springs—Boney, Koch, Jones, and Trolinger—contain abundant remains of extinct large animals along with some artifacts. As long ago as 1840, Albert Koch investigated the spring seeps and made sensational claims of cultural remains in association with mastodons (Koch 1857). Recent work, however, has shown that each spring has a central feeder conduit, as at Tule Springs, in which materials of different ages have been thoroughly mixed by artesian roiling (Haynes 1976; McMillan 1976; Wood 1976). Further, artifacts found in the springs, including Koch's, are all late. No firm evidence suggests contemporaneity of man and mastodon in the lower Pomme de Terre Valley (Wood 1976:107).

CRYSTALTURBATION: GROWTH AND WASTING OF CRYSTALS IN SOIL

Crystalturbation is a soil-mixing process that is common to subhumid lands of the world. There are two principal ways in which soil mixing occurs. One is simply a matter of soil particles' and objects' increasing their distance from one another as crystals in the soil gradually grow from precipitating solutions. An example is when caliche intermittently precipitates in soil over a long period of time, eventually engulfing the soil as a calcic or petrocalcic horizon (Figure 9.27). The model in Figure 9.27 shows how the process works. The crystals that form may be calcium carbonate (caliche, tufa, travertine), sodium carbonate, sodium chloride (salt, halite), calcium sulfate (gypsum), or silicon dioxide (quartz), plus other compounds, such as iron, and aluminum. Carbonate engulfment in many dry land soils is such an effective disturbance agent that argillic horizons are commonly obliterated by the process (Gile *et al.* 1966, 1969:281; Gile 1975b:325; Gile and Grossman 1968:15).

The other way in which crystalturbation occurs is through repeated cracking, re-solution, and reprecipitation of salts in soil. Such processes lead to the development of patterned ground amazingly similar to that formed by frost action: sorted circles, sorted and nonsorted polygons, sorted and nonsorted nets, sorted steps and stripes, salt wedges, heaved stones, and other heaved objects (Hunt and Washburn 1960; Malde 1964:14; Hunt 1975:55–65) (Figures 9.28, 9.29, and 9.30).

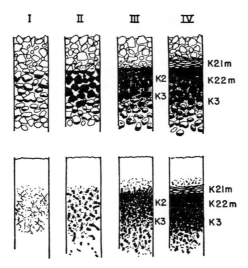

Figure 9.27. Diagram of stages of caliche accumulations in gravelly (top) and non-gravelly (bottom) parent materials. Carbonate accumulations are indicated in black. (Adapted from Gile *et al.* 1966.)

Figure 9.28. Twigs, stones, and other debris are uplifted by salts crystallizing beneath them. (From Hunt 1975. Copyright © 1975 by The Regents of the University of California, reprinted by permission of the University of California Press.)

Figure 9.29. (A) Polygonal patterns in gypsiferous ground at the shoreline of a Holocene lake, just north of a road crossing a valley at Devils Golf Course, Death Valley. Polygons are formed by cracks in a layer of rock salt 6–8 in. (15–20 cm) below the surface; the salt is at least 3 in. (8 cm) thick, and perhaps much thicker than that. It formed at the capillary fringe above the water table, which extended into the hill when the lake existed. Surface cracks in the salt are marked by troughs in which stones have collected. (B) Hillsides in Tertiary playa beds in the Mustard Canyon area are crusted with salt 6 in. (15 cm) or more thick and are cracked into polygonal slabs up to 10 ft (3 m) in diameter. Cracks are perpendicular to the slope. (From Hunt 1975. Copyright © 1975 by The Regents of the University of California, reprinted by permission of the University of California Press.)

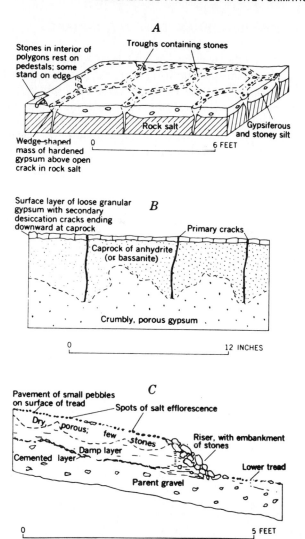

Figure 9.30. Sketch and cross sections of ground patterns in Death Valley, California. (A) Diagram of sorted polygons above a layer of rock salt. (B) Cross section of nonsorted polygons in anhydrite caprock on gypsum. (C) Cross section of sorted step (terracette). (From Hunt and Washburn 1960:Fig 185.1.)

SEISMITURBATION: DISTURBANCE BY EARTHQUAKES

Seismiturbation is the moving of soil by earthquake action. Among earthquake effects is the production of cracks, usually accompanied by lateral or vertical motion of the earth. Such cracks may fill with sand or other water-borne sediments, and they may be quite conspicuous. Several examples of such disturbances in archaeological sites are known in southeastern Missouri and adjoining areas, a product of the New Madrid earthquake of 1811 and successive years (Figures 9.31 and 9.32). This series of shocks wrought profound changes in the Mississippi Valley alluvium. At the Campbell Site, a Mississippian town and cemetery, Chapman and Anderson (1955:72, 79) found two burials disturbed by faults. In both instances the crevices that had formed along the fault trace were filled with sand, and lateral movement had displaced the lower extremities of one of the inhumations (Figure 9.32).

The Dry Creek Site in interior Alaska displays extensive faulting in eolian and other sediments and paleosols, with dip–slip displacements of up to 3 m (Figure 9.33). Many small fault blocks occur at the site, each of which has rotated clockwise (Thorson and Hamilton 1977:162). Paleosol 4a of the site is cut by 25 faults with offsets up to 20 cm. The faults are

Figure 9.31.   Fault trace (light-colored sinuous zone) at the Zebree Site, Arkansas. Note how it curves around the pit outline at lower right. (Photograph courtesy of Dan Morse and the Archeological Survey of Arkansas.)

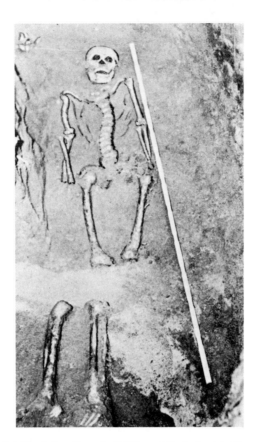

Figure 9.32. Burial 19 at the Campbell Site, a Mississippian Cemetery in Pemiscot County, southeastern Missouri, showing sand-filled cracks and displacement of the lower extremities, probably a result of the New Madrid earthquake. (From Chapman and Anderson 1955:Fig. 31.)

believed to have been caused by vigorous shaking of the bluff in which the site occurs during a high-intensity earthquake.

It is possible that, in high seismic areas, artifacts and other objects within a loose sand matrix could actually rise to the surface over a long period, just as shaking a mixture of sand and pebbles causes the latter to rise to the surface (Hunt 1975:80).

It is sometimes difficult if not impossible to distinguish between faults formed by graviturbation (subsidence) and those formed by seismiturbation. For example, the normal faults mentioned earlier that appear in the lacustrine sediments at the margins of Lake Texcoco at the Tlapacoya Site near Mexico City were likely caused by subsidence, which is still

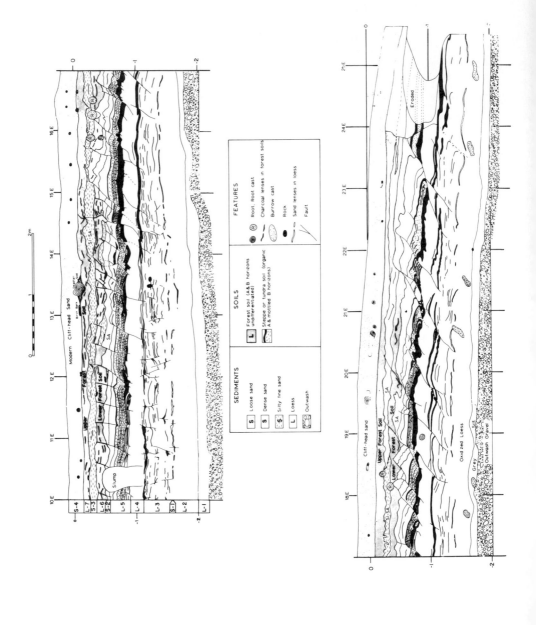

SEDIMENTS

S Loose sand

S Dense sand

Silty fine sand

L Loess

Outwash

SOILS

Forest soil (A&B horizons undifferentiated)

L Steppe or tundra soil (organic A & mottled B horizons)

FEATURES

Root, Root cast

Charcoal lenses in forest soils

Burrow cast

Rock

Sand lenses in loess

Fault

occurring in the area. Subsidence of lake sediments is a common phenomenon. On the other hand, faults that transect the Dry Creek Site in Alaska are most likely seismically induced. To complicate the picture, Mexico City, like Dry Creek, is in a highly tectonically unstable area. In any event, the results in both cases are the same—pedoturbated soil and sediments.

CONCLUDING STATEMENTS

Soils are not static bodies—they are dynamic, open systems in which numerous processes operate to pedoturbate profiles, and to move objects vertically and horizontally within them. These processes may operate singly or in combination in additive or subtractive fashion, in all environments and at all latitudes.

Fingerprint topography and linear gilgai, for example, express the combined effects of *argilloturbation* and *graviturbation* in subtropical latitudes. At high latitudes and altitudes, gelifluction lobes are produced by *graviturbation* and *cryoturbation,* and to some extent by *aquaturbation.* In many well-drained soils, *faunalturbation* by ants and earthworms may well offset the effects of *cryoturbation* (exemplified by the burial of objects by earthworms cited earlier), whereas in poorly drained soils the reverse seems to be true—except perhaps where crayfish are present!

Cultural materials, then, may sink into the soil, may be concentrated into layers at depth, may be reoriented within the soil, may be thrust to the surface, or may be moved horizontally on a plane or downslope. Various processual permutations can be envisioned. The result can be a spurious association of artifacts, with concomitant distortion in interpretation. Before we proceed to make interpretations that depend on artifacts' being in their original position, we *must* demonstrate that they were not moved by one or another form of soil mixing—or qualify our interpretations according to the types of soil mixing possible in a given soil. In sum, we must pay more attention to the dynamic nature of the medium in which we dig.

At this point the reader may conclude that we are doomsday prophets for archaeology, and that many if not most sites may be hopelessly pedoturbated. On the contrary, we believe that many (perhaps most) sites

Figure 9.33. Fault-disturbed sediments at the Dry Creek Site, Alaska. While the principal purpose of this figure is to show faulting, note that other forms of pedoturbation have operated as well (see comments in concluding statements). (From Thorson and Hamilton 1977:Fig. 5.)

are not. The Dry Creek Site in Alaska, cited earlier, should underscore this point. At least six pedoturbative processes operate or have operated at the site: *graviturbation, seismiturbation, faunalturbation, floralturbation, cryoturbation,* and *crystalturbation.* Yet, in spite of the complex pedoturbatory processes that have occurred, the site still retains enough contextual and stratified integrity that meaningful interpretations of the Quaternary archaeology and paleoecology can be made (Thorson and Hamilton 1977). Such was not the case at Engigstciak, however, where some parts of the site have been completely pedoturbated (Mackay *et al.* 1961).

Very few archaeologists have the training to interpret soil dynamics as subtle as some of those we have outlined in this paper. In truth, many of the processes are as yet poorly understood, even by soil scientists. Consequently, we have not offered advice on how to recognize and identify various pedoturbation features. Some of the processes are more easily recognized than others; rodent and other burrows, root casts, and tree-tipping, for example, pose few problems in identification. They are visible and relatively self-explanatory, and they can be recognized without special training. At the other end of the scale, however, are the more subtle effects of other soil fauna (for example, earthworms), freeze–thaw action, shrink–swell action of clays, crystal growth, and artesian action, which challenge the capabilities of soils specialists. An effort to offer criteria for the identification of each of the processes discussed would easily double or triple the length of this chapter if we were to avoid misleading and oversimplified interpretive strategies. Rather, we recommend that the archaeologist become familiar enough with the processes detailed here that one can reasonably expect to recognize potential problems, and then consult a specialist. In any case, *each instance of pedoturbation must be evaluated individually,* especially for its effect on cultural remains.

In sum, a reasonably accurate assessment of the pedoturbatory history of the soils and sediments at every archaeological site is absolutely prerequisite to valid archaeogeological interpretations. This, in addition to calling attention to the range and implications of pedoturbation processes in archaeological site formation, is the essential point of this chapter.

REFERENCES

Anderson, D. M.
    1970   Phase boundary water in frozen soils. *U.S. Army Corps of Engineers, Cold Regions Research and Engineering Laboratory, Research Report* No. 274, 19 pp.

1971 Remote analysis of planetary water. *U.S. Army Corps of Engineers, Cold Regions Research and Engineering Laboratory, Special Report* No. 154, 13 pp.

Ascher, R.
1968 Time's arrow and the archaeology of a contemporary community. In *Settlement archaeology,* edited by K. C. Chang. Palo Alto, Calif.: National Press Books. Pp. 43–52.

Barr, D. J., and D. N. Swanston
1970 Measurement of creep in a shallow, slide-prone till soil. *American Journal of Science* **269:**267–480.

Baxter, F. P.
1967 Genesis of upland soils. In Soil resources and forest ecology of Menominee County, Wisconsin, edited by C. J. Milfred, G. W. Olson, and F. D. Hole (Soil Series No. 60). *Wisconsin Geological and Natural History Survey Bulletin* No. 85, 91–101.

Baxter, F. P., and F. D. Hole
1967 Ant (*Formica cinerea*) pedoturbation in a prairie soil. *Soil Science Society of America, Proceedings* **31:**425–428.

Beckmann, G. C., C. H. Thompson, and G. D. Hubble
1973 Linear gilgai. *Australian Geographer* **12:**363–366.

Benedict, J. B.
1976 Frost creep and gelifluction features: A review. *Quaternary Research* **6:**55–76.

Benedict, J. B., and B. L. Olson
1978 The Mount Albion complex: A study of prehistoric man and the Altithermal. *Center for Mountain Archeology Research Report* No. 1.

Beskow, G.
1935 *Soil freezing and frost heaving with special application to roads and railroads.* Stockholm. (Translated by J. O. Osterberg, Technical Institute, Northwestern University, Evanston, 1947.)

Best, T. L.
1972 Mound development by a pioneer population of the bannertailed kangaroo rat, *Dipodomys spectabilis baileyi* Goldman, in eastern New Mexico. *American Midland Naturalist* **87:**201–206.

Binford, L. R.
1964 A consideration of archaeological research design. *American Antiquity* **29:**425–441.

Blancaneaux, P.
1973 Notes de pédologie guyanaise. Les Djougoung-Pété du bassin-versant experimental de la crique Grégoire. (Sinnamary-Guyane Francaise.) (Notes on Guyana pedology. The "Djougoung-Pété" on the experimental basin slope of the Grégoire Creek, Sinnamary, French Guyana.) *Cahiers O-K-S-T-O-M Serie Pédologie* **11:**29–42.

Bocock, K. L., and O. J. W. Gilbert
1957 The disappearance of leaf litter under different woodland conditions. *Plant and Soil* **9:**179–185.

Booij, A. H.
1975 Storm als oorzaak van microrelief in de ondergrond. (Storms causing a microrelief in subsoil.) *Boor en Spade* **19:**30–31.

Bourlière, F.
1964 *The natural history of mammals* (3rd ed.). New York: Knopf.

Bouyoucos, G. J., and M. M. McCool
  1928 The correct explanation for the heaving of soils, plants, and pavements. *Journal of the American Society of Agronomy* **20**:480–491.
Bowley, W. W., and M. D. Burghardt
  1971 Thermodynamics and stones. *Transactions, American Geophysical Union* **52**:4–7.
Buntley, G. J., and R. I. Papendick
  1960 Worm-worked soils of eastern South Dakota, their morphology and classification. *Soil Science Society of America, Proceedings* **24**:128–132.
Buol, S. W., F. D. Hole, and R. J. McCracken
  1973 *Soil genesis and classification.* Ames: Iowa State University Press.
Caine, T. N.
  1964 Movement of low angle scree slopes in the Lake District, northern England. *Revue de Geomorphogique Dynamique* **14**:171–177.
Canada Soil Survey Committee
  1970 *The system of soil classification for Canada.* Ottawa: Canadian Agriculture Queen's Printer.
Carson, M. A.
  1976 Mass-wasting, slope development and climate. In *Geomorphology and climate,* edited by E. Derbyshire. New York: Wiley. Pp. 101–136.
Chambers, M. J. G.
  1967 Investigations of patterned ground at Signy Island, South Orkney Islands, II: Temperature regimes in the active layer. *Bulletin, British Antarctic Survey* **12**:1–22.
Chapman, C. H., and L. O. Anderson
  1955 The Campbell Site. *Missouri Archaeologist* **17**:Parts 2 and 3.
Childe, V. G.
  1956 *Piecing together the past.* London: Routledge and Kegan Paul.
Cooke, R. U., and A. Warren
  1973 *Geomorphology in deserts.* Berkeley: University of California Press.
Cornwall, I. W.
  1958 *Soils for the archaeologist.* London: Phoenix House.
Corte, A. E.
  1962a The frost behavior of soils, I, Vertical sorting. *Highway Research Board, Bulletin* No. **317**, 9–34.
  1962b The frost behavior of soils, II, Horizontal sorting. *Highway Research Board, Bulletin* No. **331**, 46–66.
  1962c Vertical migration of particles in front of a moving freezing plane. *Journal of Geophysical Research* **67**:1085–1090.
  1963 Particle sorting by repeated freezing and thawing. *Science* **142**:499–501.
  1966a Experiments on sorting processes and the origin of patterned ground. In *Permafrost International Conference, Proceedings of the National Academy of Science–National Research Council* No. 1287, 130–135.
  1966b Particle sorting by repeated freezing and thawing. *Biuletyn Peryglacjalny* **15**:175–240.
Coster, C.
  1938 Bovengrondsche afstrooming en erosie op Java. *Landbouw (Buitenzorg, Java)* **14**:457–563.

Crooks, K. A. W.
  1958   "Finger-print" pattern on certain calcareous soils—a suggestion. *Bulletin, American Association of Petroleum Geologists* **42**:3001.
Culling, W. E. H.
  1963   Soil creep and the development of hillside slopes. *Journal of Geology* **71**:127–161.
Curtis, J. T.
  1959   *Vegetation of Wisconsin: An ordination of plant communities*. Madison: University of Wisconsin Press.
Czerrvinski, Z., H. Jakubczyk, and J. Petal
  1971   Influence of ant hills on the meadow soils. *Pedobiologia* **7**:277–285.
Darwin, C.
  1896   *The formation of vegetable mould through the action of worms*. New York: Appleton.
Daubenmire, R. F.
  1959   *Plants and environment: A textbook of plant autecology* (2nd ed.). New York: Wiley.
Davies, J. L.
  1969   *Landforms of cold climates*. Cambridge, Mass.: MIT Press.
Davis, E. L.
  1975a Ancient Californians: Paleo-Indians of the Lakes Country. Unpublished abstract on deposit (China Lake manuscript), Los Angeles County Museum of Natural History.
  1975b Clovis population shifts from Great Basin to Great Plains: An hypothesis. Paper presented at the 41st Annual Meeting of the Society for American Archaeology, Saint Louis.
Davis, E. L., and D. E. Fortsch
  1970   Extinct fauna and early man in the Mojave Desert, California. Paper presented at the 35th Annual Meeting of the Society for American Archaeology, Mexico City.
Davis, E. L., and R. Shutler, Jr.
  1969   Recent discoveries of fluted points in California and Nevada. *Miscellaneous Papers on Nevada Archaeology 1–8, Nevada State Museum Anthropological Papers* No. 14.
Decker, A. M., Jr., and T. S. Ronningen
  1957   Heaving in forage stand and in bare ground. *Agronomy Journal* **49**:412–415.
Denny, C. S., and J. C. Goodlett
  1956   Microrelief from fallen trees. In Surficial geology and geomorphology of Potter County, Pennsylvania. *U.S. Geological Survey, Professional Paper* No. 288, 59–66.
Dostovalov, B. N., and A. I. Popov
  1966   Polygonal systems of ice wedges and conditions of their development. In Proceedings, First International Permafrost Conference. *National Research Council of Canada, Publication* No. 1287, 102–105.
Dudal, R.
  1963   Dark clay soils of tropical and subtropical regions. *Soil Science* **95**:264–270.
  1965   (editor) Dark clay soils of tropical and subtropical regions. *FAO (Food and Agricultural Organization of the United Nations)* Agricultural Development Paper No. 83.

Duffield, L. F.
  1970 Vertisols and their implications for archaeological research. *American Anthropologist* **72**:1055–1062.
Dylik, J.
  1969 Slope development under periglacial conditions in the Lódź region. *Biuletyn Peryglacjalny* No. 18, 381–410.
Edelman, C. H., F. Florschütz, and J. Jesweit
  1936 Über spätpleistozäne und fruhholozäne Kryoturbate Ablagerungen in den Östlichen Niederlanden. *Verhandelingen van het Koninklijk Nederlands Geologisch Mijnbouwkundig Genootschap, Geologische Serie* **11**:301–336.
Embleton, C., and C. A. M. King
  1968 *Glacial and periglacial geomorphology.* New York: St. Martins Press.
Evans, A. C.
  1948 Studies on the relationships between earthworms and soil fertility. IV. On the life cycles of some British *Lumbricidae. Annals of Applied Biology* **35**:471–493.
Evans, A. C., and W. J. Guild
  1947 Studies on the relationships between earthworms and soil fertility. I. Biological studies in the field. *Annals of Applied Biology* **34**:307–330.
Everett, K.
  1963 Slope movement, Neotoma Valley, southern Ohio. *Ohio State University, Institute of Polar Studies, Report* No. 6.
Eyles, R. J., and R. Ho
  1970 Soil creep on a humid tropical slope. *Journal of Tropical Geography* **31**:40–42.
Fahey, B.
  1974 Seasonal frost heave and frost penetration measurements in the Indian Peaks region of the Colorado Front Range. *Arctic and Alpine Research* **6**:63–70.
Fortsch, D. E.
  1976 Late Pleistocene vertebrate fossils from China Lake, California. Manuscript on deposit (written for the Pacific Section), Friends of the Pleistocene, China Lake, California.
French, H. M.
  1976 *The Periglacial environment.* New York: Longman Group,
Gabert, P.
  1964 Premiers résultats des mesures d'erosion sur des parcelles expérimentales dans la région d'Aix-en-Provence (Bouches du Rhône, France). 4th report, International advancement in research on slope morphology. *Zeitschrift für Geomorphologie Supplementband* **5**:213–214.
Gaikawad, S. T., and F. D. Hole
  1961 Characteristics and genesis of a podzol soil in Florence County, Wisconsin. *Transactions of the Wisconsin Academy of Science* **50**:183–190.
Garner, H. F.
  1974 *The origin of landscapes.* London and New York: Oxford University Press.
Gerasimov, I. P., and K. K. Markov
  1968 *Permafrost and ancient glaciation* (Translation T499R). Ottawa: Defense Research Board. Pp. 11–19.
Gilbert, O. J. W., and K. L. Bocock
  1960 Changes in leaf litter when placed on the surface of soils with contrasting humus types, II. Changes in nitrogen content of oak and ash leaf litter. *Journal of Soil Science* **11**:10–19.

Gile, L. H.
  1966   Coppice dunes and the Rotura soil. *Soil Science Society of America, Proceedings* **30:**657–660.
  1975a Causes of soil boundaries in an arid region: I. Age and parent materials. *Soil Science Society of America, Proceedings* **39:**316–323.
  1975b Causes of soil boundaries in an arid region: II. Dissection, moisture, and faunal activity. *Soil Science Society of America, Proceedings* **39:**324–330.
Gile, L. H., and R. B. Grossman
  1968   Morphology of the argillic horizon in desert soils of southern New Mexico. *Soil Science* **106:**6–15.
Gile, L. H., R. B. Grossman, and J. W. Hawley
  1969   Effects of landscape dissection on soils near University Park, New Mexico. *Soil Science* **108:**273–282.
Gile, L. H., F. F. Peterson, and R. B. Grossman
  1966   Morphological and genetic sequences of carbonate accumulation in desert soils. *Soil Science* **101:**347–360.
Grassé, P. (editor)
  1955   *Traité de zoologie. 17. Mammiféres. Les ordres: Anatomie, éthologie, systématique.* Paris: Masson.
Grave, N. A.
  1968a Merzyle tolshchi zemli. *Priroda* **1:**46–53.
  1968b *The earth's permafrost beds* (Translation T499R). Ottawa: Canada Defense Research Board. Pp. 1–10.
Green, R. D., and G. P. Askew
  1965   Observations on the biological development of macropores in soils of Romney Marsh. *Journal of Soil Science* **16:**342–349.
Grinnell, J.
  1923   The burrowing rodents of California as agents in soil formation. *Journal of Mammalogy* **4:**137–149.
Halsworth, E. G., and G. G. Beckmann
  1969   Gilgai in the Quaternary. *Soil Science* **107:**409–420.
Halsworth, E. G., G. K. Robertson, and F. R. Gibbons
  1955   Studies in pedogenesis in New South Wales. *Journal of Soil Science* **6:**1–32.
Harrington, M. R., and R. D. Simpson
  1961   Tule Springs, Nevada with other evidence of Pleistocene man in North America. *Southwest Museum Papers (Los Angeles)* No. 18.
Harris, C.
  1972   Processes of soil movement in turf-banked solifluction lobes, Okstindan, northern Norway. *Polar Geomorphology, Institute of British Geography, Special Publication* No. 4, 155–174.
Harris, S. A.
  1968   Gilgai. In *Encyclopedia of geomorphology,* edited by R. W. Fairbridge. New York: Reinhold.
Haynes, C. V.
  1967   Quaternary geology of the Tule Springs area, Clark County, Nevada. In Pleistocene studies in southern Nevada. *Nevada State Museum, Anthropological Papers* No. 13, 15–104.
  1976   Late Quaternary geology of the lower Pomme de Terre valley. In *Prehistoric man and his environments: A case study in the Ozark Highland,* edited by W. R. Wood and R. B. McMillan. New York: Academic Press.

Heath, G. W.
  1965   The part played by animals in soil formation. In *Experimental pedology*, edited by E. G. Hallsworth and D. V. Crawford. London: Butterworth. Pp. 236–243.
Hesse, P. R.
  1955   A chemical and physical study of the soils of termite mounds in East Africa. *Journal of Ecology* **43:**449–461.
Hole, F. D.
  1961   A classification of pedoturbations and some other processes and factors of soil formation in relation to isotropism and anisotropism. *Soil Science* **91:**375–377.
Hole, F. D., and Nielsen, G. A.
  1970   Soil genesis under prairie. *Proceedings, Symposium on Prairie and Prairie Restoration.* Galesburg, Ill.: Knox College. Pp. 28–34.
Hole, F. D., and Schmude, K. O.
  1959   Soil survey of Oneida County, Wisconsin. *Wisconsin Geological and Natural History Survey, Soil Survey Division, Bulletin* No. 84.
Holmes, R. M., and G. W. Robertson
  1960   Soil heaving in alfalfa plots in relation to soil and air temperature. *Canadian Journal of Soil Science* **40:**212–218.
Holmes, W. H.
  1893   Are there traces of glacial man in the Trenton Gravels? *Journal of Geology* **1:**15–37.
Hopkins, D. M., and J. L. Giddings
  1953   Geological background of the Iatayet archeological site, Cape Denbigh, Alaska. *Smithsonian Miscellaneous Collections* **121**(11).
Hugie, V. K., and H. B. Passey
  1963   Cicadas and their effect upon soil genesis in certain soils in southern Idaho, northern Utah, and northeastern Nevada. *Soil Science Society of America, Proceedings* **27:**78–82.
Hunt, C. B.
  1975   *Death Valley: Geology, ecology, archaeology.* Berkeley: University of California Press.
Hunt, C. B., and A. L. Washburn
  1960   Salt features that simulate ground patterns formed in cold climates. *U.S. Geological Survey, Professional Paper* No. 400B, B403.
Inglis, D. R.
  1965   Particle sorting and stone migration by freezing and thawing. *Science* **148:**1616–1617.
Jacks, G. V.
  1963   The biological nature of soil productivity. *Soils and Fertilizers* **36:**147–150.
Jackson, K. A., and D. R. Uhlmann
  1966   Particle sorting and stone migration due to frost heave. *Science* **152:**545–546.
Jahn, A.
  1960   Some remarks on the evolution of slopes on Spitsbergen. *Zeitschrift für Geomorphologie, Supplementband* No. 1, 49–58.
  1961   Quantitative analyses of some periglacial processes in Spitzbergen. *Nauka O Ziemi II, Seria B* No. 5, 3–34.
Jessup, R. W.
  1960   The stony tableland soils of the southeastern portion of the Australian arid zone and their evolutionary history. *Journal of Soil Science* **11:**188–196.

Johnsgard, G. A.
  1971 Pedoturbation by artesian action. *Soil Science Society of America, Proceedings* **35**:612–616.
Johnson, A. W.
  1952 Frost action in roads and airfields. *Highway Research Board, Special Report* No. 1.
Johnson, D. L., and K. L. Hansen
  1974 The effects of frost-heaving on objects in soils. *Plains Anthropologist* **19**:81–98.
Johnson, D. L., and N. C. Hester
  1972 Origin of stone pavements on Pleistocene marine terraces in California. *Proceedings of the Association of American Geographers* **4**:50–53.
Johnson, D. L., D. R. Muhs, and M. L. Barnhardt
  1977 The effects of frost heaving on objects in soils, II: Laboratory experiments. *Plains Anthropologist* **22**:133–147.
Kaplar, C. W.
  1970 Phenomenon and mechanism of frost heaving. *Highway Research Record* No. 304, 1–13.
Kirkby, M. J.
  1967 Measurement and theory of soil creep. *Journal of Geology* **75**:359–378.
Koch, A. C.
  1857 Mastodon remains in the state of Missouri, together with evidence of the existence of man contemporaneously with the mastodon. *Transactions of the Academy of Science of St. Louis* **1**:61–64.
Kojan, E.
  1967 Mechanics and rates of natural soil creep. *U.S. Forest Service Experimental Station (Berkeley, California), Report* pp. 233–253.
Krause, R. A., and R. M. Thorne
  1971 Toward a theory of archaeological things. *Plains Anthropologist* **16**:245–256.
Laycock, W. A.
  1958 The initial pattern of revegetation of pocket gopher mounds. *Ecology* **39**:346–351.
Leary, R. M., J. L. Sanborn, and J. H. Zoller
  1968 Freezing tests of granular materials. *Highway Research Record* No. 215, 60–71.
Lee, K. E., and T. G. Wood
  1971a Physical and chemical effects on soil of some Australian termites and their pedological significance. *Pedobiologia* **7**:376–409.
  1971b *Termites and soils.* New York: Academic Press.
Leopold, L. B., W. W. Emmett, and R. M. Myrick
  1966 Channel and hillslope processes in a semiarid area, New Mexico. *U.S. Geological Survey Professional Paper* **352**:193–253.
Limbrey, S.
  1975 *Soil science and archaeology.* New York: Academic Press.
Lutz, H. J.
  1960 Movement of rocks by uprooting of forest trees. *American Journal of Science* **258**:752–756.
Mabbutt, J. A.
  1965 Stone distribution in a stony tableland soil. *Australian Journal of Soil Research* **3**:131–142.

Mackay, J. R., W. H. Mathews, and R. S. MacNeish
  1961 Geology of the Engigstciak archaeological site, Yukon Territory. *Arctic* **14**:25–52.
McMillan, R. B.
  1976 Man and mastodon: A review of Koch's 1840 Pomme de Terre expeditions. In *Prehistoric man and his environments: A case study in the Ozark Highland,* edited by W. R. Wood and R. B. McMillan, New York: Academic Press.
Malde, H. E.
  1964 The ecologic significance of some unfamiliar geologic processes. In The reconstruction of past environments (Proceedings of the Fort Bergwin Conference on Paleoecology, 1962), assembled by J. J. Hester and J. Schoenwetter. *Fort Bergwin Research Center* No. 3, 7–15.
Matelski, R. P.
  1959 Great soil groups of Nebraska. *Soil Science* **88**:228–239.
Milfred, C. J., G. W. Olson, and F. D. Hole
  1967 Soil resources and forest ecology of Menominee County, Wisconsin (Soil Series No. 60). *Wisconsin Geological and Natural History Survey, Bulletin* No. 85.
Mitchell, R. J., and W. J. Eden
  1972 Measured movements of clay slopes in the Ottawa area. *Canadian Journal of Earth Sciences* **9**:1001–1013.
Mueller, O. P., and M. G. Cline
  1959 Effects of mechanical soil barriers and soil wetness on rooting of trees and soil mixing by blow-down in Central New York. *Soil Science* **88**:107–111.
Neumann, T. W.
  1978 A model for the vertical distribution of flotation-size particles. *Plains Anthropologist.* **23**: 85–101.
Nielsen, G. A.
  1963 Incorporation of organic matter into the A horizon of some Wisconsin soils under native vegetation. Unpublished Ph.D. thesis, University of Wisconsin, Madison.
Nielsen, G. A., and F. D. Hole
  1964 Earthworms and the development of coprogenous A_1 horizons in forest soils of Wisconsin. *Soil Science Society of America, Proceedings* **28**:426–430.
Oakes, H., and J. Thorp.
  1951 Dark clay soils of warm regions variously called *Rendzina,* Black Cotton Soils, Regur and Tirs. *Soil Science Society of America, Proceedings* **15**:347–354.
Ollier, C. D.
  1959 The two cycle theory of tropical pedology. *Journal of Soil Science* **10**:137–148.
  1966 Desert gilgai. *Nature (London)* **212**:581–583.
Olson, G. W., and F. D. Hole
  1967 The fragipan in soils of northeastern Wisconsin. *Transactions, Wisconsin Academy of Science, Arts and Letters* **56**:174–184.
Owens, I. F.
  1969 Causes and rates of soil creep in the Chilton Valley, Cass, New Zealand. *Arctic and Alpine Research* **1**:213–220.
Parsons, R. B., L. Moncharoan, and E. G. Knox
  1973 Geomorphic occurrence of Pelloxerets, Willamette Valley, Oregon. *Soil Science Society of America, Proceedings* **37**:924–927.
Paton, T. R.
  1974 Origin and terminology for gilgai in Australia. *Geoderma* **11**:221–242.

Penner, E.
    1959   The mechanism of frost heaving in soils. *Highway Research Board Bulletin* No. 225, 1–22.

Pissart, A.
    1966   Expériences et observations á propos de la genese des sols polygonaux triés. *Revue de Belge Géographie* **90**:55–73.
    1970   Les phénoménes physiques éssentielles liés au gel, les structures périglaciaires qui en résultent et leur signification climatique. *Annales, Société Géologique de Belgique* **93**:7–49.
    1973   Resultats d'experiences sur l'action du gel dans le sol. *Biuletyn Peryglacjalny* **23**:101–113.

Popov, A. I.
    1962   *The origin and development of massive fossil ice* (Issue 11). Moscow: Academy of Sciences of the USSR, V. A. Obruchev Institute of Permafrost Studies. (National Research Council of Canada, Technical Translation No. 1006, 5–24.)

Price, L. W.
    1971   Geomorphic effect of the Arctic ground squirrel in an Alpine environment. *Geografiska Annaler, Series A* **53A**:100–106.

Rick, J. W.
    1976   Downslope movement and archaeological intrasite spatial analysis. *American Antiquity* **41**:133–144.

Roche, P.
    1954   Mesures de l'érosion et du ruissellement sous différentes cultures dans la région du lac d'Alaotra (Madagascar), 2nd Conf. Interafr. Sols Léopoldville **1**:547–567.

Rudberg, S.
    1962   A report on some field observations concerning periglacial geomorphology and mass movements on slopes in Sweden. *Biuletin Peryglacjalny* **11**:311–323.

Russell, J. S., and A. W. Moore
    1972   Some parameters of gilgai microrelief. *Soil Science* **114**:82–87.

Salem, M., and F. D. Hole
    1968   Ant (*Formica exsectoides*) pedoturbation in a forest soil. *Soil Science Society of America, Proceedings* **32**:563–567.

Schiffer, M. B.
    1972   Archaeological context and systemic context. *American Antiquity* **37**:156–165.
    1976   *Behavioral archaeology.* New York: Academic Press.

Schreiber, K. F.
    1969   Beobachtungen über die Entstehung von Buckelweiden auf den Hochflächen des Schweizer Jura (Observations on the formation of "hummocked fields" on the upper areas of the Swiss Jura). *Erdkunde* **23**:280–290.

Schumm, S. A.
    1956a Evolution of drainage systems and slopes on badlands at Perth Amboy, New Jersey. *Geological Society of America, Bulletin* **67**:597–646.
    1956b The role of creep and rain-wash on the retreat of badland slopes. *American Journal of Science* **254**:639–706.
    1964   Seasonal variations of erosion rates and processes on hillslopes in western Colorado, *Zeitschrift für Geomorphology* **5**:215–238.

Scully, N. J.
    1942   Root distribution and environment in a maple-oak forest. *Botanical Gazette* **103**:492–517.

Sharma, V. N., and M. C. Joshi
  1975 Soil excavation by desert gerbil *Meriones hurrianae* (Jerdon) in the Shekhawati region of Rajasthan desert. *Annals of the Arid Zone* **14**:268–273.
Sharp, R. P.
  1942 Periglacial involutions in northeastern Illinois. *Journal of Geology* **50**:113–133.
Sharpe, C. F. S.
  1938 *Landslides and related phenomena.* New York: Columbia University Press. (Reprinted: Pageant Books, New York, 1960.)
Shcherbakov, Y. A., and V. V. Bakanin
  1969 Low hillock relief in the Sikhote-Aline (in Russian). *Izvestiya Vsesoyuznogo Geograficheskogo Obshchestva* **101**:358–360.
Shumskii, P. A.
  1964 *Ground (subsurface) ice.* (National Research Council of Canada, Technical Translation No. 1130, 118 pp.)
Shumskii, P. A., and B. I. Vtyurin
  1966 Underground ice. In Proceedings, First International Permafrost Conference. *National Research Council of Canada, Publication* No. 1287, 108–113.
Soil Survey Staff
  1975 Soil taxonomy: A basic system of soil classification for making and interpreting soil surveys. *U.S. Dep. Agric., Agric. Handb.* No. 436.
Springer, M. E.
  1958 Desert pavement and vesicular layer of some soils of the desert of the Lahonton Basin, Nevada. *Soil Science Society of America, Proceedings* **22**:63–66.
St-Onge, D.
  1965 La géomorphologie de l'Île Ellef Ringnes, Territoires du Nord-Ouest, Canada. *Canada, Ministére des Mines et des Relevés Techniques, Direction de la Geographie Étude Géog.* No. 38, 46 pp.
Taber, S.
  1916 The growth of crystals under external pressure. *American Journal of Science, Series 4* **191**:532–556.
  1929 Frost heaving. *Journal of Geology* **37**:428–461.
  1930 The mechanics of frost heaving. *Journal of Geology* **38**:303–317.
Tanner, W. F.
  1958 "Finger-print" pattern on certain calcareous soils. *Bulletin, American Association of Petroleum Geologists* **42**:438–440.
Ter-Stepanian, G.
  1965 *In-situ* determination of the rheological characteristics of soils on slopes. *Proceedings, International Conference on Soil Mechanics and Foundation Engineering, 6th* **2**:575–577.
Terzaghi, K.
  1952 Permafrost. *Journal of the Boston Society of Civil Engineers* **39**:1–50.
Thompson, R. H., and W. A. Longacre
  1966 The University of Arizona Archaeological Field School at Grasshopper, East Central Arizona. *The Kiva* **31**:255–275.
Thorp, J.
  1949 Effects of certain animals that live in the soil. *Science Monthly* **68**:180–191.
  1957 Report on a field study of soils in Australia. *Science Bulletin (Earlham College, Richmond, Indiana)* No. 1, 169 pp.
Thorson, R. M., and T. D. Hamilton
  1977 Geology of the Dry Creek Site; a stratified Early Man site in interior Alaska. *Quaternary Research* **7**:149–176.

Troll, C.
  1944 Strukturboden, solifluktion und frostlklimate der Erde. *Geologische Rundschau* **34**:545–694. [SIPRE Translation No. 43 (1958).]
Vessel, A. J., and R. W. Simonson
  1958 Soils and agriculture of the Palau Islands. *Pacific Science* **12**:281–298.
Washburn, A. L.
  1956 Classification of patterned ground and review of suggested origins. *Geological Society of America, Bulletin* **67**:823–865.
  1967 Instrumental observations of mass-wasting in the Mesters Vig District, Northeast Greenland. *Meddelelser om Grønland* **166**:1–297.
  1969 Weathering, frost action and patterned ground in the Mesters Vig District, Northeast Greenland. *Meddelelser om Grønland* **176**:318 pp.
  1970 An approach to a genetic classification of patterned ground. *Acta Geographica Lodziensia* **24**:437–446.
  1973 *Periglacial processes and environments.* London: Arnold.
Watson, J. P.
  1967 A termite mound in an Iron Age burial ground in Rhodesia. *Journal of Ecology* **55**:663–669.
Wiken, E. B., K. Broersma, L. M. Lavkulich, and L. Farstad
  1976 Biosynthetic alteration in a British Columbia soil by ants (*Formica fusca Linné*). *Soil Science Society of America Proceedings,* **40**:422–426.
Wilde, S. A.
  1958 *Forest soils, their properties and relation to silviculture.* New York: Ronald Press.
Williams, M. A. J.
  1973 The efficacy of creep and slopewash in tropical and temperate Australia, *Australian Geographical Studies* **11**:62–78.
Williams, P. J.
  1966 Downslope movement at a subarctic location with regard to variations with depth. *Canadian Geotechnical Journal* **3**:191–203.
Wood, W. R.
  1976 Archaeological investigations at the Pomme de Terre springs. In *Prehistoric man and his environments: A case study in the Ozark Highland,* edited by W. R. Wood and R. B. McMillan. New York: Academic Press.
Young, A.
  1960 Soil movement by denudational processes on slopes. *Nature (London)* **188**:120–122.

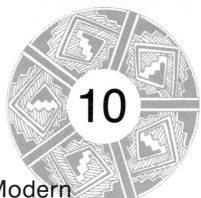

Decision Making in Modern Surveys

STEPHEN PLOG, FRED PLOG,
and WALTER WAIT

In the last decade the investment in and significance of results obtained
from survey archaeology have increased dramatically. Some archaeologists are now devoting most of their field effort to survey work,
and in some parts of the world the relative importance of survey and
excavation as field techniques is approaching equality. Although the growing importance of cultural resources surveys in the United States is in part
responsible for this trend, the discovery of techniques for making increasingly significant inferences about the prehistoric past from site surfaces,
as well as the growing cost of excavation and its heavy impact on the
available archaeological record, has markedly increased the archaeological potential of surveys.

With more surveys has come greater diversity in the kinds of survey
techniques applied. Some of these have been intentional—the effort to
implement statistically based sampling strategies in survey work and the
variety of random, systematic, and stratified designs that have been
applied is one example. Some have been unintentional, however. For
example, the average distance that survey crews were asked to maintain
from each other has usually been set in the field, with little thought to the
consequences of varied spacing. It has become increasingly clear that
these different decisions, however they are made, result in drastically
different survey results. Archaeologists are recognizing the need to de-

ADVANCES IN ARCHAEOLOGICAL METHOD AND THEORY, VOL. 1

scribe systematically the decisions that must be made in designing a survey and to identify the alternative consequences for data recovery of different strategies. In no way are we suggesting that there is or should be evolution toward a standardized set of survey procedures—only that the consequences of different strategies must be well known.

At the same time, we would argue that archaeological sophistication has been growing dramatically. Of particular importance to our argument is the growing awareness that it is virtually impossible to avoid introducing biases into our data and completely impossible to avoid making a variety of observational and recording errors in the field. The growth in sophistication and maturation that we see involves a recognition that, although such biases and mistakes cannot be avoided, they can be compensated for and corrected. Awareness of likely errors and biases, awareness of techniques for identifying them, and awareness of means of correcting for them are a clear necessity.

What we shall attempt to describe in this essay are some of the decisions that arise and the problems that must be overcome in doing a survey. We suggest no panaceas, only alternatives. Although we have tried, we have not been able to avoid using the Southwestern United States as a paramount case in the discussion, since that is the survey context in which all of us have worked. Each of the sections that follows considers a major problem in the design of an archaeological survey.

SELECTION OF A SURVEY UNIVERSE

The most basic decision that any archaeologist makes in undertaking a survey is where that survey is to be conducted. Ideally, such a choice is based on the theoretical, methodological, and empirical issues underlying the research topic on which the survey is to focus. In reality, the location of a particular survey project is being determined with increasing frequency by a variety of political and economic considerations ranging from the "military sensitivity" of areas in foreign countries to the need for "cultural resources assessments" of localities and regions in the United States. We are convinced that it is not justifiable to undertake surveys in areas where the choice of survey locale has been forced unless meaningful research issues have been identified there. At the same time, it is important to recognize that some such projects prove to be more problematical in this regard than others.

The primary issue underlying such problems is the boundary of the survey universe. Basically, three kinds of boundaries can be identified: arbitrary, cultural, and natural. Natural boundaries are those defined over some topographic or vegetative pattern. A survey of a drainage, a mountain range, or a ridge line is one circumscribed by natural boundaries. Cultural boundaries are those defined over artifactual criteria. Arbitrary boundaries are those defined over criteria insensitive to either natural or cultural patterns.

Ideally, archaeologists would always choose in solving most problems to survey a culturally bounded area, whether the boundary is conceived as encompassing an entire culture or a subsistence-settlement unit within that culture. Delineation of such cultural boundaries is not simple, nor even possible in some cases, since these boundaries are dynamic, not static. When surveys are done over areas that cross one or more cultural boundaries, the difficulty of distinguishing cultural from seasonal from organizational patterns becomes immense, if not impossible. Surveys defined over completely arbitrary criteria, of which many cultural resource management projects are an example, are especially problematical.

Naturally bounded survey units represent an intermediate case. Natural and cultural boundaries do not always correspond. At the same time, rivers and mountain ranges do frequently prove to be important cultural boundaries. Thus, when the natural or cultural evidence represented in particular situations is largely or wholly unknown, the selection of a ridge line, a drainage, or the areas between two mountain ranges as a survey universe is an efficient and logical choice. By the same token, when the boundaries of areas identified for cultural resource inventories have some correspondence with natural features, the problem of arbitrariness is considerably reduced.

Archaeologists are sometimes in a position to select the boundaries of the area they will survey; sometimes they are not. To the extent that it is possible to identify a cultural boundary for the area that will be surveyed, this course of action is preferred. To the extent that it is not possible, natural boundaries represent an effective second choice. Surveys in arbitrarily bounded units that correspond to neither cultural nor natural divisions represent the most significant methodological and interpretive problems.

SITE DEFINITION

One of the most critical decisions we must face if we are to develop survey data with an iota of comparability is the question of what is and what is not a site. Upon the discovery of artifacts, a surveyor must make a "yes" or "no" decision concerning site status. Chenhall (1975) (citing

Gardin) has suggested that the adequacy of this decision is a reflection of archaeological perception, and we agree. He suggests that at every stage in the "process of doing archaeology, decisions are being made to 'keep' some objects and/or data and to 'refuse' other objects or data" (Chenhall 1975:8). The adequacy of a survey, then, depends in part on the surveyor's perception of the importance of certain classes of archaeological data. Fifty years ago an archaeologist could simply ask local residents in a given area, "Where are the sites?" and locate most of the substantial occurrences in the area. Smaller sites, dwellings, activity areas, and even substantial artifact scatters without visible architecture were not important to the kinds of questions being asked. For all practical purposes, these informal, unsystematic surveys resulted in the compilation of a reasonable inventory of a specfic class of archaeological sites—large pueblos with dense artifact scatters. Small sites or sites with low artifact density are another issue, however.

We feel that many surveys have systematically excluded such sites. This exclusion may be the result of conscious decisions made on the basis of the research objectives of the survey or, more likely, an unconscious decision made on the basis of the archaeologist's perception of what a site was or was not. Unfortunately, our perception of what a site should actually look like on the ground is too often influenced by the larger, more visible, but less frequent sites present in an area. For example, a recent survey of 52 km² (20 mi²) of Chaco Canyon National Monument recovered a total of 1130 sites, of which 1.3% (about 15 sites) were considered "pre-ceramic" (Judge *et al.* 1975:96–97). In contrast, a survey of the Star Lake area of New Mexico, roughly 24 km from Chaco Canyon National Monument, discovered 109 pre-ceramic sites within a survey area of 60 km² (23 mi²) (Wait 1977). This survey was similar in intensity to the survey of the Chaco Canyon area and covered similar topographic and vegetation zones. Is the difference in the density of pre-ceramic sites between the two areas a real difference in the utilization of the two areas prior to about A.D. 500, or is it the result of the difficulty of perceiving sparse lithic scatters as sites when one is working in an area such as Chaco Canyon, where multiroom pueblos with standing architecture and dense artifact scatters are common? Such lithic scatters may be more visible in an area such as Star Lake, where puebloan sites are virtually absent.

This problem is also exemplified by a survey of the Roosevelt Lake and Horseshoe Reservoir areas in central Arizona. The following statement is made in the report on this survey:

> No pre-pottery sites were recorded within the reservoir areas. . . . Many scatters of lithic debris, mainly primary flakes and cores, were noted during the survey. While these scatters were not recorded as sites because of a lack of certain site criteria, there

is the possibllity that they represent the presence of a pre-ceramic, non-sedentary occupation [Fuller *et al.* 1976:192].

As will be noted below, the definition of a site used by the crew doing this survey is biased toward the large puebloan sites found in many areas of Arizona.

Ultimately, these problems are related to the definition of sites with which surveyors are instructed to work, if such definitions are made explicit at all (and much of the literature on surveys suggests that they are not). And definitions vary considerably. For example, the Southwest Anthropological Research Group (SARG) has defined a site as "any locus of cultural material, artifacts or facilities" with an artifact density of at least 5 artifacts per square meter (Plog and Hill 1971:8). The Arizona State Museum also uses an artifact density criterion for site definition, but in addition specifies that a site must have more than one definable locus of past human activity and must exhibit definable limits in time and space (Fuller *et al.* 1976:68).

These definitions have several weaknesses. Using data from our own survey work, we have found that sites having an artifact density of 5 or more artifacts per square meter are the exception rather than the rule. For example, the lithic sites discovered during the survey of the Star Lake area had densities ranging from .004 to .95 artifact per square meter (Wait 1977). No site came close to the minimum of 5 artifacts per square meter specified in the above site definitions. This is true not only for early lithic sites such as those at Star Lake, but also for the more typical Southwestern puebloan sites found on Black Mesa and in the Chevelon drainage in Arizona. Average artifact densities on sites in these areas were 3.0 and 2.1 per square meter, respectively. Ninety-five percent of the sites in these areas had artifact densities lower than 5 per square meter. An archaeologist participating in a low-intensity ("intensity" is defined below) survey and having a conception of a site as an area with an average density of 5 artifacts per square meter might easily walk over sites and merely record in his daily journal, "Saw a lot of sherds but recorded no sites today. There must be a site around here somewhere!" Rigid application of density-based site definitions may thus result in the systematic exclusion from analysis of significant components of the archaeological record.

In addition to the problems with density-based definitions of sites, we feel that, for certain types of sites, definable limits and multiple definable activity loci are extremely difficult to ascertain. Thomas (1975:81), for example, has argued that nonsedentary populations "often leave scanty, widely scattered evidence of their lifeway," and Taylor (1972:67) has noted that the "vestiges of nomadic people are scanty, diffuse, and offer very little to the archaeologist in the way of stratified deposits'' (see also Klinger 1976). With these populations, it may be unlikely that locations where activities were carried out will have ''more than one definable locus of past human activity.'' It may also be the case that the distribution of artifacts deposited when activities were carried out is so diffuse that it is difficult to define the limits of the site in space. Thus, in using criteria for site definition such as multiple activity loci and definable spatial limits, significant components of the archaeological record may again be excluded from discovery and analysis, as exemplified by the survey of the Horseshoe Lake and Roosevelt Dam areas described above. We argue that this exclusion is a result of the bias, in choosing criteria for site definition, toward the larger sites on the site-size continuum that are more characteristic of sedentary populations.

More investigators are, however, beginning to recognize the value of the ''trailing edge'' of the archaeological site spectrum—that is, those loci of cultural material where artifact distributions are sparse and diffuse. Thomas (1975), for example, has suggested that for some analyses the site concept could be abandoned entirely. For such ''non-site'' investigations he suggests that the cultural item (the artifact, feature, individual piece of debitage, etc.) could be utilized as the minimal unit of analysis and that the type of artifact distribution classified as culturally insignificant by many surveys may in fact be of primary interest to those archaeologists dealing with nonsedentary peoples in particular (1975:62). He argues (1975:81) that the activities of nonsedentary groups often do not involve ''sites'' in the conventional sense of the term.

There have been a number of recent attempts to operationalize the non-site concept (Rodgers 1974; Doelle 1975, 1977; Goodyear 1975; Thomas 1975; Wait 1977, n.d.), which suggest that this component of the archaeological record will receive increasing attention in future surveys. At the same time, these attempts to operationalize the concept are not without their problems. For example, Doelle (1977) has argued that ''sites'' and ''non-sites'' cannot both be recorded during a single survey of an area. He recommends a ''wide-spaced, rapid paced'' survey to provide a reliable inventory of the sites in an area, since sites are ''generally large and visible,'' and a second survey to sample non-site manifestations (Doelle 1977). As noted above, however, we feel that the vast majority of sites in many areas of the world are neither highly visible nor large in size. In the following section, we shall present evidence that ''wide space, rapid paced'' surveys will miss a large number of sites in an area. In addition, we feel that Doelle's suggested survey strategy is inefficient in its use of time and money and note that surveys have been conducted in which both site and non-site information has been collected as part of a single survey (Rodgers 1974; Goodyear 1975; Thomas 1975).

Despite some of the weaknesses in recent attempts to operationalize the non-site concept, we believe that the concepts of site and non-site manifestations are both useful for designing archaeological surveys. We would distinguish between the two as follows. A *site* is a discrete and potentially interpretable locus of cultural materials. By discrete, we mean spatially bounded with those boundaries marked by at least relative changes in artifact densities. By interpretable we mean that materials of sufficiently great quality and quantity are present for at least attempting and usually sustaining inferences about the behavior occurring at the locus. By cultural materials we mean artifacts, ecofacts, and features. The emphasis on sites as a locus of cultural materials rather than as a locus of past behavior follows the reasoning of Schiffer and Gumerman (1977). A non-site area is a potentially interpretable but not spatially discrete locus of cultural materials. The materials either (*a*) are so limited in quantity or (*b*) cover so broad an area, or both, that meaningful boundaries cannot be defined by normal survey procedures. Designing a basis for recording both site and non-site manifestations in any survey effort is, we believe, critical.

Similarly, the notion of a density limit on site definitions is problematical but not absurd. Such a definition should never be an absolute, and this is where we believe that the proponents of such an approach have erred. On the one hand, it should be tied to some notion of interpretability in the specific context in which the survey is being conducted. On the other hand, it should be regarded by each member of every survey crew as a standard about which arguments are to occur and judgments are to revolve. The occurrence of such arguments and the focusing of such judgments are the most important effect of quantitative definitions of sites.

INTENSITY

One of the most basic decisions an archaeologist must make in conducting a survey is the degree of *intensity* of the survey. We use the term intensity to refer to the degree of detail with which the ground surface of a given survey unit is inspected, whether that survey unit is a large region or a small sample unit. One potential justification for sample surveys is that they allow a high-intensity inspection of a limited area, resulting in superior evidence (House and Ballenger 1976). There is substantial variation in the intensity that is characteristic of archaeological surveys that have been undertaken and are being undertaken—for example, in the Southwestern United States. In the not-too-distant past, it was not atypical for a region to be surveyed by automobile, the investigator stopping periodically to check the likely location of sites or to check areas where local residents indicated that sites would be found. Such surveys were very low in intensity; the proportion of the ground surface that the investigator neither saw nor inspected was quite high relative to what he did see and inspect. However, there is considerable variation in intensity even among surveys that archaeologists claim to be complete or thorough. Intensity in these instances can be measured by the amount of distance separating members of a survey team or by the number of person-days spent in surveying a particular area. For example, in a survey of part of the Hay Hollow Valley by the Southwest Archaeological Expedition of the Field Museum, survey members were spaced 3 to 10 m apart (Plog 1974b:83), whereas in a survey of the Paria Plateau by the Museum of Northern Arizona, survey members were 50 to 150 m apart (Mueller 1974:10). Both surveys were designed to discover all the sites in the respective areas (Mueller 1974:8; Plog 1974b:83), but there is a large difference in the intensity of the two surveys.

What is the justification for surveying at high levels of intensity? Clearly, intensity is costly, and, unless there is good justification for keeping surveyors 10 m apart rather than 50 to 150 m apart, much more can be accomplished with a low-intensity survey. Two examples will now be presented to illustrate the problem with low-intensity surveys.

First, on surveys in the Apache-Sitgreaves National Forest in east-central Arizona by the Chevelon Archaeological Research Project, we have found that the average site is approximately 500 m² in area, or approximately 22 by 22 m. Imagine employing a level of intensity requiring that surveyors be 150 m from each other. Allowing for minimal distance between sites, six sites could be present side by side at any one point between the lines walked by the two surveyors. More realistically, in many areas of the Southwest two to three sites could easily be missed. Even if surveyors are 50 m apart, an average-sized site could easily be missed. "Average" in this instance includes sites with architecture. Unless walls or at least a rubble mound stands well above the ground surface, it is unlikely that sites with habitation units will be seen from a distance of 100, 50, or even 10 m. This evidence suggests that unless the intensity of a survey is high many sites will be missed—not simply atypical or very small sites, but typical and relatively large sites. That is, the higher the intensity of the survey, the larger will be the number of sites that will be found.

To test this hypothesis and to see whether there is a rate of diminishing return in terms of the number of sites found as survey intensity increases, information was collected from several surveys, which the archaeologists conducting the surveys state were *complete* inventories of different parts of the Southwest. For each survey, the number of person-days required to survey a square mile is used to measure the intensity of the survey, and the number of sites found per square mile is used to measure the number of sites found. (We emphasize that the person-days per square mile are *estimates,* as only the length of the field season, rather than actual field days, was given for some surveys.) The particular surveys used and the values of these two variables for each survey are shown in Table 10.1. These surveys are not a random sample. They include all surveys found for which the needed information was presented.

If this hypothesis—that the higher the intensity of the survey, the larger will be the number of sites that will be found—is valid, we would expect a high positive correlation between person-days per square mile and site

TABLE 10.1

Estimates of Site Density and Survey Intensity for Surveys in the American Southwest

Survey location	Area of survey (mi²)	Person-days/ mi²	Pre-historic sites/ mi²	All sites/ mi²	Reference
Roosevelt Lake, Arizona	2.8	24.2	9.3	10.3	Fuller *et al.* (1976)
Horseshoe Reservoir, Arizona	1.7	38.2	37.0	37.0	Fuller *et al.* (1976)
Hopi Buttes, Arizona	82.0	1.0	2.6	2.6	Gumerman (1969)
Black Mesa, Arizona	48.5	30.3	16.3	24.4	Layhe *et al.* (1976)
Star Lake, New Mexico	22.0	26.8	6.0	11.9	Wait (1977, n.d.)
Hay Hollow Valley, Arizona, 1967	5.0	80.0	50.2	50.2	Plog (1947a,b)
Hay Hollow Valley, Arizona, 1968	5.0	80.0	65.0	65.0	Plog (1974a,b)
Chevelon Canyon, Arizona	3.0	40.0	39.0	39.0	Plog (1974a)
Paria Plateau, Arizona, 1968	61.3	6.0	6.4	6.4	Mueller (1974)
Lower Chaco River, New Mexico	68.5	12.6	4.5	10.5	Reher (1977)
Buttes Reservoir, Arizona	15.2	56.5	18.0	18.0	Debowski *et al.* (1976)
Eastern Hueco Bolson, Texas	103.0	5.7	4.0	4.0	Whalen (1977 and personal communication)

density. Variation from a perfect correlation is expected, owing to factors such as real differences in site densities between areas, the effect of vegetation type and density and terrain on the speed at which one can walk, and differences in the length of a work day from one project to another. With the values shown in Table 10.1, the degree of correlation was measured by using a Pearson's product–moment coefficient. Correlation coefficients were calculated by using only the density of prehistoric sites, and by using the density of all sites, both prehistoric and historic. The values of these coefficients are .888 and .893, respectively, which are significant at the .01 level (although we re-emphasize that the data do not represent a simple random sample, and thus one of the assumptions of the significance test is violated), indicating a strong positive correlation between survey intensity and site density as predicted. A scatter plot of the relationship between person-days per square mile and site density per square mile is shown in Figure 10.1.

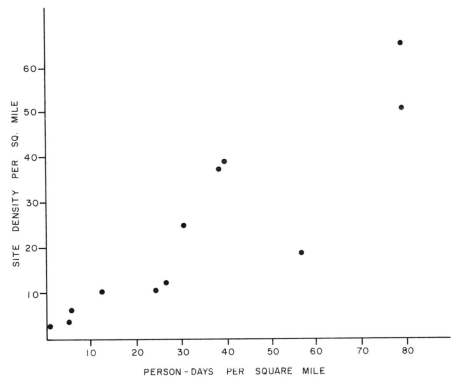

Figure 10.1. Scatter plot of the relationship between survey intensity and site density for 12 surveys in the American Southwest.

It can be argued that such a positive correlation could result simply from the fact that, if more sites are discovered in an area, more time must be spent in recording them and making collections. However, the regression equation for the surveys analyzed indicates that, for each additional site discovered, 1.51 additional person-days are required. Thus, to argue that the positive correlation is solely the result of the increased amount of time needed for recording and collecting would mean that 1.51 person-days were spent recording each additional site. However, dividing the average person-days per square mile involved in all 12 surveys by the average number of sites discovered per square mile produces a figure of .70 person-day per site, assuming that no time is required to find the sites. In addition, the descriptions of the procedures for recording and collecting sites on these surveys suggest that a considerably smaller amount of time was required for these activities.

Two additional comments should be made concerning this test. First, these same results can be replicated in the case of a single survey project. Judge (1977, personal communication) has obtained results similar to ours for different field seasons of the Chaco Project in New Mexico. Second, the scatter plot (Figure 10.1) does *not* suggest a point of diminishing return. Rather, a linear relationship between survey intensity and site density is suggested. However, as Judge (1977, personal communication) has argued, it is logical to expect the rate of return in terms of the number of sites discovered to drop off at some point as survey intensity increases. Clearly, this is an important question that must be addressed by future research. To summarize, these tests substantiate the assertions that, unless the intensity of a survey is high, many sites will be missed, and that many of the surveys in the Southwestern United States that purport to be complete inventories fall far short of that goal.

The second example of the effects of survey intensity pertains to the characteristics of habitation sites discovered. In surveys in the Apache-Sitgreaves National Forest by the Chevelon Archaeological Research Project, roughly ten times as many sites per square kilometer have been located, as compared with typical surveys done in surrounding areas. At the same time, the average number of rooms found on these sites is roughly one-tenth of that of sites in surrounding areas. Although there is an outside chance that these figures reflect simple differences in the nature of the prehistoric occupation of the areas in question, it is more likely that variation in the intensity of the studies of the areas is primarily responsible for such a difference. The archaeologist's interpretation of the prehistory of an area will vary drastically if he finds 2 as opposed to 20 sites per square kilometer, or 2 as opposed to 20 living units on a typical site. These examples illustrate that very unrepresentative pictures of the prehistory of an area will be obtained if high-intensity surveys are not carried out.

The variety of issues that must be taken into consideration in establishing an acceptable level of intensity is ultimately both large and specific to particular survey situations. We cannot suggest any particular level of intensity that will always be optimum. All that can be said is that, the greater the level of intensity, the higher will be the percentage of all sites in an area that will be found. Clearly, however, rather than stating that surveys are "complete" or "100%," archaeologists should specify the level of intensity of the survey (e.g., Moratto 1976).

We have considered the issue of intensity primarily in terms of spacing between crew members. There are, however, situations in which spacing may be less relevant than defining some means of inspecting for materials that are not clearly visible on the ground surface. Some surveys in the Northeastern United States have employed the technique of placing shovel test pits at intervals of 10 or 20 m because of growing evidence that many sites in the area have no surface manifestation (cf. Baker 1975; Weide 1976; House and Ballenger 1976; Williams 1977). In other areas the removal of vegetation or of litter derived from that vegetation may be necessary in order even to see if there are sites on the ground. Finally, resistivity, phosphate, and a variety of other physical and chemical techniques for subsurface examination are being tried and in some instances have proved useful (Baker 1975). [Such techniques are not without problems, however, since they implicitly embody definitions of the concept "site" (Rothschild 1976).] Even in arid areas, rapid sedimentation may result in deeply buried sites with little or no surface manifestation. The nature of the topography, vegetation, geology, and geomorphology of an area, not to mention the nature of the cultural evidence anticipated there, must all be taken into account in making decisions concerning intensity (see especially Rothschild 1976).

SAMPLING STRATEGIES

Having determined the degree of detail with which the ground surface is to be inspected, a decision must be made concerning whether all or part of the area to be investigated will be surveyed. In many types of cultural resource management studies, relatively complete inventories are required, and the area must be completely covered with a high-intensity survey. In many contract and research situations, however, the area in question needs only to be sampled. Although most archaeologists would agree that the areas to be surveyed should be chosen through a probability sample when only a sample is needed, decisions concerning sampling size and fraction, unit size and shape, and sampling design are not so clear-cut. Much effort is currently being invested in experimental and applied efforts to understand the merits of alternative strategies (Mueller 1974; DeBloois 1975; Judge *et al.* 1975; Benson 1976; House and Ballenger 1976; Plog 1976; Ritter and Hanks 1976; Plog *et al.* 1977). In the sections that follow, we shall discuss aspects of each of these decisions.

Sample Fraction and Sample Size

Sample fraction refers to the percentage of some target population that is included in a sample. *Sample size* refers to the number of observations that are made. The two are clearly different. One can imagine, for example, doing a 10% sample of a 100-km² area by surveying a single 10-km² block. Alternatively, a 10% sample could be undertaken by surveying 1000 blocks of .01 km² each. Balancing sample size and sample fraction in designing a survey is an important concern for a number of reasons (see Raab 1976 for an excellent, concise discussion of this relationship).

First, for most of the statistical techniques that are employed in making inferences about a target population on the basis of a sample, the sample size—the number of observations—is critical. The probability that a particular inference can be accepted or rejected increases as the sample size increases. Yet, because increasing the sample size with the sampling fraction held constant means employing smaller and smaller areal units, the logistical problems increase drastically. The number of units that a crew or an investigator can survey in a day increases, and the need for transportation from one sample locus to another rises dramatically, as do transportation costs. Thus, logistical and statistical factors must be balanced.

Second, it is important to note that inferences can successfully be made on the basis of very small sample fractions. Political polls are a good example—the sampling fraction is typically below a thousandth of a percent, and the sample size is quite high, often involving thousands of individuals. Such samples are based, however, on an extremely precise understanding of critical characteristics of the target population. (Such samples are typically highly stratified, an issue that will be discussed shortly.) That archaeologists have so substantial an understanding of their target populations and the variables influencing site distributions is doubtful. Nevertheless, important inferences about the prehistory of some regions have been supported on the basis of extremely small sampling fractions.

Finally, we should note that archaeologists approach a sampling problem from a comparative disadvantage. When most scientists employing sampling techniques discuss a 1% sample, they refer to a sample that will encompass 1% of the entities in the target population (100 of 10,000 people, for example). But, in beginning a survey, we do not know how many entities (archaeological sites) there will be or where they are. Our only option is to base the sampling fraction on the percentage of the land surface to be studied, recognizing that there is no guarantee that this will correspond neatly to the percentage of archaeological sites in the target population. That is, on the basis of sampling theory we can expect that, on the average, a 10% sample of a region will discover 10% of the *total area* of sites in the population but not necessarily 10% of the *sites* in the population.

As previous experimental studies of sampling in archaeological surveys (Mueller 1974; Judge *et al.* 1975; Plog 1976) have not addressed this problem, an experiment was conducted using survey data from the Valley of Oaxaca in Mexico that have been utilized previously for sampling studies (Plog 1976). Twenty-five simple random samples were drawn with five different sampling fractions—2.8, 5.6, 12.5, 25.0, and 50.0%—for the Etla area in the Valley of Oaxaca. The average number of sites found on the 25 samples at each sampling fraction was computed and was then expressed as a percentage of the total number of sites in the Etla area. The average percentages of sites discovered at each sampling fraction are shown in Table 10.2. These figures indicate that, on the average, the percentage of sites discovered by a sample is higher than the percentage of the land surface of the population surveyed. For example, a 12.5% sample of the land surface of the Etla region, on the average, resulted in the discovery of 21.6% of all the sites in the Etla region. Of the 125 random samples drawn, only 34, or 27.2%, of the samples located a percentage of sites that was lower than the sampling fraction. In addition,

TABLE 10.2

Comparison of Sampling Fraction with the Average Percentage of Total Sites Recovered with Each Sampling Fraction Using Twenty-Five Simple Random Samples with Each Sampling Fraction

Number of sampling units	Sampling fraction (%)	Average percentage of total sites discovered	Percentage difference	Ratio of column 3 to column 2
2	2.8	5.2	2.4	1.86
4	5.6	11.8	6.2	2.11
9	12.5	21.6	9.1	1.73
18	25.0	39.1	14.1	1.56
36	50.0	62.8	12.8	1.26

the ratio of the percentage of sites discovered to the percentage of land surface surveyed tends to decrease as the sampling fraction increases. As the figures in Table 10.2 indicate, a 5.6% sample discovers, on the average, a proportion of sites that is double the sampling fraction. However, a 50% sample discovers a proportion of sites that is only slightly higher than the sampling fraction.

That surveys will, on the average, "discover" a percentage of the total sites that is greater than the percentage of the area is also suggested by the following example. Assume that in a region that is 100 km² we take a random sample totaling 10 km². If sites were points, the probability that we would find a given site would be the area surveyed divided by the area of the region, or 10 km²/100 km². As noted above, a 10% sample should, on the average, discover 10% of the sites. However, sites are not points but areas. Furthermore, a site is "discovered" on a survey as long as it at least touches the boundary of the area surveyed. That is, we normally do not care (except when the sample is being used to estimate population parameters) whether or not 100% or 1% of the site lies within the area surveyed, since in either case we discover the site. The probability that a given site will be found is thus greater than 10 km²/100 km².

To express the same idea from a different viewpoint, assume that within the above area all sites have a radius of 100 m and that we have sampled the area using squares that are .25 km², or 500 m on a side. When a given square is surveyed, all sites totally within the square will be discovered, *in addition to* all sites whose centers lie within 100 m of the square. In surveying the quadrat, we will find all sites whose centers lie within an area of approximately .49 km², an area almost double the size of the actual quadrat. Therefore, if we survey a 10% sample of a 100-km² area by selecting 40 squares (40 × .25 km² = 10 km²), we are "hypothetically covering" 19.6% of all possible locations of site centers (40 × .49 km² = 19.6 km², 19.6 km²/100 km² = 19.6%). We thus might predict that we shall discover approximately 19.6% of all sites in the area. The exact percentage will be different in a real situation because of the simplifying assumption that every site has a radius of 100 m. The actual percentage will also be lower in a real situation to the extent that adjacent sampling squares are selected, as the "hypothetically covered" areas of such squares will overlap. Thus, it would be expected that, as the sampling fraction increases and the probability of selecting adjacent squares also increases, the difference between the percentage of the area actually surveyed and the percentage of the area hypothetically covered will be lower. In addition, the amount of difference between the percentage of the area surveyed and the percentage of sites found will decrease as the percentage of the area surveyed increases, as shown in Table 10.2.

This hypothetical situation can be tested somewhat by returning to the above experiment using sampling data from the Etla area in the Valley of Oaxaca. The samples drawn from this area utilized square sampling units, each of which was .25 km². The average radius of the sites in the Etla area is approximately 60 m, excluding one large site that is over forty times as large as the remaining 16 sites. Utilizing this average radius, we can predict that each sample unit will hypothetically cover an area of .384 km², since all sites within the unit and all sites whose centers lie within 60 m of the quadrat will, hypothetically, be discovered. Taking the five sampling fractions utilized in the above experiment, we can then calculate the percentage of the area hypothetically covered and compare it with the total area that was actually surveyed and the average percentage of sites discovered. These figures are shown in Table 10.3. They indicate that the percentage of area that is "hypothetically discovered" is much closer to the average percentage of total sites actually discovered than is the percentage of the area actually surveyed, for the first four sampling fractions. In fact, for the latter sampling fractions, the percentage of sites that are expected to be discovered is still lower than the percentage of sites actually found. This is most likely due to the exclusion of the one large site when the average site size was calculated. The overestimation of sites to be discovered with the 50% sample using the hypothetical coverage method is most likely due to the high probability of having a large number of adjacent sampling units with a sampling fraction of 50%. This factor has not been controlled for in the above comparison.

The above examples suggest that *on the average* a survey of a given proportion of a region will discover a percentage of the total sites in the region that is greater than the percentage of the region that is actually surveyed. The magnitude of the difference in the percentages will be a function of the size and shape of the sampling unit, the average size of the

TABLE 10.3

Comparison of Percentage of Etla Area Surveyed Using Five Different Sampling Fractions with the Percentage of Total Sites Discovered and the Percentage of Area "Hypothetically Covered"

Sampling fraction (% of area actually surveyed)	Percentage of area hypothetically covered	Average percentage of total sites discovered
2.8	4.3	5.2
5.6	8.5	11.8
12.5	19.2	21.6
25.0	38.4	39.1
50.0	76.9	62.8

sites in the area, and the sampling fraction. For example, four square sampling units that are .25 km² each and cover a total area of 1.00 km² will hypothetically cover an area of 1.44 km², assuming that an average site has a radius of 50 m, whereas two square sampling units that are .50 km² each and cover a total area of 1.00 km² will hypothetically cover an area of only 1.30 km². In addition, a square that is 300 m on a side, covering an area of .09 km², will hypothetically cover an area of .16 km², whereas a rectangle that is 900 by 100 m, also covering an area of .09 km², will hypothetically cover an area of .20 km²—an area over twice as large as the area of the sampling unit itself. This is illustrated in Figure 10.2. Thus, the smaller the size of the sampling unit, the higher the length-to-width ratio of the sampling unit, the larger the average size of the sites, and the lower the sampling fraction, the greater will be the magnitude of the difference. Given this information, the real density of

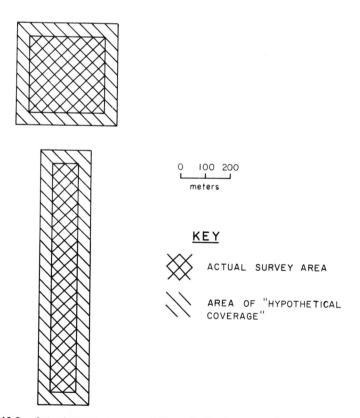

0   100 200

meters

KEY

ACTUAL SURVEY AREA

AREA OF "HYPOTHETICAL COVERAGE"

Figure 10.2.   Actual survey areas and "hypothetical coverage" areas for a square 300 m on a side and a rectangle 900 by 100 m. A constant site radius of 50 m is assumed.

sites in an area can be computed from a simple correction factor based on site size and sample unit shape and size.

Finally, one other important implication of the above discussion should be pointed out. Given that archaeologists doing surveys sample space rather than sites, the larger sites will usually have a greater probability of being found. The exact probability depends on the ratio between site area and the area of the sampling unit. For example, if sites range in size from .3 km² to .01 km², and 40 sampling units .1 km² in area are used, then a site .3 km² in area will have a better chance of being found than a site .01 km² in area. The largest site will fall into at least 3 sampling units and will thus have at least a 7.5% chance of being discovered if 1 sampling unit is chosen, whereas a site .01 km² in area will usually lie completely within 1 sampling unit and will have a 2.5% chance of being discovered. If, however, 4 sampling units 1.0 km² in area are used instead of 40 units .1 km² in area, then the site .3 km² in area will have only a slightly greater chance than the site .1 km² in area of falling into more than 1 sampling unit, and only a slightly greater chance of being found.

That larger sites are, on the average, found with greater frequency than small sites can be shown by returning to the Oaxaca survey data. The number of times that a site was found was tabulated for the 25 random samples at each of the five sampling fractions. Sites were then grouped into three size classes, and the frequency with which sites were found was averaged among the sites in each size class. The average frequency of discovery for sites in each size class is shown in Table 10.4. The area of the sampling units was .25 km². These figures support the assertion that, the larger the site, the greater is the probability that it will be found in a sample. Thus, large sites will be disproportionally discovered by samples, providing a biased, inflated estimate of the frequency of larger sites and of the average size of sites.

TABLE 10.4

Frequency (in Percentage) with Which Sites of Different Size Classes Are Discovered at Five Different Sampling Fractions

Site area (ha)	Number of sites	Sampling fraction				
		2.8%	5.6%	12.5%	25.0%	50.0%
291	1	24.0% of all samples	32.0	68.0	92.0	96.0
2–8	5	2.4	11.2	21.6	34.4	60.0
.6–1.8	11	4.7	9.8	17.1	34.2	58.9

Unit Size and Shape

Given a sample fraction and sample size, an investigator must next select a unit of a particular shape and size that will be used in drawing the sample. A number of studies have been undertaken on this issue (Plog 1976; Mueller 1974; Judge *et al.* 1975). The choice is typically between a quadrat or rectangular unit and a transect, which can be thought of as either a long, skinny rectangle or a line. Although the evidence is not conclusive, there is substantial indication that transects are more effective from a strictly statistical perspective. The one study (Mueller 1974) done to date suggesting that quadrats are superior is based on a highly problematical data base that would inherently favor quadrats. In addition, rotational transects were utilized in Mueller's comparisons of quadrats and transects, rather than the parallel transects used in other experimental studies (Judge *et al.* 1975; Plog 1976). Previous comparisons of these two types have shown that parallel transects are superior to rotational transects (Haggett and Board 1964). A second reason for favoring transects is that they "hypothetically cover" a larger area than a quadrat of the same size, and thus can be expected to discover a greater percentage of sites than the quadrats. That such is, in fact, the case can again be demonstrated by using the settlement data from the Valley of Oaxaca. Considering simple random samples with small and large quadrats and transects drawn in a previous study (Plog 1976) for three survey blocks in the valley, transect samples found a greater number of sites than the comparable quadrat sample in all six cases. The figures are shown in Table 10.5. Four of the six differences are statistically significant at the .10 level, and three are significant at the .05 level using a *t*-test. Although transects have been shown to be superior in the few studies conducted, it should be noted that only a limited number of population parameters have been considered in the comparisons of the estimation precision of different shapes of sampling units.

All studies done to date suggest that smaller units are more efficient estimators than larger units. In addition, we have noted other reasons for and against choosing smaller sampling units (for example, sample size for statistical inferences, increasing logistical problems, and the increase in the area of hypothetical coverage as the unit size decreases). Examining the figures in Table 10.5, we can see that, owing to the greater area of hypothetical coverage of the smaller sampling units, smaller units find more sites than larger units. From our own survey experience, we have found that sampling units that can be surveyed by a crew of two to four people in either half a day or one day are the optimal compromise between the desire to increase sample size and area of hypothetical coverage

TABLE 10.5

Average Numbers of Sites Found by Different Sampling Techniques in Experimental Studies Using Survey Data from the Valley of Oaxaca

Survey area	Sampling technique and unit size	Number of samples	Average number of sites found per sample	*t*	Significance level
Etla	Quadrat—small	100	2.99	−1.75	.08
Etla	Transect—small	100	3.50		
Etla	Quadrat—large	100	2.17	− .92	.36
Etla	Transect—large	100	2.41		
Valdeflores	Quadrat—small	100	6.28	−1.62	.11
Valdeflores	Transect—small	100	6.76		
Valdeflores	Quadrat—large	100	4.60	−2.34	.02
Valdeflores	Transect—large	100	5.29		
Zaachila	Quadrat—small	100	4.58	−2.16	.03
Zaachila	Transect—small	100	5.06		
Zaachila	Quadrat—large	100	2.97	−2.24	.03
Zaachila	Transect—large	100	3.47		

and the need to minimize the amount of time and money spent in moving from one sampling unit to another.

Sample Designs

There are three major design principles around which survey strategies are developed: randomization, systematization, and stratification. Combinations of these design principles serve as the basis of some of the most incisive sampling techniques (Cheek *et al.* 1976). Randomization involves selecting according to a random numbers table or some other device that randomizes the location of particular sample units, and ensures that the probability of a given unit's being chosen is equal to the probability of other units' being chosen. The advantage to randomization is that it reduces observer bias—the kinds of problems that arise archaeologically, for example, when an investigator believes that he knows where sites will be located. Randomization also permits investigators to state precisely the biases that have occurred in the sample. Systematization involves locating sample units at equal distances from each other. This technique is useful for many sorts of mapping projects where an even distribution of data points over a study area is needed.

Stratification is also a technique used to ensure a relatively even spatial spread of sampling units over the universe. It frequently involves dividing an area into strata of equal size, each of which will be sampled equally.

However, it may also involve breaking a target population or study area into units of equal or unequal size that will be sampled unequally—more observations will be made in some units than in others—because of evidence indicating that the distribution of some important variable over the study area is in fact unequal. For example, a type of soil that is better for agriculture may be restricted to certain areas, and as a result site density may be high in the areas where the soil occurs and extremely low in areas where it does not occur. In such a case, better estimates of population parameters can be made by surveying more sampling units in the areas where the site density is high and likely to be *more variable,* and fewer sampling units where site density is low and *less variable.*

As noted previously, sophisticated samples in other disciplines are typically based on substantial stratification. Stratified samples provide estimates that are superior to those provided by random samples to the degree that strata are homogeneous internally and there is heterogeneity between strata. Unfortunately, our understanding of prehistoric site distributions is not always sufficient to permit meaningful stratification on any other than areal grounds. However, studies have suggested that areally stratified samples provide statistically more precise estimates of population parameters than either random or systematic samples (Judge *et al.* 1975; Plog 1976).

A fourth type of sampling design, which has received a considerable amount of attention, is cluster sampling. Some recent discussions of this method have created certain misconceptions, which we should like to rectify. First, the use of probability samples in surveys is not always cluster sampling as Mueller (1975:39–40) has stated. Mueller (1975:39) has argued that archaeological field research is always cluster sampling. For example, he states:

> Archaeologists are constantly sampling space during survey and excavation. . . . Each spatial unit contains a cluster of cultural and/or paleoenvironmental data that are the elements of study. Each spatial unit actually conforms to the definition of a cluster and of a sampling unit. In this way, *archaeologists engaged in first-stage fieldwork, the discovery of previously unknown data, are actually cluster sampling* [1975:39; emphasis mine].

This statement is incorrect, because not all archaeological fieldwork is cluster sampling. The question of whether a particular sample is or is not a cluster sample depends not on whether one is doing fieldwork or laboratory analysis, as Mueller (1975:39) states, but on the unit of analysis, or sampling element, and the sampling units. For example, if a comparison of artifactual assemblages of sites (the elements) from a region that has been randomly sampled using 2 by 2 km units is being carried out, then this is a cluster sample, as Mueller (1975:38) states. The sampling element—the sites—and the sampling unit—the 2 by 2 km squares—are not the same; each sampling unit may include several elements, *each of which will be analyzed separately*. However, if the object of the analysis is simply to estimate the density of sites in a region, and we take a random sample of 2 by 2 km units and count the number of sites in each unit, this is *not* a cluster sample. Site densities in the different sampling units are being compared. The unit of analysis and the sampling unit are the same—the 2 by 2 km squares. We are simply measuring one characteristic of each square—the number of sites (just as one can estimate the total weight of people in a classroom by totaling the number of pounds on a sample of individuals from the class)—and no analysis of the individual sites is being made. Thus, it is not always the case that surveys are cluster samples. In many cases we are simply attempting to estimate population parameters on the basis of characteristics of sampling units—spatial units of different sizes and shapes—and when this is the case the sample is not a cluster sample. An excellent, in-depth discussion of this problem in terms of questions being investigated by one individual survey project is given by Thomas (1975).

The Data Base and Multistage Sampling

Whatever the specific data base in question, there are important aspects of the archaeological data base in general that affect sample designs. One of the most important aspects concerns the relative desirability of finding out where sites are and where they are not. For understanding prehistoric man-land relationships and for a variety of cultural resource management problems, it is as important to know where sites are not located as to know where they are located. Yet, understanding the prehistory of an area and managing its cultural resources necessitate some evidence concerning the sites that are there. This problem is typically overcome by employing a multistage sampling design (Redman 1973; Ritter 1976). A first phase of sampling is done on a random or areally stratified basis. A density map is constructed on the basis of this first phase, and a second phase or stage of sampling is undertaken in which the proportion of new units done in each area varies with the previously observed density of sites in that area. More sample units containing archaeological sites are therefore likely to be surveyed in the second sample stage, resulting in more data concerning the prehistory and archaeological resources of the area in question. The use of multistage sampling is an efficient sampling method that has been underutilized in previous archaeological research.

Judgment versus Probability Samples

It should be clear from the previous discussion that a great number of decisions or judgments must be made in designing a probability sample. In this sense, the often-voiced opposition of judgment and probability sampling is a poor conceptualization of the circumstances in which most of us operate most of the time. To rely exclusively on judgmental sampling assumes that existing archaeological knowledge of an area is complete—that nothing remains to be known. But to rely blindly on probability sampling reflects an equally unjustifiable refusal to assess and take into account pre-existing information. We suspect that, as our knowledge of survey design alternatives becomes more precise and refined, the opposition of judgmental and probability sampling will disappear as archaeologists learn at what points it is wise and at what points it is unwise to bring information to bear in the design of largely probabilistic survey strategies. We also suspect that most projects will reflect an evolution from a relatively heavy reliance on probabilistic devices in the early stages of the research process, when the dangers of bias are greatest, to a heavy reliance on judgmental criteria at later stages, when the need for specific categories of data can be more precisely identified.

SURFACE COLLECTIONS

The design of a strategy for recovering artifacts from site surfaces is the next issue. It has normally been the case in the past that the collection of artifacts from site surfaces was a regular component of archaeological surveys. However, it has been suggested that the collection of artifacts be avoided, and some institutions have adopted this as their policy (Fuller *et al.* 1976:68). Several reasons for doing no-collection surveys have been presented (Schiffer and Gumerman 1977), but paramount among these is the loss of provenience information when uncontrolled surface collections are made. Given a correlation between surface and subsurface deposits on a site, the lack of provenience information for surface artifacts hinders future work at the site. Thus, the analysis of artifacts in the field has been advocated in order that artifactual information can be obtained without losing provenience data.

Although the question of collections versus no-collections should be a project-specific consideration, as Schiffer and Gumerman (1977) have argued, we maintain that collections will have to be taken in the majority of cases for several reasons. First, as Schiffer and Gumerman (1977) have stated, ''Many research designs require detailed analysis of materials that simply cannot be performed in the field.'' Thus, a no-collection policy severely limits the range of questions that can be answered on the basis of the surface artifactual data. Second, the lack of collections prohibits any reanalysis of the artifacts by other researchers to answer research questions not posed by the original investigators or to retest the conclusions reached in the initial study. Finally, information from different areas of a site are necessary to isolate multiple occupations or functionally specific areas on a site—information that is critical to many of the research problems that archaeologists use survey data to solve, or to the assessment of the significance of sites in cultural resource management studies. In addition, some type of sampling design is necessary to guarantee that there is no selection bias when artifactual information is recorded. Given the need for sampling and for information from different areas of a site, artifacts might as well be collected in most cases, since loss of provenience data, the primary problem with uncontrolled surface collections, can be avoided simply by bagging artifacts by collection unit and recording the location of the collection unit on the site.

Collection Strategies

Although collections are necessary for most surveys, the archaeological literature indicates that the collection strategy most frequently used is the grab sample, which suffers from selection bias and loss of provenience information and is, therefore, inadequate. This problem becomes especially acute in light of evidence that large artifacts are overrepresented either on site surfaces or in surface collections (Baker and Schiffer 1975). Although probability sampling in surveying has become common, the application of probability sampling to the surface collection of every archaeological site discovered on a survey is, unfortunately, infrequent, despite discussions of alternative strategies (Whallon and Kantman 1969; Redman 1974). Rather than describe a ''cookbook'' approach to obtaining surface collections, we shall focus on some of the decisions that must be made in designing a collection strategy and on some of the relevant considerations in making these decisions. The information needed from surface collections will have to be gathered by different methods in different areas, depending on the characteristics of the sites and the research problems. For example, efficient collection strategies in areas where sites average 100,000 m² in area will differ from efficient collection strategies in areas where sites average 1000 m² in area (see Dancey 1975 for a related experimental study). However, it is important that at least part of the samples collected be probability samples in order to minimize selection bias and to allow us to state the degree of confidence we can have in estimates of population parameters.

In choosing collection strategies for surface collections of artifacts, the same decisions must be made as when designing a sampling strategy for surveys. That is, one must choose a level of intensity (Bellis 1975), a sampling design, the size and shape of the sampling unit, and the size of the sample to be collected. As noted above, a variety of sampling designs can be used to make surface collections. Whallon and Kantman (1969) and Redman (1974) provide descriptions of alternative probability sampling techniques, and these will not be repeated here. In choosing a particular design, two considerations are most important. First, one must ensure that collections are made from different parts of the site in order that information can be obtained on the range of occupational periods repre-sented at the site and their spatial extent, as well as information on the functional similarity of artifacts from different areas. Simple random or nested or cluster samples will not be advantageous because with these designs there is the possibility of not obtaining collections from some areas of a site. Some type of stratified or systematic sample is needed. Second, the speed with which the sample can be drawn and the sampling units located is critical. No one wants to spend half the time on a site drawing random numbers and then trying to locate the sampling units chosen. Some type of systematic sample, whether checkerboard or un-aligned (interval in Redman's 1974 terms), for which one need only draw one random number and for which the sampling units are located at specified intervals from each other, will normally be more advantageous than a stratified design. An unaligned systematic sample is superior to a checkerboard systematic sample in that the latter may provide highly inaccurate estimates of population parameters if there are spatial periodicities in artifact frequencies across the site.

The primary consideration in regard to the shape of the sampling unit is the loss of provenience and artifact association information as sampling units become more elongated. For example, if collections are made in rectangular units 16 m² in area with dimensions of 16 by 1 m, one would be collecting artifacts in one sampling unit that may be up to 16 m apart. In contrast, if collections are made in units 4 m on a side, also 16 m², the artifacts collected in one sampling unit will be no more than 5.7 m apart. Provenience information for any particular artifact is thus more precise when collection units are square rather than rectangular, and there also is less chance of mixing artifacts from different activity areas or from differ-ent occupational periods.

The most relevant characteristics in determining the sampling unit size and the sampling fraction are the sizes of sites in square meters and the artifact density (House and Schiffer 1975:50). It makes little sense to collect five sampling units 1 m² in area on a site that has an average artifact density of less than 1 artifact per square meter. Neither does it make sense to use units 20 m on a site if the site is only 400 m². Clearly, these factors have to be balanced along with data needs for the research problems being addressed in making decisions for surveys in different areas and, in some cases, perhaps on a site-by-site basis within an area. For example, in a survey on Black Mesa in northeastern Arizona, a sampling unit 4 m on a side was used to make surface collections. Given the average size of sites in the area, about 650 m², and the average artifact density, about 2 artifacts per square meter, it was felt that units of that size would provide sufficient samples of artifacts from different areas of the site and would provide a sufficient number of different units within different areas of the site. Determinations of the sampling fraction for each site discovered varied with the size of the site, with the sampling fraction increasing as site size decreased in order to ensure that a sufficient number of artifacts from the site as a whole was collected. Although consideration of artifact density is necessary in designing collection strategies, we do not find the argument that there should be at least 100 artifacts per sampling unit (Redman 1974) convincing. Such rules of thumb do not take into account differing research problems and the very different types of sites that are found in different parts of the world or even within a single research area.

Non-Sites and Low-Density Sites

The discussion to this point has revolved around the case of well-bounded sites with relatively high artifact densities. It is clear that a variety of problems not yet considered arise when the site is characterized by very low artifact density or when the boundaries of the site are difficult or impossible to assess. In such circumstances, even more precise records of artifact proveniences may be a necessity.

First, artifact density may be so low that, unless collection units are very large (resulting in poor provenience information), much time may be spent locating the sampling units to be collected only to find that many are void of artifacts. Such was the case for the lithic sites in the Star Lake area. Not only may such a method be inefficient in terms of time, but it also may not provide large enough samples of artifacts for meaningful analyses to be done. Second, Sterud (n.d.) suggests that precise provenience information may be critical in developing statements concerning the function not only of small sites, but of larger, more complex assemblages as well. He suggests that the identification and understanding of more limited and hence less complex units may provide clues to the interpretation of larger sites. By identifying small, recurring activity locations or sets of artifacts representing the conduct of specific activities, activity locations on more conplex sites might be identified (see also Wait n.d.). This type of research has been conducted by a number of archaeologists (Moseley and Mackey 1972; Dillehay 1973; Sterud n.d.; Wait n.d.). Examples of the collection of precise provenience information on low-density sites are the work of Rodgers (1974), Davis (1975), Bandy (1977), and Wait (1977, n.d.). In his study, Rodgers drew a 10% sample of a survey area where non-site manifestations were common, with circles 45 m in radius as the sampling units. The location of all artifacts within these circles was recorded with Brunton compasses and measuring tapes. Artifacts were bagged as found. Tightly clustered groups were rebagged as a unit. Goodyear (1975) used Rodgers' method during his investigations on the Papago Reservation, south-central Arizona. He stated that sample circles yielded three times as many artifact loci as in previous surveys of adjoining areas (Goodyear 1975:49). Goodyear (1975:49) concludes that these earlier surveys must have missed many "small, isolated and subtle types of remains." By recording exact placement of artifacts, arguments concerning non-site distributions of artifacts could be made and analyses of the spatial relations of artifacts within clusters could be attempted. Goodyear cautions, however, that sampling in the manner described "is not always compatible with analyzing for past behavioral systems" (1975:51). Indeed, limiting the intensive search areas to predefine circular radius seriously detracts from Goodyear's work. Dispersed distribution of artifacts that extend past arbitrary circular boundaries was not recorded. This prevents the use of Goodyear's data for statements concerning artifact density, site size, or total artifactual composition of a site.

Wait (1977, n.d.) used a collection method similar to Rodgers' and Goodyear's on the sparse lithic sites in the Star Lake area. However, the technique was used in conjunction with a complete survey rather than a sample. Each artifact, on its discovery, was flagged with a wire 91-cm (36-in.) pin flag. The area surrounding the find was searched by the field crew, and all additional artifacts were likewise flagged. A rope was then laid through a centrally located datum point on a north–south axis and was utilized as a guide in a systematic survey of the site by the field crew. The site was swept along this axis, with parallel sweeps being made until no new artifacts were discovered. The distance between searchers was no more than 2 m. The distance and compass bearing to each flag were then measured. Collected samples were bagged separately and labeled with the distance, coordinate, site number, and bag number. In this manner, all visually apparent artifacts were recovered. A map of the distribution of lithics on one of the low-artifact-density sites from Star Lake that was generated from the provenience information is shown in Figure 10.3. In a variant of this approach, Chomko (1974) flagged functionally different artifacts with varied colored flags, providing a quick, albeit unverified, notion of activity areas.

Pin-flagging the location of artifacts in this manner proved to be an efficient way in which to establish parameters for low-density sites. Not only does this method allow rapid field judgments to be made concerning the extent of the site, it also paves the way to controlled surface collection. Low-density sites, unobservable to the single surveyor, can easily be located once the survey crew begins to place flags at every artifact encountered. Perhaps one of the biggest advantages of this method is the

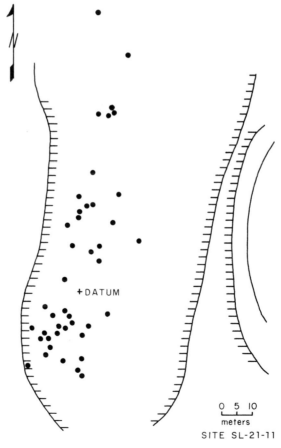

Figure 10.3. Map of the distribution of lithics on a site in the Star Lake region, New Mexico, generated from the precise provenience information collected during the surface collection.

flexibility it affords the researcher. Site area, for example, can be computed in a quantifiable manner so that comparisons of site size can be made between sites and between survey areas. We feel that this cannot be done with most published information on site size because of the bias embedded in judgmental boundary determinations. For example, estimates of site length and width were recorded for six sites at Star Lake using conventional "eyeball and pace" methods. Since the location of each surface artifact was mapped for these sites, we could compare the actual distribution with the judgment estimates. We found that short distances were consistently underestimated and that long distances were consistently overestimated, although the amount of bias fluctuated from crew to crew.

Time and Labor Costs

One of the primary questions that may arise concerning the use of sampling strategies or point provenience for surface collections is the amount of time and money required to make such collections. Although such collection strategies require more time than a grab sample because the spatial units or individual artifacts to be collected must be located and defined, techniques can be used that minimize the amount of time required. For example, in the survey on Black Mesa mentioned above, a movable grid system made of ropes was used to define quickly the sampling units to be collected. With this system, a crew of five individuals collected an average of nine sampling units on each site (144 m²) and recorded all necessary information concerning the site in an average of 45 to 60 minutes per site. This is considerably less time than the estimate of 1 man-day per site for probability samples of site surfaces on similar sites in central Arizona (Fuller *et al.* 1976:69). At the same time, the larger sites characteristic of other areas of the world would require a much greater investment of time for a probability sample. However, it is important that archaeologists obtain, at all levels of data collection, samples of data that are not influenced by selection bias, in order to ensure that inferences made from these data are as sound as possible. It is ironic and unfortunate that many recent surveys that have utilized sophisticated sampling techniques to select areas to be surveyed have utilized unreliable grab samples to collect artifacts from the sites discovered.

SITE RECORDS

Of equal importance to the nature of artifactual collections made from sites is the nature of the description of the location and attributes of the occurrence. The kinds of notes that it is worthwhile to make concerning particular sites will vary with the nature of specific projects. At the same time, there is some responsibility for each surveyor to record information on a site sufficient for the purposes of a number of archaeologists who may never see, but have an interest in, the area. As the magnitude of research problems that archaeologists have investigated using survey data has grown, so has the form of the site records. The form currently in use at Arizona State University, for example, is 12 pages long and is accompanied by a 20-page instruction manual.

We suspect, however, that the growth of such forms also reflects an effort to standardize the information that is being recovered from sites. Although the specific site attributes recorded must remain a matter of individual decision, the nature of the recording process should not. Two issues are primary. The first concerns whether site records are to be made in a largely free-hand format—using a day journal or site log—or whether specific pieces of information are required for each site—using a questionnaire or code sheet. It is our belief that the latter approach is preferable. Achieving an even reasonably comparable record of sites in an area is difficult at best. The use of a code sheet at least provides a common and repeated set of stimuli for those who are making the site records and thereby helps to achieve comparability. Admittedly, any such record should still allow room for individual comments and observations. But an attempt to generate a parallel set of data for each site seems critical.

The precision with which the location of sites is recorded is a similar issue. We have heard different archaeologists argue that the best information base for developing such records is a topographic map, a compass, and an areal photograph. We suspect that under different environmental circumstances the utility of these devices is different. In most circumstances all three, if they are available and can be used, are necessary for developing a precise record of site locations.

What precision means, in this circumstance, is extremely problematical. It depends, in the first instance, on the accuracy with which field observations are made and, in the second, on the degree of detail required for the inferences that the investigator is attempting. The difficulty with the first issue is illustrated in Table 10.6. This table shows the magnitude of the locational error that would result if one assumes that archaeologists typically make 1%, 2%, and 5% errors (obviously, we are assuming that we all make errors) in using a compass to locate sites. Basically, these figures suggest that an archaeologist who typically makes a 2% error (or records 2% errors because of nearby powerlines or ore bodies) in siting on features 2 km away can, using three observations, at best, place a site within an equilateral triangle 126 m on a side. Of course,

TABLE 10.6

Magnitude of the Locational Error Resulting from Errors of 1%, 2%, and 5% in Compass Sitings

Assumed error	Distance to object sited on:		
	.5 mi	1 mi	2 mi
1%	28 yd	55 yd	111 yd
2%	55 yd	111 yd	221 yd
5%	138 yd	276 yd	553 yd
Assumed error	Distance to object sited on:		
	.5 km	1 km	2 km
1%	16 m	31 m	63 m
2%	31 m	63 m	126 m
5%	79 m	157 m	314 m

with more observations, this error can be reduced. But it is not always possible to make more observations, and it may be unwise, temporally and monetarily.

What sort of precision is *necessary* is now largely unknown. Clearly, the claim of some investigators to be able to locate sites plus or minus 10 m must be suspect. On the average, such a claim is almost godly. But what degree of error is tolerable? At what point do sketches of site distributions become sufficiently warped that intuitive impressions of them are misleading? At what point does the calculation of a nearest-neighbor statistic become biased and unreliable? Clearly, we do not know the answers to such questions. Equally clearly, we must find out because, until we know, it will be impossible to determine the amount of time that it is necessary and justifiable to spend in recording site locations.

INDIVIDUAL VARIABILITY AND MEASUREMENT ERROR

An important source of bias that enters into information obtained from archaeological surveys, and that has received little attention, is the amount of variability between different crews or different individuals working on the same survey in recognizing and defining sites. That is, how good are archaeologists as measurement instruments? How certain can we be that a significant part of the variability that we find between sites in an area is not a product of differences between individuals or crews in site recognition and definition?

We know of no studies that have addressed this question. In an attempt to provide some initial information relating to this problem, four characteristics were tabulated for sites recorded by four crews involved in a recent survey of Black Mesa in northeastern Arizona. These characteristics were the average size, in square meters, of sites recorded by the crews, the average ceramic density of sites recorded by each crew, the percentage of all sites recorded by each crew that were smaller than 100 m², and the percentage of all sites recorded by the crews that had rubble mounds. The figures for each of these characteristics for each of the four crews are shown in Table 10.7. The figures show little variability among crews in the percentage of sites with rubble mounds, a greater amount of variability in the percentage of sites less than 100 m² in area, and considerable differences in the average size and ceramic density of sites recorded by each crew. The figures thus suggest that a significant part of intersite variability in site size and artifact density on Black Mesa could be due to differences among crews in how site size was defined, and that some crews may have missed or not recorded some very small artifact scatters. That this is actually the case is uncertain, because the sites recorded by each crew were not a random sample of the sites in the survey area. Rather, each crew primarily surveyed one large block of land within the 48.5-mi² area.

To provide an initial estimate of how much of the variability in site sizes is due to differences between crews in how site boundaries were defined, 12 of the sites originally recorded by crew number 3 were revisited by one of the individuals that had been in charge of crew number 2. The size of these sites was redefined by this individual, without prior knowledge of the size estimates made by the original crew. The average size of the 12 sites as defined by the original crew was 2704 m², whereas the average size of these sites as defined by the chief of crew number 2 was 1611 m². The original size estimates were higher than the later size estimates in 9 of 12 cases. The higher site-size estimates for crew number 3 for the 12

TABLE 10.7

Variability between Crews in Their Recognition and Definition of Sites on Black Mesa, Arizona

Crew number	Average site size (m²)	Average ceramic density (per m²)	Percentage of sites recorded with areas of less than 100 m²	Percentage of sites recorded with rubble mounds
1	803	1.2	29.1	19.1
2	507	1.7	44.2	17.7
3	838	1.6	48.1	19.3
4	464	0.9	42.9	19.8

revisited sites are consistent with what might be expected, given the figures shown in Table 10.7. Furthermore, the data indicate that additional tests must be made to evaluate the hypothesis of intercrew differences before meaningful studies can be made of intersite variability in site size on Black Mesa. This example also demonstrates that measurement error is a factor that should be, but has not been, considered in explaining variability in site characteristics, not only on Black Mesa, but in other areas also.

A similar problem arises in the case of the accuracy with which crews are able to locate sites. Approximately 30 sites in the Black Mesa survey area were revisited and were located on small-scale (1 in. = 400 ft) topographic maps using local relief, and compass sitings and taped measurement from nearby (10 to 150 m) drill holes whose locations were present on the maps. This study showed that there is considerable variability in the accuracy with which the sites were originally located on the topographic maps. Some sites were located correctly, whereas others were over 200 m from their correct location. Analysis has indicated that there are no statistically significant differences between survey crews in the accuracy with which they located sites. The amount of topographic relief in the immediate vicinity of the sites also cannot explain the variability in locational accuracy. Clearly, other explanatory variables must be examined in order that we can understand when sites are likely to be located accurately and when they are likely not to be. That is, when is an individual or crew likely or unlikely to locate a site correctly on a map? It is only after problems such as these have been addressed, after the degree of measurement error has been identified, that we can be somewhat certain that the variability we see in survey data, such as variation in site size or in nearest-neighbor distances, is real and is an accurate representation of the variability in the cultural systems being studied.

ANALYTICAL FRONTIERS

Much of what we have been able to describe in this essay reflects a growing attention to the effects of the assumptions that archaeologists have made about sites and surveys and the alternative survey strategies that they have attempted. There remains much room for improvement that will further increase our control over the quality of results that we are able to obtain. Examples of such ongoing research efforts may be cited.

A number of years ago it was not uncommon to hear archaeologists, working in areas of extensive modern agriculture, claim that surface evidence in their area had been so thoroughly degraded by farming that it was unusable. (This same claim was made of subsurface or plow-zone sites.) In the last few years, a great deal of attention has been given to "plow-zone" archaeology. No one has claimed that the contextual quality of plow-zone sites is equivalent to that of buried ones. A number of archaeologists have observed, however, that buried and unburied sites may often occur in distinctive vegetative, topographic, and geomorphological locations and that to write them off involves a high risk of systematically excluding an important component(s) of the archaeological record. With this assumption as a starting point, a variety of experiments have been attempted with plow-zone data (McManamon 1976; Roper 1976; Rudolph 1977; Sterud and McManamon 1976, Trubowitz n.d.; Weide 1976). There is no sense in which these provide a satisfactory definition of a standard approach to working with plow-zone materials. They do, however, clearly identify the direction in which future research must go—more explicitly defining what can and what cannot be accomplished with plow-zone materials. Although it is still clear that the plow moves artifacts, it does not do so infinitely. Archaeological interpretability is degraded by the plow, but it is not always, or even typically, destroyed. Until we more adequately understand the effect of this transformation process, the circumstances under which particular approaches to working in plow-zone situations should be taken will remain unclear.

The impact of casual surface collecting on archaeological sites is a similar example. On the one hand, some archaeologists have cited the effect of several decades or even centuries of amateur collecting as one reason why surface remains are an unreliable basis for inference. On the other hand, those archaeologists who have continued to work with surface remains have not been quick to address this issue. Yet, it is ultimately not a difficult phenomenon to treat. Lightfoot (n.d.) and Francis (n.d.) undertook to study the impact of casual collecting on archaeological sites in the vicinity of Springerville, Arizona. They attempted to associate variation in a variety of different characteristics of the ceramic and lithic artifacts occurring on sites in the area with variables such as the number of potholes on the site and the distance from roads. For some cultural characteristics, they discovered that up to 60% of the intersite variation could be explained on the basis of these measures of casual collecting. For other characteristics, the results were negligible. They were ultimately able to define zones based on proximity to roads in which the impact of casual collecting was increasingly less severe. Once such a phenomenon is identified, it can be controlled for in subsequent analyses. The argument described early in the paragraph is ultimately a product of ignorance; it can be obviated by collecting appropriate data and undertaking appropriate research.

Although the first two examples pertain to cultural effects on sites, natural phenomena that must be investigated are equally evident. Perhaps the phenomenon most familiar to survey archaeologists is the "regeneration of site surfaces." We have revisited sites that were completely collected a few years previously, only to discover that the surface evidence was superior quantitatively and qualitatively to that originally obtained. On the one hand, this phenomenon is not a pure reflection of time but may be, for example, a reflection of the intensity of thunderstorms within an area. On the other, it is undoubtedly variable for different environmental and cultural settings. Moreover, in one study of surface regeneration, Ammerman and Feldman (n.d.) were able to demonstrate that successful collections from which parallel inferences were made could be taken from a site in Italy in successive years (see also Williams 1977; Trubowitz n.d.). The primary differences among the collections could be related to the climatic conditions at the time the collection was made.

In none of these areas is our current understanding so complete as to permit any of us to rest on our laurels. These research areas clearly demonstrate a critical lesson. If we wish to do surveys and surface archaeology, and if we wish to do so without simply ignoring the many and honest criticisms that can be leveled at this approach to the archaeological record, then it is essential that we undertake research designed to allow us to recognize and alleviate the effects of many of these problems.

REFERENCES

Ammerman, A. and M. Feldman
  n.d.   Replicated collection of site surfaces. Manuscript on deposit. Department of Anthropology, State University of New York, Binghamton, New York.
Baker, C. M.
  1975   The Arkansas Eastman Archeological Project. *Arkansas Archeological Survey, Research Report* No. 6.
Baker, C. M., and M. B. Schiffer
  1975   Archeological evidence for the size effect. In The Arkansas Eastman Archeological Project, edited by C. M. Baker. *Arkansas Archeological Survey, Research Report* No. 6, 117–122.
Bandy, P.
  1977   Report and test of a new technique for mapping and recovery of "exposed" archeological sites. Paper presented at the 42nd Annual Meeting of the Society for American Archaeology, New Orleans.
Bellis, J. O.
  1975   The controlled surface pickup on the Mound House Site in the Lower Illinois River Valley. Paper presented at the 40th Annual Meeting of the Society for American Archaeology, Dallas.

Benson, C.
   1976   Assessing the adequacy of a regional sampling design: Cedar Mesa, Southern Utah. Paper presented at the 41st Annual Meeting of the Society for American Archaeology, St. Louis.
Cheek, A., S. Hackenberger, S. Purves, and K. Leehan
   1976   Report on the ten percent archaeological reconnaissance of the proposed McGee Creek reservoir. *Archeological Research Associates, Research Report* No. 4.
Chenhall, R.
   1975   A rationale for archaeological sampling. In *Sampling in archaeology*, edited by J. W. Mueller. Tucson: University of Arizona Press. Pp. 3–28.
Chomko, S.
   1974   A survey technique for delimiting activity areas within a site. *Missouri Archaeological Society, Newsletter* No. 278, 1–5; No. 279, 1–7.
Dancey, W.
   1975   Surface collecting in Central Washington: An evaluation of archeological survey technique. Paper presented at the 29th Annual Meeting of the Northwest Anthropological Conference, Ellensberg, Washington.
Davis, E.
   1975   The "exposed archaeology" of China Lake. *American Antiquity* **40**:39–53.
DeBloois, E.
   1975   Elk Ridge Archeological Project: A test of random sampling in archeological surveying. *U.S. Department of Agriculture, Forest Service, Intermountain Region, Archeological Report* No. 2.
Debowski, S., A. George, R. Goddard, and D. Mullon
   1976   An archaeological survey of the Buttes reservoir. *Arizona State Museum, Archaeological Series* No. 93.
Dillehay, T.
   1973   Small archaeological sites investigations for interpretation of site activities. *Texas Archaeological Society, Bulletin* No. 44, 169–177.
Doelle, W.
   1975   Prehistoric resource exploitation within the Conoco Florence Project. *Arizona State Museum, Archaeological Series* No. 62.
   1977   A multiple survey strategy for cultural resource management studies. In *Conservation archaeology: A guide for cultural resource management studies*, edited by M. B. Schiffer and G. J. Gumerman. New York: Academic Press. Pp. 201–209.
Francis, J.
   n.d.   The effect of casual surface collection on variation in chipped stone artifacts. *Arizona State University Anthropological Research Paper* No. 13 (in press).
Fuller, S., A. Rogge, and L. Gregonis
   1976   Orme alternatives: The archaeological resources of Roosevelt Lake and Horseshoe Reservoir. *Arizona State Museum, Archaeological Series* No. 98.
Goodyear, A. C.
   1975   Hecla II and III: An interpretive study of archeological remains from the Lakeshore Project, Papago Reservation, South Central Arizona. *Arizona State University, Anthropological Research Paper* No. 9.
Gumerman, G. J.
   1969   The archaeology of the Hopi Buttes district. Ph.D. dissertation, Department of Anthropology, University of Arizona, Tucson.

Haggett, P., and C. Board
  1964 Rotational and parallel traverses in the rapid integration of geographic areas. *Annals of the Association of American Geographers* **54**:406–410.
House, J., and D. Ballenger
  1976 An archeological survey of the Interstate 77 Route in the South Carolina Piedmont. *University of South Carolina, Institute of Archeology and Anthropology, Research Manuscript Series* No. 104.
House, J., and M. B. Schiffer
  1975 Archaeological survey in the Cache River basin. In The Cache River Archeological Project: An experiment in contract archeology, assembled by M. B. Schiffer and J. House. *Arkansas Archeological Survey, Research Series* No. 8, 37–53.
Judge, J., J. Ebert, and R. Hitchcock
  1975 Sampling in regional archaeological survey. In *Sampling in archaeology*, edited by J. W. Mueller. Tucson: University of Arizona Press. Pp. 82–123.
Klinger, T.
  1976 The problem of site definition in cultural resource management. *Arkansas Academy of Science, Proceedings* **30**:54–56.
Layhe, R., S. Sessions, C. Miksicek, and S. Plog
  1976 The Black Mesa Archaeological Project: A preliminary report for the 1975 season. *Southern Illinois University, University Museum, Archaeological Service Report* No. 48.
Lightfoot, K.
  n.d. Casual surface collecting's impact on archeological interpretation through regional surface surveys. *Arizona State University Anthropological Research Paper* No. 13 (in press).
McManamon, F. P.
  1976 Cultural resource management in the plow zone. Manuscript on deposit, Massachusetts Historical Commission, Boston, Massachusetts.
Moratto, M.
  1976 New Melones Archaeological Project—Stanislaus River, Calaveras and Tuolumne counties, California: Phase VI, Part 3, Archaeological inventory. *San Francisco State University, Archaeological Research Laboratory, Conservation Archaeology Papers* No. 3.
Moseley, M., and C. Mackey
  1972 Peruvian settlement pattern studies and small site methodology. *American Antiquity* **37**:67–81.
Mueller, J. W.
  1974 The use of sampling in archaeological survey. *Society for American Archaeology, Memoirs* No. 28.
  1975 Archaeological research as cluster sampling. In *Sampling in archaeology*, edited by J. W. Mueller. Tucson: University of Arizona Press. Pp. 33–41.
Plog, F.
  1974a Settlement patterns and social history. In *Frontiers of anthropology*, edited by M. Leaf. New York: Van Nostrand. Pp. 68–92.
  1974b *The study of prehistoric change.* New York: Academic Press.
Plog, F., and J. Hill
  1971 Explaining variability in the distribution of sites. In The distribution of prehistoric population aggregates, edited by G. J. Gumerman. *Prescott College, Anthropological Papers* No. 8, 7–36.

Plog, F., J. Hill, and D. Read
  1977 Chevelon archeological research reports: I. *UCLA Archaeological Survey, Monograph* No. 2.
Plog, S.
  1976 Relative efficiencies of sampling techniques for archaeological surveys. In *The early Mesoamerican village,* edited by K. Flannery. New York: Academic Press. Pp. 136–158.
Raab, L. M.
  1976 Research proposal—archeological sample survey of the Caddo Planning Unit, Ouachita National Forest, Arkansas. Manuscript on deposit, Arkansas Archeological Survey, Fayetteville.
Redman, C.
  1973 Multistage field work and analytical techniques. *American Antiquity* **38**:61–79.
  1974 Archeological sampling strategies. *Addison-Wesley Modular Publications in Anthropology* No. 55.
Reher, C. (editor)
  1977 *Settlement and subsistence along the Lower Chaco River: The CGP survey.* Albuquerque: University of New Mexico Press.
Ritter, E.
  1976 Second stage archaeological sampling in the Red Mountain Geothermal area. Paper presented at the 1976 Annual Meeting of the Society for California Archaeology, San Diego.
Ritter, E., and H. Hanks
  1976 Archaeological probability sampling and multiple-use planning in the California desert. Paper presented at the 1976 Annual Meeting of the Society for California Archaeology, San Diego.
Rodgers, J.
  1974 An archaeological survey of the Cave Buttes Dam alternatives site and reservoir, Arizona. *Arizona State University, Anthropological Research Paper* No. 4.
Roper, D.
  1976 Lateral displacement of artifacts due to plowing. *American Antiquity* **41**:372–375.
Rothschild, N.
  1976 Stranger in a strange land: A consideration of survey and sampling. Paper presented at the 41st Annual Meeting of the Society for American Archaeology, St. Louis.
Rudolph, J.
  1977 Experimental replication of the effects of agriculture on an archeological site. Unpublished M.A. thesis, Department of Anthropology, Southern Illinois University, Carbondale.
Schiffer, M., and G. Gumerman (editors)
  1977 *Conservation archaeology: A guide for cultural resource management studies.* New York: Academic Press.
Sterud, E.
  n.d. Small site methodology. Manuscript on deposit, State University of New York, Binghamton.
Sterud, E., and F. McManamon
  1976 The identification of activity loci in plough zones: An example from New York State. Paper presented at the 41st Annual Meeting of the Society for American Archaeology, St. Louis.

Taylor, W.
    1972   The hunter-gatherer nomads of N. Mexico: A comparison of the archival and archaeological records. *World Archaeology* **4:**167–178.

Thomas, D.
    1975   Nonsite sampling in archaeology: Up the creek without a site? In *Sampling in archaeology,* edited by J. Mueller. Tucson: University of Arizona Press. Pp. 61–81.

Trubowitz, N.
    n.d.   The persistence of settlement pattern in a cultivated field. Manuscript on deposit, State University of New York, Buffalo.

Wait, W.
    1977   Identification and analysis of the "non-sedentary" archaeological site in northwestern New Mexico. Unpublished Ph.D. dissertation, Department of Anthropology, State University of New York, Binghamton.
    n.d.   *Archaeological survey of Star Lake, New Mexico.* Carbondale: Southern Illinois University Press.

Weide, M.
    1976   I-88 Archaeological Project: 1975 summer season. Manuscript on deposit, Public Archaeology Facility, State University of New York, Binghamton.

Whalen, M.
    1977   Settlement patterns of the eastern Hueco Bolson. *University of Texas at El Paso, Centennial Museum, Anthropological Paper* No. 4.

Whallon, R., and S. Kantman
    1969   Early Bronze Age development in the Keban Reservoir, east central Turkey. *Current Anthropology.* **10:**128–133.

Williams, K.
    1977   A preliminary assessment of techniques applied in the FAI-255 survey. Paper presented at the 42nd Annual Meeting of the Society for American Archaeology, New Orleans.

Subject Index